Daniel P. Wood

RE-UNION

OF THE

SONS AND DAUGHTERS

OF THE OLD

TOWN OF POMPEY,

HELD AT

POMPEY HILL, JUNE 29, 1871,

PROCEEDINGS OF THE MEETING, SPEECHES, TOASTS AND OTHER INCIDENTS OF THE OCCASION.

ALSO,

A HISTORY OF THE TOWN, REMINISCENCES AND BIOGRAPHICAL SKETCHES OF ITS EARLY INHABITANTS.

Publication Committee:

WM. W. VAN BROCKLIN, LE ROY MORGAN, RICHARD F. STEVENS,
EBENEZER BUTLER, HOMER D. L. SWEET.

POMPEY:
Published by Direction of the Re-Union Meeting.
1875.

SYRACUSE, N. Y.:
COURIER PRINTING COMPANY.

1875.

To the Descendants

—of—

The Pioneer Residents of the Old Town of Pompey,

this book

—is—

Most Affectionately Dedicated;

hoping

That the Bright and Shining Example of their Fathers and Mothers

herein transmitted to them,

May be ever their Guiding Star through the Voyage of Life.

PREFACE.

The undersigned committee, appointed to supervise the publication of the proceedings at the Re-Union of the former residents of Pompey, have felt, and upon inquiry have found, that a simple history of that day's proceedings is not all that will be expected at our hands. We have accordingly obtained, by considerable effort, material for a more extended book. In the following pages will be found, not only the re-union meeting, including speeches, toasts, &c., but also an historical sketch of the town of Pompey, and short biographical notices and reminiscences of some of the prominent and early settlers, to which we have added a directory of the names, post-office address, occupation, &c., of as many of her distinguished men and women as we have been able to obtain, with a brief mention of their public life.

The publication of this volume has been long delayed, hoping that we might be able to give biographical sketches of many more early citizens of Pompey than will be found in the following pages. Our efforts for the last year and a half in reference to this book, have been directed to this end. Notwithstanding our appeals repeatedly made through the press, and personal applications to the descendants of the fathers of old Pompey, the absence of many sketches we had hoped to obtain is annoying to us, and will be painfully manifest to all acquainted with the names to which we refer. While our desire has been to produce such a volume as would meet the approbation of all, we are sensible that many things worthy of remembrance have been omitted.

For the production of the volume as it is, we have cheerfully given our services, and hope that it may prove a pleasant visitor at the fireside of Pompey's children wherever they may be, and a source of lasting happiness to us all.

WM. W. VAN BROCKLIN,
RICHARD F. STEVENS,
LEROY MORGAN,
EBENEZER BUTLER,
HOMER D. L. SWEET.

A BRIEF ACCOUNT

—OF—

Measures Taken which Resulted in the Re-Union.

A desire seems simultaneously to have possessed the minds of many of the Sons of Pompey to revisit the home of their childhood, and very naturally this desire was communicated to others only to find a hearty response. Some time during the year 1870, Hon. Horatio Seymour, Hon. William G. Fargo, Hon. E. C. Litchfield, Leonard Jerome, Esq., Dr. Lucien B. Wells, and others, having expressed a very strong desire that a meeting of former residents of Pompey should be held, Dr. L. B. Wells, of Utica, communicated by letter with E. Butler, Esq., of Syracuse. The following is Dr. Wells' letter:

UTICA, July 10th, 1870.

DEAR SIR:—A few days since, meeting Gov. Seymour, he stated to me that he had been urgently solicited by W. G. Fargo, of Buffalo, to have a movement initiated for a re-union of former residents of the town of Pompey. The Governor expressed the same desire and promised to be present on such occasion, and requested me to write to some of my friends who may feel an interest in the matter. From your extensive acquaintance in Pompey, and in Syracuse, where so many families reside who were former residents of Pompey, I have taken the liberty to present the subject for your consideration, earnestly desiring that this proposed re-union shall take place at no distant day.

Respectfully Yours,

L. B. WELLS.

To Ebenezer Butler, Esq., Syracuse.

This was the first measure taken which finally culminated in the Grand Re-Union of June 29th, 1871. Very soon the substance of this letter became known to many former residents of Pompey, then residing in Syracuse and elsewhere, and a very general interest was created in the subject. Citizens of Pompey were informed of the stat of feeling existing abroad, and at Pompey initiatory steps were taken to bring about a re-union. Accordingly, meetings were held at Pompey, and finally, one on the 6th day of August, 1870, at the Presbyterian Church, of which Wm. W. Van Brocklin was Chairman, and Wells M. Butler, Secretary, it was then resolved to invite the Sons and Daughters of Pompey from abroad to a Re-Union, to be held sometime in September following, and a committee of arrangements was appointed. The committee met on the 13th day of August, and after full consultation it was decided, in view of the magnitude of the enterprise, the distance from Pompey many of her children reside, and the lateness of the season, that adequate preparations could not be made in time to secure a full attendance. The committee therefore adjourned to June, 1871, to meet at the call of the chairman. In the month of May, 1871, some fifty or sixty former residents of Pompey, then residing in Syracuse, held a meeting at the office of Dr. R. F. Stevens to make arrangements for co-operating with the citizens of Pompey in preparation for a re-union. Levi S. Holbrook, Esq., was called to preside, and on motion, it was resolved that a committee be appointed by the chair, to attend the contemplated meeting at Pompey, and to co-operate with the Pompey committee in making arrangements for the coming re-union. The chair appointed the following gentlemen as such committee:—Henry L. Duguid, Dr. R. F. Stevens, Calvin S. Ball, Jr., Wm. A. Sweet, Edward S. Dawson and Ebenezer Butler.

At subsequent meetings held at the same place, efforts were continued in aid of the re-union, and preparations made to ensure success.

During the time intervening between August, 1870, and

June, 1871, a continued intercourse was kept up among those who were in earnest in reference to the matter, to the end that the residence of all entitled to an invitation should become known; and especially were the more eminent and active descendants of Pompey informed of the enterprise, so that they might be able to accommodate their business or pleasure to an attendance at the contemplated re-union.

A delegation of the Syracuse committee visited Pompey, and were present at a meeting held June 3d, 1871. It was then determined that the Syracusians should co-operate with the citizens of Pompey, and Dr. R. F. Stevens was appointed Corresponding Secretary. It was also resolved to publish an invitation circular, to be sent to all former residents of Pompey and their descendants, which should be signed by the invitation committee, inviting them to a re-union to be held at Pompey Hill, June 29th, 1871.

The daily press of Syracuse was enlisted in the project, and notices published calling the attention of the public to the high degree of enjoyment anticipated, and the large number of distinguished guests expected.

The invitation circular was also published, and these papers and hundreds of the circulars were sent to every part of the Union, wherever a Pompey man or woman could be traced. The office of the Corresponding Secretary assumed the proportions of an immense business corporation, sending and receiving mail.

At the meeting of June 3d, held at Pompey Hill, various committees were appointed, and the committee of arrangements enlarged and sub-divided, so that everything calculated for the comfort, pleasure and convenience of the expected gathering of the clans of Pompey, should receive attention. The names of the persons who constituted the different committees, and the officers selected for the re-union day, are all noted in their appropriate place. From this time up to the time appointed for the re-union, the town of Pompey, and especially the village of Pompey

Hill, was the theatre of constant plans and labor, and numerous other meetings were held for the purpose of consumating the arrangements projected at the meeting of June 3d.

It is highly appropriate in this connection to acknowledge the obligation the committee of arrangements were under to the Press of Syracuse, and especially to the *Standard*, *Courier* and *Journal*, for the interest taken by them in publishing the invitation circular and notices of the Re-Union, both before and after the occasion. The following resolution was unanimously adopted by the committee of arrangements:—

Resolved, That the citizens of Pompey are under high and lasting obligations to the Press of Syracuse for the unselfish interest manifested by each of the daily papers in gratuitously publishing the notices and circulars of our Re-Union, and giving to the public so just and full an account of the interesting proceedings on that occasion, and in their behalf, and also in behalf of her sons and daughters abroad, we tender them our sincere and heartfelt thanks.

The following is the invitation circular above referred to, printed on tinted note paper. On the outside,

RE-UNION AT HOME.

POMPEY, Onondaga Co., N. Y., June 1, 1871.

You are most cordially invited to attend a Re-Union of the former residents of the old Town of Pompey—now Pompey and Lafayette—which will be held at Pompey Hill on Thursday, the 29th day of this month.

	WELLS M. BUTLER,
RICH'D F. STEVENS,	FRANK JEROME,
Cor. Sec'y, Syracuse, N. Y.	Rec. Sec'ys, Pompey, N. Y.

On the inside, the following appeal, signed by the committee:—

AULD LANG SYNE.

A desire has been implanted in our natures to visit, in after life, the graves of our ancestors and the homes of our childhood—to renew old acquaintance and revive reminiscences of by-gone days.

Most of the early settlers of Pompey are gone, and the survivors are fast passing away. They, with those of younger years, join in inviting the sons and daughters and former residents of the old Town, to a joyous Re-Union, promising them all a warm welcome to their old and honored home.

It is desirable that all should arrive at the village as early in the day as possible, and the time will be occupied with meetings, (both day and evening,) addresses, music, feasting, visiting and recreation, with ample arrangements for the comfort and happiness of all.

Addresses are expected by ex-Governor Horatio Seymour, of Utica, ex-U. S. Senator Geo. H. Williams, of Oregon, Judge Charles Mason, of Washington, Maj. Gen. Henry W. Slocum and Judge Lucien Birdseye, of Brooklyn, Hon. L. R. Marsh, Leonard W. Jerome, Esq., and Hervey Sheldon, Esq., of New York, Hon. Wm. G. Fargo, of Buffalo, E. C. Litchfield, Esq., of Cazenovia, Hon. R. H. Duell, of Cortland, Hon. D. G. Fort, of Oswego, Dr. Chas. W. Stevens, of St. Louis, Mo., Judge Leroy Morgan and Hon. C. B. Sedgwick, of Syracuse, and others who have signified their intention to be present; also a poem is expected to be read by "Grace Greenwood" (Mrs. Lippincott) who intends to be present and join in the festivities of the occasion.

From Syracuse persons can reach the Hill by the Binghamton Railroad to Lafayette Station, or by private conveyance.

Each one receiving this, is requested to extend the invitation to other old residents of Pompey, and all who accept this invitation, will please communicate their intention to be present, by letter, to the Corresponding Secretary—Dr. R. F. Stevens, Syracuse, N. Y., at their earliest convenience.

Committee of Invitation.—Jehiel Stearns, Asa H. Wells,

Beach Beard, Harvey M. Woodford, John J. Taylor, O. Jarvis Wheaton, Merit Butler, Chas. R. K. Hill, Noah Palmer, Zenas A. Jones, Elias Barnes, David Hibbard, Edmund O. Clapp, Manoah Pratt, Samuel Baker, Hiram Clement, Miner B. Murray, Alvin M. Ball, Alanson P. Benson, Chester Baker, Luther Cole, Elijah Parks, C. C. Midler, Sandford K. Newell, Warner Butts, Isaac C. Wicks, Geo. Doolett, Gersham Wheelock, Uriel Wilson, John H. Clarke, Lewis O. Hill, Victory J. Birdseye, John C. Jerome, John Smith, Warren Sloan, William Savage, Reuben Edgarton, Harry Knapp, D. G. Southard, Taber D. Williams, Julius Mason, Joseph Wallace, John Hatch, Joseph Jennings, Silas L. Holbrook, Hiram Sutherland, Daniel Kellogg, Orace Newman, Benjamin F. Wheeler, Reuben Billings, David Williams, Chas. Hill, Matthias Berry, Henry Candee, Russell Duguid, Nicholas VanBrocklin, Parker Borden, Ira Dodge, Hiram Perry, Myron Sharp, D. E. Hayden and Orrin Bishop.

Committee of Arrangements.—Marshal R. Dyer, Geo. E. Wells, Frank Jerome, W. B. Sweet, R. D. Slosson, Levi Wells, W. W. VanBrocklin, Frank Porter, Henry Doolett, O. G. Dibble, Ira Ellis and Rensselaer Northrup.

Committee of Reception.—O. C. Pratt, Col. M. B. Birdseye, A. H. Clapp, Morris Beard, J. Haskell Stearns, Frederick R. Murray, Samuel A. Hibbard and Samuel Jerome.

Other Committees were subsequently appointed as the work of preparation progressed, but the names of those who constituted those Committees have not been preserved.

The Committee to prepare the tables—as near as can be ascertained—were Jas. VanBrocklin, Chas. E. Hopkins, Nicholas VanPatten, Geo. Kenyon and Eli Pratt.

The following are among the persons who served on the Committee on Decorations, the Committee to prepare various Refreshments and Furnish the Tables, and the Committee to wait upon the Guests at the tables. Many of them served on two or three Committees, and some, doubtless, whose names do not appear, were active in helping:—

R. Northrup, Melvin Webster, Frank Robinson, Josie Downs, Laura Beard, Gertrude Beard, Mr. and Mrs. A. S. Hale, Mr. and Mrs. Levi Wells, Dr. O. G. Dibble, Fannie Wheaton, Ada Wheaton, Lizzie Wills, Dora Ellis, Phoebe Curtis, Alice Dunham, Olive Corwin, Lucia Robinson, Minnie Beard, Irving Robinson, Frank Waters, Fletcher Soule, Wm. Mason, Mr. and Mrs. E. Pomeroy, Mr. and Mrs. O. C. Pratt, Mr. and Mrs. John Soule, Wm. H. VanBrocklin, Ellen VanPatten, Sarah J. Robinson, Ida Soule, Celia Butterfield, Sophrona Hayden, Mr. and Mrs. J. V. Butts, Sophrona Wilby, Orlando Robinson, Fannie Fisk and Julia VanBrocklin.

All the arrangements having been perfected in detail that were deemed necessary, all awaited the approach of the appointed day with eager expectation.

THE RE-UNION DAY.

The morning was chilly, and clouds overcast the sky. A heavy rain had fallen the night before, but the roads were in fine condition; a light shower fell during the forenoon of the Re-Union Day, but soon after noon the clouds disappeared, leaving one of those beautifully clear and transparent atmospheres that so grandly displays the gorgeous scenery of the surrounding hills and valleys—the pride and glory of old Pompey. Many from abroad had arrived the night before, and the early morning saw the Hill busy with life. A large tent had been spread on the village green, sufficient to accommodate three or four thousand people; evergreen banners had been thrown across the various avenues leading to the village, and one spanned the village green from the Presbyterian Church to Capt. John J. Taylor's store, bearing the magic word "WELCOME."

A special train had been prepared at Syracuse to convey guests to the Hill by the Syracuse & Binghamton Railroad, via. Lafayette, and it was filled with an eager and expectant throng. Teams had been sent by the citizens of Pompey, and at Lafayette Station awaited the arrival of the train. A procession was soon formed, consisting of sixty-eight well filled farmers' wagons, which was met near the "old Anderson Home" by two mounted marshals and an escort, sent from the village. Dresher's full band, from Syracuse, was at the head of this procession, and as they came in sight of the village the band struck up "Home, Sweet Home," and as they reached the village, about nine o'clock in the morning, a wild scene of enthusiastic welcoming greeted them. About this time every avenue leading to the village, (of which there are nine,) was full of vehicles of every description, conveying thither its freight of human hopes and expectations for a glorious Re-Union. From Syracuse, in addition to the special train, hundreds came with their own conveyance, among whom was Hon. D. P. Wood, the chosen President of the Day, Gen. John A. Green, Jr., of Syracuse, and Hon. Wm. G. Fargo, of Buffalo, who, with his family, Judge Verplanck and Hon. Joseph Warren, of Buffalo, came in his mammoth family carriage drawn by six splendid horses, which he had transported from Buffalo for the occasion, affording him an opportunity to pass the home of his childhood in the vicinity of Watervale. From Cazenovia, Fayetteville, Manlius, Delphi, and the eastern portion of Pompey, came an immense throng, over three hundred carriages passing the Academy Green upon their approach to the village green. Among these was Governor Seymour, who came from Cazenovia with friends with whom he had stopped the night before. From the south, also, came an equally large concourse, and as the immense streams of humanity from every direction poured in upon the village green, they mingled together in serene confusion. Here met those who had been separated for many long years, and on every side was seen the greeting of relatives and friends —the aged fathers and mothers living over the sunny days of childhood. Tears and smiles, sorrow and joy, chased each other over the gathered multitude. Here was a crowd listening to the reminiscences of the early days of Pompey by Harry Hopkins. At another point might be seen the tall and commanding form of Senator Williams receiving the congratulations of the friends of his youth. While yet again, in the conscious dignity of a virtuous life, moved the presence of Governor Seymour, greeting the playmates of his youthful days. And yet again, at various points, might be seen Hon. Wm. G. Fargo, Ex-Mayor of Buffalo; Hon. Charles Hayden, Ex-Mayor of Rochester; Hon. Daniel G. Fort, Ex-Mayor of Oswego; Hon. Charles B. Sedgwick and Hon. Horace Wheaton, Ex-Representatives in Congress; Hon. LeRoy Morgan, Judge of the Supreme Court, and many others, surrounded by groups of admiring friends, relating incidents of early life in Pompey. And yet again, among the multitude were a large number who, though not so distinguished, have yet an equal claim to our esteem for their consistent and upright lives of integrity, honoring, as they have God, humanity and their native town. Such scenes of happy greeting as were witnessed from the time the people began to assemble till the closing of the day, and especially from 9 to 11 o'clock, on the village green, are seldom witnessed in a life time. No words can convey an adequate idea of the emotional feeling which the occasion called forth.

At eleven o'clock, the hour appointed for the meeting in the tent on the green, the loud-mouthed cannon and the joyfully sad peals from the old bell in the Congregational church, that had in early days summoned many present to the house of worship, now announced the hour for the formal exercises of the day. The tent was already crowded to its utmost capacity, and thousands were unable to gain admittance. Dr. Richard F. Stevens called the vast assembly to order, and Hon. D. P. Wood assumed his position, by order of the Committee of Arrangements, as President of the Day. The Vice-Presidents were as follows:—

Dr. Jahiel Stearns, Asa H. Wells, John C. Jerome, O. J.

Wheaton, Myron Sharp, Morris Baker, Dr. E. Parks, Miner B. Murray, Harry Knapp, Harvey M. Woodford, Orace Newman, Zenas A. Jones, Samuel Baker, Charles R. K. Hill, Joseph Jennings, Warner Butts, Silas A. Holbrook, Horace Wheaton, Manoah Pratt, H. W. Van Buren, Nathaniel Foster, Dr. L. B. Wells, C. J. Hayden, J. M. Taylor, A. T. Dunham, Solomon Judd, Addison G. Williams, Merrit Butler, Wm. J. Curtis.

RECORDING SECRETARIES.—Frank Jerome, W. M. Butler, of Pompey.

CORRESPONDING SECRETARY.—R. F. Stevens, of Syracuse.

The services were commenced by the band playing the "Anvil Chorus."

The Throne of Divine Grace was then invoked by Rev. Mr. Cooper, pastor of the Congregational church, in a solemn and impressive prayer, the language of which, it is to be regretted, has not been preserved. The immense concourse then sung the words, "Praise God from whom all blessings flow," &c., to the good old-fashioned tune, "Old Hundred," accompanied by the band.

At the conclusion of the singing, the President, Hon. Daniel P. Wood, said:—

Sons and Daughters of Pompey:

Upon an occasion of so much interest and importance, when those who have been long absent from their childhood's home have returned to visit the companions of their youthful days, and to look again upon the places familiar in life's fresh morning, it is eminently proper that some present resident of Pompey be called upon to address appropriate words of welcome to the returning pilgrims. I therefore have the pleasure of introducing to you Wm. W. VanBrocklin, who will now address you.

Wm W. Van Brocklin

MR. VAN BROCKLIN'S ADDRESS OF WELCOME.

Fellow Citizens, Sons and Daughters of Pompey from Abroad:

The occasion which has called together this vast assembly, is one which will ever be remembered as the brightest period of our earthly existence. To-day, Pompey welcomes home her sons and daughters. And as one who still lingers upon this soil, consecrated by the sacred ashes of your fathers, I have been commissioned by the present citizens of Pompey, without distinction of party or creed, in their behalf to express their most sincere and cordial greeting—to extend to you who have come hither from every quarter of our great and glorious land, the hospitalities of the town—to assure you that every door in Pompey is thrown wide open to receive you, and that you may feel the same degree of freedom that a child would, upon returning after a long absence to visit the parental roof. Thus are you welcomed; yet the occasion is so fraught with recollections of our early life, and so eminent are the characters of those who have come back to honor the place of their nativity, that I cannot dismiss the subject without briefly expressing a few thoughts that seem to me appropriate. You are welcomed; not as the prodigal son, yet with an equal degree of affection. Unlike him, in poverty you left us, with nothing but your unblemished reputations, which, thank God, you have kept pure, and your stern purpose and firm resolves to do and conquer upon the battle fields of life. Unlike him, you have not spent your substance in riotous living, yet, while Plenty has crowned your efforts, in the various appointments, which, under God, you have been called to fill, and "want goes smiling from your door," we have killed the fatted calf, and upon it will you be feasted, in token of our appreciation of your exalted worth; and as you will soon surround the table of your re-union with the loved and cherished companions of your youthful days, you will find, while joy and gladness shall abound, and mirth and song and dance shall speed along the happy hours of this day, that this is not entirely an occasion of unmixed festive enjoyment. Room will be left to drop the tear of affection over the vacant chairs, and over the graves of those we loved and honored, twenty, forty, sixty years ago. To them is due much of your success in life. Their careful supervision of your early education, the sterling worth of the early settlers of Pompey, their examples of economy, virtue, honesty and strict integrity have left an imperishable impress upon your characters. And so we find that this re-union of Pompey's sons and daughters is composed of an array of talent seldom equalled, never excelled, and it impresses the mind with the transcendant value of our institutions, which open to the rich and poor alike, throughout our vast domain, opportunities to acquire fortune and fame. Within my own recollection, Pompey has furnished to our State Legislature thirteen members, six representatives in our National Congress, one United States Senator and member of the recent Joint High Commission, two Governors, five Mayors of cities, three Supreme Court Judges and one Major-General of our victorious armies, while we have heard with pleasure and pride of the promotion of many who have left their Pompey homes to posts of trust and honor in other States, not to speak in detail of the large list of minor offices and nominations for important trusts that would tire your patience to hear. In addition to all these, the agriculturists, artisans, commercial men, citizens who represent all the industrial pursuits of life that Pompey has thrown forth upon the world, challenge the respect and admiration of every community from Plymouth Rock to the golden shores of the Pacific. Nor are the learned professions wanting in illustrious examples reared upon this sacred soil. Of them I need not speak, for soon they will speak for themselves in yonder grove, in strains of stirring native eloquence. And yet again, Pompey's sons and daughters have plucked the fairest roses from the field of science, and the literary world does homage to the artless word painting of the unapproachable Grace Greenwood. While all I have said, and more, is true of Pompey's children, I am not left in wonder that in your hearts welled up a yearning desire to visit once more the magic spot that has given to the world so rich a legacy. There is a philosophy closely connecting a people with the land of their birth. God, nature, divine revelation, and humanity in its normal condition, are all in harmony. Hence the transcendently lovely scenery, beautiful landscape views, healthful, invigorating breezes, enlarged and comprehensive views of nature in her sublimest moods, witnessed and enjoyed by your mothers and yourselves during your early existence, have left an impress upon your minds and assisted to form characters that will continue to exert a salutory influence which will reach ever onward and upward throughout the boundless cycles of eternity. This glorious old town of Pompey, of classic name, overlooking the lakes Onondaga and Oneida in yonder fertile valleys—with landscape views extending into seven counties of the State, itself but a succession of lofty, luxurient hills and fertile valleys, with its beautiful rivulets and cascades, separating the waters upon this inhabited summit of the Empire State, to find their meandering way to replenish the exhausted streams under the burning suns of a Southern clime, as well as to mollify the freezing current of our Northern lakes, is one of the spots upon this green and rolling earth where the true lover of nature would like to be born. Therefore, in conclusion, I repeat, welcome to these sylvan shades and cool retreats; welcome to these academic halls, where, under the tuition of a Stebbins, who now sleeps 'neath the clods of Chenango's beautiful valley, a fit resting place for the ark of a spirit so noble and so good, we together learned to climb the hill of science; welcome to the holy places where sleep your buried dead; welcome to our mountain homes; welcome! thrice welcome to our hearts! and should we never meet again on earth, be assured it is ours to know that this re-union we to-day are permitted to witness and enjoy, is typical of that never ending re-union, that God, the Father of our spirits has reserved for all his children.

The band then played "Home, Sweet Home."

Hon. Horatio Seymour was next introduced, and responded to the address of welcome, as follows:

GOVERNOR SEYMOUR'S ADDRESS.

There is a living cord which binds men and animals to the spots where they first feel life. A wonderful instinct guides the fish of the sea through the dark floods of the ocean to the streams where their existence begins; that directs the bird through the vast expanse of the air back to the hidden spot where it was born, and enables the beast of the forest to track its way through dense shades to its native lair. A secret vague yearning for our first home draws to-day to this retired village men from all parts of our broad country. They have left the exacting busy pursuits of their several stations at the bidding of this instinctive demand of nature at no small cost of time, of effort, and of means. They are here from the shores of the Atlantic and the Pacific; from the great valley of the Mississippi; from Northern and from Southern States. Whatever their stations in life may be, and although they may have become old men, the spirit of childhood comes over them when they stand again in the places where everything recalls the feelings and the associations of early youth. But beyond an instinctive desire to revisit our native homes, there are moral and intellectual reasons which have moved us to accept the invitations of the citizens of this town to meet here on this occasion. We sometimes think of the sorrows and joys of childhood as trivial things, and we smile at the deep feelings they once excited. As we grow older we look upon them in a different light. We find they had much to do in forming our characters and shaping our fortunes. Their memories have gone with us through life. They are golden threads woven into the warp and woof of our existence· They grow brighter as the rest of the fabric fades and decays. No man comes back alone to this spot thus hallowed. Each is surrounded with a crowd of those whom he has in imagination called back from their graves. On this day and in this place he sees with vivid clearness their forms and aspects, and he holds with them a closer communion. If each of us could see the cloud of such visions, which fills the minds of this assemblage, we should then feel that we are in the awful presence of the multitude of the spirits of those who once lived and acted here, and whose memories we cherish among the sacred things of our hearts.

Beyond those instinctive thoughts which crowd upon our mind, there are many matters of historic interest connected with this town and this vicinity. They would make ample topics for a more full address than would be in place at this time. This is not an occasion for any one man's speech, but for an exhibition of the feelings of each and all who meet here to indulge their memories with the past and to do honors to their forefathers. I will therefore say but a few words, and I will then give way to others.

Those of us who have reached the age of three score years will remember this spot as one of the frontier stations of civilization. The land was covered as with a pall by great and gloomy forests. The first settlers placed their homes upon the hill tops, where they could most readily get air and light and an outlook over the land then covered as if by a great ocean with the green and waving foliage of lofty tree tops. The deeper and darker valleys were shunned. Their luxuriant but excessive vegetation was fraught with disease and death. We used to look off upon the lower lands, where the city of Syracuse now stands with its population of fifty thousand, as a pestilential place to be avoided. It was then an unsightly swamp, in whose miasamtic air many sickened and died. At that day the toil and energy of the country were given to cutting down the overshadowing forests. The trees were felled in the winter months. In the spring their huge trunks were piled up and burned, filling the country with smoke of the log heaps; in the summer the crop was cultivated with painful toil amid the stumps and roots that covered the ground with a net work of decaying wood; in autumn they gathered the slender harvests, which gave them their simple food and scanty clothing. For these blessings they thanked God and were content. It took a lifetime of hard and patient work to make a cleared farm in this hill region. I do not think the men of this generation are equal to the work done by their fathers. I will not recount the events and changes which have taken place since their days. They are constantly forced upon our attention when we turn our mind towards the past. It is enough to say that we who saw the forest cut down in this region, who watched the retreating steps of savage tribes, and who witnessed the destruction of the wild beasts of the woods, have lived through social changes and a material progress equal to that of ten centuries of English history. We have seen changes in the condition of our people as marked as those which have occurred in Britain from the reign of Alfred the Great to that of Queen Victoria. We have witnessed the first steps, and the highest achievement of civilization.

Let me say a few words about the social condition of this town at the beginning of this century. The people were poor; their condition was one of constant toil and hard struggles to gain food and clothing; but these evils were relieved by the kindly sympathies which sprung from common wants. All intercourse was upon a level. Where all were poor there was no glare of wealth to shame poverty or to cause repining. In this respect this community was then like all others in Central New York. But there was one fact which every native of this town loves to speak of, which sent so many of its sons forth into the world to become prosperous men, which brings so many of them back to-day with feelings of gratitude to their fathers. Amidst all their poverty, toil and privation, their first thought was to get schools for their children, and to found an academy which should give instruction in the higher branches of education. To do this, great efforts were made, and in some instances men put mortgages upon their lands to enable them to do their share towards building up this institution. For a long time it was the only academy in a large section of this State, and many pupils were sent to it from adjoining counties. The people of Onondaga have always given the founders of this town great credit for their wisdom and foresight. Among the first in-comers were persons of culture and ability, who did much to form the characters and shape the policy of their townsmen. At one time all the four members in the Legislature of the State from this county, and at or about the same time the representatives in Congress, were natives of the town of Pompey.

It can be claimed for its academy that it was of National consequence. In the Senate of the United States, in the House of Representatives, in the Judiciary of the Nation and of New York, in the Legislatures of the States, in the armies of the Union, in the pulpits of our churches, in the learned professions, and in all useful pursuits, those born and educated in this town have held positions of honor and responsibility. One of the earliest recollections of my childhood is that of looking upon a meeting of the friends of that academy, on a winter's evening, in a room which was lighted, as well as warmed, by a huge wood fire, which roared and flashed in the cavernous fire place. All the means and efforts of its founders could only put up an humble building for academical uses. If seen now, we might smile at its rude workmanship and its meagre endowment of books and apparatus, but it we could see it in the light of the benefits it has done, we should bow reverentially to the memories of those who founded it, amid all the wants, trials and poverty of frontier life.

The social condition of this country has changed in the last half century. At the outset it was rude, but it was free and void of shams and hypocrisy. They had a kind of teaching too, which, in some ways was better than that gained by modern improvements in books and schools. At an early day; in poor communities only those who were able to put up comfortable houses could entertain travelers.

Hence fifty years ago Inn-keepers were among our leading men. The village bar-room was not only made attractive by its ample space, and made cheerful by its great fires of logs and sticks, which would be called logs in those days, but it was also the place of common resort for all classes. Here the lawyer, the doctor, clergyman, and men of business and of labor, met to talk over the affairs of the town, the State and nation. These discussions were open to all of the wide circle which filled the room.

Men then heard both sides of the questions of the day. They learned to temper their prejudices, and to correct their opinions. Nor was the gain to the uneducated only. The members of the learned professions were taught much that was valuable to them in their pursuits. Clergymen and lawyers knew more of human nature then than now. Opinions were not formed in studies alone, or from association with one class of minds. Hence they were not put forth in those terms of bitterness, and with those feelings of bigotry which are apt to mark those who see but one side of questions. The village bar-room had its evils and its temptations. If these could be done away with, and its cheerful rooms and bright fires could be restored, and above all, if the old kindly and free intercourse among all classes could be renewed, we should not only have better order and morals throughout our social system, but we should all have wiser and better men at the bar, in the pulpit, and in the halls of State and National legislation.

The amusements of those old days were more robust than at this time. Physical strength and activity were admired. Each town had ambitions of having the swiftest runner and the most skillful wrestler. The battle with the forest could only be fought and won by hands hardened to toil and endurance. These were the qualities most admired, for they were most needed. Our deacons would not now think of calling out the country to aid in lifting up the frames of their churches by a promise that some adventurous man would stand upon his head on the highest ball on the steeple's top, and twine his feet in the tines of the lightning rod. Yet, if my memory serves me right, the church which stands in its fair proportions on this village green was helped up by some such inducements. I am sure the deacons would not try to stimulate the sale of pews by putting a pail of punch on the pulpit stairs to warm up the liberal spirits of the church members. I know that was the case when the pews were sold in the church just by.

It has been said that those were the "days of pure liquor, sound Democracy and vital piety." We can dispense with the liquor, pure or impure. Of Democracy in a partisan sense, I have nothing to say, but as it is held by all classes and all parties as a part of our political system, I think it is true that in all social intercourse, in public morality, in official virtue, it was better practiced then than now. So far as piety is concerned, I can only say I believe that then, as now, devoted men preached the truths of religion, and toiled with faithfulness in their Maker's cause. Many of those who rest in yonder grave-yard went down to their resting place soothed and comforted by an assurance of future joys, and I trust all of those who stand before me are animated by the same hopes, and will, in their last hours, be sustained by the same consolation.

The President, with some appropriate remarks, presented Governor Seymour with an exquisite bouquet, the gift of Mrs. P. P. Miller, of DeWitt, whereupon Governor Seymour responded as follows:—"I am very much gratified for this beautiful bouquet. I have said already how I reverenced the memories of the fathers of Pompey, and how I admired their sons. I can now only say how much I love their daughters." [Applause and laughter.]

Governor Seymour, in a few moments, rose and said:—"My friends, pardon me for lifting up my voice one more. [Applause.] I spoke of the early men in my county. I tried in very feeble and inadequate terms to tell you what their claims were upon our respect. I can do more now.

I want to give you an example of one more of them in presenting to you Judge Strong, a gentleman ninety years of age, who has spent his whole life honorably and well, trying to serve his fellow-men, to honor his God, and to uphold the institutions of our country. I now present you Judge Oliver R. Strong, of Syracuse, one of the early settlers of the town of Onondaga."

The aged patriarch stood uncovered before the immense assemblage, his clear eye indicating a vigorous intellect in his green old age, and in eloquent silence he gracefully bowed his acknowledgements to the hearty welcome of applause he received.

After Judge Strong had resumed his seat, the entire assemblage arose and joined in singing the following beautiful anthem, the effect of which will ever be remembered by all present on the occasion. It seemed as though one soul animated the vast concourse and one sympathetic cord united all the people. At the close of the singing a solemn stillness pervaded the place, and a happy expression beamed forth from thousands of tearful eyes.

AULD LANG SYNE.

Should auld acquaintance be forgot,
  And never brought to mind?
Should auld acquaintance be forgot,
  And days of auld lang syne?
For auld lang syne we meet to-day,
  For auld lang syne;
To tread the paths our fathers trod
  In days of auld lang syne.

We've passed through many varied scenes,
  Since Youth's unclouded day;
And friends, and hopes, and happy dreams,
  Times hand hath swept away.
And voices that once joined with ours,
  In days of auld lang syne,
Are silent now, and blend no more,
  In songs of auld lang syne.

Yet ever has the light of hope
  Illumed our darkest hours,

And cheered us on life's toilsome way,
  And gemmed our paths with flowers:.
The sacred prayers our mothers said
  In days of auld lang syne,
Have ever kept us in the right,
  Since days of auld lang syne.

Here we have met, here we may part,
  To meet on earth no more,
And some may never see again
  The cherished homes of yore;
The sportive plays and pleasant days
  Of childhood's auld lang syne—
We ne'er shall meet to know again
  Those joys of auld lang syne.

But when we've crossed the sea of life
  And reached the heav'nly shore,
We'll sing the songs our fathers sing,
  Transcending those of yore;
We there shall sing diviner strains
  Than those of auld lang syne—
Immortal songs of praise, unknown
  In days of auld lang syne.

The President stated that he was compelled to make an announcement that would undoubtedly be painful to all; Grace Greenwood can not be present. He then read the following telegram:—"It is impossible for me to be with you to-day, my aged mother is not well enough."—Grace Greenwood.

The President then announced that Mrs. Dr. H. V. Miller, of Syracuse, would read a paper of "Reminiscences of Pompey," in place of the poem by Grace Greenwood.

Mrs. Miller then read as follows:—

It is related by that famous traveler, Bayard Taylor, that far up among the fastnesses of the Pyrenees he found a race of sturdy mountaineers, who for centuries have preserved intact a Republican form of government, despite the threats of the two Despotisms of France and Spain, that crouch on either hand. Strong only in their patriotism and their natural defences, they have defied intrigue, diplomacy and brute force, and still maintained the letter and spirit of a pure Republic. The same traveler tells us of a similar instance among the Alps, where he found in the "little Land of Appenzell," a hardy nation, of limited numbers, but strong in the patriotic principle, and the love of freedom, who refuse even to join the confederacy which unites the Cantons around them; whose rulers are chosen directly by the people, and who have preserved, along with their free institutions, a simplicity of life and manners almost patriarchal.

When the shores of what is now Great Britain were invaded by foreign hordes, first of Saxons and afterwards of Normans, the Cymry, the ancient people of Wales, retreated to their mountain fastnesses, and long after the plains had become the prey of the invaders, they retained their independence, and only yielded when war and hardship had reduced the race nearly to extinction.

From these, and other similar facts, we cannot resist the conclusion that the continuous toil of a mountaineer's life, the contest with the elements that rage unobstructed around the high lands, the daily habit of climbing and overcoming obstacles, and above all, the pure and invigorating air of the hills, tend to develope strength of character, independence of thought and action, sturdiness of purpose, and physical force, as well.

It is said that during the Crimean war, the regiments of Scotch Highlanders were so affected by home sickness, that the regimental bands were forbidden to play the national airs, "Bonnie Doon" and "Annie Laurie," so greatly were the spirits and health of the men affected by the remembrance of their native land. I believe it is an acknowledged fact that love of home prevails most powerfully with those born and reared among the hills. This numerous assemblage of the sons and daughters of the hills, who have gathered from all points of the compass to this common center, like pilgrims to a holy city, is proof that we are true to our instincts; that though some of us have felt in former times, and while under the spur of youthful ambition, that "Pompey was rather slow," that "we wanted to get away from this knoll," still the home of our childhood has power to win us for a time from the pursuit of fame, or wealth, or pleasure.

And the noticeable fact, that of all this crowd so large a proportion have won for themselves a competence of this world's goods; so many have become men of mark in our country's annals; so many have helped to raise the general average of morality and prosperity in the community at large, goes far to prove the correctness of the conclusion that a youth passed among the hills is a good preparation for the arena of life.

In the case of many here present, years have passed since they parted from the home of their youth, while others have by frequent visits, kept fresh and bright the links of memory's chain. With all of us it is love and loyalty to old Pompey that brings us here. I remember, some years since —when House's Printing Telegraph was first invented—being taken by a friend to the office in Syracuse, to inspect its operations. My friend introduced me to the operator as from Pompey, whereupon the latter telegraphed my name and address to the office in Rochester; in a few minutes the answer was unrolled before me, it ran thus:—"God bless old Pompey! Are the old wind mills standing yet?" It seemed as if I could see that man swing his hat as he gave that telegraphic cheer for his old home, and though I have forgotton his name I cherish for him a kindly feeling still. Many such pleasant surprises I have enjoyed, when by a word and a grap of the hand old associations have been called up, and long buried memories revived. I have stood in a crowd of strangers, and felt all the dreariness incident to such a position entirely dispelled, when some familiar voice has said "I used to know you in Pompey!" or, "I was in the same class with you in school!"

We are *proud* of our native town, and it is an honest, well grounded pride that we cherish. The annals both of our State and nation, bear honorable witness of the part her sons have borne in the history of both. We are proud of her far-reaching landscapes, of her broad emerald slopes, now bathed in sunshine, and now swept by the trailing skirts of a passing cloud; of her atmosphere of such crystaline purity that objects which are miles away "as the crow flies," seem at the distance of only a few minutes walk. Down yonder among the "low landers," we boast even of her superior snow drifts, though we are not anxious to face them, and until lately we have been ready to venture our last dollar that Pompey *winds* cannot be beaten. But this summer a *son-in-law* of Pompey has found a place near the summit of the Rocky Mountains, where a head wind absolutely stopped the train. Now we are forced to acknowledge that no *Pompey* breeze was ever known to brow beat a train so as to force it to a stand still; possibly, because no railroad ever ventured to climb her heights. So that, for the present, Pompey meekly yields the pre-eminence in this respect to her Rocky sisters across the continent.

I have heard the following anecdote, which illustrates this feeling of pride and attachment to Pompey: In the town of Lysander, lived some years ago, a blacksmith known as "Dutch Jake;" around him had settled several farmers who had emigrated from Pompey, and who were accustomed frequently to apply to him for work in his line. They were not satisfied with his work, however, and did not hesitate to declare it inferior to similar work done in Pompey. On one occasion "Dutch Jake" lost patience at a remark of this kind, and exclaimed with emphasis, "Its all Pompey! Pompey! I believe you folks dat come from Pompey, you tinks *you go to Pompey ven you die!*"

In the early history of this region, this town held a conspicuous position. The reputation of the place for wealth, intelligence and refinement, and the energy and talent of its principal men, called hither a great amount of business, and made it a sort of commercial emporium for the country around. I remember to have heard from the lips of the late Squire M. Brown, of Elbridge, accounts of his frequent journeys hither when a young man, with loads of grain from the farms of his father and his uncles, the Munroes of Elbridge and Camillus, this place being their most accessible market. Here they sold their grain to Henry Seymour and carried back groceries, dry goods, &c., purchased of him. The old wind mills near the academy were erected by Mr. Seymour for grinding purposes, and supplied the needs of the inhabitants for a long time.

The following facts (obtained from Samuel Baker, Esq.,) concerning the first church organized here, will show that the early settlers here were men of good moral and religious principles and energy and perseverance to carry out the plans. The First Congregational church of Pompey was formed October 19th, 1796, by Rev. Ammi R. Robinson, pastor of the church in Norfolk, Conn., and comprised twenty-two members. Its first deacons were Levi Jerome and Daniel Dunham. It first settled minister was the Rev. Joseph Gilbert, whose remains lie interred in the village cemetery. In 1803 the Rev. Hugh Wallis was installed as pastor, and in the year 1810 the church became a member of the Onondaga Presbytery. About this time the Rev. Artemas Bishop, a native of this place and a pupil of the academy, was sent by the American Board as a missionary to the Sandwich Islands and is now living there. In the year 1836 Mrs. Crane (Julia Ostrander) went with her husband as a missionary to India. As fruits of the religious training of this church and the academy, we offer the following list of faithful ministers of the Gospel who have gone out from our midst:—Rev. Jared Ostrander, Rev. Charles Jerome, Rev. H. C. Hayden, Rev. Carlos Swift, and Rev. Delos E. Wells.

The large folio Bible given to the church by Mr. Henry Seymour at the time of its dedication, remains in a good state of preservation, although made to give place to a more modern one, which, with a handsome silver communion service, was given by another sister in the church.

For many years the above church was the only one in the place; but in process of time three others have been organized, and now occupy their respective places of worship. From these facts it will be seen that this first church must have exercised a powerful influence upon the early moral and religious character of the community.

To the high standard of education, also, which prevailed here at an early date, may be attributed much of the influence which the children of Pompey have exerted in the community at large. In regard to schools, she has been the pioneer, having established the first academy in this region. The original building was erected about 1805, stood nearly upon the site of the present edifice, and by one whose early years were largely passed within its walls, is described as follows:—A frame building, two stories high, and painted yellow. On the first floor were two rooms, used respectively as a high school and a district school. On the second floor was a large room, used as occasion required, for a town-hall or chapel. Up to the time that the present church edifice was built, in 1817, the Congregational society worshipped in it, and my informant retains a vivid remembrance of its bare walls and its uncomfortable high-backed pine benches, where he spent the time of service in vain endeavors to touch the floor with feet and to see the minister over the shoulders of his grown-up neighbors.

In this room, the Rev. Joshua Leonard, (more familiarly known as "Uncle Jock,") preached on the Sabbath, greatly to the edification of his hearers, for he was a man of great eloquence and power; but during the week he presided over the youth of the community, congregated in the room below. It is related of him that he always prayed with open eyes, and generally standing in front of the large open fireplace by which the school room was warmed. On one occasion a young man, a new scholar, entered the room while the Reverend teacher was engaged in the opening prayer. While the stranger waited near the fire place for the conclusion of the exercise, a roguish boy, the son of the principal, stepped slyly behind him and dropped a live coal into his open hand. Uncle Jock, whose watchful eyes saw the performance, broke off his prayer, administered condign punishment to the offender, then quietly resumed the broken thread of his devotions, and finished as if there had been no interruption.

Edward Aiken, Flavius Littlejohn, (a brother of D. C. Littlejohn, of Oswego, who afterwards became a noted lawyer of Michigan,) Henry Howe, since for twenty-five years a teacher of youth in Canandaigua, and Andrew Huntington, were Mr. Leonard's successors in the old academy. It was under the tuition of Mr. Leonard that Charles Mason and Seabred Dodge received their thorough mathematical training, which fitted them for the responsible positions which they have since filled.

In the new academy, built in 1834, we, of later days, recall Samuel S. Stebbins, classical and stately; Ensign Baker, renowned for his hobbies, successively, of elocution, agricultural chemistry, and—*circular swings!* T. K. Wright, eminent as a drill-sergeant, and a host of younger men, whose term of office were so short that they failed to impress the public memory as did the earlier teachers.

Among those who presided over the female department in the new academy may be mentioned Miss Anne Hopkins, afterwards the wife of Professor Kendrick, of Rochester; sweet, saintly Harriet Rand, whose blessed influences have not yet ceased to echo in the hearts of her pupils; Mrs. Elizabeth Stone, late Mrs. Niven, whose dignity and rare culture still grace the society of Syracuse; Julia Reynolds, whose magnificent physique, winning ways and charming conversational powers secure for her the admiration of all who know her; and Adelia Payson, who, a few years since, left a large circle of friends and pupils to bear the tidings of a free gospel to the women of China.

A few facts in regard to the district and select schools, held here at an early date, may be of interest. Before the year 1800 a school was taught in a log house near where Colonel Kellogg's house now stands. Miss Lucy Jerome, afterwards the wife of James S. Geddes, and mother of Hon. George Geddes, of Camillus, was the first teacher. Later, a frame building was erected upon the village green, about due west from the hotel. In this building a district school was taught by Leman H. Pitcher, father of L. B. Pitcher, of Salina. It is supposed that about the year 1801, Miss Hepey Beeber taught this school. Merrit Butler remembers that his father, one of the trustees, sent him for her with a horse, to her home on Newman's Hill, and that he rode home behind her. When the first academy was built, the district school was removed thither, and Manoah Pratt, Daniel F. Gott and James Robinson, were among the teachers.

One of the earliest select schools was taught by Miss Philene Hascall, afterwards Mrs. Samuel Baker, in the front chamber of what was known as the "Joe Colton" house, afterwards occupied by Dr. Stearns, and later still by Joseph Beach. Another was taught about 1819, by Charlotte Hopkins, (Mrs. Beardsley) in the north west room of the hotel kept by her father, Col. Hezekiah Hopkins.

In these two schools, Charles B. and Henry J. Sedgwick, Mary, Sophia and Horatio Seymour, Victory J. and Ellen Birdseye, Charles, Richard and William Stevens, Cornelia Stearns, and many others, who are now in the prime and vigor of life, received their earliest instruction. Later, probably, about forty-five years ago, Miss Rowena Wells, (Mrs. Jared Ostrander,) taught a select school in the upper story of the building next north of the church, known as the Stevens house. The family chronicle of the writer abounds in anecdotes of this institution, only one of which will be recorded here. One of the numerous sons of the family, had received in his face a paper wad, skillfully snapped by his next neighbor, who immediately became absorbed in his studies, and kept his face buried in his book that he might not be exposed to a return of the compliment. The other urchin prepared *his* paper missile and awaited his opportunity but none came. The little fellow tried various stratagems to no purpose, and at last in his ecstasy of impatience resorted to extreme measures, "Miss Rowena, Miss Rowena," he called out, "Mayn't Dave Porter look here?" "Dave Porter, look there!" replied the teacher. *Dave did* look, and received full compensation for the injury he had inflicted, whereupon order was restored and the operations of the school resumed.

The district school house, from about the year 1820 to 1845, stood west of Dr. Stearns' office. In this building many present will remember, as among tbe teachers, Asa H. Wells, Calvin S. Ball, Jno. Doolett, Alfred Sloan, and Harry Gifford. Since this latter building fell to decay a more commodious one has been built on the opposite side of the street, which was burned down in the year 1867, and replaced in 1868 by the purchase and remodeling of the church near by.

Thus have I endeavored in brief to span the interval between the present and the rapidly receding past; to offer some slight tribute to the memory of those who have borne a part in preparing the children of Pompey for positions of responsibility. The task has been a pleasant one, and lovingly performed.

To the aged who in spite of the burden of years and infirmities have come to visit the scenes of their past, this day must wear a tinge of sadness, for of many whom they once knew and loved, the only memento they will find will be a monument on yonder marble-crowned hill-top. Let us who are in life's prime, go forth to our toils, refreshed by the air of our native hills, cheered by the greeting of old friends, remembering that "old age creeps on apace," and to us, the time may come, when the scenes of middle life will, to our backward vision, grow dim and indistinct, compared with the vividness with which we shall recall the scenes of our early years.

At the close of Mrs. Miller's paper, the quartette from Syracuse, Joseph Durston, Mrs. S. B. Wood, Mr. and Mrs. J. E. Van Cleeck, sang with thrilling effect, "We have come to our homes in the old Empire State."

The President next announced that they were fortunate in having one of Pompey's younger sons present who had been remarkably busy since he had gone forth from his old home to the busy world. He had represented a distant State, on the Pacific coast, and more recently had been a member of the Joint High Commission, and his name would be handed down to future generations in enduring remembrance. He introduced Senator George H. Williams.

SPEECH OF SENATOR WILLIAMS.

Mr. Chairman and Friends:—

One of our distinguished poets has written beautifully of the "Voices of the Night," but under some circumstances the daytime too, has its voices, and from the suggestive surroundings of this day I seem to hear a voice saying, "Backward, flow Backward, Oh tide of the years." Our lives, it appears to me, may properly be divided into two periods. One is when every thought, passion and emotion of our natures is absorbed in visions of the future—sorrow, repentance and regret for misfortunes, misdeeds or mistakes suffered or committed are then unknown—our life appears to be spread out before us like a beautiful panorama, in which we see the green fields, the flowery pathways, the bright and cloudless skies, but in which, the pitfalls, the thorny acclivities, the clouds and darkness, are artfully concealed from our view. This was the period of life through which I passed in the town of Pompey. Imagination easily carries me back from this stand point to that time, when I was one of those poetically described as "whining school boys," with satchels and shining morning faces creeping to school. The tender associations, the happy scenes and the sportive incidents of my boyhood now comes back to me, like the half remembered pictures of a morning dream. Life then was little more than a succession of ecstatic sensations.

Whether I chased the butterflies in the summer sunshine, or like Maud Muller "raked the meadow sweet with hay," or whether I toiled through the snow to my allotted labor, or joined in the pastime of snowballing or sleigh-riding metaphisically speaking there was "no snow in my song or winter in my year." Well do I remember the day when like another youth of whom we read bearing aloft a banner with the strange device, "Excelsior," I come up from the district school of the country to the Academy on the Hill—yonder stands the old Academy—foundation and superstructure, walls and windows, roof and belfry as they were more than twenty years ago. Unattractive and inanimate that time-worn and weather beaten pile of stone and mortar seems to be, but every crevice and nook and corner is quick with the memories of youthful friends and by-gone years. They inhabit every room. They occupy every seat. They sit at every desk. They are regular at the morning prayer and at the recitation. They are as bright and joyous as ever. Unseen and unheard, they steal out of those portals with which so many of us are familiar, to take part in the proceedings of this day. Many things crowd upon my mind from the reminiscences of that old Academy, but none are more prominent or pleasing than those connected with its then flourishing Lyceum. The beauty and the chivalry of Pompey were accustomed to meet there. Debate was not confined to those connected with the school; but Gott, plausible, persuasive and eloquent, Birdseye, always lawyer-like and logical, Dodge, with his strong practical views, appeared upon that arena of intellectual combat. They were "giants in those days," as it then appeared to me, and I still think that their speeches compared favorably with those I have heard in bodies of much higher pretensions. I have met with a reasonable share of success and prosperity since I left this town, but whenever I review my life, I always decide that the happiest of its days are those I passed in the Pompey Academy.

Circumstances of fortune as many of you know were not very favorable, but I had a heart for controversy with these. Spurning all such embarrassments, I only looked up that ladder which I had set out to climb, whose top appeared to penetrate the shining temples of fortune and fame. Time and experience have satisfied me, I am sorry to say, that the enjoyments of this world unmixed with trouble, are found more than elsewhere in these illusions of early life. When I considered myself sufficiently prepared I applied to one with whose name most of you are familiar, and whose memory I shall always revere, to pursue the study of the law in his office. Do you know said he, in answer to the application, " How long Jacob was compelled to serve for his wife Rachel ? " Being a little more familiar with the scriptures then than I am now, I was quite ready with the answer.

He then said what I have since found to be true, that the law for its favors demanded the same fidelity and devotion that Jacob displayed for Rachel, and pointed out with paternal kindness the difficulties and discouragements I would have to encounter. I told him that my resolution was made and could not be changed ; three years for the most part of the time, I passed in his presence, and among the books of his office, and I can only say that if Jacob enjoyed his service for Rachel as much as I did then my service for the law, it is probable that he was quite as happy in his protracted courtship as he was in his wedded life. (Laughter and applause.) I ventured, about the time I decided to be a lawyer, to visit the Court House, in Syracuse, while the Circuit Court was in session. Judge Moseley was presiding, his hair was as white as silver, and he was the very personification of Judicial propriety. Around him and in the bar were Noxon, Lawrence, Hillis, Gott, Birdseye, with other lawyers, and bailiffs, with long pikes, moved around with noiseless steps to preserve perfect order and stillness in Court. I can remember how much I was overawed by that presence, and what misgivings crossed my mind as to whether I could ever appear with credit to myself in such a forum.

I am reminded of my first and greatest professional victory. One citizen of this town sued another to recover the value of a horse gored to death, as it was alleged, by an unruly ox. Mr. Gott, my preceptor in the law, appeared for the plaintiff and I was employed by the defendant. My point to defeat the action was not that the ox did not gore the horse but that the owner of the ox did not know at the time that he was a vicious animal. I marshalled my authorities and made a desperate effort for my client, but no Pompey jury could withstand the persuasive powers of Mr. Gott and he recovered a judgment of eighty dollars. Confident that I was right, I appealed the case to the Common Pleas. James R. Lawrenee, Esq., represented me as I was not then admitted to practice. Failing there as in the Court below, to prove the *scienter* on his motion, Judge Pratt nonsuited the plaintiff and I had won the case. No doubt the Emperor William was proud to witness the triumphal entry into Berlin of his victorious legions returning from the conquest of France, but it is not at all probable that he experienced that keen sense of pride and satisfaction which I felt at this my first professional victory. (Laughter and applause.)

When I reached the age of twenty-one, I applied for admission to the Common Pleas of this county; Judge Pratt appointed a committee for my examination, of which the Hon. C. B. Sedgwick was chairman. I appeared before that committee with fear and trembling. The chairman enquired what I would do to collect fees for professional services which were not voluntarily paid. I made as I suppose, a satisfactory answer, and was admitted, and I have since found that one of the first accomplishments of a lawyer is to know how to collect his own fees. (Laughter and applause.)

Twenty-seven years ago, with the proof in my pocket that I was a lawyer, signed by Judge Pratt, and a small library of law books, I started in that direction in which it is said,

"The star of Empire takes its way." I have many reasons to believe that I was accompanied by the good wishes of those who had known me here. One act of generous kindness I cannot forbear to mention upon this occasion. Determined to go west, I had neither money or books. David F. Dodge and John S. Wells borrowed for me what money I needed. I repaid the money within three years, but the debt of gratitude I can never pay. Twenty-seven years ago is an expression that forcibly and in some cases sorrowfully suggests to the mind the idea of change; what changes have occurred since 1844? Some who were then in their nurse's arms I now see before me full grown men and women. Some who were then boys and girls I now find presiding over flourishing households. Some who were then in the prime and vigor of middle life, now bend under the weight of accumulated years, and not a few have passed away to

> "The land of the great departed ;
> Into the silent lands."

When I left Syracuse in the canal boat that was to carry me away from friends and home, the convention by which Silas Wright was nominated for Governor, was then and there in session. He is dead, and so are most of the great men associated with him in the government of the country. Parties and opinions have changed wonderfully since that time. Administrations have come and gone. War has stricken the land with its multiform afflictions. Great discoveries in science and art have been made. Telegraphic wires have been stretched across the ocean. Thousands of miles have been added to our railway system. Six times have I crossed from ocean to ocean, on the trans-continental railroad. Many new States have been added to the Union, two of which I have helped to make. Our country, though not without some suffering, has grown greatly in wealth, power and glory. I believe in freedom, education and progress, and have faith, though the indications are not always favorable, that mankind is slowly but surely advancing to a higher and better plane of existence. I have said that life may be divided into two periods. One is, when the prospective absorbs all, and the other is, when the faculties of the mind loosening their hold upon the future, seek pleasure in a retrospective view of passed events. I will not say on which side of the line separating these two periods, I stand, but I am obviously near enough to it, to find my attention divided between what of the past is unforgotten, and what of the future is unrevealed.

Time and change have scattered many of the associates of my early life far and near. Some have gone in one direction and some another, and I have found a home upon the shores of the Pacific ocean. I live in a populous and flourishing city, where but a few years ago rolled "the distant Oregon and heard no sound save the dash of its own waters." I would not entice any away from the good old town of Pompey, but if any of you are disposed to emigrate, I invite you to the land where I live. Come where a great, genial ocean, snow-capped mountains, majestic rivers, with woodland and prairie will give you every variety of soil, climate and scenery. Oregon is not a land "flowing with milk and honey," but it is a land of health, plenty and beauty. This is a re-union of the old residents of Pompey. Some have come here from the "cool sequestered vales," and others from the conflicts of professional and public life. All are here to revive old associations, renew old acquaintances and especially to do honor to our old home; various have been my experiences since I left here, I have been in the whirl and vortex of political life, I have lived thousands of miles away, but I have never forgotten my old friends in Pompey, or "the old folks at home." Accept my greetings and congratulations. I am about to return to my distant home upon the Pacific, but I shall remember this occasion with pleasure, and as long as I live, shall cherish the hope that peace, plenty and happiness may be and remain in the old town of Pompey.

After music by the band the President stated, I have now the pleasure of introducing to you one whose boyhood was spent in this village, and all present who then resided here will quickly recall the pleasant recollections of his active, sportive young life; and I will only say that the physical energy and intellectual promise thus early manifested have developed into the successful competitor among the gifted intellects of our great Metropolis, for the highest honors of his profession. I refer to Hon. Luther Rawson Marsh, of New York.

REMARKS OF LUTHER R. MARSH.

My Townsmen, old and young, one and all:

I am glad, this day, to meet you; glad to talk with you of the present and the past; and, in doing so, we should miss, to some extent, the object of our brotherly reunion if we did not gossip a little of ourselves, and push our personalities somewhat to the front. Let us then commune in freedom and with unconstrained joy.

It is curious to notice how a little town like this will ramify its influence through all the land, and bind itself with every part of the country. What portion of the Union, North or South, or on either ocean—what essential business or interest, private or public, but is represented here to-day?

These town celebrations have, of late, come much in vogue amongst the old settlements of New England—a custom that should extend throughout the land. They have an interest beyond the pleasure of the meeting and the renewal of broken ties; they are the best historians, gathering materials for the home life of the nation; they help to collect and preserve the facts and domestic reminiscences connected with the starting and growth of our country, as the line of population, with a rapidity unknown in history, advanced across the continent. Every town may thus contribute its quota; and, ere those who saw the beginning are removed, their memories are evoked and recorded.

Though we stand, now, on land so recently reclaimed from aboriginal sway, and though we are assembled on the One

Hill, and not on the ancient Seven, yet are we on classic ground. We meet at the villas of *Pompey.* We bear the name of him—a foremost soldier of the world—at the stamp of whose foot armies arose, and at the base of whose statue "great Cæsar fell." Our allies are near; and our Roman friends, like sentinels, are all around us—*Fabius* and *Tully*, *Marcellus* and *Cicero*, *Camillus* and *Manlius Torquatus*—while within our Eastern border, we may consult the mystic utterances of *Delphi.*

Nor is the history of our town so recent as it seems. The mists of antiquity rest upon it. It was by no means the beginning when the present dynasty started here. There had been enacted, in this locality, at some period of the unknown past, events which no pen has written and no tradition preserved. Generations and races have preceded us on this chosen spot and disappeared. Whence they came, whither went, is not yet ascertained; mystery enclouds their origin, their life and their departure; conjecture starts her various theories, but authentic history is silent. The evidences of a former population, now wholly extinct, are thick around us. A second growth of trees, of such age and magnitude as to take rank with the original forest, astonished those who thought they had come to a place entirely new. If, when we were boys and girls, a museum had been established here to hold the *reliques* discovered in our soil, this would have been a famous resort for the curious and scientific. Here would have remained your stone tablet of Anno Domini, 1550, now reposing in the Institute at Albany, whose hieroglyphs so many Champollions have endeavored to decipher. Here would have been collected not only the rude arrow-heads and granite tomahawks of the savage, but the proofs of aformer and unkn own civilization—the blacksmith's forge, iron implements of husbandry, fragments of earthenware and church bells, and numerous coins and medals, whose devices and inscriptions age has obliterated. Long before the ancestors of the present residents clambered here—long before the time when a bounty of five dollars was offered for a wolf's scalp—there was imbedded in the soil, since upturned by the coulter, not only the utensils of peace but the weapons of civilized warfare—if warfare can be said ever to be civilized—guns, and cannon, and cannon ball; indicating advance in the arts both of living and killing; showing that wherever man goes cruelty goes with him; and that he is ever ready to unite the elements of destruction with those of progress. It was because of this profusion of antiquities, no doubt, that, after modern chisels had done their artistic work, the soil of our town was chosen for the clandestine deposit of the Gypsum Giant; but he was a stranger, not a native—not indigenous, but imported—the only humbug, as with due modesty we claim, Pompey ever turned out.

How different the scene this day from that presented to our fathers, as, at the close of the last century and the beginning of this, they clomb these hills, to plant here a new community. There were no roads to guide them up the wooded acclivity but the Onondaga's trail. Soon, however, they mingled the echoes of their industrious axes with the roar of the wild beast and the sigh of the wind. Cleared fields appeared. Fruit-bearing trees supplanted the towering monarch, and grass and grain invited the sickle. The red man and the wolf, who had so long held a divided dominion, retired before the rifle and the plow—reluctantly retired, for some still lingered to a recent day. The Indian, with his wampumed moccasins and beaded leggings, his silver-banded hat and ornamented ears, his blanket and his bow, yet remain, vivid frescoes on the walls of our memory; and some present, no doubt, remember when Bruin came over the hill, strolling and swaying leisurely on the green, as if to attend town meeting, then in progress. But, though native born, he was not permitted to exercise the rights of citizenship till he had shown a prowess worthy of it. Accordingly, Major Case, the constable, stepped forth to test his credentials. The amiable visitor rose on his haunches to give the bailiff welcome, quickly struck his extemporized tip-staff from his grasp, and gave him the bear salute—a back-hug so pressing as to leave no doubt of its cordiality. Old Hawkeye, himself, would never have tempted it a second time. Possibly the grizzly stranger may have anticipated the service of some process upon him—for Bears, even to this day, in Wall street, sometimes receive such documents—as he put his mark of cancellation, like a railroad conductor, through many a summons and execution in the officer's pocket-book, till his teeth met in the Major's breast; who only escaped (to die from his wounds some three years after) when the axe of Canfield Marsh sank in the victor's skull.

The new settlement grew and flourished. Adventurous men and women, chiefly from the New England hive, came hither—bringing with them the Yankee's outfit of good habits, indomitable pluck, and a desire for education. This lovely village arose, cresting the mount, near two thousand feet above the sea—so high, that no Vesuvius can ever shower it, like ancient Pompeii, with its ashes; an elevation from which eye-shot may sometimes touch the blue of Ontario, some fifty miles away; nested here, as it seemed, where old Hyem lived and feathered down his "Beautiful snow;" where two fountains, but a few rods apart, and bubbling from the same field, send their sparkling salutations to the ocean—one, through the Susquehanna and the Chesapeake, the other coasting the thousand isles of the St. Lawrence. It soon became a centre of influence; men of character and might, and genuine grit, were developed. For years this village was a power in the politics of the County and the State. When, some forty-seven years ago, a Senator from Onondaga applied to the Council of Appointment, at Albany, for the re-appointment of one Luther Marsh to the office of High Sheriff, DeWitt Clinton slapped him on the knee, saying: "Squire Birdseye, I wish you to understand, that the good people on Pompey Hill cannot have *all* the offices in the State of New York."

I fancy, however, that the Sheriff received his re-appointment, for as he was riding through Christian Hollow—as

Edwards states in his "Pleasantries of the Bar"—he saw a man in the field suddenly drop his hoe and run for the woods. The officer quickly dismounted, tied his horse to the fence and gave pursuit. After a long chase he captured the panting fugitive, who gasped that it was what he feared. "Well," said the Sheriff, "I have no process against you now, but I thought I would let you know that if I ever should have, *it wouldn't do you any good to run.*"

He was a man, I think, of pretty strong impulses. Mr. Sedgwick has just told me that, at a time happily now past, when political hostility implied personal as well, a bitter opponent, who was usually kept in salutary restraint by the will and physical endowments of the Sheriff, presumed, on the occasion of seeing a wounded right arm in a sling, to press his personalities so far that he received an *argumentum ad hominem* from the left, which sent him not only against but through the door—latch and hasp and hinge giving way—and the offender fell, at full length, in an adjoining room.

At another time, Mr. Sedgwick tells me, a Deacon from a distant part of the town, while waiting for blacksmith Davis's services, was accustomed to tie his team to one of a cherished row of sapling maples—now, as you can see, quite fully grown—which the Sheriff had planted in front of his house. One of them was nearly girdled by the teeth of the horses, at which the Deacon received an indignant remonstrance and prohibition. The next time he came to town, however, he repeated the offence, whereat the Sheriff cut the reins and let the horses run. Fortunately, only the wagon was seriously damaged; but the lesson was thorougly taught, and the Deacon, ever after, gave a wide berth to the maples.

The Academy of Pompey—to build and maintain which the early settlers, with a large wisdom, sacrificed so much—was presided over by a succession of accomplished scholars. Among, and of the earliest of them, the Rev. Joshua Leonard, remarkable as a linguist and mathematician—with a condensing engine in his head—and of so sweet a voice that when from the pulpit he gave out his favorite hymn, Wesley's, "Jesus, lover of my soul," and joined in singing it, both audience and choir stopped, entranced, that they might hear the minister carry it through alone. He was succeeded by Rev. Eleazar S. Barrows, a sermonizer of much power, Dr. Edward Aiken, Henry Howe and Flavius Josephus Littlejohn. This institution, standing so long alone in Central and Western New York, drew to this conspicuous summit crowds of youth from the surrounding counties.

When Victory Birdseye, with his large and accurate learning, and the eloquent Baldwins, and Sedgwick, a man of strength, and Daniel Gott, with memory of steel and voice of deep and solemn music, displayed their powers before a Justice of the Peace, the entertainment richly repaid the thronged attendance.

Here Henry Seymour, that courtly gentleman, laid the foundations of the fortunes, social and political, of the future Governor.

But new times came on. Great arterial thoroughfares were established on easier grades, and our native village has been compelled to stand aside, somewhat solitary in her loftiness and her lovliness, and see the increasing inland travel and freightage of the country passing by her, as, in its transit between the commercial East and the abounding West, it veined the distant valleys. The law of gravitation is a mighty agency in advancing or retarding the growth of localities, and determining the routes of trade. We may not soon expect to see a railroad depot on the top of Holyoke, nor cotton mills on Mount Washington. A position in alliance with the eternal laws of Nature receives perpetual aid from an exhaustless fund in the sky. And so it has occurred that our native peak, though rejoicing in its beauty, its fertility, its healthfulness and its traditions, has not been able to solicit the currents of modern traffic up its steep sides. They seek, rather, the furrowed channels and the level plains.

And therefore, also, has it happened that through the last half century, Pompey has sent away so many of her sons and daughters, to fulfil, elsewhere, their various spheres of duty; taking nothing from the homestead but the dowry of good birth, fair education and strong constitutions—the last not the least in the long struggle of life. In a letter from a brother on the Pacific coast, he says: "Though the frosts are on my head I feel *like a 'colt.'*" I must confess to something of the same exuberance, as if the tonic oxygen of these hills, inbreathed in youth, still continued to invigorate.

Though Pompey, as we see, still remains a pleasant place to *stay at*, yet it has certainly been, as Webster said of his own New Hampshire, an excellent place to *go from*. Accordingly, these Onondaga highlanders have swept down on the lowlands and invaded the valleys. When, not long since, the Census Marshal inquired at my door the names, ages and birthplaces of the inmates, he could hardly think us serious when he was told that the owner was born on Pompey *Hill* and his wife in Cherry *Valley*.

Indeed, they seem to have interlinked themselves with distant parts of the world, for, when the late Jas. T. Brady was in Rome, he desired his brother, Judge John R. Brady, of New York, to tell me that he had paid his respects to my cousins, the *Pontine Marshes*. Now that was a branch of the family quite intimate, in his day, with our sponsor, *Pompey Magnus*, who used to visit them and traverse their estates, whenever, as he often did, he led his legions along the Appian Way.

And now, to-day, for the first time since their dispersion, does a common impulse move her children to return—and they come bearing their sheaves with them. The thousands under this tented roof, and the thousands for whom there is not room, attest the interest felt in this family festival.

We cannot permanently return to the home we left so early. We may not deck with our cots her upswelling dome, nor hang them on her slopes, nor join our hands in

Luther R. Marsh

friendly cordon around her base. Our lines are cast, some by the eastern, some by the western sea, while others dot the intervening space; and there we dwell, enriched only by boyhood's possession of these high citadels. But one there is—our good President, Daniel P. Wood—who is not willing that a day shall pass without regaling his eyes and refreshing his soul with glimpses of the sightly top; and who has so chosen his home, that, from the observatory in his own grounds at Syracuse, he may send at will his loving glances through fourteen miles of sky, to the beloved towers of Pompey.

We tread the ancient *green*, where the athletes used to gather to jump, to run, to wrestle, to throw and catch the rapid ball and pitch the heavy bar. The intervening years, and all the cares and din of active life, are, for the moment, swept away, and we seem again to partake in

> "Those healthful sports that graced the peaceful scene,
> Lived in each look, and brightened all the green."

Was there ever a daintier wrestler at arm's end—our favorite game—than *Palmer*, a slender and cultured youth, whose fustian coat seemed made to withstand the grips of the strongest, but which, while it enclosed the lithe and graceful form, the strongest could never lay upon its back? When, with electric spring, he gave his toe-lock trip, how often have I seen the sturdiest champion, who had been allured from a distance by the fame of our Olympians, go down.

Since Asahel—"as light of foot as a wild roe"—overtook the Hebrew Captain, could man ever swallow the ground like *Gridley?*

We revisit the *strawberry fields!* Has any one forgotten the *Birdseye* lot, by the old barn, flush with its lowly treasures, where summer strewed the earth with fragrant rubies, too lavish to be hidden beneath the clover? Whose taste gave realization to the quaint saying of an English writer, "Doubtless God *might* have made a better berry, *but he never did.*" A little cousin came up from Onondaga to make a visit. He crept into this crimson field through the fence he was too small to surmount, and when his capacities were satisfied, he sought in vain the fissure by the broken rail. A passer by, hearing his despairing sobs, inquired the cause. "I came,' the urchin cried, "to Pompey Hill to see my cousin, and can't find the hole out." More fortunate have we been in retracing our steps to the well remembered haunts.

We stray among the *orchards!* Even to this day, through the memories of more than forty years, can I pick you out, whether in the orchards of Elihu Parsons, or Jasper Bennett, or Merrit Butler, or in the bordering Sedgwick nursery—which seemed a garden of the Hesperides—the very trees, if standing, which bore the golden prizes of the autumn; delicious globes, which Eve nor Adam could have resisted—which Atalante would have lost the race for—which would have comforted King Solomon, and their nectar stayed him with flagons—and which, whether by your leave or without your leave, it were hard to blame a boy for taking; apple-trees as worthy to play a part in the history of the world as the one which gave Newton the suggestion of an universal and planetary law—as the one under which the great rebellion was quenched at Appomattox.

But, alas! the full tufted pear tree in my father's garden, so long and widely known, has bowed its bowery head before the vandal chopper—no longer a stimulus to rising with the lark, lest earlier boys should find the juicy bells shaken down from grafts by the night winds. Oh, Woodman, thou should'st have spared *that* tree on whose limbs many a Sunday school lesson has been learned—honored for service rendered, for its fair fame, and for the menories clinging to every bough. This tree, the cradle of the robin and the nursery of song—and the windmill, beating the air with its mighty wings—and the liberty pole, from whose top the bunting caught the earliest gales, are missing features in which the present reality differs from the youthful photograph.

We walk again the halls of the old *Academy*, and listen for the *arma virumque cano*, or for the lisping echoes of Grecian verse.

We turn in to the venerable mansions in which we were first launched on this ocean of human life—an ocean sometimes lit up with roseate clouds, sometimes swept by relentless storms, but ever its gulf stream bearing us on to a destination and a destiny which only heavenly revelation can interpret.

Reverently we press the verdure between the hollowed mounds and marble records on yonder ridge—a place of taste, suggestiveness and beauty—from whence extends an unbroken circle of lovely landscape, till the earth rounds it out of view. There, is the history of our town, carven in stone. There, are its biographies, short and condensed, but veracious and comprehensive, recording the two great events in each one's life—birth and death—the Alpha and Omega; no, not the Omega—but rightly viewed, the Alpha, rather, of another life. And there, on the very crown of the knoll, with dewy eyes, and thronging memories, and holier resolves, I trace the letters of a mother's name.

We give a hearty hand shake to those we left here and who yet remain, some of whom are patriarchs indeed, whose vigor vouches the salubrity of this upland village; and we interchange with each other the recollections of the past, the gratulations of the present, and the best wishes for the future.

But list! I hear the Marshal's trump summoning us to a more attractive feast in yonder wood. Let us go thither.

[*The President.*—We will consent to adjourn to the grove for dinner, now awaiting us, on condition that Mr. Marsh will afterwards continue his remarks.]

After dinner he was called on to resume.

If you will insist on making two bites of a cherry, I am afraid your ivory will touch the cherry pit at last. This breezy grove is not unfamiliar ground. Though in yore a frequent resort, it was never the "shade of melancholy boughs;" and to-day the hills break forth into singing, and all the trees of the grove clap their hands. Never, in the olden time, when Fays nestled under every leaf, and Dryads

"and sylvan boys, were seen,
"Peeping from forth their alleys green,"

and Romance ruled the hour, have I known the holt so charmed with wood nymphs, nor these shadeful branches drop such manna on the tables. I knew, yesterday, that the coming hours were filled with good assurances, for when, toward nightfall, while bordering fields on either hand waved their bearded heads with a growth unequalled even in the fat soil of the valleys, we breasted the uprise, wet with the tribute of the passing clouds, as our native village burst on the sight, lo! God's seven prismatic colors came and blent and bent in beauty their glorious span, against the dark ground of the retreating storm, pointing, with rainbow promise, to the heart of the hamlet.

When I came up the hill I brought another Hill with me—one J. H. Hill, from Lenox. He was a Delphinian and Pompey born. We knew him in boyhood as *Hull Hill*, and he has acted, ever since he came, as if he owned the *whole hill.* I speak with some severity, for, with insufferable audacity, he has doubted my veracity. I would have him know that the word of a Pompey boy is steadfast, and that though his foot may be on his native heath, his name is neither Micawber nor Munchausen. I beguiled his way with many a story of our good old town; how the sun earlier rose and later set, than elsewhere; how Boreas whistled and Euroclydon roared; how we jumped from barn roofs into the deep drifted snow; how many yards we leaped, how many miles we ran; how, at dawn, we used to brush the morning gems from the meadow grasses in quest of the errant kine; how we learned to skate by the roadside and to swim in the goose pond; how long leagues of wild pigeons, week after week, in their annual migration, winnowed the air with million wings; how the brook at Pratt's Falls, after pouring its energies through crank and cog, in grinding the neighbors' grain, shoots the perpendicular abyss of a hundred and sixty feet—down which, one day, a woman fell, but escaped unhurt; with many another truthful recollection—all which, as he should, he greedily devoured, till I came to a story of the steeple, at which his unfaith arose, and he declared it threw discredit on all the rest. Now, there are many here who know that when our church steeple was completed, Smith the builder, ascended to the very top of the spire, and, twining his limbs in the tines of the fork, hung with his head downwards, suspended only by his legs; at which Dominie Chadwick strode out in front of the church, and cried loudly to the reckless architect, "In the name of Jehovah, God Almighty, I command you to come down." Now, though I have brought some twenty of our best citizens to verify this incident, and though it is attested in the Governor's address, yet *Hull Hill* still doubts. He is a Judge, somewhere down in Massachusetts. I wonder what rules of evidence he has established for his Court? a tribunal where parties should always demand a jury on questions of fact, and never trust to the stubborn incredulity of the Judge. I felt this imputation the more keenly, as I left this burgh with a fair record; for, about that time, Nathaniel Baker—whose son is owner of this grove—desired me to bring a bag to his house; which done, he filled it to the mouth, as full as Benjamin's sack, with butternuts, saying, "There, Rawson, I give those to you, for you "are the only boy in town who hasn't secretly visited my nut grove." No doubt Hull Hill was there—every dark night.

[Mr. Hill:—I am converted.]

Some honor have these sons of Pompey rendered to their native town. But they are present, and I may not recount it. I may only say that one of them, Horatio Seymour, rising to many a station of trust, has filled the highest office in our State. I see him—plainly as at this moment—as he stood by the pillar, glibly scanning his dactyls and spondees, the first day I entered the Academy. We began our admiralty studies together; he, as a shipwright, whittling buoyant vessels out of corn stalks; while I, the mariner, for want of other water than the clouds dropped on us—a habit they have not forgotten, you perceive—fearless of reefs or cyclones, navigated the stately flotillas—in the rain trough. And afterwards, under the tuition of Capt. Alden Partridge, at Middletown, we pursued our military education together, which fitted him, as Governor, to be the *ex-officio* Commander-in-Chief of the forces of the State; and me, to marshal—pleadings. I take some credit for this production of Pompey, for, but the nuptials at which *my grandfather* officiated, you would have had no Governor talking to you to-day.

Another, Charles Mason, who, at West Point, from the beginning of his course standing at the head of each successive class, took, at last, the highest of the graduating honors, though many of his competitors—among them the late leader of the late Confederate armies—have since won distinction for superior abilities. He has since administered the Patent Office, and given law from the Supreme Bench of Iowa.

Another, Henry W. Slocum, also a West Point graduate, as a Major-General in our army, consecrated his sword and rare abilities to the service of his country, in her recent contest for life.

And still another, George H. Williams, a representative in the National Senate from distant Oregon—fresh from his labors in the accomplishment of the great international treaty—the inauguration of a new mode of determining disputes between nations; a new departure in the settlement of belligerent claims; a victory of civilization, in which arbitrament takes the place of war; where arguments are not pointed by bayonets, nor rounded reasons rendered from columbiads; where Peace no longer stands with ensanguined feet, lifting her misty head above the smoke of battle; a sacred stadium in the journey of our race a millenium herald in the East.

You come, also, from professional chairs, from Congressional seats, from high judicial stations, from sculptor's studios and places of influence, and some stand in rank with the kings of finance. While others of us assemble from less conspicuous, though not less laborious posts of duty in the world.

But a celebration of hermits, unsunned by the smiles of Pompey's daughters, would have bereft our programme of its cheer. They also come with an equal enthusiasm. The voice of one of them, Mrs. Miller, has just wafted its musical reminiscenses to our ears. Yon Laurel, it is true, shadows a vacant chair, around the brow of whose destined occupant Grace Greenwood, its bays might fittingly be bound, and who speaks to us to-day only in her song; but then, in consolation for her absence, our *Greenwood* is full of *Graces*, at sight of whom we sigh to be foresters, and to spend our days in the witching shade.

Some there were, starting life with us, or not long before, who are not here; or, if here, not visble through the vale. Among them, *Charles Baldwin*, the genius of our town—not permitted to acquire the future honors to which his gifts seemed so justly to entitle him. Judge Hiram K. Jerome, from Palmyra—of Pompey growth—has just told me that it was his fortune to room with Baldwin in yonder office of Daniel Gott, and that neither Joshua A. Spencer, nor Henry R. Storrs, nor Elisha Williams more deeply impressed him as a speaker. In a Masonic address, he came to speak of the origin of that ancient fraternity. Some, he said, placed it at the time of Josephus, others even earlier; but for himself, if called on to state the period, he should say it was at the time when the Almighty said, "Let there be light and there was light."

And *Seabred Dodge*, the giant of our town—physical and

intellectual—whom I have seen toss a barrel as a plaything, its hoops and staves tumbling together in their fall, and of whom I remember to have heard Joshua Leonard say—no small praise to those who knew the men—" his attainments in mathematics are superior to those of Dr. Aiken, Priest Barrows and myself, all combined."

I said this was the first time the children of Pompey had gathered, from their scattered homes, to the bosom of the mother. It probably is the last. Other and younger generations may come. This, it is likely, never again. So there is joy for our re-union, and there is sadness for our parting. And many a day shall go by, and many a year close on its bleak December wing; but the radiant hours which have inlaid this social re-union shall glow and purple with thoughts of the princely hospitalities which have welcomed home the Pompey legion—true to the memories of their ancestral hearth-stone. And oh, how much richer are we for the fond meeting of heart with heart; and back to our busy haunts we take fresh inspiration from this beacon hill-top, that ever looks up to the heaven's broad face, lit by God's constellation of watchful stars. And now, having climbed the upland together, and together mingled our joys, and hopes, and recollections, and pledged anew our fealty to the dear old eminence, we will descend, as pilgrims from a sacred shrine, with the maternal blessing on our heads, and giving back, as with one voice, the filial benediction, " May the summits of Pompey, as they catch the earliest and latest gleam of the sun, so also receive, and ever retain, the favor of our Lord."

At the point in Mr. Marsh's remarks, where he refers to the Marshal, there was a postponement of the speaking, and the vast concourse repaired to the grove where refreshments awaited them. The last part of his remarks were made after dinner at the grove. The place chosen for the pic-nic, was in a large grove owned by Deacon Samuel Baker, situated a short distance north-west of the village. The road leading to it was through an arched gateway, handsomely decorated with evergreens, with the figures 1793, the date of the organization of the town of Pompey, and 1871, the date of the re-union. The grounds were thickly shaded, and in every way adapted to the purpose. The scene presented was alike pleasing to the sense of sight and taste. Three long tables running north and south, and with ais les between them, were set apart for the accommodation of visitors and guests. They were laden with substantials and delicacies, including strawberries and ice cream in great profusion. They were spread with white linen, and decorated with boquets and evergreens. They were the model of neatness and good order, and attracted universal attention. To the west of them Reuben Wood, of Syracuse, the well known caterer, was superintending the preparation of immense quantities of coffee. To the east was a long row of "family tables," set at right angles with those just mentioned, where family re-unions took place. Among them were those of Hon. W. G. Fargo, the Birdseys, Mr. Sloan, Orrin Bishop, John Soule, Messrs. Northrup, O. J. and Daniel G. Wheaton, Eli Pratt, Joseph Wallis, Morris Bush, John P. Robinson, Julius and W. E. Mason, Edmund O. Clapp, Messrs. Beards, of Fayetteville and Pompey. Frank Jerome and Chas. Cook had a table with an evergreen arch in the centre, bearing the word "greeting," handsomely wrought, and underneath the symbolic device of crossed hands. The Pompey Center and Manlius and Fayetteville tables were neatly and tastefully arranged, and attracted general attention. On the south the Sweet and Garrett families had a fine table and capacious tent; and the family and friends of John Q. Smith of Syracuse, occupied another tent to the west, where one of the finest collations on the grounds was spread. Miner B. and Fred. Murry also had an elegant table to the north-east, and bountifully spread. Evergreen arches were also made over the principal tables. Means for preparing coffee were provided at various points, and common use was made of them. Large wooden tanks of lemonade, as cold as a January day on Pompey Hill, occupied a prominent position, and also a tank of ice water. Long before the procession reached the grove, hundreds, aye, thousands of people had congregated and were enjoying themselves in a most rational manner, and from many gatherings song and music echoed through the wood. At about 2 o'clock the sound of music in the distance was heard, and the words "they are coming," brought all to the margin of the route.

The young people who were to wait upon the tables dressed in uniform, with badges and flowers, arranged themselves on either side of the route of the procession, and all was in readiness for the reception. The procession entered the grove, headed by the Marshal and his assistants, mount ed, and Dresher's full band, and in good order the guests took seats at the tables. The Rev. Mr. Brace offered thanks to the Throne of Grace. The waiting committee filed in in good order, and the work of destruction commenced. The attack was long and perseveringly continued, but the committee was too well armed to be defeated, and when the tables were cleared two hours later, the fragments gathered up were sufficient to have maintained a small army during a short seige. There was an abundance of everything, and right heartily were the bounties partaken of by the entire assemblage. Before Mr. Marsh concluded his address after dinner was served, the Durston quartette favored the assemblage with another of their choice selections, singing, "Oh, how I love my mountain home," and were followed by music by the band.

At the conclusion of Mr. Marsh's address, the President read the following toast and sentiment.

The Old Town of Pompey—Glorious in her past memories, proud of her fertile soil, magnificent scenery and noble sons and daughters. To these she points with pride, and says in the language of the Roman matron, "These are my jewels," and called upon William Barnes, Esq., of Albany, to respond.

RESPONSE OF MR. BARNES.

Mr. Chairman:

For unknown cycles of years, before any white man settled in the county of Onondaga, there lived and ruled over these pleasant hills and lovely valleys, those celebrated tribes of Indians known as the Confederate, or United Five Nations. These Romans of the New World had subjected to their sway most of the other tribes from the Hudson to the Mississippi rivers, and from the Carolina's to the Great Lakes. The hills of Onondaga formed the grand Council Chamber, where their dusky Senators convened and counselled, and where the painted Chiefs and Warriors planned their far-reaching campaigns. This soil was classic in the annals of tradition, reaching back to an era of which the memory of man knows not the beginning. The advance of the white man, from the time of King Phillip's war in the east to the present Indian warfare raging on the outskirts of our civilization in the west, has been but an ever repeated history of the yielding of the native red man to the Anglo-Saxon race.

This is not the time or the occasion for Aboriginal enquiry or discussion—but at this glorious re-union at the household shrines of our fathers, we cannot fail to remember the sadly eloquent sentiment which runs, like a minor chord, through all the speeches of their orators, and seems to have nerved the Savage arm in almost every Indian conflict that has occurred on this continent—"You ask us to leave the homes of our ancestors; you are attempting to drive us from the graves of our Fathers!"

To this sentiment, certainly every human heart assembled here to-day can thrill. We all feel that we are treading to-day a soil consecrated to us, also, as the chosen home of our fathers, and which contains within its bosom all that of them is earthly. I am proud to say that in your quiet church-yard at the base of Pompey Hill, I have a grandfather and grandmother quietly reposing. My grandfather, Deacon William Barnes, emigrated from Great Barrington, Mass., to Otsego County, N. Y., and from thence in 1798, to a farm about one mile south of the village of Oran. In the immediate neighborhood three of his brothers, Phineas, Roswell and Asa Barnes, had previously settled. My grandfather was a farmer, and had upon his farm a small blacksmith shop, as it was not unusual in those days for the farmer to understand and practice, occasionally, some mechanical trade. Animated by that stern monitor necessity, as well as by the promptings of his Puritan blood, he painted in conspicuous letters, first above his forge, the motto which was the guide of his life, "Work or Die," and alternating between the two pursuits of blacksmith and farmer, laying down the ponderous hammer only to assume the equally severe labor of felling primeval trees four or five feet in diameter, and guiding his oxen through virgin acres, where the stumps impeded every onward step—his life stands as the representative of the lives of nearly all those early settlers in Pompey, whose memory we revere to-day.

These early settlers were mostly God-fearing New Englanders of Puritan origin, and fervently inspired with religious zeal and enthsiasm. In my grandfather's house, no secular book or newspaper could be read upon the Sabbath day, the sacredness of which was kept with punctillious rigidity. An amusing incident has been recently related to me by one of the parties, still living, and now in his eighty-sixth year, (Mr. Luther Buell of this town.) In the early part of the present century he was working for my grandfather, and one Sunday afternoon, being sent to drive up the cows from the woods to be milked, a young deer was found with the herd, and by quiet and shrewed management was driven up also to the barn yard with the domestic cattle. Young Buell, much elated at the prospect of a fine haunch of venison, hastened into the house to notify my grandfather of his prize, but alas! for the impatient Nimrod—the sun had not yet set in the west, and the sacred day could not be profaned by secular pursuits—venison or no venison, no gun could be discharged on those premises, and the young man was compelled to watch and stealthily guard his game until the sun had fairly sunk below the horizon, and the New England Sabbath had terminated. Then the deer was duly shot, and my grandfather's conscience preserved inviolate.

Our present generation have little conception of the herculean task lying in the pathway of the early pioneers of Central New York. It was no small undertaking to travel through dense forests in search of the military lot which the settler had purchased from the soldier of the Revolution, by whom it had been drawn as a reward for military services during the war. Once upon his lot, (perhaps a dozen or more miles from a Doctor, a neighbor or grist-mill,) he was confronted not alone by wild beasts and Indians, but by the no less stern realities of a primeval forest out of which he must by his strong arm alone, create and build up a Christian home. What was to be done? Wife and children were there, needing food and shelter; sometimes in addition, a mortgage upon the lot with a no less ravenous appetite for interest on each recurring anniversary of the purchase. We read of heroism on the field of battle, where frantic men rush on to death, nerved by the maddening stimulus of martial music and the cannons roar, but here in the solitary wilderness was no flag flaunting in the breeze, no flying artillery, no support from other thousands of sympathetic hearts throbbing in unison, no pensions, no honors, no promotions, no glory, no immortality. No; none of these—here were only the wife and children, born and yet to be born, two strong stalwart arms, and a loving, honest and manly heart, intent only on serving God and performing its duty here on earth.

The sturdy faith which led these men into the wilderness, did not desert them when they faced its dangers, and the settlers axe soon resounded through its majestic solitudes. One by one the stalwart monarchs of the forest were laid low, until the sunlight crept coyly into the modest "clearing," and laughed with the wife and children, as the open space was consecrated to the *Lares and Penates* of the Christian home. Those days were not without their sunshine. Did you ever hear of the tender friendships and hearty hand-grips of those early pioneers? If not, watch closely when you see any of the survivors casually meet. The whole combined energy of "Fifth Avenue," could not concentrate as much soul and electricity as was generated in one "barn-raising," or town-meeting. And then the midnight fires when the log-heaps were lighted in the dry season of June; no costly illuminations in the N. Y. Parks, in Paris, or in London, could equal the quiet joy of the farmer at the ever-changing pyrotechnics of the "fallow" and "log-heap." And then for the children; could Delmonico with all his art furnish a dish equal to fresh warm maple sugar to be eaten on the pure and unsullied snow of the vernal equinox?

And after churches were erected, what holy joy welcomed the quiet Sabbath, the day of peace and rest, and how soul-satisfying the sermons of those pioneer clergyman, teaching their earnest hearers to look "from Nature up to Nature's God."

The church was often a Log-House or Barn, but it mattered little to the true Christians there assembled. The fervent prayers and aspirations that arose to Heaven from those humble walls, let us devoutly believe were as acceptable to God as the anthems of Westminster, or the formalisms of Ecumenical Councils, convened in the broad aisles of St. Peters, at Rome.

In this stern conflict year after year, with poverty and want, many noble men and martyred women died a premature death, overborne by their excessive burthens. The mass, however, came out victorious, the mortgages were gradually satisfied, comforts and conveniences were added to the household, from year to year, while numerous stalwart sons and handsome daughters joined hands with them in the crusade of labor, until the earth began generously to reward the faithful husbandman, and the wilderness blossomed as the rose.

I have been asked to-day to respond to a sentiment honoring the memory of these men—how can I speak of them, without laying also my tribute of grateful reverence upon the graves of the honored mothers and grand-mothers of these early days, who with scanty means literally created the food and clothing for their families, and trained and taught us, their children, with all the fidelity and devotion of guardian angels. Many of them had disciplined intellects which were stimulated and fed only at the fount of classic English literature, and in the intervals of their daily toil, they were often able to talk with you more critically, and quote more freely from the Spectator, from Pope, Addison and the earlier poets than would be possible for many of the so-called literary women of to-day, while they gave to Humanity and to the State, not merely one or two feeble and dyspeptic offsprings, but well-endowed, fully perfected children, (sometimes numbering more than a dozen,) and all nursed at their own bosoms, and trained to manhood and womanhood, in the fear and admonition of the Lord.

My revered Father, Orson Barnes, (with whose name many of you are familiar, although he has been dead for twenty years,) having removed from this neighborhood during my childhood, I had few opportunities to become acquainted with your older citizens. As a law-student, I well recollect the Websterian brow of Daniel Gott, and the able, honest and cheerful face of Victory Birdseye. They belonged to that honored class of lawyers, not yet I trust, entirely extinct, who performed their professional duties with all the honesty, zeal and conscientiousness of ministers of the gospel. I well recollect when studying law in Baldwinsville, with the late lamented Judge Geo. A. Stansbury, walking twelve miles, day after day, to the Court House, at Salina, to hear such lawyers as Noxon, Lawrence, Hillis, Gott and Birdseye, and feeling amply repaid for the physical fatigue.

Among the many men of mark, who have been born in the town of Pompey, and who I see around me to day, I miss one face that should have lent its geniality and charm to this gathering. I refer to the celebrated artist and greatest of American sculptors, E. D. Palmer, of Albany, N. Y. Born upon these hills, almost within sight of our festivities, and early inured to toil, his hardy frame gathered and consolidated year by year the strength and vigor which at manhood vitalized and invigorated his genius, and enabled him without the training of the European schools or having even seen the classic models of the old world, to wrest from his trans-Atlantic rivals a fame that grows brighter and brighter, with each succeeding effort of his genius. Pompey has produced great orators, lawyers, statesmen and financiers, but I recall no other of her sons who has achieved a wider reputation, or who wears his honors more worthily, than Erastus D. Palmer. A representative American in every pulse and fibre of his being, the town of Pompey honors herself when she honors him.

Mr. Chirman—I have already occupied too much of your time, and the lengthening shadows admonish me that the afternoon is rapidly passing away, but I cannot leave you without referring to one historical fact connected with the settlement of the military tract in Central New York. The twenty-six towns composing this tract, were with the exception of four, named from ancient Romans and Grecian Generals, Orators and Statesmen. Our own township, No. 10, comprising 60,000 acres, received the name of Pompey, from Pompey Magnus, the son of Strabo, who was born in the year of Rome, 647. He was as you all know, a brave, successful General, and was honored with three Roman triumphs for his victories over Africa, Europe and Asia, and was esteemed the conqueror of the world. Having been elected consul and invested by the Roman Senate, with extraordinary powers, he ruled the Empire with almost supreme authority, and was considered as the rival of Alexander the Great. One incident in his life occurs to me, which I desire to relate, not merely to "adorn a tale," but to "point a moral," which it may be well for us in these latter days to heed. Rome, the haughty mistress of the world, was suffering from famine, and cries for bread arose in her streets. By a *Senatus Consultum*, Pompey had been entrusted with the important duty of providing and importing corn and other provisions. He sailed with his fleet to the coast of Africa, and having obtained vast supplies, was preparing to return, when a fearful storm arose, threatening the destruction of the whole expedition. His mariners refused to re-embark, and were on the point of mutiny, when Pompey seized the helm of his vessel and ordered them to weigh anchor, with these decisive words, "*It is necessary that we should go, it is not necessary that we should live.*" It was this spirit which animated the early pioneers of the town which bears his name. Fidelity to duty first of all, and after that, considerations of personal safety and ease; this was inculcated in their daily teachings, and in every action of their lives, and on this festal day, as we meet to commemorate their virtues and emulate their example, let us consecrate ourselves to the same high ideal, and make ourselves worthy inheritors of their heroic blood, always remembering that

> "Ill fares the land to hastening ills a prey
> Where *wealth* accumulates and *men* decay!"

At the conclusion of Mr. Barnes' speech the President said:

The fair daughters of Pompey—we never forget them—We cannot marry them all, (laughter,) if we would—They would not let us if we could. (Laughter). But Pompey has long been the hunting ground for wives by outside barbarians. (Laughter). I propose to give a toast appropriate to that class of men, and shall call upon a distinguished individual from yonder city to respond. He has become a son-in-law of Pompey, by uniting in marriage with one of the Daughters of the late Doctor Urial Wright, so well and so favorably known to all the residents of Pompey, and who for a number of years held the office of "Superintendent of the Onondaga Salt Springs," and discharged its duties with marked ability. The widow of Doctor Wright—four daughters, two sons, two grandsons, and two sons-in law, are present with us on this occasion. I offer the following toast: "Old Pompey's sons-in-law, their good judgment in the selection of their wives prove them worthy of the true and noble women who have captured them."—(Applause.) I call upon Hon. James Noxon, of Syracuse, to respond.

MR. NOXON'S RESPONSE.

Mr. Chairman and Fellow Citizens:—

It is a pleasure to be called upon to respond to the sentiment given by your chairman, relative to the fair daughters of Pompey and the men who have been captured by them. The introductory remarks of the President upon the reading of the toast, inspires me with more than ordinary feeling at the present time, to reply in a manner worthy of the sons-in-law of Pompey. The sons of Pompey have spoken well for her in her younger days. They have justly and proudly referred to the men and women who laid the foundations of this good old town, which has sent forth so many good and worthy daughters and sons. Our acquaintance with the history of the State and the men who have taken part in the transactions relative to its policy and government, leads us to point with pride to the men who have gone forth from these hills and inscribed their names high upon the roll of honor in every department of life. The reputation and character of the men who have gone forth from Pompey, extends far beyond the limits of the county of Onondaga, and who does not well remember in casting his eye over the State, that no individual locality has produced better or greater men than she. It well behoves the young men, not only here in this locality but everywhere in the State, to look about them and around them, and see where they had better be born—(laughter)—I wish my voice could reach the ears of the young men of the valley below us, not alone those who have been accustomed from youth to gaze admiringly upon these mountain tops, but those living far-distant and beyond the bounds of our county. I would point them to the fertile hills, and ask them to look well to it, that their sails were well trimmed, and if they loved high places, and to be honored and distinguished among men to come here, and if they could be born again, be born in the good old town of Pompey, (applause and laughter). It produced great men, and the record of this day will long be remembered as a day of treasuring up and recounting her jewels. Why was it that the town of Pompey and the other hills of the county of Onondaga, whose tops were away up among the clouds, were so early settled by the hardy men who emigrated from New England? It was because here was a fertile soil, beautiful mountain streams, fine breezes, a county unaffected by the low and marshy region of the valleys, and hence the early settlements were made here, and the pioneers from other counties, and other States pitched their tents on these proud eminences, where the physical and mental condition of men best flourished, and where great men must and will be born. I beg you will note that it was not altogether my fault that I was born on yonder Hill, in the town of Onondaga, instead of this more elevated one in Pompey. Onondaga has proud old hills, and she too, has a noble record of good and great men who have gone forth from her majestic hills and been leaders in the van of civilization. It may not be amiss to state that those hills, like the hills of Pompey, have been subject to the depredations of the venturesome young men of the valleys, who have committed trespasses upon the estates of the good farmer, and been captured and made Sons-in-Law by their fair daughters. (Laughter and applause).

Now, my friends, be it known to you, one and all, that at an early day I made the discovery that I was laboring under a most difficult and embarassing perplexity, which it was hard to overcome, while in dreams I yearned and desired to be born here, my lot had been cast elsewhere, and I could not if I would be born on both these glorious Hills. This difficulty I managed to overcome as best I could, next to being a son I reckoned a son-in-law would be pre-eminent, so I ventured to try these hunting grounds, and extended my heart and hand to one of the daughters of this venerable town; and we together walked down into yonder valley, where our lot is cast in full view of these magnificent hills. (Applause). Young men of the valleys who hear me this day, whether you live far or near, I say try on, you may grieve and mourn over the misfortunes of your lives, that you were not born here. It is not probable your tears and griefs will alter the Providences which has cast your lot elsewhere, but the way is open, your tears and grief can be turned to smiles and joy, when I teach you by a joyous experience that the best work of your lives is to be captured by one of the fair daughters of Pompey, as you surely will, if you venture upon these hill tops, and then your baptism will be complete, and although not a son, the law will recognize you as such, and you will be a *son-in-law*. (Great laughter and applause). I have no doubt our President, who for so many years roamed over these hills, knew well when he framed the beautiful sentiment to which he has called me to respond, that I had never had cause to regret that my fortune had been united with one of Pompey's daughters, and that the son-in-law and daughter rejoiced alike in this re-union of kindred spirits on this delightful occasion. Allow me to say to the daughters here present, you need have no fear of the young men from these valleys. If they have the heart and the bravery to climb these hills, and face the storm king upon the top of your mountain heights, they are worthy of your kindest solicitudes, and should be warmly received. If laudable ambition rivits them here to be engrafted into this great family of joyous and loving spirits, I entreat you to receive them kindly, and if needs be, and heaven approves, walk hand-in-hand down into the valley together; and when the centennial year of the foundation of the town of Pompey shall roll around in 1894, let them, and you, and your children, and all the rest of us who shall live to that day, come around another festive board, and rejoice in the pleasures of another re-union of the sons and daughters of Pompey.

Mr. President—sometimes the question of our birth is invested with peculiar interest. I remember not long since of hearing of a speech made by one of our citizens, (a friend of mine), who had occasion to allude to his parentage, and the stock from which he came. He said that on his mother's side he came from Plymouth Rock—that on his father's side he came from Blarney Castle, and he gloried as well he might that this union produced sons and danghters worthy of memorable sires. (Laughter) This speech was called out in a political contest of great excitement. I shall not refer to the questions at issue, we came here to lay aside and bury politics, this day we flock aro und this common altar, and know nothing beyound the words, loveliness and women—and on that altar we swear allegia nce. Not long after this speech I was called upon to address a public meeting, in which seemed to me if there was any thing to be proud of in stock and ancestral glory, I was entitled to a small share, and said to my hearers that on my father's side, I boasted of Scotch desc ent, and that my forefathers came to this country from the romantic hills of Scotland, about 250 years ago. That on my mother's side, was German, and rejoiced in the good old Dutch appellation of Van attached to the name of my mother and her ancestry. My audience was pretty well attended by Irish citizens, and I added playfully, that I came very near being born an Irishman—one of my auditors who was a native of the green Isle, demanded of me in his own peculiar brogue, "How is that?" To which I replied, I was born on St. Patrick's day. (Laughter). My friends, the thought now strikes me how much glory it would have been to me, if I could on this occasion claim I had running in my veins the Scotch, German and Irish blood, and then on top of all, been born on these hills of old Pompey. (Laughter and applause).

You, Mr. Chairman, knew well when you called me to this platform, that nothing could intimidate me from telling the most solemn truth, relating to the sons and daughters. (Laughter). I invoke the women of Pompey who have got husbands in the valleys to stand by me and fortify every word spoken as being true as gospel. (Laughter). Sir, I speak from sweet experience on the subject of this toast. My wife is here present and if she was in the habit of speech making, she, too, might speak of her experience. She has graciously permitted me to speak for both of us, and we here rejoice together with you on the success of the sons and daughters, and sons-in-law, and daughters-in-law of Pompey.

We mourn over the fate of one poor Pompey boy who came to this re-union after many years of absence, and who ventured to kiss one of the fair daughters of Pompey, but his pleasure was nipped in the bud by being unceremoniously introduced to her husband, and then made a second effort to kiss the daughter of her whom he had first attempted to kiss, when again he was introduced to the husband of the daughter. Our friend had evidently kept no note of time, and exclaimed much to our merriment that he would shortly go home and kiss the mother and daughter he had left behind him, both of whom were Pompey-ites of blessed memory. (Laughter). Fellow citizens of Pompey, may God bless your town, may God bless your men and women, and may God bless the girls of the town of Pompey. (Applause).

At the conclusion of Mr. Noxon's speech, President Wood, in proposing the next sentiment, said:—A speech was made a few days ago in the British House of Lords, by that distinguished man, Earl De Grey, which has been transmitted to us by telegraph, under the Atlantic Ocean, a sentiment in which is very appropriate to be used on this occasion, and a fit one to call out one of the noble sons of Pompey. It is this:—"The American Members of the Joint High Commission; they were men of business, knew what they wanted, and asked for it,"—and (added the chairman) *got* it I call upon the Hon. George H. Williams to respond.

MR. WILLIAMS' RESPONSE.

Mr. Chairman Ladies and Gentlemen :—

I have exhausted the time to which I am entitled on this occasion already; and I have heard others refer to many incidents in the history of this town with great pleasure. All professions and all trades, and all sections of the country are represented here to-day. They all ought to have an opportunity to speak to you, and you ought to have an opportunity to hear them. It is not right that any one person should monopolize the time. I shall, therefore, do little more than to express my acknowledgements for the compliment which was implied in the sentiment proposed by the chairman.

To adjust understandingly the complicated question, arising between two great, free and powerful nations, is, of course, a business attended with no little difficulty. Fortunately for both countries, the British Commissioners came to the consideration of the questions involved in a spirit of candor and fairness; and the American Commissioners endeavored to meet them upon the same ground. No doubt many of our countrymen feel as though enough was not conceded by the representatives of the British government. But a question appears very different when both sides are thoroughly argued instead of only one. Proceeding to a consideration of the difficulties between the two countries, of course the arguments and the reasons by which the British government is influenced in her actions were presented to our minds in a most forcible and persuasive manner, and we endeavored to meet these arguments and these reasons by showing the claims of our country growing out of the conduct of Great Britain during the late rebellion. Our effort was to make a treaty consistent with the interest, the dignity, and the honor of this nation, and conducive to the best interests of the whole world. (Applause.) We supposed that the question was simply one of skillful negotiation, as of a war between the two countries. Manifestly every expedient had been exhausted for the purpose of adjusting the questions between these two nations, and this Commission was the only peaceful mode that was left for their settlement. Had those Commissioners failed to agree, then the two countries must necessarily have resorted to the sword for the settlement of these great questions. Our true policy is peace. Our country at this time is not prepared for war. War would have inflated our currency; war would have increased our taxes; war would have depreciated our public securities, to say nothing of the sufferings and sorrows, the vices and crimes that follow in the footsteps of war.

I am happy, fellow citizens, that the services which I rendered upon that Commission have redounded to the advantage of this country and to the advantage of the world. That is compensation enough for me. I think the universal acceptance of this treaty in both countries, without any considerable distinction on party grounds, is evidence that the Commissioners struck as near as possible the golden mean upon these questions.

I find, however, that I am, contrary to my determination, making a speech. (Cries of "Go on.") I am proud and happy, fellow-citizens, to meet you here to-day. I am proud to have been a resident of the town of Pompey, and to have been a son of the great Empire State. While I had the honor to hold a seat in the Senate, there were nine members of that body who were born in the State of New York, and this is a State, on account of its size, its population, its wealth, and its power, *entitled* to such a representation in the Senate of the United States.

I met here persons from all parts of the country; some have come from the north, some from the south, some from the east, some from the west to greet each other; to revive the reminiscences of early days. I have come from the hot atmosphere of Washington to look upon the green trees and the waving fields once more, and breathe again the pure fresh air of Pompey Hill. Ladies and gentlemen, I can hardly express the feelings that I entertain upon this occasion. But I am rejoiced at this opportunity of meeting once more so many of my friends of Pompey, and I express the earnest hope that all honor, happiness and prosperity may attend them through the future days of their lives. (Applause).

The President then read the following:—

Pompey Academy—A light set upon a hill, which has spread its effulgence afar.

And said: "I call upon the Hon. LeRoy Morgan to respond, an honorable descendant of this old town, and now Judge of the Supreme Court, living in the city of Syracuse:"

JUDGE MORGAN'S RESPONSE.

Mr. President, Ladies and Gentlemen, and Fellow Townsmen—

I wish it was in my power to make my voice heard over this vast congregation. I think I would give you some of the history of the early struggles of the young men who graduated from Pompey Academy, some of whom have since become the most distinguished men in the State and nation. But my voice is entirely inadequate to be heard for a distance. I shall therefore content myself with saying a very few things. It would have been gratifying to me to have held a class meeting somewhere in this vicinity, and to have had each old resident of this town, who has become distinguished and who now resides abroad, tell you his early experience, and to tell you how he contrived when a young man to win his way into public favor, and finally, to attain the highest positions known to our government.

Now, our forefathers who emigrated to this town, mostly from the Eastern States, built wisely, wiser, perhaps, than they knew. One of the first things they did was to endow an institution for the education of their children.

If you want to know why it is that Pompey has produced so many eminent men, go back to your fathers; ask them what it meant after they emigrated, when they collected together in council to forecast the future! They first collected themselves together and built up this Seminary of learning or Academy, which, for a long time, was the only one within reach.

Well, we all remember that our fathers, many of them were poor—many of us were born—of "poor, but respectable parents."

How was it that we were enabled to educate ourselves? It was by working in summer and teaching school in winter, thus mostly paying our own way with the wages which we were able to earn by our own labor. Now, it is not a miracle that Pompey should be the most distinguished town in the State; there is no great end attained without some adequate cause to produce it; and the only reasons that you can give as to the origin of the great fame which your own town has reached in her distinguished sons, flowed naturally from the incipient steps which your fathers took at that early day in buildng up the institution called the Pompey Academy, then the great nursery of learning.

You sent your boys, or rather they sent themselves, to that institution until they arrived at an age suitable to enter upon the business of life. One would seek one vocation, another another, and occasionally a man desired to become a lawyer. Many of such applied to be admitted to a clerkship with a distinguished lawyer of this village,—and I am proud to mention his name,—Daniel Gott, who always held out his kindly hand and received every applicant that came to him with the patronage of a father.

Many men, distinguished now, can go back to their early history, and remember with a kind recollection his manhood. They always admired his talents; and they cannot but recollect with gratitude the kindly good feelings, he always manifested towards the young men of the country. It is not best Mr. President, by any means, that I should occupy much time. I have said perhaps all that is necessary to say.

John F Seymour

I am proud that I was born in Pompey. A certificate showing we graduated from Pompey Academy has become a sort of title of nobility which we love to carry around with us.

I see before me "Great Pomp," and there is "Little Pomp,"—Horatio Seymour and John F. Seymour, born in this town; their early life spent here. They left here at an early day and took up their residence in Utica, and their name of "Pomp" followed them. I should like to hear now from the younger "Little Pomp." But if he is little, gentlemen, he has got a heart as large as any man in this crowd.

There are a great many from whom I would like to hear. I see here several distinguished men who left at an early day. Let them step up here and tell you their experience; and I think when one of the graduates of the Pompey Academy who has actually won his way to fame, gets upon this stand and tells you his whole experience, every young man of ambition will know exactly how to go and do likewise. (Applause.)

He closed by calling on John F. Seymour. Mr. Seymour came out after repeated calls, and spoke as follows:—

REMARKS OF JOHN F. SEYMOUR.

I was a child, Mr. Chairman, when tossed upon the top of a wagon load of furniture and carried from this place to Utica, but I recollect my playmates, the village green, the old Church, and the garden and brook behind my Father's house, and I can with truth, repeat Hood's beautiful lines,

I remember, I remember,
The house where I was born,
The little window where the sun
Came peeping in at morn.

I remember, I remember,
The fir trees dark and high;
I used to think their slender tops,
Were close against the sky.

It was a childish ignorance,
But now 'tis little joy

To know I'm farther off from heaven
Than when I was a boy.

"Pompey Hill," as a name is not attractive. It is a common saying that school masters have been abroad in this land, and some may think that this, and similar names are their stately, pedantic steppings. We will do them the credit to believe they would have chosen the descriptive and more appropriate Indian, rather than unmeaning Latin and Greek words. We regret that our Surveyor-General, Simeon DeWitt, has fastened the worn out names of the old world upon our towns and villages, but when we look at these meadows dotted with cattle and sheltering woods, at the fields of waving barley, and the pure streams of water, which with beautiful falls, leap down yon hill-sides into the valleys far below us, then the feelings of home, and nativity become masters of us, and we exclaim with all our hearts,

Thy *name* I love,
I love thy rocks and rills,
Thy woods, and templed hills.

What a crowd of people throng up here to-day, who with me, feel more than we have the power to express.

What a multitude have lived here and called it home, and then have gone forth reaping success in every department of life, in every portion of our country. I think I know the reason of this success. I might not care to mention it much abroad, but the truth is, the first settlers were brought up on potash. The thick forests which covered these hills were cut down, and burned, and their ashes converted into potash. Potash paid for their farms, potash bought flour and merchandise of every sort, it was the staple, the money of this country, and the people who could live on potash, could live on anything and anywhere, and so when they went down into the valleys, they swept everything before them. Some of us, Mr. Chairman, were born a little too late for that potash!

As this is an occasion when records are sought and made of all the families which have resided here, I will briefly mention that of my father, Henry Seymour. He was a son of Moses Seymour, of Litchfield, Conn., his wife the only child of Jonathan Forman, of Middletown Point, New Jersey, her mother was a Ledyard, of New London, Conn. The children left by my father and mother were six, this was their original number, and death has not broken it, the gray hand of time has scarcely touched the eldest, and all of them are in the midst of their several family circles, with almost the full health and strength of youth. In the order of their ages, they are as follows: Mary, the wife of Rutger B. Miller, of Utica, Horatio Seymour, of Utica, Sophia, the wife of Edward F. Shonnard, of Yonkers, John F. Seymour, of Utica, Helen Clarissa, widow of Ledyard Lincklaen, of Cazenovia, and Julia, the wife of Roscoe Conkling, of Utica. We trace back to these hills many of the tastes and principles of our lives, not only to that Academy founded and sustained by a noble race of men, but to a home influence, maintained by a noble race of mothers, and we must not on this occasion fail to pay our tribute to such women, who were help's meet for such men. They were the descendants of revolutionary heroes, and knew more of genuine elegance and honest poverty than most of the present day. If they had fewer books than we, they knew more of what was in them. They were familiar with the best English authors of the time, both of prose and poetry. With fewer schools they gave more personal attention to the education and discipline of their children. They were not ashamed of work, but were taught to be as skillful in the kitchen as in all the graces and refinements which adorn social life; the same hands which were accustomed to the choicest books and the rarest flowers, nursed the sick, and prepared tables which would excite the envy of an epicure.

If fortune favored them they avoided all display of any disparity between themselves and their neighbors, and they endeavored by self-denial to build up instead of dragging down their husbands. Their toil on these hills did not unfit them for any place in life elsewhere. They may have heard and known less of what are now called the rights of women, but they knew as much, if not more, of their duties. Believing their highest sphere was that of true wives and faithful mothers, they were rewarded by the admiration and devotion of men, and by children who gather here to-day to pay a tribute to their worth, and influence, more noble and lasting, than any which can be won in a political arena.

The President then read the following sentiment:

The City of Syracuse—Pompey greets her younger though more ambitious sister on this glad and festive occasion. Though above her *always*, we consent to stand on a level with her to-day.

In obedience to loud calls, Hon. D. G. Fort, of Oswego, took the stand, and delivered the following address.

MR. FORT'S RESPONSE.

My Old Friends and Neighbors:

I can hardly understand upon what principle I have been sandwiched in here to-day, between Governors and Senators and Judges, to make a speech, unless it is upon the principle that the painter, when he makes a picture, paints upon the background something dark, that the picture itself may be more distinctly seen. It is almost forty years since first I came among this people. I brought with me few years, little knowledge, and less experience. My lot was cast upon these hills, with parents who had come out West to seek their fortune. I was educated in these schools—long live the memory of the old academy there; I have worshipped in your churches, and some of my kindred are sleeping in yonder cemetery. My lot is now cast among others, and standing here to-day, I say with pleasure, that no memories of my past life come home to me stronger or furnish keener emotions of pleasure than those connected with my residence among this people and the anticipation of occasional returns here. I remember, also, when a boy, and first began to have youthful aspirations and build air castles of what I would be in the world. In the neighborhood where I lived was a man—doubtless many of you will remember him—who spent his summers upon the Erie Canal as captain of a line boat, an occupation much more honorable then than now, and his winters with his family in their country home. Evening after evening have I sat and listened to his well-told stories of startling adventures and experience in the life which he had chosen. My mind filled with delight at the greatness that he had achieved, and I then resolved that when sufficient years and wisdom had gathered around my head, I would strive for the same high position that he occupied. But, as many have found, I too found that frequently " the best laid plans of mice and men gang aft aglee." Many years have come and gone since then, I have never forgotten the ambition of my early life; but alas, alas, the dream of my childhood has never been realized and it seems to me to-day to be further off than ever before. (Applause). "Man proposes, but God disposes." I look around upon this vast audience, and endeavor to find the faces of those that were so familiar to us in the days that are past. Thanks to a kind Providence, they are not *all* gone. A few still remain, like ancient landmarks in the well-settled country, but they are fast growing less, and soon we shall find them, "like angels's visits, few and far between." I ask myself, "Where, where are the friends that to me were so dear?" and the answer comes swelling up, some have gone away from us, many of them are lying in yonder church-yard, sleeping quietly, and the remainder have come out here to-day, with warm hearts and whitening locks to welcome Pompey's children home again. All that remains now of many warm hearts that beat with life and love a few years ago, is the stone in yonder cemetery, marking the place where they sleep. May the grass grow green and fresh over their graves, and may the memory of their many acts of love and kindness be as fresh and enduring in the hearts of their children. Here again we meet under these old shades, while familiar voices of the past call up recollections that long since had slumbered in forgetfulness. It is a source of pride and gratification that we who have always pursued the common and private walks of life, can point to so many old friends from this town who have achieved the greatness which has been denied to us; but here we meet to-day; and meet as brothers; here for once we meet upon one common level, as we sit and chat around the old hearthstones and these well-filled tables. But boys and times have changed since then; years ago we were in the habit of greeting the boys or Pompey Hill as Horatio, George, Charley, Leroy, Lucien and Henry; but to-day when we speak to Horatio, we must take off our hat and address him as Governor, and George, who used to be so well acquainted with all of us, comes here to-day from the golden shore, and we must greet him as Senator of the United States; while Charles, Leroy and Lucien, have dropped the old names that we used to give them, and come here to be introduced to our people as Judge; and the epulets on Henry's shoulders speak to us of noble service he has rendered his country, and bid us address him only as General. Well, well, boys! you have done nobly. Although we belong to the class where high privates are always needed, we can assure you that while our children cannot hear their fathers called "Governor," "Senator," "Judge," or "General," it is with pride that we tell them that we were once permitted to attend school and play marbles with boys who have since achieved that high distinction. But I must stop. I will, however, tell you that I well remember a lesson that was taught me in yonder Academy by Mr. Stebbins, an old teacher there. I am not going to let this vast audience pass from here without endeavoring to press upon them the lesson he taught me. He was trying to teach his class what so many of us have tried to teach others—not to talk too much. (Laughter). The doctrine he held out to his class was, if we would only sit still and "look wise," we might pass off for great men; whereas, if we undertook to talk, we must talk *sense, for nonsense* would surely expose shallowness. I remember the story he illustrated it by. He said there was a certain man who had a son who was a fool. One day the man was to be visited by his minister and a deacon in the church; he told his son, "Now, John, when these visitors come, don't you speak a word; it don't make any matter what they may say to you, don't you speak a word to them." The boy promised; the visitors came. In the afternoon the father had occasion to leave the room, and the visitors began to talk to the boy, but not a word would he answer. At last one of them remarked, "I believe our brother has one son that is a fool, and I guess this is the one." The boy jumped up and rushed to his father, saying, "Father, father, they have found it out, and *I never said a word!*" (Laughter). Just here I am reminded that perhaps I had better make a personal application of this lesson to myself. (Laughter). If I had kept still, and tried to look wise in silence, perhaps some of these strangers might have taken me for a Governor or a Judge, but inasmuch as I have not done that, I will do the next best thing and leave the floor for some one who is to follow. (Applause).

President Wood, then stated that he was about to call upon one who had come from beyond the Mississippi to engage in the festivities of this occasion. One who received his early education in Pompey Academy, and who has since become eminent in the medical profession, and for the last twenty-four years has filled the Professorship of Anatomy and Physiology in the St. Louis University. He then called upon Dr. Charles W. Stevens, of St. Louis, Mo.

Dr. Stevens then took the stand and said:

Friends and Associates of my early life:—

I take pleasure in responding to the call made upon me by our President. We have heard eloquent and appropriate speeches, full of wit, humor, and sentiment, from the gentlemen who have preceded me.

They are all lawyers, and eminent in their profession; they have praised each other magnificently, and have done so in heartfelt sincerity, and we are well assured that the recipients have well earned, and well merited such eulogy. I am indeed proud of the fact, that so many who were, in years long gone by, my schoolmates and playmates, have attained such high position and excellent reputations. But I would ask you to call to mind the many worthy men who have in other callings, or in other professions done service, entitling them to worthy mention.

He that does the most to benefit his fellow man, should stand highest on the roll of honor, and could honors be bestowed or made commensurate with the good accomplished, many who are now unknown, or in comparative obscurity, would stand highest in good repute. In making this remark I have an object in view, and that is to call to your minds the name and services of a man who was a Pompey boy, and who has accomplished more of substantial good, and is more of a benefactor than any lawyer or any doctor who ever went from Pompey, or Pompey Academy. The man about whom I have thus awakened your curiosity, is the inventor of the melodian—Jeremiah Carhart. He worked at his trade as a cabinet maker in this village for some years, and while following his occupation in the city of Buffalo, he invented this soul-stirring instrument. I venture to assert that no instrument ever invented has been so fully adapted to the purpose of rousing those ennobling sentiments or feelings which music is capable of doing, as the melodian, and were it now at once swept from existence, an hiatus would be created that could not easily be filled. It has been manufactured by thousands upon thousands, and is found everywhere from the Atlantic to the Pacific. You find it in the houses of the rich, but oftener among middle classes, and very often in the cottages and log cabins of the poor; you find it in thousands of churches, even way off on the verge of civilization, in the frontier settlements, in the humble churches of the prairies have I seen it and have been charmed by its vibrations. Perhaps you will not find it in St. Paul's or in Trinity, but look into all those churches like the "little one round the corner," where there is true piety and hearty devotion, and there you will find it. The man then, who has made music for the million, who has made so many hearts and homes more cheerful, bright and glowing with inspiration and happiness, who has added life or heightened the enjoyment of the religious worshipper deserves to be ranked as a benefactor, and truly may it be said of him, "that the world is better for his having lived in it," Jeremiah Carhart sleeps in Greenwood, but the good he has done lives after him. Well, my friends, I am glad I am here to-day, I have come from beyond the Mississippi, and would have traveled twice twelve hundred miles to join you on this festive occasion. My life in the great west, I am proud to say, has not been mis-spent, I have practiced my profession nearly thirty years, and during twenty-four of these years I have been engaged in Medical institutions as a teacher of Anatomy, and am now ministering, as best I can, to the "mind diseased" of three hundred unfortunate fellow beings. I saw St. Louis in its infancy, when it had but sixteen thousand inhabitants. She now numbers over three hundred thousand, and is the fourth city in the Union. There she sits as a Queen, on the bluffs of that mighty river; she is sweeping into her lap the products, the wealth of that great valley; she is the center of over twenty thousand miles of inland navigation, and is now the terminus of fourteen railroads. She is now demanding to be made the capital city of the nation, and mark my prediction, that in ten years, the marbles, the beautiful columns, and cornices of yonder splendid edifice will travel across the continent in the direction where it is said the "star of Empire wends its way;" and I am not certain but if we had a half dozen of the energetic sons of old Pompey there, we might accomplish the matter in half the time.

Well, I have said enough about St. Louis, and I trust you will excuse me for my enthusiasm; but I am glad I was born in Pompey. I look back to my boyhood, and my early manhood, as the happiest period of my life, and as I stroll over these hills and valleys, the rocks, the trees, and streams call up most pleasing reminiscences, and I wish I were a boy again. I see about me here, the familiar faces of several who were my teachers; there is Miss Charlotte, who taught many of us our A. B. C., and I see yonder Manoah Pratt, who afterwards in a room of the old Academy, taught me other rudiments, and here on my left stands Asa Wells, who taught me geography and grammar, and I see all around me the boys and girls of those days, now most of them happy husbands and wives, or fathers or mothers; but how are we all changed; time has made his mark, most of us have come to that period when we look at the short future and contrast it with the long past.

We have had here a grand and joyful re-union, soon we must shake the parting hand, and by the lightning train speed to our distant homes. May the sunset of our lives be bright; and

"In life's closing hour when the trembling soul flies,
And death stills the heart's last emotion,
Oh! then may the seraph of mercy arise
Like a star on Eternity's ocean."

Dr. Stevens having concluded his remarks, the melody of "music" from Dresher's full band again filled the grove. After which the President said: "We have heard much from Pompey's sons and it may be pleasant and interesting now to hear from some person who was not born in Pompey, not that there is any want of material here, for Pompey has yet remaining some thousands more of statesmen and orators. I therefore, propose the following toast:

"The unfortunates of the human race born outside of the town of Pompey. They have our hearty sympathy and condolence, and we can only say that we hope they will do better the next time."

I call upon Col. Andrew J. Smith, of Syracuse. Col. Smith responded in a humorous and amusing speech, and closed by reciting in an effective manner, "Miles O'Reiley, after the fall of Richmond."

The next toast proposed by President Wood, was as follows:—

"The towns of Onondaga County—The town of Pompey extends fraternal greeting to her sisters, and invokes for them a future as bright, honorable and prosperous as her past has been." And called for a voluntary response, when F. W. Fenner, Esq., of Lysander, took the stand and spoke as follows:—

MR. FENNER'S SPEECH.

Mr. Chairman, Ladies and Gentlemen:—

I have been listening with feelings of pleasure to the remarks that have been made by the *distinguished* ex-residents of Pompey—those who have "gone out" from the old town, and made themselves distinguished as Governors, Statesmen, Judges, Lawyers, Doctors and Poets. But I think it is fair that those from old Pompey, who have not gained a handle to their names should have a representation upon this platform.

I claim to hail from the old town, although it was my misfortune not to be born on the hill, but down in the valley. In 1818 I was carried with my father and his family, by the force of circumstances, to the forlorn and forsaken town of Lysander, and from there to Camillus, where but few then lived. Well, my father lived until 1851, an industrious farmer, a good citizen, and a credit to the old town of Pompey. He was a tiller of the soil, a hewer of the timber; but he came out victorious, with nine children, but no lawyers or professional men among them! However, the old fathers and mothers of Pompey taught their children good morals, industry and economy, and may God be praised that we have been blessed with such fathers and mothers. Pompey may well be proud of them; for *without them* none of our distinguished and honorable friends who have addressed us to-day, could have said that they were born in Pompey! (Laughter).

I am not a public speaker, I plow the soil, but I did think

that we of the hardy hand ourselves, needed a representative here, and I determined to be that one, as no other responded. We cannot all be statesmen, judges and lawyers, and we don't want to be, and we would not be if we could. (Laughter). Some of us must look to the soil, and to the genuine, hard honest workers the country owes its prosperity, and I think the dear old town has abundant reason to be proud of her farmers, as well as of her other great men, for without them the professions would come to naught. (Applause).

The Chairman then announced that an original poem, entitled "A Fragment," would be read by H. D. L. Sweet, of Syracuse. Mr. Sweet then read the following poem :

We who boast that our grand-parents formed that noble little band
Who subdued the mighty forests that encumbered this fair land ;
They who made the howling wilderness to blossom like the rose ;
In their dusky neighbors finding friends, and not insatiate foes,
Should remember that the relics which we find in all our fields
Point to people who once dwelt here that no history reveals.

I have sought the tomes historic, I have roamed tradition's shade,
For some hidden written record that this people must have made ;
I have watched for the revealing by some dusky Indian Chief,
Such a legend as would strengthen every link of my belief;
But alas, in vain I've sought them, still they all elude pursuit ;
All conjecture ends in chaos, every witness still is mute.

Thus I thought and thus I'd written, it was only yester night,
That once more I roamed the forest in a sad disheartened plight,
And I saw as it was near a mighty monarch of the wood,
Quite unthinking I approached it, and beneath its branches stood.
All unconscious I addressed it, as I viewed its form with pride ;
Few, and simple were the questions, and in whispers it replied:—
"Mountain pine tree, standing in the glory yet,
Half forgotten of the nation which this hill
Once supported with its plenty?" "I forget?
Sooner cease the murmur of yon little rill ;
Brothers fell by fire and ax in sight of me ;
Fields were cleared of forests and the waving corn
Grew in place of beeches, maples, that you see,
Years, and years before the eldest ones were born.
Rudely, bleakly whistled winds around my form ;
Lonely, bravely stood I in a century's storm."

Carry back your mental vision through the far receding years,
When these trees you now term monarchs could have formed the shaft of spears;
'Ere the Plymoth rock was trodden by those puritanic feet,
Or the classic James was rippled by a Newport's modest fleet;
Ere the Spaniards built Augustine, or the Frenchmen reared Quebec;
Or the Dutchmen on the Hudson found that little island speck;
Here a colony resided, these the fields that once were tilled
By a purely peaceful people, in the arts of war unskilled.

Here the sound of rural labor in the sweetest gentlest strains,
Filled the breezes with their music, where no jar of discord reigns;
Where no sound of selfish traffic could be heard within the mart;
And disasters born of commerce brought no anguish to the heart.
Here were no conflicting dogmas; here no quarrels of the press,
Here the wealthy were not worried by pale poverty's distress.
Here the poor were free from envy of a neighbor's greater wealth,
For the man was counted richest who enjoyed the finest health.
Politics were uninvented, office-seekers all unknown,
Non-producers lean and stinted lived on what they earned alone.

Women knew no height of fashion, wore no ribbons, pearls or lace;
Decked their forms in simple vesture, with a modest native grace;
Won their men with love, not passion, that divine but subtle force;
Raised their babes to honest manhood, (never seeking a divorce);
Novels then did not attract them, no, nor Saratoga Springs,
Or a thousand dollar Cashmere, or a pair of diamond rings;
Ignorant of all around them, save their duty—is it queer
They enjoyed the rights God gave them, each in her respective sphere?

Years and years this people flourished, in the plentitude of peace,
Giving praise with hearts unsullied, as each harvest brought increase.
Huts were built of trees and branches, covered o'er with curling bark,
Round which trailing vines were clustered, bearing blossoms rich and rare
In the spring-time; but in autumn stripped of all their foliage stark,
Giving fruitage to the people as a recompense for care,
Fields were cleared, and plowed and planted, smaller seeds were deftly sown,
Corn we hoed and flocks were tended, blooming grass was duly mown,
Smiling plenty crowned their labors, gentle peace encircled all,
Till the jealousy of Indians reached its climax, wrought their fall.

It was in the early autumn, when the evening breeze was mild;
That arose a midnight tempest, louder rose the war-whoop wild;
Flashed the lightning sharp and vivid, but as quick the forest child
Whirled the gleaming bloody hatchet, buried in some settler's brain,
Freeing souls from earthly bondage, trials, troubles, cares and pain;

Flowed the red tide like a torrent, fuller, freer, flowed the rain,
Washing from the reeking greensward every spot of bloody stain!
Wailing went the tearing tempest, as its moans grew low and soft,
Rose the flaming lights more fearful, leeping terribly aloft,
From the cabin, barn and cottage—in the valley, on the hill,
When the morning blessed the landscape, all was gone and all was still."

At the conclusion of Mr. Sweet's poem, George H. Jerome, of Niles, Michigan, was loudly called for, who stepped upon the platform and said:

Mr. President:—

At the call of my friends about me here, I have consented to come forward to show you what grand old Pompey has done and can do in the way of her *physical* productions. While the brains of Pompey have been well represented here to-day, and her moral average has been shown to be a good deal above par, none have had the courage to stand up for *physical men.* I stand before you as a pretty fair representative of a well-preserved physical Pompey boy—do I not? Look at me and see if you detect any egotism in that. Well, *muscle* has its advantages as well as any thing else, as an incident or two this day occurring, and on these grounds will show. As we this morning came down from the Globe Hotel in Syracuse, we saw standing on the side walk, two or three boys—one of them a good chunk of a fellow, as we passed, spoke out, "there's some good looking men"—"I'll bet they are going up to that Pompey re-union." "By George, I wish I had been born on Pompey Hill." Now, Mr. President I ask you if ever a neater cleaner compliment was paid to physical development than that? Another incident. A little while ago, a lean Cassius-like friend of mine, one whom Euclid must have had in his eye when he defined a straight line—"the shortest distance between two given points," stepped up to me and said, Henry, you seem to be doing more of hand-shaking and kissing than is your share; why, my friend, said I, don't you know that the Committee of Arrangements decided to have the *hand-shaking and bussing* principally done by Pompey's fat, well-to-do physical sons—men whom that kind of business don't tire? My longitudinal friend almost instantaneously collapsed, and has been seen but once since, and that was at a refreshment booth, making a most vigorous effort to recruit.

Some pretty tall bragging, as I take it, has been done here to-day, about the glory of birth. Why you can't find in all this vast crowd, a man, woman or child, who will admit that they have been born anywhere else than in old Pompey. Now, if there is any bragging to be done on the score of birth I can beat at that game every mother's one of you, for I was not only born in old Pompey, but I was born *twice*. I had here a *dual* birth. And if you don't believe me, I can produce a two hundred avoirdupois witness, a *twin* brother, nearly as big as myself, to swear to it. Beat that who can, for although Pompey has given birth to Governors, M. C.'s, Judges, and lots of big men, as we have to-day often been told, yet she has sent out but mighty few men of *double birth*. Why, I have a brother, whenever he looks at me, I mean at my dual—duplicated self, involuntarily exclaim, "what a birth!"

Now, Mr. President, not a word has been said about the Lyceums of old Pompey. A moment about that and I am done. We all remember the Lyceum fever and furor during the reign of Stebbins. Not a place, not a time, not an occasion was too sacred for spouting and debate. You, Mr. Chairman, must recollect the time when you under the hill, just below where you used to live, waxed eloquent, with nobody but stones, trees, fences, and G. H. Jerome well concealed under the fence, for your auditors. Don't you? Your honest blush gives the answer. I was one of a number of the Academy boys who organized a Lyceum, appointed a chairman and held grand discussions in the belfry of the old Baptist church. Nor was our discussions in that *heavenly* locality always *spiritual*. Aye more, I was a member, in good and regular standing of a debating club, organized and its meetings held in a seven-by-nine ice house. And it was at one of those debates on a political question, that a brother of mine, Wm. Watson, was converted from Whiggery to Democracy, and the very next day after his conversion, he borrowed the money of a Whig brother, and enclosed it to Edwin Croswell, for the Albany Argus, the first Democratic paper ever seen in my father's house. After that he held office as a Democrat, and lived a Democrat up to the passage of the Kansas-Nebraska bill. So it is, I hail with quickened and glad remembrance those Lyceums, for it is to them that we are so largely indebted here to-day, for those Ciceros and Demosthenese, who have fulminated so acceptably at this memorable re-union.

But, Mr. President, I came not here to talk, I simply consented to stand up here for a moment in defense, and if you please, *in illustration* of Pompey's *physical* renown—to tell you, that not alone is Pompey's fame *intellectual*, nor yet alone is her grandeur *moral*—that wherever bold adventure and physical heroism have thrown their gauntlet and piled their monuments—that wherever *sinew* and *pluck* have recorded their victories—that on those cannon-riven battle-fields, where liberty was the guerdon and *muscle* the implement of its achievement, there—there too—Pompey's boys are seen at the front, in no spirit of self-glory, shouting to their comrades born of the lowlands, Come on! Come on!!

At the close of Mr. Jerome's address, Dr. R. F. Stevens, of Syracuse, made a few remarks, as follows:

DR. R. F. STEVENS' STATEMENT.

Mr. President, Ladies and Gentlemen:—

For some strange reason or other, the committee of arrangements from the town of Pompey seemed to think it necessary to have a corresponding secretary in the city of Syracuse, and it fell to my lot to be named for that office.

I will not detain you now further than to mention that for the last three weeks, I have not had any opportunity to attend to a single item of my own business; I have a great many letters with me, thirty or forty of which would be very interesting to you, and I will mention some of the names of those that you will readily recognize.

Charles Mason, who says it was impossible for him to be here. I would be glad to read it, but it is too lengthy. Rev. Jared Ostrander and his wife, Lucien Birdseye, several letters from the Marshes, Murrays, Fargoes, Jeromes, Bostwicks, Wrights, and others, are in my possession. I will state as corresponding secretary, that I have sent out over fifteen hundred letters of invitation, and I will state also that I have distributed to-day, among the multitude here assembled, over six thousand circulars or programmes of the exercises of the day.

This will indicate to you very clearly, the magnitude of this re-union, and I merely mention it as secretary of the organization, that I regard it most extraordinary, I have not the slightest doubt, we have here to-day, over eight thousand people.

One more toast will be read, to be responded to by Mr. VanBrocklin, and then so far as I know, the exercises of the afternoon will be closed after hearing from the quartette again, a piece selected by themselves.

The day being nearly spent, the President announced that he would propose but one more toast, as follows:—

The present residents of Pompey—Worthy sons of noble sires. In their hands the fair fame of the old town will suffer no reproach. Its escutcheon will remain bright and untarnished. He called upon Wm. W. VanBrocklin, Esq., to respond.

MR. VAN BROCKLIN'S RESPONSE.

Mr. President, Ladies and Gentlemen:

This is no occasion to render an excuse for this unexpected call. From what has already been said during the exercises of this day, which will ever remain sacred and fondly cherished in our every heart, and from what we have seen, we have a fair account, and a clear demonstration of what

Pompey has produced. What the future shall be, depends upon her present citizens. I noticed that an idea that I ventured to suggest this morning, in the address of welcome, "that there is a philosophy closely connecting a people with the land of their birth," was somewhat elaborated in that appropriate essay delivered on this occasion by one of my early schoolmates, Mrs. Miller, who so opportunely occupied the vacancy occasioned by the regretted absence of the accomplished Grace Greenwood. You will remember that she demonstrated the proposition, by facts observed by the celebrated Bayard Taylor, among the rugged Pyrenees, and the majestic snow-crowned Alps. Governor Seymour, too, gently, almost poetically touched the same cord, in his beautiful allusion to the fishes of the sea and the wild denizens of the forest. Now, while I firmly believe that nativity has much to do with the characteristics of mankind, I just as frankly confess, that all the transcendent excellencies of character, that individualize the great and good of earth, do not depend entirely upon the spot upon which they happened to be born. It has been said that Pompey is a good place in which to be born, and a still better place from which to emigrate. I think I can accommodate both of these propositions, with the stamp of truth. The first has been demonstrated. As to the second, I would say, if you have ambition for wealth, or fame; if you would acquire distinction in forensic debate, or in legislative halls; if you would reach the highest niche among the kings of finance, or the ultimate goal of the statesman's ambition; leave these glorious old hills, and go where wealth, and worldly honors will be showered upon you, for "a prophet is not without honor, except in his own country." But if you would hold a closer communion with God, and be enabled placidly to view the jarring elements of strife and contention, raging in the world around and beneath you, then still linger around these sacred peaks—Nature's self-appointed temples, that the faithless and the false should ne'er pollute. I can assure you from experience, having had a mixed existence of excitement from without, and repose among the verdant hills of this my native town, that for comfort, and the full enjoyment of the amenities of social life, and the cultivation of the more ennobling faculties of our nature, a country life is the true condition of our being, where we can oft when returned from the field, "drink deep drafts from the old oaken bucket, the iron-bound bucket, the moss-covered bucket, which hangs in the well." A country life is conducive to temperance. There remains, moreover, much good cheer in the good old town of Pompey.

You have seen it here to-day, in the sumptuous tables spread, from which so many thousands have been refreshed. Health and happiness, innocence and virtue, too, are the conditions of a life among these pure breezes of our mountain homes. This you have seen to-day, in the honest sparkling eyes of the young sons and daughters of Pompey as as with nimble feet, and gushing hearts of welcome, they have passed through these aisles, administering to the physical wants of this vast multitude; while the bounding blood of youthful vigor coursing their veins, has given them a vivacity and earnestness, which has assured you how welcome you have been made to your early home. And while the keeping of the enviable reputation of old Pompey, rests with such as have to-day met and welcomed home the wandering clans, I can confidently affirm the truth of the proposition, "That in the hands of the present residents of Pompey, the fair fame of the old hill-town will not degenerate." For this we have good reason, as it has been demonstrated, that Pompey cannot naturally produce any but great men and women. Yet, you will find in the future, that there will not be that pre-eminent notoriety among Pompey's children, that there has been in the past. This I am constrained to say, as I am more in the habit of dealing with facts, than to amuse or flatter.

As I have said, the land of our birth, however dearly we may love it, does not entirely form our characters. And it is so with those who have acquired eminent distinction in life, whose birth place was Pompey. Other circumstances have had a controlling influence upon their destiny—to-wit: the good character and example of their parents—the fact that they, at great sacrifice, established in this then pioneer town, good schools and churches—nurseries where the young mind, naturally adapted to growth and cultivation, has been fully developed, and thrown forth upon the world, to achieve great good for God and humanity. Other localities have caught the spirit, which at that early day founded the Pompey Academy, and emulating the bright example of our fathars, set high up among the clouds, radiant with light to illumine the surrounding hills and valleys, we find that other institutions of learning have sprung up, in Onondaga Valley, Cazenovia, Homer, and other places in this vicinity, which, in their turn, will send forth great and good men and women, to elevate and refine society. They are to-day educating Pompey's children, and I apprehend it is the duty of the foster fathers of our venerable Academy, to entertain enlarged and comprehensive views of the necessities of the situation, and command at any price, the services of an excellent corps of instructors, who will call within its sacred walls as of old, students from the valleys, and all the surrounding country. It is thus, in this age of competition, of enterprise, and of progress, that the present citizens of Pompey can maintain her ancient glory and renown. It is thus that the good character inherited from our ancestors, and the principles inculcated by our fathers, will be experienced generations yet to come. It will not do for Pompey to rest upon the laurels already won. She no longer enjoys the monopoly of Academic lore. And while she may not degenerate, surrounding towns have already reached the high plane of excellence it has so long been her privilege to occupy.

I have been amused to-day as I cannot amuse you, especially with the speech of Senator Noxon, in which he tells us how near he came to being an Irishman. And this calls to mind a class of present citizens of Pompey, unknown to us, Mr. Chairman, in our school boy days. The town is being filled up with emigrants from the "Green Emerald Isle," and of them it need not be said, "That they were born upon St. Patrick's day, to make them full blooded Irishmen. They were born, not in Pompey, but upon the green sod of old Ireland. And they come it seems, to inherit through their economical and industrious modes of life, what you and your fathers have left—the green hills and valleys of your native town. Already upon the ruins of a church, they have erected another, giving it a different name, and there they worship the same God your fathers worshipped, upon the same spot, sixty years ago. The future of Pompey will somewhat depend upon this class of its present citizens, and I am happy to believe, that under the genial influence of our institutions, and the desirable opportunities offered in this land to which they come, their future, will give to their adopted country, the home of their choice tho' not of their birth, the Currans, the Emmets, and the St. Patricks of the United States. I look then for a brilliant future for Pompey, not only from the descendents of the original settlers, but from those as well who have made it the home of their adoption. Another new church has arisen, and within its consecrated walls, many worship the God of our fathers, who were the playmates of your early life. In other portions of Pompey, religious changes have not been so marked. In Delphi, near where dwelt the Litchfields, Slocums, Sheldons, Blowers, Barbers, Hills, McClures, and many other old familiar names, you will find the present citizens, still worshiping in the Baptist and Methodist churches. The society of Pleasant Valley, too, at Oran, still remains, whose liberal creed embraces within the covenant of Divine grace the whole human family. Here you may find the hospitable home of Noah Palmer, of Elias Barnes, a walking encyclopedia of that portion of Pompey, the genial Joseph Scoville, D. D. Denison, whose father the old Doctor Denison, was noted for his sound democracy and skill in curing diseases, Col. C. C. Midler, of military fame, when general trainings were in fashion, and many other scions of a worthy stock, whom I have not memory, or time to name. At the four corners four miles north of Pompey Hill, the church erected by the Westons, the Clements, the Hibbards, the Hinsdales, the Clapps and others, many of whose descendents yet remain, is now no more used as a church, its membership having been absorbed by Manlius, Jamesville and Pompey Hill. And where once the bread of Heaven was dispensed to the hungering multitude, the bread which perishes is now sheltered upon the farm of Addison Clapp.

But of all the churches familiar to the early days of Pompey, located upon this venerable hill, none remain except the Methodist and Congregational churches; and especially in the latter you will to-day find very many names familiar to the early settlers of Pompey. There still you will find the Jeromes, the Stearns, the Bakers, the Wells, the Woodfords, the Butts and many other descendants from the "old stock," whose rigid discipline, and bright example of the christian graces, continue to yield copious harvests of "peace on earth, and good will to man." May they remain to the latest generation, land-marks upon the shores of time, where the future pilgrim, returning like you to-day to the home of his childhood, shall find a familiar spot, known and prized in life's young day. I regret that the time has been too short, in which to prepair sentiments appropriate to every trade and occupation, represented here to-day. We would have been pleased and instructed, had the artisans whom Pompey has sent forth, greatly to her honor, been called upon to respond to an appropriate toast. You will not be under the necessity of going farther than the city of Syracuse, to find shops conducted by sons of Pompey. They can make machines, as well as machine poetry. I allude to the Sweet brothers.

By Mr. John F. Seymour.

Palmer the sculptor, was he not born here?

By Mr. Van Brocklin—I believe he was, and so was Carhart, the inventor of the Melodeon. But should the Melodeon, notwithstanding the vast amount of happiness it has conferred upon mankind, be struck entirely from existence, we should not suffer much, as long as we have the "human voice divine," which can discourse such heavenly music, as that to which we have this day listened, from the "Durston Quartette." The only mistake I apprehend, made in this glorious re-union, is, that we did not appreciate the magnitude of the occasion, and resolve to have it continue three days, instead of one, to give an opportunity more thoroughly to renew the scenes of early life. As it is, so soon we meet, so soon to part; and while the lingering farewell dwells upon our lips, the moistened eye of the thousands who hear me, indicates the deep feeling that pervades this sacred place. And let us remember, with a faith that reaches beyond the shores of time, and spans the endless cycles of eternity, that upon the resurrection morn will be another re-union of Pompey's children, past, present, and future, more glorious and enduring, when we shall see, high upon the scroll of eternity, amid the honored names of the remotest generations, and the succession of generations, down through the long vistas of the ages past, the name of Pompey, encircled with an immortal wreath of perennial flowers, and all her children redeemed and purified, for the society of a higher and purer life.

The exercises at the grove were closed by the Durston Quartette singing a farewell song. The time intervening between this and the evening meeting was spent in social intercourse, in taking rides and walks to familiar places, which awakened the slumbering memories of early days. Some visited the Academy and the grounds upon which once stood the "old wind mill." Some hastened to pay a tribute of respect and veneration to the "old homestead," now in the hands of strangers. Many repaired to the village cemetery, a beautiful spot located on the highest land in Pompey, affording a comprehensive view of the surrounding country. Here rests the sacred ashes of the fathers, mothers and friends of early life. And as the various parties sought the places most to memory dear, and walked again upon the soil that gave them birth, who can catch, in imagination the panorama of thought and feeling, that must have passed in review, as the thousand recollections of youthful days crowded upon the minds? Who delineate the varied emotions, that such a visit must have developed? While many remained to attend the evening meeting, and to visit for a few days, friends and early homes, very many, characteristic of American life, exchanged the hasty farewell, and were off to distant homes, to mingle again in the busy scenes of life.

EVENING MEETING.

At seven o'clock, the old bell that had in "olden time," summoned to religious duty, pealed forth its familiar tones announcing the time for the final meeting of the day.

Soon the Presbyterian church was filled to overflowing; on motion of Victory J. Birdseye, Dr. Richard F. Stevens was appointed chairman, who upon assuming the duties of his position, made appropriate remarks, as follows:—

Ladies and Gentlemen:—I thank you for the partiality shown in calling me to preside at this the last meeting of this most interesting re-union occasion. I am reminded by these sacred walls of times long gone by of childhood days, when here I was taught the words of Holy Writ in Sunday lessons, and my eye rests upon the family pew where I sat with my parents more than fifty years ago, and listened to religious teachings from the pulpit. I see before me, men and women who were children with me, whose heads are already silvered, and whose changed appearance tells its fruitful story of many years. I see also before me those who were the active men and women of those early days, now full of years, and bent with age. It would much more comport with my feelings to remain silent, when I remember that on the spot where I now stand I have seen deposited, on funeral occasions, the encoffined remains of my parents and many dear friends and neighbors who rest in the quiet old burying-ground on the hill. I see at my right my former school teacher, Mr. Asa H. Wells, and in yonder pew, I see Mrs. Beardsley, formerly Miss Charlotte Hopkins, who taught me my A. B. C's. The house adjoining this church, was my birth-place, and in this immediate locality, many who now listen to my words, ran and played with me in all the joyous sports and pleasures of childhood's happy days. To one returning after so many years, everything that remains is vocal with reminiscences of early days, the churches, the houses, the village-green, the shade trees I helped to plant, now a foot in diameter, the gardens, the apple-trees, everything however small, has its history of some childhood event.

I cannot express the gratification I feel in being permitted to enjoy with you this re-union of so many of our former friends and neighbors as have been assembled here to-day. From all parts of our country the descendants of the old town of Pompey have come to meet and revive recollections, to shake the friendly hand like brothers and sisters in a common family, to call each other by familiar names, to tell of the passing events of life, and, as the hours of the re-union draw to a close, to give the parting aud affectionate "good-bye."

We have met this evening to listen to those who may be pleased to give us such reminiscences as will be most interesting to us all.

It is to be regretted, that no stenographic reporter was secured for the evening meeting, and therefore, no full report of the proceedings has been preserved. Historical reminiscences, and interesting remarks were made, in their order by the following persons: Rev. Samuel W. Brace, of Utica; Rev. Charles Jerome, of Clinton, Oneida Co., since deceased; Victory J. Birdseye, and Wm. W. VanBrocklin, of Pompey; Leman B. Pitcher, of Salina; Ebenezer Butler, of Syracuse, since removed to Whitehall, N. Y.; Dea. Asa H. Wells, of Pompey, since removed to Manlius; Hon. Wm. Barnes, of Albany, and Hon. Daniel G. Fort, of Oswego.

An original poem was read by Flora Butterfield, daughter

of Mrs. Catharine Clarke Butterfield, a cousin of Grace Greenwood. Miss Flora was only thirteen years of age at the time of the re-union, and her production, not designed for rehearsal or publication, is here produced without correction:

TO OUR GUESTS FROM ABROAD.

BY FLORA BUTTERFIELD.

The old residents of Pompey have here again met,
That your old native land you might not forget;
To renew old acquaintance with the few that are here
That you hold to your hearts, by memories dear.

There's but few that are left where in childhood you played,
To welcome you home from the lands where you've strayed;
But your welcome is *warm*, as we all can proclaim,
For long years it will be 'ere you all meet again.

Alas! what sad memories this day brings to some,
As fresh to your minds come the days past and gone!
When children, you played 'round this dear old Hill
With kind friends you loved, who in death are now still.

As you gaze once again on each familiar spot,
How they rush to your mind, scenes long since forgot;
And a sadness steals o'er you as of the past you tell,
And you turn once again to take a farewell!

Yes, farewell! 'till we meet above
In a blest re-union of peace and love!
Where no ties will be broken, for all will be there,
And happiness forever, free from all care.

REMARKS OF HON. WILLIAM BARNES.

Mr. Chairman:—

Interested I have been, and deeply, in the many narratives of early events and incidents in the settlement of this town, which I have heard this evening. These stories from eye-witnesses and participants cannot long be enjoyed by any of us, as the tottering steps and white hairs of some of the speakers too plainly indicate. I grieve that my beloved father, (the late Orson Barnes,) personally known to many of you, is not with us this evening in body as I know he is in spirit, for he could add many items interesting to you all, relating to the original settlers, their trials, privations and triumphs.

During my term of office as Superintendent of the Insurance Department of this State, I noticed one New York City Fire Insurance Company, the annual statements and accounts of which were always marked with especial fullness and accuracy. Analyzed however critically, and subjected to any accountant's rules or legal tests, everything was found to be sound and correct.

Its stockholders numbered on its roll several of the richest and most influential men of New York City. From year to year certain delinquencies required more full returns from the Companies, and detailed lists of bond and mortgage securities of stock loans, lists of stockholders, and other requirements; which additional and specific requirements met with serious, determined, and even personal opposition on the part of several Companies.

I always anticipated that the Fire Insurance Company to which I allude would interpose the strongest objections to these new and onerous requirements, but I was always disappointed in my expectations, for every new blank form which was presented to the New York Bowery Fire Insurance Company, however full, or complicated, or onerous, was promptly filled up and sworn to, and generally the first return on file made by any of the Insurance Companies.

For ten years this fact was a matter of wonder and astonishment to me, and it is only to-day that I have had a satisfactory explanation, by learning that its respected President, Dr. William Hibbard, was born in the town of Pompey, and belonged to the "Hibbard" family of Pompey Hill.

The above are all that have been preserved of the evening meeting.

The following resolutions were adopted, when the evening meeting adjourned:—

Resolved, By the guests at Pompey from abroad, that we

tender to the citizens of Pompey our earnest and sincere thanks for the magnificent entertainment which we have to-day enjoyed, and for the ample provisions made, and the arduous and well directed efforts used to make our re-union pleasant and agreeable to all.

Resolved, That our thanks are especially due to the Committee of Arrangements and Officers of the Day—their wise and admirable conception of the necessities of the occasion, in providing for the immense multitude of visitors, with wants so numerous, and for the good order manifest in every department of the day's doings.

Resolved, That we most cordially tender our thanks to the Orators, Singers and Musicians of the Day, for the pleasing and instructive speeches to which we have listened, and for the songs and music which have attuned our hearts in unison, to appreciate the sublime and transcendently glorious spectacle to-day witnessed, of a re-union on earth of the sons and daughters of Pompey.

OF THE INCIDENTS OF THE DAY.

Numerous incidents occurred during the day, to mention all of which would fill a volume. A few only will be related, as illustrating the spirit that pervaded the entire assembly. The greetings of long absent friends were interesting to witness, and that none should be slighted, the friendly hand was extended to all. A gentleman of some sixty summers, met a lady of about the same age who had been his schoolmate of fifty years ago; after recognition and a cordial greeting, unbidden he extended his hand to a lady in company with his former schoolmate, "and this," said he, "is?" "My daughter," responded the lady, "and this is her husband." And extending the friendly hand to still another lady, he said "and this is another daughter?" "O, no; that is my grand-daughter, and this is her husband." Then as the obtrusive tear filled his eye, he turned to his schoolmate, on whom the rolling years had apparently made but little impression, and said "truly, Mary, we must be growing old, and yet to-day I feel as though I were a child again."

Again, at various points might be seen groups of friends and acquaintances, long separated, calling up the incidents of early days, and occasionally might be heard a brief speech. Lloyd Slade, of Kelloggsville, N. Y., in the fullness of his heart was constrained to speak substantially as follows to a group of friends:—"I was not born in Pompey, but like many fortunate sons of other towns, I married a wife from the fair daughters of Pompey, who is now present, and whose father, Willoby Millard, was one of the Board of Education in 1800, and who did much to erect the first Academy building and establish the Pompey Academy. As to-day it is customary to push personalities to the front, I would say of myself that I taught school thirty winters, and one of them in Pompey, as many present will remember. From among my scholars in that humble school, have arisen self-made men—as successful financiers and noble philanthropists as ever honored a nation. I refer to Hon. Wm. G. Fargo and his brothers. Now, my hearers, this is probably the last re-union of the present sons and daughters of Pompey that we shall ever enjoy on earth; but let us lay aside mourning and sadness, and with an eye of faith behold the resurrection morn; when the re-union of cherished ones departed and those journeying with us, will occur at our Celestial Home, where pleasures never end, and joys immortal bloom."

Another indication of the universal interest in the occasion, was the rehearsal by Homer A. Billings, to some of his companions of the following poem:

POMPEY, THE LAND OF THE BRAVE AND THE HOME OF THE FREE.

Hurrah for old Pompey! the land of the free,
I think that you *still* are the right place for me,
Within thy fair borders I chanced to be born,
To own thee my birth-place, I never shall scorn
To sing of thy beauties—my theme it shall be
Hurrah for Old Pompey, the land of the free.

Our scenery's delightful, our climate is healthy,
Our wants are but few, our farmers are wealthy ;
The heighth of our land makes us know well our station,
(Since we know that "High standing's the pride of our Nation)
For reasons like these, you're the land still for me.
Hurrah, &c.

We're a free happy people, contented we are,
In haps and misfortunes, we never despair,
Our government's mild, and wholesome our rules,
Interested we are in our *Common Schools*,
Oh ! Yes, I will say, you're the land still for me.
Hurrah, &c.,

Thy name, old Pompey, oft' puts me in mind
Of the great Roman general, in hist'ry we find,
Who lived in the days of "Cæsar the great,"
That noted old Emp'ror and great potentate,
We all trust thy downfall *never* will be.
Hurrah, &c.,

How oft' have I traveled thy fair meadows o'er,
Where the wild beasts and savage had traveled before ;
How oft', o'er thy valleys and landscapes I've gazed
With fancies bewildered, confounded, amazed,
Old Pompey ! thy landscapes are dear unto me.
Hurah, &c.,

My own native Home—in the Cot on the hill,
The place of my birth ! Oh ! it gives such a thril
Of joy and sensation ! I cannot forget
The little Log Cottage—I honor it yet,
When long years have pass'd—still remember'd 'twill be—
Hurrah, &c.,

Oh ! Home of my birth ! will it e'er be my lot
To find in this world, so endearing a spot ?
How true is the saying—that "search the whole earth
No spot's so endeared, as the home of one's birth,"
In life's last decline, I shall oft think of thee.
Hurrah, &c.,

May this meeting, to-day, and these social communions
Be but a prelude to future re-unions—
And may *this* re-union, of Friendship and Love
Foreshadow a blissful re-union above,
Where "*Forever and ever,*" *re-united* we'll be
And from sin and temptation, and sorrow set free.

But adieu ! for these days will not last long with me.
For in other lands soon, perchance I may be,

But of *this* I am *sure*—" wherever I dwell,
Of the scenery of Pompey to others I'll tell—
Yea, tell it with pleasure, with joy and with glee,
As the Home of the Brave, and the land of the free.

LETTERS.

The following are among the many letters received by the Recording Secretary:

BROOKLYN, 20th June, 1874.

R. F. Stevens, Esq., Sec'y, &c.

DEAR SIR:—I regret very much that I shall not be able to attend the re-union of the former residents of the town of Pompey, which is to take place on the 29th inst., as I sail on to-morrow's steamer, for Europe.

It would give me great pleasure could I be with you on that occasion, and thus meet many of those whom it has been my good fortune to know personally, as well as many others, whom I have known only by reputation. Should the former residents of Pompey, generally avail themselves of this opportunity for visiting their native hills, you will have a gathering of which you may well be proud, for you will find there assembled, many who are eminent in the various walks of life. The pulpit, the bar and the bench, the Legislative Hall, and the business Exchange, the official rolls of civil and of military life, each can show distinguished representatives of the old town of Pompey, while many others of her sons, to fame unknown, have well performed their part in life by the honest and successful discharge of the duties pertaining to the various positious in which Providence has placed them, and I repeat that it would be a great pleasure to me could I be present to witness the return of these wanderers to the scenes of their childhood, and to listen to the eloquence of the heart which such a gathering will be sure to inspire. Trusting that you may have a full attendance, I am,

Yours, very truly,

EDWIN C. LITCHFIELD.

BROOKLYN, N. Y., June 26th, 1871.

Richard F. Stevens, Esq.

DEAR SIR:—I wrote you some days since in reply to your kind invitation of June 1st, saying that I should endeavor to be present at the re-union of the former residents of Pompey; I regret now to inform you that the illness of a member of my family will deprive me of the anticipated pleasure.

As a former resident of "The Hollow," it grieves me to think that this important meeting, and one which will probably be the most pleasant and longest remembered of any of the assemblages ever held in our native town should be held on "the Hill." I can recall to mind a time when every man in Delphi would have "died in the last ditch," rather than to allow such an event to take place. We should have contended that Delphi was entitled to the honor, but for the sake of harmony we might have compromised on Green's Corners. Now, I suppose from your high stand-point, poor old Delphi will be entirely over-looked, and little will he heard at your re-union, except in glorification of "The Hill," its great eminence, its bracing breezes, its time-honored Academy, and the great and good men and women it has sent forth.

The fact that Delphi quietly submits to all this, convinces me that the old village has greatly changed since the days when we demanded for the Hollow its fair share of all the town offices, down even tc the sealer of weights and measures, and would under no circumstances consent to the holding of a town meeting at any point west of the Corners. The Hollow must have been "re-constructed" since my day, or this re-union would not have heen held on the hill without a terrible struggle. However, if Delphi can stand it, I can, and I sincerely hope all your pleasant anticipations connected with this meeting will be realized, and that the re-union will result in renewing and strengthening the attachments of all present to our noble old town.

Very Truly Yours,

H. W. SLOCUM.

H. W. Slocum

PRATTSBURGH, June 23d, 1871.

Mr. Richard F. Stevens.

SIR:—I have just received your circular inviting me to a re-union at Pompey Hill, on the 29th inst., I regret that circumstances will prevent my attendance. Age alone would render it difficult, as I was 86 years old in April last. It would be extremely gratifying to have an interview with many friends who may be there present. In addition to the associations of a former residence, it may be said, that the place has a most salubrious air, and is richly worth a visit for a view of its far-stretching landscape. Memory recalls the list of strong men who have resided there; and from time to time have officiated in our National and State councils. On this topic, the limits prescribed to this note forbid my expatiating. As I cannot be a participant in the approaching

"Feast of reason and the flow of soul,"

I must content myself with the hope that we may all finally meet in that higher and better world where our re-union will be perpetual, and our happiness without alloy.

I am, very respectfully Yours,

R. S. ORVIS.

SYRACUSE, June 19, 1871.

Dr. R. F. Stevens.

DEAR SIR:—An invitation to attend a re-union of the old residents of Pompey came to me a few days since—A "re-union of the old residents of Pompey!" I read that sentence with many a heartfelt throb, for

"They are *not* all here
Some are away
The *dead* ones dear!"

From off *my* family altar nearly every flower hath withered, faded and died. Gone from us in early life! But one (and he far away in a western home,) is left me of my once joyous home-circle. Oh! not for me is that re-union! Too many sad memories of the past cluster around that dear old "hill-side home."

The grass hath grown green and long upon the eloquent dumb mounds, where sleep my dead! *Can* I go up to the re-union? There will be the school-mates of my girlhood. The teachers I both loved and feared in childhood. The friends of later years, my father's and my mother's friends. All will be there! Shall I too go? Yes! I will take the dear ones "God hath given me," and climb those hills "sublime and glorious still," Up! up! to the "re-union," and for one day I will strive to prove in social greetings that "clouds have their silver linings," and after storms, comes ever the bright sunshine.

Yours, in hopes of a blessed re-union, "Up Higher,"

ESTHER A. CLAPP DORWIN.

SYRACUSE, July, 1871.

Dr. R. F. Stevens:

DEAR SIR:—For *us* the "glorious re-union at old Pompey" hath come and gone, but the memory of that day can never pass away—with us it liveth forever! Like the sunny dreams of childhood, its memory will brighten our future pilgrimage down the shady slope of life; it revived old memories long since dead; it taught us, though we had years ago learned, that life was "real and earnest," that there was still left for us much of love, of poetry and sentiment.

There old friends, and perchance old lovers met, and as they grasped the hand the "light of other days" beamed from the eye, and the eager "God bless you! are you here?" was not a studied expression, but an outburst from the abundance of the heart. What if the brown hair of the one *was* threaded with silver, and the jetty locks of the other grown thin and grey? What if the voice once so musical *had* acquired, by contact with the world, a harsh note, and the bright eye become less bright? Did we note these changes?

Ah, no! the heart was young again, and the expressions "I know you! how little you have changed!" were heartfelt, no matter if our mirrors at home told a different tale, and after this, how proud we were to say to such a friend, "this is my son," as we presented our noble, stalwart boy, or, this my daughter, as we led up our *girl*, just blushing into womanhood.

Proud day for ancient Pompey! Proud day for fathers and mothers! for young and old—proud day for all! And yet with all the pride and joy of the occasion, there were sad hearts there, hearts desolate of love; hearts which amid all these fond greetings continually cried out "where is my father, my mother, brother or sister?" Kindred and friends were around them, but those loved first and best, were gone. A green spot in the church yard answered the wailing heart, gone home! Safely housed from wind and storm! A family around the Great White Throne! Would you wish them back to-day?

You, my friend, visited the home of your fathers; I went to mine beneath the hills, the home of my grand-sire, my father, and the home where my childhood flitted by. Thirty-five years ago its halls echoed to the tread of fond parents, and the tiny feet of children. There the treble of my fair haired foster sister, the rich tenor of my gentle mother's voice, the second of my loved elder brother, my noble father's bass, with the accompaniment of cousin Charlie's viol, floated at eventide among the hills, while Willie and "Sis" and I frolicked upon the grass or climbed the stately Balm of Gilead at our door. Now what a change! The echoing halls resound to the step of the sons and daughters of the "Emerald Isle," and our fathers, where are they? The little red school house on the green still reared its head in humble pride, as in years gone by; it looked to me smaller than when I there stood up at spelling, and battled for the "head;" and, to, its sombre sides had taken on a shade of brown; but as I looked at its high windows, out of which I had slily peeped many a time, and its quaint old benches and desks, bearing many a mark of mischievous girls and boys, and saw my own name rudely cut with the knife of one of my boy lovers, I knew it was the same dear old school house; every bench and desk seemed to tell a tale of school girl's joys and sorrows, of school mates and masters gone; for

"None were there to greet me now,
And few were left to know,
That played with me upon the green
Full forty years ago."

There, to, stood the old elm tree upon the corner; though shorn of much of its original beauty and grandeur, it still spread its gnarled branches far and wide, showing how nobly it had braved the fury of "Old Pompey's" winds for centuries. Beneath its cool shades I remember sleeping, and dreaming such dreams as come to us but once, and that in our sinless, happy childhood. I remember standing on tip-toe and spelling out the bills which told of the wonderful things to be found in the city of salt, for the old tree was used as a bulletin board in those days by the agents of the merchants of the infant city of Syracuse.

The ancient Columbia Poplars too, were there near by; which *seventy years* ago shaded the house of my *grand-father.*

How familiar they looked, tall and straight, their dark leaves whispering as they did years ago. Many a whip I have cut from their leafy sides, with which to urge on my "Arabian Steeds," which so often in *those* days bore me "o'er the hills and far away!"

But do *you* know Doctor, how sadly I missed the dear old country church? How desolate the green looked without it? for it had been borne away, as a store house, for a thrifty farmer; who instead of "pulling down the *old* and building greater" chose rather to take the *old church*, with its ample dimensions; and now in place of the *voice* of *prayer*. we daily hear the *cooing* of *doves* from its high dome. Fondly and tenderly, do I remember the church of my early love; when *first* my infant lips learned to join in the *Response* the devout *Litany* and prayer. There, too, when but a child I took the solemn vows of confirmation; promising to love God and keep my spirit "free from earth-taint." Still do I feel the kindly pressure of the good Bishop's hands upon my head; and hear the accents of his gentle voice;

"When he spoke, what tender words he used,
So softly that like flakes of feathered snow
They melted as they fell."

I was but a light-hearted child then of thirteen, and long years have passed since the echo of that good man's voice died away in that dim old country church; and he with many of my loved ones "rests from his labors."

Ah! Dr. it is good for us to live over the past, as we did on that never to be forgotten day! We shall ever look back upon it as a "bright green spot in the desert sands of life!" We will remember it ever, and teach our children to echo the cry which daily goes up from our hearts. Thank God for the Re-union.

Yours, very Truly,

ESTHER A. CLAPP DORWIN.

MANTORVILLE, MINN., June 23d, 1871.

Dr. R. F. Stevens:—

Your favor, inviting us to attend a re-union of the former residents of the old town of Pompey, has been received, and has awakened many thoughts of the "Auld Lang Syne." Again and again, through all the "halls of memory," have been stirred anew the long-slumbering echoes of the past. Half forgotten forms have reappeared with sharper outlines and more than usual distinctness, claiming former appreciation. Few things would be more gratifying to us than to meet and greet once more the many surviving friends of "long ago" on the grand old hills of Pompey; but growing infirmities, a long and wearisome journey, with other reasons, will compel us to forego the pleasure. But we shall be with you in spirit and measurably share the festive joy of your gathering. And should any there still kindly remember "Jared" and "Miss Rowena," and enquire of our wellfare and *whereabouts*, please tell them that we now hail from the "Land of the *Dakotas*," just over the eastern line of what we here call the "West," *alias* Minnesota; and like many who were young when we left our native hills, are far in the "sear and yellow leaf." Our lot has been cast among the Pioneers of the West. Left the "Hills" when the first railroad pointing westward was being built, from Utica to Auburn. Found Milwaukie a small village. Preached the first sermon ever preached in Madison, the Capitol of Wisconsin, standing behind a dry goods box covered with an Indian blanket, in the upper story of a store, the best meeting house the place could afford. Now it is a beautiful and proud city, full of churches and elegant public buildings, and the whole country, a few years since the home of a few filthy Pottawatomies, Menominies and Winnebagoes, now blossoms out with cities, villages, and homes of culture and refinement. The Indian trails, once the only guide to the Wisconsin pioneer, have given place to a net-work of railroads, which bear along their iron traceways the burden of a great and growing commerce. All these changes have we witnessed within the last thirty-five years. The last five years have been spent in Minnesota. This State, twenty years ago, had but a few hundred inhabitants. Now her population of half a million can take excursions on a thousand miles of her railroads; and as they witness the rapid movements in building the N. P. Railroad, some fancy they can *almost* hear the thunder of the iron horses from Puget Sound, as they rush over the mountains, bringing the commerce of China with them, and gathering up, as they course the great Plains, the products of a thousand industries already being opened up from a territory large enough to make twelve or fifteen States as large and as good as New York.

Our three score years and ten are nearly filled; but with such a western experience, and such an *outlook* still *westward*, our old friends will not think hard of us if we express a willingness to live a few years longer to see what we may see in the West.

I can but think your gathering will make a proud day for Pompey, and that you will realize, as never before, that your town has furnished her full average of notables, and that the old Academy, and olden churches, (however imperfect in their workings,) have had much to do in moulding the character and in shaping the destiny of those that meet in your union.

Could I have the pleasure of meeting the multitude that will gather at your union, and hear recalled the names of others that have passed behind the vail, I would gladly recall the memory of one, now perhaps half forgotten by the older inhabitants, and entirely unknown to the new. I refer to Theodore E. Clarke. His life was scarcely considered a success, even by his best friends. His powers were too restive to be curbed down to those pursuits necessary to give success. But among the long list of gifted minds Pompey has produced, I have long regarded Theodore's as the *tallest* of them all. For pure intellection, for logical acumen, for profound abstract thought, for far-reaching and comprehensive views, for bold excursions into the unknown in search of hypothesis to explain known facts, he probably had few equals in this or any other country—in this or any other age. But he passed away in middle life, comparatively unknown, and has gone where thinking is a *business* and profound logic appreciated.

Through you we would send our kindest greetings to old friends, hoping that the renewal of old acquaintances—the stirring memories that will be awakened there—the lessons of instruction that will be suggested by the occasion—will better qualify for a grander, nobler and enduring re-union beyond the *River*.

We hope to meet you on the other shore.

Yours, in memory of past,

Jared F. Ostrander.

MANTORVILLE, MINN., Aug. 29th, 1871.

Dr. R. F. Stevens.

DEAR SIR:—Your request for a few items from my pen shall be cordially complied with. The grand gathering of the scattered sons and daughters of Pompey, on the 29th of June, is an era in the history of that place. The friendly meetings and greetings of those who came back to the homes of "other days"—the reminiscences awakened—the long past brought back with its memories of sadness and of gladness—all conspire to invest the day with an interest which will live when other days are forgotten. Thanks for the papers sent, giving an account of the doings and sayings of that day, that grand event, in which it was my misfortune not to participate, has, nevertheless, more than any other of my life, stirred up memories of the past, brightened up scenes of my childhood and youth, until they seem but a little ways back in the dim distance, although my three score and ten years are nearly told. The schools of Pompey Hill are among my earliest recollections. The one taught in the school house, near D. Kellogg's residence, I attended and remember—the teacher, I think, was Leman Pitcher. The house was used for meetings on the Sabbath, and the Rev. Mr. Wallace was the minister. The desk used as a pulpit was sometimes, also, used to shut up naughty scholars in. One day Hugh Wallace, the minister's son, was sent there for some misdemeanor, and after looking around to view the situation, exclaimed: "I don't want to be shut up in father's pig pen." After my father removed to his "wilderness home," half a mile east of the Academy, it was my lot, with sister Chloe, to go to school through the woods by marked trees, with only a faint foot-path that led to the hill. One morning, as we were leisurely wending our way to school with our dinner bag and books, we heard a terrible crash in the bushes near us. We halted, and on turning around saw a big black animal near the path, sitting on his haunches and looking at us. As we had not been frightened with stories of bears, we had no fears. We stood facing the animal and wondering what it might be, until Bruin, not being in want of a breakfast, or taking pity on us poor, unprotected children, walked majestically away, leaving us to pursue our course. On telling of our adventure to the scholars, and they to the teacher, quite an excitement was produced; and our return home after school was guarded by two or three big boys, around the road, nearly a mile and a half. We were not allowed to tread that path alone again.

You ask me to say something of the schools I taught. My first attempt at teaching was in the chamber of your father's house. You probably recollect it, for there you learned your "A, Be, Abs." Mrs. Miller, in her address, alluded to that school, though I think she must have been too young to have been a pupil. It was forty-eight years ago this summer. I remember the circumstance to which she alluded. It occurred in this wise: Her sister Ellen was wanting a "copy set," as we then termed it, and I was obliged, while writing, to turn my back to the school. It has always been my impression that it was James Beebe, a cousin of Mrs. M.'s, who called out—"Miss Rowena, mayn't David (not Dan.) Porter turn his face this way?" Without stopping writing, I said: "Yes, David, turn around." "I don't want to," said he, "for James wants to spit in my face." By this time I was ready to attend to matters. One of the Birdseye boys, (Eben,) in that same school, was, one day, for playing truant, compelled to stand in the middle of the room and study his lesson. This he did with unusual energy and application. Looking off his book, he said: "Miss Rowena, do bears have chickens?" This called out a burst of laughter from teacher and pupils, and he was sent to his seat without any new light on the subject of natural history.

This school was succeeded by one taught the next Summer, in the house near the Academy; then occupied by David Hines. After that I taught five terms in the School-house then standing near the spot now occupied by the new church. The path of life has led me far away from those scenes of labor, and of interest; but I have ever looked back to them as among the pleasantest of my life; and with very kindly feelings towards all those who were my pupils. Among them I saw the names of ten or more, who were to be present at the gathering on the Hill, and I felt an honest pride in the thought, that perhaps my feeble endeavors were not all lost. It has always given me pleasure to hear of the welfare of my pupils, and have ever sorrowed with them, when hearing of their afflictions. I have ever regretted that in my occasional visits to the home of my early life, I met so few of them. They were scattered here and there, and some were sleeping their last sleep. On a visit to the cemetery in Pompey, sixteen years ago, I counted sixteen stones erected to the memory of those who were my pupils. In other lands some have found their last resting-place, and perhaps some repose on the battle-fields of our late distracted and bleeding country. I regret that Grace Greenwood was not with you in the re-union, to add to the interest with her poetical talent. She, too, learned from me her alphabet, and "a, be, abs." A few years ago, I received a letter from her with a graceful acknowledgement of my endeavors to instil into her young mind the first rudiments of knowledge, and start her on her literary career. I do not forget among my hundreds of pupils, the three brothers, William, Charles and Richard Stevens, who were some of the first on whom to try my hand at teaching. Especially the latter, a feeble little boy, who had so much of my sympathy, that he was left to "run loose," and awakened the envy of the others for my partiality.

Yours, Respectfully,

ROWENA M. OSTRANDER.

Perhaps you will deem me intrusive, but I will venture to make a few more suggestions; altho' others may do the same. You may cast mine aside, if so, as though they were not made. Pompey, will after this, gain a new celebrity.

Perhaps very few dreamed of the great wealth of intellect and influence, that has gone out from that town, to enrich the world. Besides the notables mentioned in connection with the grand re-union, there are others, who are entitled to a remembrance, among the great and good of Pompey's sons and daughters. They are found in all the professions, in all the walks of usefulness. Many* are the ministers of the gospel of peace, who have gone, here and there, some to the privations and hardships of our western land, and some to carry the gospel to the heathen. Two, certainly, were Pompey's children. Artemas Bishop, who, some now living, will remember, left the grand old hills, and the home of his childhood and youth, to preach "Jesus and the resurrection," to the far-off islands of the sea. It was, I think, in 1821, he sailed from Boston for the Sandwich Islands. Mrs. Julia A. (Ostrander) Crane, sailed from the same port, in 1836, as a missionary to the benighted Hindoos. The year before, (1835,) Mrs. Theresa Patten Howard left her home and friends, to labor as a missionary in Burmah.

Among the earlier teachers in Pompey, who deserve a passing notice, at least, were the Rev. Eli Burchard, J. J. Deming, and Miss Upham. Among the many names that will pass into oblivion, I would snatch two which might have been ennobled upon the annals of literary fame, had not death interposed. Almira Campbell and Adelaide Delia Clarke, sister to Grace Greenwood. But few ever knew of the wealth of intellect hidden away in these young minds. I possess a few poems of the former, written between the ages of fourteen and twenty, which show more than ordinary perception of the beautiful and the true, even in older persons; and her letters, a maturity of thought and judgment far above her years. I cannot forbear quoting from her obituary notice written by Seabred Dodge, for the Onondaga Journal. "She was a young lady of distinguished accomplishments and virtues. She possessed a mind well

*Perhaps, I am mistaken in the many.

stored with useful knowledge. She courted not the society of the gay and thoughtless; unassuming in her manners, she made no pompous display of her mind, conscious that the great and majestic river makes its way in silence to the ocean; it is the little rill that froths and frets as it rolls. "As pure her life, its close as calm, as bright, as moonbeams radiant with their softest light; as whispering winds or shades which twilight throws, peaceful she sunk, in nature's last repose." She died in 1823, in the twenty-third year of her age.

R. M. OSTRANDER.

Mr. Richard F. Stevens, Cor. Sec'y of the "Re-union at Home," and Gentlemen, committee of invitation.

SIRS:—"When silent time wee lightly foot had trod on thirty years," I find myself honored by an invitation from you to join with the friends of other days in a social and friendly re-union to be held at Pompey Hill on the 29th inst.

Gentlemen, I should be very glad to be able to mingle with you on that day; but I regret to say that the sore affliction of inflamatory rheumatism forbids my attendance, and I fear that I shall be doomed to my chamber. However, I shall be with you in spirit, and in fancy shall enjoy the refining pleasures to be derived from the humanizing emanations that will flow from the poets, orators and large hearted, who will assemble together on the appointed day to join in the mutual and agreeable essay of reviving the joys and pleasures of Auld Lang Syne.

Praying that pleasant weather and all things auspicious may be vouchsafed to you all, I am fraternally yours, &c., &c.

SANFORD THAYER.

Syracuse, June 26, 1871.

BURLINGTON, Iowa, June 16, 1871.

My Dear Sir:—

Your favor of the 12th instant, enclosing an invitation to

the Pompey re-union on the 29th, is just received. It would afford me the highest gratification to join in that jubilee, but other engagements will probably prevent. But in compliance with your alternative request, I take occasion to express some of the reflections and reminiscences which the occasion elicits.

It calls up the past with all of its hopes and anxieties and vicissitudes. The panorama of a life time stands unveiled before me; I watch its dissolving views as they follow each other in quick succession on the curtain of memory. The child whose wondering gaze at first scanned the blue dome of Heaven, supposing it to shut down at equal distances on all sides of his humble house, and who hardly attempted to speculate as to what was beyond, changes in rapid gradation to the boy, the youth, the man—all the while enlarging the scope of his knowledge, but finding the suggested unknown, to increase in perhaps still greater proportion, until with whitening locks he looks forward to the limitless future and backward to the equally limitless past, and all around to the infinitudes of space, and forms perhaps just as inadequate and erroneous notions as to what is beyond the scope of his enlarged but still narrow comprehension as had been those of any previous period. When I had mastered my first exercise in arithmetic, I was in my own estimation much nearer the *ultima thule* of mathematical knowledge than I have ever found myself since, and never did I feel myself so far from home as when I was first at Green's corners, though then but one mile distant from the paternal roof.

How vivid are many of the thronging recollections of my school boy period. The noonday sport, so full of interest, and which was so suddenly interrupted, never to be resumed, by the inexorable summons from the lord of the school-room, was but an epitome of a human life. The voices of my young playmates seem almost still ringing in my ears, I watch the staid demeanor and listen to the grave conversation of our old puritan fathers, who have long since been succeeded by their sons and daughters, and those again by a third generation of men and women.

All these seem but the occurrences of yesterday, after a long and troubled dream from which it almost seems as though I was yet to awake and witness their repetition. And yet half a century has intervened between that time and the present. Forty such intervals placed consecutively backward, would reach beyond the Christian era, a hundred and twenty would ante date the creation according to the letter of the Mosaic history. But still, this whole time is not so very long. Do not the results of our own experience in this respect satisfy us that if Adam had lived till now, he might still have regarded his life as short, and that he would have looked back upon his days of primeval innocence and ignorance with regrets, perhaps more piognant but with feelings nearly akin to those called forth by the voices of our own memories?

My earliest recollections of things outside of my own home neighborhood are of the old Pompey Academy. And ever since, its well remembered dingy and weather-worn exterior has excited a veneration unequalled by that of any other structure. This is partly due to intrinsic causes, but none to the effect of early associations. Its commanding position made it distinctly visible from the play-grounds of our district school house, which was situated on a more humble but parallel ridge to the eastward; I well remember with what feelings of awe it was always regarded by me in those earlier days, as something superior to the sphere in which I was born and to which I seemed confined. I sometimes attended "meeting" in its large upper hall, which was fireless in winter as well as in summer, and supposed that this was all the connection I should ever have with its venerable existence. I looked upon the students who were so fortunate as to enjoy its full advantages as a privileged order, and could imagine no earthly condition which I should pride so highly as to become one of their happy number.

Chas Mason

My wishes in this respect were destined in some degree to be gratified. A few weeks of mathematical instruction, under its most distinguished principal, Mr. Leonard, just at the close of his connection with that institution, was followed by a longer period of both classical and scientific study, under his successor, Mr. Aikin, and the supervision of the Rev. Mr. Barrow.

Brief as was the relation of instructor and pupil between Mr. Leonard and myself, it was sufficient to give me an exalted estimate, and a life-long recollection of his capabilities in that connection. I have never known a more lucid expositor of an abstruse subject, or one who would present any idea more clearly with the same number of words. He was the soul of the Academy and gave it most of its well-merited celebrity; and whenever memory calls up that institution from among the shadows of the past, prominent in the foreground, is the figure of Mr. Leonard, with his cane and spectacles and with his erect military bearing.

Mr. Barrow was a gentleman of high intelligence and culture, and manifested the greatest interest in the welfare of those under his charge. He gave a new direction to the current of my life by inducing me to change my intention of soon bringing my academical studies to a close, and to attempt by my unaided efforts to acquire a full collegiate education. The usual recourse in such cases that of teaching school a portion of the year to supply the means of studying during the remainder was suggested and adopted.

During my seasons of study I lived at home, walking every morning and evening nearly three miles to and from the Academy. This instead of being a disadvantage, doubtless contributed not only to my health but also to my educational progress. It gave me the needful exercise without any loss of time. In fact I always regarded this long walk as the most favorable opportunity for studying such subjects as did not involve the necessity of carrying a burden of books. The distance was passed over mechanically and almost unconsciously with less to interrupt the intellectual current than though I had been all the while seated at my desk. And ever since from force of habit or otherwise, whenever I have had an intricate and perplexing subject to untangle, I have resorted to walking as a means of rendering my mind more active and less liable to confusion.

Among the many pleasing recollections which cluster around the Pompey Academy, were the exhibitions (as they were called,) with which the students and the public were sometimes indulged. These I always anticipated with the liveliest interest, long before I was in a condition to become an actor therein. And if as a spectator I could obtain a position where I could see and hear all that there took place, I was on one of the pinnacles of human happiness.

The dramatic portions of the exercises on those occasions were most completely to my taste, and no theatrical exhibitions which I have ever witnessed since that time, when measured by the effect produced on my own mind, were superior to those there presented. Among the actors I particularly remember Orange Butler, who would have made his mark as a comedian on any stage and before any audience, had he turned his chief attention and devoted his studies to his histrionic art.

I have also a vivid recollection of the effect produced on my young mind by Miss Charlotte Hopkins, now Mrs. Beardsley, as a vocalist on one of those occasions. I have since heard the voices of Jenny Lind, and Parepa Rosa and Miss Nilsson, with many others of wide celebrity, but the sensations produced by any of these were tame in comparison with those which thrilled the soul of the rapt boy as he listened to the rich warblings of a strain from "the bards of Ayr," by Miss Hopkins. The echoes of that music have never yet wholly died away.

Much of the effect in these cases was doubtless due to the recaptivity of my own youthful nature. The keenness of my moral and intellectual appetites had not been blunted by time or indulgence. Paucity of amusements caused a fuller appreciation of those we were privileged to enjoy. But after making full allowance for all these considerations, very much of the effect to which I have alluded was doubtless due to the intrinsic excellence of what I then witnessed.

In illustration of this idea, I will refer to another of the few amusements of that early period, I mean the general trainings which annually took place on Pompey Hill. One of the chief charms on those occasions was the gingerbread made by a baker name Nettleton, which was then sure to be awaiting our expectant shillings. Its appreciated excellence was doubtless, partly due to a healthful appetite, which had then been rarely gratified and never pampered. But after making full allowance for this cause, no one whose memory extends back to those times, will ever question its intrinsic merits. Nettleton's gingerbread was one of the beneficent institutions of that day. Its manufacture is one of the lost arts. Perhaps the world is never again to know the secret of its perfection.

But there are other memories which the present occasion elicits, and to which I will briefly allude. Pompey Hill was then a village of no inconsiderable pretensions. It raised its head above its rural surroundings as high socially, as it stood geologically, and this pre-eminence was tacitly acknowledged by all the country people around. Thither they went for law, medicine and merchandise, thither they carried to market the products of their farms and of their handiwork, and thither they wended their way annually to elections, town meetings and general trainings, and on every Sunday to "meeting."

My earliest recollections are of the large upper room in the old Academy, to which I have already alluded, as the most pretentious place of religious worship for the Presbyterians, who were then the most numerous and wealthy denomination. In the progress of improvement, a new church was built by them in a more central portion of the village, and the Academy was occupied by the Baptists, who, after a few years, erected a building of their own. In the mutations to which all human affairs are subject, this building has since passed into the occupancy and ownership of the Roman Catholics. I was present when the erection of the steeple of the Presbyterian meeting house was completed, and saw a hair-brained man seat himself upon a three-pronged fork which was fixed by a socket upon the point of the spire. I turned away my eyes with a shudder, and when next I looked, he was coming down the spire head foremost like a squirrel. The bare thought of that transaction almost makes my blood run cold to this day.

I remember the time when most of our country people dwelt in log houses, and how I used to be impressed with the odor of aristocracy that seemed to surround the village habitations, all of which were of frame work, and most of them were even painted. The population of the town was considerably greater then than now, for all these log houses were crowded with children. The country had been chiefly settled by men in the prime of life, who had immigrated almost simultaneously, and purchased small farms averaging little if any more than one hundred acres each. David Green, owned three hundred and twenty acres, the two Newmans, John and Amos, had each about the same number. Conrad Bush had twice as many, but these were rare exceptions. The consequence was that the whole country was densely populated at a very early day. The process which has since been going on has been that of *uniting* farms instead of *dividing* them. A considerable proportion of the country habitations have become tenantless, and have disappeared, in consequence of the emigration of their former occupants with their families, until the number of scholars in the district wherein I received my rudimentary education, is not now more than one-third, or perhaps one quarter of what it was when I was one of them; and this diminution would have been still much greater, but for the new element of Irish immigration which has filled in part the vacuum created by the causes above mentioned.

Away down the vista of the years that have forever fled, come visions of many more of the early inhabitants of Pompey, who have passed from this mortal stage, to many of whom I was connected by ties of respect and gratitude in consequence of the salutary influence they have exerted over my destiny. Prominent among these, I will mention Daniel Wood, Victory Birdseye, Elisha Litchfield, Ansel Judd, Asa Wells, David F. Dodge and Daniel Gott. It was while struggling with an unfriendly fortune that these and others of lesser note by kindly counsel or otherwise, strengthened me in my purposes and aided in their accomplishment. A suggestion from the first named of these individuals induced me to consult the second, who by a letter to the third, then our representative in Congress, secured me an appointment in the Military Academy, which thus unexpectedly changed again the current of my life.

But the advantages thus presented for my acceptance were not obtained without cost. They involved the necessity of a separation from home and kindred and friends, from all that constituted the world in which I then lived, and of entering upon a new and untried state of existence. One in whom the domestic ties were unusually strong, and who was called for the first time in his life away from their almost immediate influence, may well be supposed to feel the sacrifice of all he has ever loved or valued; but the measure of that sacrifice can only be fully appreciated by him who has had a like experience. It was the mental anguish of death while yet the life pulses were beating warm and healthful, while the senses were all unclouded, and while relief from physical agony afforded no part of a compensating equivalent. And when the nostalgic symptoms incident to such a state of mind and circumstances had become fairly developed, actual death with all its attendant horrors seemed attractive and even welcome, provided my mortal frame could be restored to the scenes for which my longing heart was pining with a desire as unconquerable as it may now seem extravagant.

But I persevered in the course I had chosen. The recuperative forces of youth and nature triumphed. Another world grew up around me. A new moral creation sprung into existence, which has ever since been constantly extending and consolidating itself and becoming more and more a subject of absorbing interest and affection.

Yet even still there is an inner world recognized and ever unforgotten. It lies next outside of the charmed circle of my childhood's home, and partakes of its peculiar influences, though these lessen in intensity in proportion as they increase in circumference. Its inhabitants seem different from those of the outer world. Whoever was born or has long resided in my native town, is bound to me by a tie unknown to others, and seems in some degree a relative. I have always availed myself of every convenient opportunity to keep alive the magic influence which connects my life with the place of its commencement, and the surroundings of its earlier stages, and have sometimes hoped it yet was destined to terminate near where it first began.

The great change in my life to which I have alluded, took place in 1825, a year not more momentous in my own history than in that of the human race. Railroads, in the sense in which that word is now understood, were on that year first made a practical reality. The Stockton and Darlington railway for the general transportation of freight and passengers from place to place, commenced its operations in that year, and was the first of its species.

It constituted an era in human history, a new departure in the progress of civilization. Other inventions and other causes have contributed to the great result, but an impulse was then communicated which has elevated human nature to a higher plane of existence and endued it with new attributes and new capabilities. The man of to-day is a very different being from the man of 1825. He can fly through space with the speed of an eagle. He can practically navigate the summit of mountain ranges as well as the beds of the deeper rivers. He can converse with his friends who are a thousand miles distant, and is made instantaneously conscious of its daily occurrences among the antipodes. If at the expiration of another forty-six years, he is gfted with powers attributed to the genii of Arabic fiction, the change will hardly surpass that which our own eyes have witnessed.

But this change, great and beneficial as it has been in most respects, has not been without its disadvantages in others. Our native town, and especially its chief village, have felt some of its inauspicious effects. Its elevated position and other circumstances have placed it beyond the reach of any probable railroad or telegraph. In respect to other localities, its relative movement has been backward. Its men of mark are mostly drawn to other centres. Syracuse, whose prosperity has by the cause we are considering, been so much enhanced, absorbs most of its mercantile and manufacturing enterprise. The great west which by the same causes, has been brought practically nearer to the principal markets of the world, entices its agricultural population, until like most of the other rural districts of the State, it has been constantly diminishing in comparative wealth and in actual population.

Yet while its hills remain to give their beautiful diversity to its unequalled landscapes, it will never be wanting in attractions for those who have an eye for rural beauty, wherever the places of their birth. But to one who was born and nurtured among those hills, of whose moral view they thus formed a living part and parcel, they will always possess a charm which time and distance can never dispel. Hundreds of years hence, the wanderer from this his birth place, shall wend hither his pilgrim steps, as I have often done, to gratify the irrepressible promptings of his heart, to fortify the better principles of his nature, or to give his troubled spirit rest, by contemplating the theatre of his early innocence and by watching the lights and shadows that sweep over those grand and peaceful undulations, bringing calmness to a soul that has long been tempest tossed, among the conflicts and commotions of the world without.

On the summit of the eminence which overlooks all its surroundings, and which is in the village burying ground, lies the brother by whose side I always slept in childhood, taking his final rest. Thither have I sometimes repaired on a summer's Sabbath hour, to meditate over the past and to admire the beautiful panorama which spreads on every side, as far as the eye can reach. The impenetrable veil of the primeval forest has been withdrawn so far as to diversify and unfold the beauties it can no longer conceal. The summer breezes, whose wings never are scorched by any sultry sun, are there nestling in the groves or flitting out and in at the windows of the hundreds of quiet homes that are scattered all around. Hills and valleys all verdant and beautiful stretch themselves out in endless variety on every side, until they meet and mingle with the skies in the dim distant horizon. It is the loveliest sight of nature in her mildest mood that can be found in all the earth, and never satiates or ceases to delight the heart that is all attuned to its higher, holier impulses. No one need ever seek a preferable spot on which to await the momentous events of the rapidly approaching future. I hope that I may yet again be sometimes permitted to feast my moral appetite upon its rich but unchanging treasures.

Frequent are the admonitions however, that such privileges will soon be ended. At brief intervals the news is spread that some of our old familiar friends have passed forever away. Even with your letter came the sad intelligence that Mr. Daniel Marsh, whom I remember from my earliest years, and who then and for long years afterwards resided within sight of my birth place, would never again be seen in his frequent walks around your native village. One by one the Great Teacher's call is summoning us from our game of life, which, like our schoolboy sports, is often left unfinished. The writer of these lines will doubtless precede most of those for whom they are intended, but they all will follow, and oh how soon! Faith then looks up with hopeful eye to a higher destiny prepared by Him who has shaped all things more in kindlier adaptation to our individual happiness than could have been contrived by the most exalted human intelligence. Till then we all shall never meet again, but my kindest wishes shall attend each one in life, in death and in the realms beyond. From the narrow isthmus which connects the unforgotten past with the undeveloped future, I send you all my greeting, and bid you all till next we meet, adieu.

Yours, very truly,

CHAS. MASON.

DR. R. F. STEVENS.

NEW YORK, June 24th, 1871.

Dr. R. F. Stevens, Sec'y, &c.

DEAR SIR:—Your proposed Pompey re-union has just come to my knowledge, having received from a relative this morning, a circular, in which my name appears as one of the speakers announced for the occasion.

The idea is novel, attractive, and admirably conceived.

I regret I did not know of it earlier, for I cannot think of any event, which would give me greater pleasure; but it is now too late; other matters will prevent my attendance.

It is natural to reverence my birth place, and early home. The sweetest memories cling to the familiar scenes and friends of sunny childhood and youth.

I spent several years at school and studying my profession on good old Pompey Hill, which has purer air and water, and is nearer Heaven than any inhabited place in the State.

I remember well preceptors Leonard and Huntington. The old yellow Academy with its BELL; Declamation Hall, &c. There was, as usual a great variety of talent among the pupils. Some afterwards became graduates, studied the different professions and met with varied fortune. And a few have made their mark, and have founded a lasting fame, but for pecuniary success, there was *one*, who never studied at all, and who has far excelled all the others. The son of a wealthy farmer of the county, he was sent to the Academy to get educated and prepared for business, and he was provided with the necessary new books for the purpose. But the boy understood *trade* meant business, not education, or "*Book-larnin*," and he therefore spent most of his time at the Inn of Capt. Pitt Dyer. All old inhabitants will remember the happy smiling face of the jovial Inn-keeper. This *was the Pompey Exchange*, where speculations, politics and religion were ably discussed, and where Uncle Nat stood champion of the world at chequers, and it was here the young pupil, between November and April, traded. Starting with the capital of a silver watch, he returned home in the Spring with four horses, three watches, and fifty dollars cash. The leaves of his books remained unsoiled. Uncle P. his father, was a practical man, he saw the situation at a glance, he made no farther effort in the line of the Academics, but made a virtue of necessity and allowed the talents of his son to flow in their natural channel, and it is due to the boy to say, that well he improved the opportunity, and now in middle age, he is the wealthy man, sagacious trader, able financier, and influential citizen, although his correspondence exhibits some deficiency in his early school training.

I am proud of my native town, she has always leaned toward the right, vice has found no abiding place within her limits. Her farmers for intelligence and integrity, rank among our best citizens. From my earliest recollection her common schools have been models not surpassed, if equalled, by the best of the present time, and in them a good business education was brought to the door of every one, and was well improved.

Among the able teachers in the old common school at Delphi, (my house,) which was one of the best in the county from 1815 to 1830, were Joshua A. Spencer, Elephalet

Spencer, Hiram Denio, Wm. H. Shankland, Orville Robinson, David C. Burdick and others, who afterwards became eminent men. Among their pupils I might name many who have done themselves great credit in after life.

Pompey was settled by hardy New England pioneers, who well understood the importance of schools. Their first business was to establish them, and thus they early shaped the future of this good old town.

The present generation is enjoying the fruits of their foresight and enterprise, long may they retain their just reputation as an intelligent and upright people.

In 1798, my father and mother, both from New England, settled in the then wilderness, on the hill about two miles from Delphi, the nearest neighbor was two miles away. Within ten years the beautiful little village with its churches and school sprang up, and all the neighboring farms were occupied.

I cannot omit one more fact which commands my veneration and love for my native town. In her dust lie buried my parents, brothers, sisters and many relatives.

Regretting that I cannot be present, and wishing you pleasant weather for the occasion and a grand success,

I remain,

Your Obedient Servant,

HERVEY SHELDON.

CLAY, ONONDAGA CO., N. Y., June 21, 1871.

Dr. R. F. Stevens :—

Having had an invitation to attend the "re-union at Pompey, on the 29th inst.," I hereby make known to you, my intention to be present.

I am not a native of Pompey. But in 1827, when a lad 14 years old, I went into the village of Delphi, to learn the hatting trade of Canfield Marsh, brother of Marovia Marsh, of Pompey Hill, also a hatter. In 1828, Marsh failed in business, and I was compelled to seek a new home. I went to the village of Fabius, and worked with Marvin Button, at the harness trade, until 1831. I then went to Pompey Hill, and worked with Edwin Dunbar, at the harness business, until May, 1834. That finished my residence in Pompey. October 12th, 1836, I married Miss Julia Penoyer, a native of Fabius, Onondaga Co., N. Y. In 1838, I located in this little village, known as New Bridge, but the proper name is Belgium. The name of our Post Office is *Clay*. I hold a commission as Postmaster of Clay, N. Y., executed by Montgomery Blair, (P. M. General of the United States,) bearing date May 3d, 1861. I still continue as P. M.

My father had several brothers who were of the first settlers in Pompey. He had a sister who married Capt. Pendason Avery. The descendants of the Barnes clan are very numerous, and may be found in almost any part of the Union! They were well represented in the late rebellion.

I am a native of this county; was born August 24, 1812, in what was then Cicero, but now Clay.

Pompey has very many attractions, and I feel a deep interest in the forthcoming re-union of its former residents.

David Porter, a native of Pompey Hill, a son of the late Dea. Porter, and a neighbor of mine, has been courteous enough to invite me to a seat in his carriage, to attend this anxiously looked for gathering. I accept of his kind invitation. We anticipate a glorious time, one that will pass down to posterity through the annals of history.

I have already extended this letter beyond its proper limits, still, I will venture a quotation from a native of Pompey. "Pompey has produced more men of talent, than any other town in the county." Yours,

ORRIS BARNES.

SYRACUSE, June 27, 1871.

Hon. Daniel Wood:—

DEAR SIR:—Previous engagements prevents my joining

you in the praise-worthy effort in gathering together all of the surviving former residents of the old town of Pompey, with a view to a re-union.

I do not rank as a pioneer, yet my parents came from Massachusetts to Pompey, west Hill, in 1799, where I, then an infant, resided for more than a quarter of a century, thus being quite familiar with the early settlement of said town.

Respectfully,

CHARLES A. BAKER.

PALMYRA, June 13, 1871.

Dr. R. F. Stevens, Syracuse, N. Y.—

DEAR SIR:—I am in the receipt of an invitation to attend a re-union of the former residents of the old town of Pompey. As this is my native town, and some years of early life having been spent at the old Academy, I am persuaded that the occasion will be one not only of general interest, but to myself especially agreeable. At my age, (73,) I can hardly expect to see many faces of the friends and associates of my early life. But the home of your childhood, the resting place of your honored dead, and the sweet memories of days gone by, will sanctify and hallow the "old Hill," and revive the associations of the half century gone.

Unless prevented by sickness, it will please me to attend and join in the pastimes of the occasion.

Very Respectfully,

HIRAM K. JEROME.

NEW YORK CITY, June 28, 1871.

Dr. R. F. Stevens, Secretary, &c.

MY DEAR SIR:—Your favor of the 20th inst., inviting me to the re-union of the residents of Pompey on the 29th inst., was duly received. I have delayed answering it, till this, the last possible moment, in the hope that by some good turn of fortune's wheel, I might respond in person, rather than by letter. That, however proves impossible, owing to engagements made some weeks before notice of the time selected reached me. I am, therefore, reluctantly compelled to deny myself the pleasure of joining in this re-union, and of meeting the many friends who will be present.

My annual returns to the home of my childhood have kept me familiar with the scenes of my earliest days; and it would delight me to be once more "at home," and to point out to those who, as to these annual pilgrimages, have been less favored than myself, some of the beauties of the old place. In a life not free from wandering, it has been my privilege to see large portions of my native land, and something of many lands abroad. It seems to me moreover, to be one of the peculiarities of my own mind to remember and recall, with something more than ordinary facility and distinctness, the scenes which have been laid before my eyes. But in all the countries I have been permitted to visit, I can recall few scenes more beautiful than those which at this season of the year are presented from the Old Hill. The lakes, which are set like mirrors in the landscape; the distant hills, almost swelling into mountains, the mighty sweep of vision to the east and north; the long valleys to the south-west and south-east, the rich fields nearer by, and almost at your feet, and showing, like the divisions on a chess board, farms and forests, dwellings and orchards, waving corn and ripening meadows, yellow stubble and green pastures, flocks and herds, and running brooks; all these make up a picture which is ever before my mind, and which seems to me fairer than almost any other scene ever presented to my eyes. In what stream in all the old town have I not bathed or fished? Upon which of its waters have I not skated? Down what hill have I not coasted over the deep snows, only to drag the heavy sled again and again up the steep ascent, with panting lungs and arid muscles? From what tree, or bush, or sward, in forest, orchard and field, have I not gathered nuts and fruits and berries? In how many meadows did I not make spoil of the honey of the wild bee? Through how many fields and woods did I not use to wander, hunting, or at least trying to persuade myself I was hunting? In how many of the old School houses have I not been present at some thronged "spelling school," to choose or be chosen, on one side or the other, and to contend for my standing, or yield at length, and among the last, to inevitable defeat, with an interest as keen, and a regret as bitter as have come in after years in the contests that may have *seemed*, (but were they really?) far more important? Up what precipice was it not my delight to climb? And if my poor name is not otherwise worthy of remembrance, is it not, with so many, many others, handed down to lasting immortality, in the carvings on the trees at Pratt's and Conkling's Falls? What place in all the broad landscape is not associated in my mind with some delightful recollection of itself, and of persons present or absent, living or departed? And, turning to the highest point of the old Hill, where the grave-stones point aloft, how many memories throng upon us, as we cross the enclosure, and seek the graves where rest the loved and honored of other days; parents, brothers, sisters, kinsfolk, playmates, friends, how many have there taken up their final earthly abode? How long will it be before the old Hill can be forgotten for their sakes, were every other tie that calls me thither, sundered forever?

It would ill become me now to attempt any statement of facts, whether of history or tradition, such as others who will be present will delight you with. But surely, there is something in soil and climate and country, which stamps itself on the character and shines out in all future life. Else why is such a delegation gathered to the homes of their childhood?

The steep hills, the dark forests, the deep snows, the fierce winds, the long, cold winters, the late coming springs; all these were struggled against and overcome. But, with these, were the charms of spring, with wild flowers blossoming on the edges of the snow-drifts; the summers in their beauty, the glories of sunset; and autumns rich with fruits, and bright with forest splendors. All these have left their stamp upon the lives of too many children of the old birth-place, for us to doubt that such a commencement is oftentimes the best preparations for the duties of life, in whatever occupation or station. They who come up to this re-union, from the hall of the Senate, or the Chair of the Executive, or the head of the army, or the bureau of the Cabinet, or the counting houses of merchants, or the direction of great railways, all will testify that the forces which have enabled them to surmount obstacles and conquer difficulties in their future life, if not derived from, were at least largely strengthened and developed by the life they led in childhood and youth amid the snows and storms of the old Hill.

The powers which have governed mighty States, or led great armies victors through long campaigns, and over wide realms, or held Senate's attentive listeners, or left their stamp on the history of the world in the treaty that settles National disputes, not by war with its bloodshed and devastation and misery, but by weighing grievances, claims and complaints in the just and equal balance of peaceful arbitration, or which have built and operated vast railroads, or sent forth great lines of steam ships over distant seas, the names of which were scarcely known to us in our school days. These powers were trained and developed in the common schools or the Academy, and by the libraries of the old town. What honor is not due to those who in the earliest years, in the midst of difficulties, privations and dangers, seeking new habitations, and laying the foundations of new institutions, gathered libraries and built schools and academies such as these, and left behind them influences so potent and beneficial, to rule in affairs of State, to lead in war, and to become as oil on troubled waters, soothing and assuaging the hates and quarrels of great nations, and turning the spear and sword into pruning hook and plow-share. How many through all this broad land, have been refreshed and invigorated by the writings of one who went from the old Hill. But how few, besides those who were born or bred there, know that the *graces* which are properly represented in the name they know her by, were born and trained and cultured in a simple farm house in our native town.

May these influences, so powerful and beneficent during the lives of those who may be present on this occasion, continue to bear now, increased and widened sway through all the coming generations. And may it long be the delight of those whose early years shall be spent amid the old scenes, to remember with pleasure the homes of their childhood, and with affection and gratitude the memories of those who, in hardship and privation, founded the Schools and Churches wherein they shall be trained and fitted for usefulness and power throughout the world.

Desiring to be remembered with affection to those who may come up to this feast, and not seeking to conceal my sense of their superior good fortune, and my sharp regret that I am not able to share personally in all their pleasures, I am,

Most respectfully and truly

Your friend,

LUCIEN BIRDSEYE.

POMPEY ACADEMY.

The history of the Academy in Pompey is very largely the history of the town. It is a history of labors and struggles and gifts and self denials and delays; but not of defeats or disappointments.

The first settlers of the town were almost wholly from Connecticut. Although, in entering the wilderness, they left schools and churches behind them, they were fully sensible of the advantages of churches and schools, and spared no efforts to secure the same to themselves and to their children.

In 1784, Washington, then scarcely rested from the fatigues of the Revolutionary War, had made his well-known journey up the valley of the Hudson, and as far as Crown Point, and up the Mohawk and by the Portage at Wood Creek to the Oneida Lake, that he might see for himself what means there were for communication by water between the new States just established on the sea-board, and the waters of the great lakes and the St. Lawrence.

What he saw then, as well as in his explorations, previous and subsequent, in Western Virginia and Pennsylvania, led him to the efforts, which lasted through his life, for opening communication from the seaboard to the western Rivers and Lakes. This journey, and the attention with which all his movements were followed, turned public observation more fully to the future advantages of settlements of the west, and tended in a few years greatly to promote emigration to the western wilderness.

By the Act of July 25, 1782, (1 Greenleaf's Laws of N. Y. 55,) the State of New York had set apart and assigned lands for the purpose of making grants to the officers and soldiers of the State, who had served in the then present war with Great Britain. By the Act of Feb'y 28, 1789, (2 Greenleaf, 281,) after a recital that the title thereto of the Indians had been extinguished, the Surveyor General had been directed to lay out the military county lands into townships, each to contain sixty thousand acres of land, and to be laid out as nearly in squares as local circumstances would permit, and to be divided into one hundred lots, as nearly square as might be; each lot to contain six hundred acres, as nearly as might be.

This act contains minute directions for making surveys and maps of the land, and for "balloting" for the lots; so that the soldiers, their heirs or assigns, should receive the lands they were entitled to; six lots in each town being assigned "for promoting the gospel and a public school or schools, and one for promoting literature in the State, as the Legislature might direct."

During 1789–90, Simeon DeWitt, then Surveyor General, surveyed the military county lands; laying them out into townships and lots, and displaying his classical tastes and learning by the names which he gave the townships; as Pompey, Manlius, Cicero, Fabius, Romulous, Cato, &c.

The county of Onondaga was erected from the county of Herkimer, by the Act of March 5, 1794. (3 Greenleaf, 110.) Pompey and other towns were created by this Act. The new county comprised the military county lands. It embraced all that part of the State, contained in the present counties of Onondaga, Cayuga, Seneca and Cortland, together with portions of Oswego, Wayne, Tompkins and Schuyler.

The first settlement within the bounds of Pompey, was made in April, 1792, by Ebenezer Butler, Jr., (afterwards commonly known as Judge Butler,) a native of Harwinton,

Litchfield Co., Conn.* He had in 1791 purchased military lot No. 65, in the township,† and in that year visited it; but his family were not removed thither till 1792. In 1793, his brother Jesse‡ and others, with their families, came to the town.

The movement for founding an Academy seems to have commenced very shortly thereafter. As early as January, 1800, a petition of the inhabitants of the town and vicinity, to the Regents of the University for the incorporation of an Academy at Pompey, was prepared, signed and forwarded to Albany.§

It was presented to the Regents at a meeting held on the 17th March, 1800, and was referred to a committee of examination. At a meeting of the Regents, held March 31, 1800, the report of that committee was considered. There seems to have been at that time no other Academy in the county. The Regents adopted a preamble and resolutions, by which, (after reciting that it was uncertain whether Pompey was the most proper place for an Academy in the county of Onondaga, and that there was reason to doubt the expediency of having more than one Academy in one county,) it was resolved that the secretary should transmit a copy of said petition and of that resolution to the supervisors of Onondaga county, and request that they would at their next session inform the Regents whether in their opinion there were any, and what, objections to granting the prayer of said petition. (See Appendix No. 2.)

* Judge Butler died in Ohio, Sept., 1829, aged 96 years.

† Lot 65 is that part of the town on which the Academy, Churches, burial ground, &c., &c., are situated.

‡ Jesse died at Fabius, N, Y., November 30th, 1856, aged 93 years 1 mo.

§ This Petition, like many other documents hereinafter referred to, throws much light on the history of the town. The first settlement had been made less than eight years before ; and here is a paper setting forth the advantages and necessity of a School of high character, it is signed by twenty-five different persons ; all apparently heads of families, every one subscribing money, the lowest $25 : the highest $125 ; the total amounting to $1,195. So much of useful information as to the names of the first settlers, their efforts, labors and sacrifices, and so much of family history, worthy of honest pride, may be gathered from these papers, that it has been deemed proper to print them at length, in the Appendix to this sketch. The petition here mentioned is No. 1 in such Appendix.

The supervisors of the county met at Pompey Hill in October, 1800. Their action was favorable to the views of the petitioners. (See Apendix No. 3.) The same having been certified to the Regents, the original petition and the proceedings of the supervisors were, on the 16th Feb'y, 1801, referred to a committee. (See Appendix No. 2.)

No further action being had by the Regents, the good people of Pompey seem to have become impatient; and in the winter of 1802, they prepared another petition, which was signed by *sixty* persons, and presented to the Regents March 15, 1802. (See Appendix No. 4.) On the receipt of it, and on the same day, the Regents resolved to approve of the application of sundry inhabitants of the county of Onondaga, for the incorporation of an Academy at Pompey, in said county, and that they would incorporate the same upon satisfactory evidence being given, within a reasonable time, of a compliance with the resolution passed by the Regents March 23, 1801.

This latter resolution, (after reciting that Academies were intended to teach branches of literature superior to those taught in common schools, and requiring to that end a more extensive provision for the support of well qualified instructors,) declared that in future no Academy ought to be incorporated, unless it be made to appear to the Board by satisfactory evidence that a proper building for the purpose had been erected, finished and paid for, and that funds had been obtained and well secured, producing an annual income of at least $100; and further, that there be a condition in the charter of incorporation, that the principal or estate producing such income should never be diminished or appropriated; and that such income should be appropriated only to the maintainance, or the salaries of the professors or tutors of the Academy.

The resolutions of March 15, 1802, and March 23d, 1801, were communicated to the petitioners, by certified copies thereof, which are still among the files of the Academy.

The erection of the first building for the Academy, must have been commenced in or about 1803. Mr. Samuel Baker states that when he first saw the building, in August, 1806, as his father Nathaniel Baker was moving into the village, the building was erected and covered, but was not completed or ready for occupation. William Lathrop was the builder.

On the 20th July, 1807, Wm. Lathrop and George W. Wood entered into an agreement, (see Appendix No. 5,) with Manoah Pratt, Henry Seymour and Samuel S. Baldwin, who were "a committee to build the Academy in Pompey," to do certain specified carpenter's work in completing the building designed for the Academy, for the sum of $200; the same to be paid by assignment of subscriptions which should be good aud collectable." Mr. Wood soon after retired from the job. Mr. Lathrop proceeded with it for some time, but on the 2d March, 1810, he relinquished the unfinished part of the job, and agreed to accept $140, in full of what had then been done. In July, 1810, a new subscription was raised, and in the same paper the same committee entered into an agreement to procure the Academy to be completed for the sum of $450. (See Appendix No. 6.)

It is easily to be gathered that, up to this time, the project for the establishment of the Academy had met many difficulties and much opposition; among the files of the Regents is an affidavit of Walter Colton, sworn to March 2d. 1802, and delivered to the Board at their meeting of March 15, 1802, when the second petition for the Academy was presented and conditionally granted. (See Appendix No. 7.)

In this affidavit, Mr. Colton, who had signed the first petition for the Academy, subscribing $100, but who had in the meantime removed to Onondaga Hill, charged fraud, it would seem, in the getting up of the first petition, in January, 1800.

Opposition however, proved ineffectual. The great difficulty was the raising of money to build and complete, and then to endow, the Academy. When we consider the condition of the country, emerging, as it then was, from the utter bankruptcy of the Revolutionary War, with its continental currency; and especially of this part of the country, without money, or roads, or canals, or markets, or any means of improvement or communication, we shall see how great was the undertaking to found and rear such an institution. The original subscription of January, 1800, proved wholly insufficient. A new one was raised in 1807, to pay Lathrop and Wood for finishing the then half built house. That also failed. No doubt it was true, as Mr. Colton had stated in his affidavit, that some had died, and others were insolvent and unable to pay what they had subscribed. But the public spirit of the town was sufficient to overcome all these obstacles. In 1810, the new subscription above mentioned was effected, which amounted to $2,345. (See Appendix No. 8.) It was sufficient to finish the building that had so long remained incomplete, and to furnish an endowment with such an annual income as should meet the conditions on which alone the Regents could grant the charter.

It is no doubt to the great and generous endeavor then made that the tradition of the town refers, which tells of the efforts for the raising of money, when subscriptions were doubled, and the increased value of farms and property, if such a school were established, was made the ground of appeal to the timid, the doubting and the frugal.

At length, in the Autumn of 1810, the building for the Academy was completed and paid for; and there remained $1,450, to serve as an endowment for the yielding of the net annual revenue of $100, required to warrant the granting of a charter.

In February, 1811, the final steps for the incorporation of the school were taken. A petition, (in the peculiar and well known hand writing of the late Mr. V. Birdseye,) was drawn and generally signed; and after being verified by the late Henry Seymour, (whose influence and labors for the school everywhere appear,) was forwarded to the Regents, in March, 1811. (See Apendix No. 9.)

On the 11th March, 1811, by vote ef the Regents, the Academy was incorporated, by the name of "The Trustees of Pompey Academy," Daniel D. Tompkins, then Governor of the State, was Chancellor of the Regents, and Francis Bloodgood was Secretary. The charter is signed by them, and sealed with the seal of the Regents, and bears date March 19th, 1811. It recites that a proper building for the Academy has been erected, finished and paid for, and that funds have been obtained and well secured, producing a net annual income of $100, and provides that the principal or estate producing such income shall never be diminished, and that the income shall be appropriated only to the maintainance or salaries of the professors or tutors of the Academy.

The persons named in the charter as the first Trustees were Henry Seymour, Senior Trustee; Samuel S. Baldwin, Manoah Pratt, Daniel Wood, Ithamar Coe, Asa Wells, Hezekiah Clark, John Jerome, Silas Park, Jacobus DePuy, Daniel Allen, Chauncey Jerome, Daniel Tibbals, Joshua Johnson, Derrick C. Lansing, Benjamin Sanford, Charles C. Mosely, William J. Wilcox, Jonathan Stanley, Jr., Levi Parsons, William Cook, Victory Birdseye, Jasper Hopper and James Geddes.

At a meeting of the Trustees, held April 4, 1811, Henry Seymour was elected President, Victory Birdseye, Secretary, and Daniel Wood, Treasurer. On the 20th May, 1811, Henry Seymour, Daniel Tibbals and Victory Birdseye were elected a prudential committee. On the 3d of November, 1812, the following officers were chosen: Asa Wells, president; V. Birdseye, secretary; D. Wood, treasurer; Asa Wells, S. S. Baldwin and D. Wood, prudential committee. Rev. Joshua Leonard was hired as a teacher, at a salary of $500 per annum. On 6th October, 1813, the following officers were chosen: Rev. J. Leonard, president; V. Birdseye, Secretary; H. Seymour, treasurer; D. Wood, C. Jerome and D. Tibbals, prudential committee.

OLD POMPEY ACADEMY.

INTERIOR VIEW OF THE "OLD ACADEMY."

By this time, the organization of the Academy had been substantially perfected, and its appropriate work had been begun. Thenceforth, the principal labor of carrying on the institution, devolved either on the treasurer, who had charge of the funds, or the preceptor who taught in the school-room. Henry Seymour, remained treasurer from Oct. 6, 1813, till January 10, 1821. On the 24th March, 1819, he had been appointed one of the Canal Commissioners of the State, and his labors in superintending the construction of the Erie Canal, then well advanced towards completion, no doubt prevented his continuing to serve longer as treasurer. It was, however, several years later, when he removed to Utica, and he continued to be a trustee till Oct. 30, 1833, when his resignation as trustee was accepted, and Mr. Samuel Baker was chosen trustee in his place. On Mr. Seymour's resignation as treasurer, in 1821, Luther Marsh was chosen in his stead; remaining treasurer till May 15, 1827, when Mr. V. Birdseye was elected to the office, which he held till his death, Sept. 16, 1853. Levi Wells was then elected to the office, and held it till his death, March 31, 1872, when Dr. O. G. Dibble was chosen to succeed him.

A singular fact should be noted as to the title of the Academy to its lot of land. On his accession to the office of treasurer in the fall of 1853, Mr. Levi Wells, while examining the papers that had come to his hands, found the deed for this lot of land. It was given by Jesse Butler and Louisa his wife, to Pompey Academy. It was dated "the —day of—A. D. 1811," was in the usual form of a deed, with a covenant of warranty. Consideration, $100. It conveyed in fee to the Academy, "All that certain piece or parcel of land lying on lot number sixty-five, in the township of Pompey, bounded as follows, to-wit: Beginning at a stake ninety-six links, south, fifty-six degrees west from the southwest corner of Daniel Wood's house; running from thence west, sixteen rods to a stake; thence north nineteen rods; thence east nineteen rods to the east line of the highway; thence along the highway southerly to the place of beginning, containing two acres of land, be the same more or less."

Though imperfect in the date, it was otherwise in due form, and duly signed and sealed by both grantors. And it was witnessed as to Mr. Butler by H. Clark. But it was neither acknowledged, proved or recorded. Of course it was liable to loss or destruction. It could only be read in evidence, if that should ever be necessary, by giving proof of signatures nearly half a century old at that time, and likely soon to be wholly incapable of proof. Mr. Wells lost no time in endeavoring to cure this defect. On presenting the deed to Mrs. Butler, she at once freely acknowledged it before him as a Justice of the Peace. Mr. Butler, however, refused to do the same, and it became necessary to resort to a provision of the recording act, very rarely used of late years. The genuineness of Mr. Butler's signature to the deed was proved by Mr. Samuel Baker. The genuineness of the signature, and the death of Henry Clark, the witness to Mr. Butler's execution of the deed, were proved by Mr. John H. Clark, (brother of Henry Clark.) Then, by filing the deed with the County Clerk, to remain forever on file in his office, it was admitted to record on the 5th of January, 1854, and recorded in Liber 115 of Deeds, p. 138. Thus, after a lapse of more than forty years, the title of the Academy to the site of its school building was first secured against loss and danger.

By a law passed April 13, 1813, the Commissioners of the Land Office were "authorized and required to grant by Letters Patent to the trustees of Pompey Academy, and their successors, in fee simple, Lot Number Fifteen in the town of Camillus, in the County of Onondaga, any law to the contrary notwithstanding." It was then, in the law, made the duty of the trustees, when they should "sell the said lot or any part thereof, to loan the money arising from such sale on landed security, to double the value of the sum so loaned, and on the payment of any such loan, then to re-loan the same forever, and to appropriate the interest arising from such loans forever to the support and maintenance of instruction in said Academy."

The passage of this law is believed to have been secured by the late V. Birdseye, at a time when he was in Albany, to attend the Supreme Court.

This lot of land, (15 in Camillus,) now in the town of Van Buren, lies on the south bank of Seneca River, about two miles below, or east of, Baldwinsville. It contained 638.88 acres, and was originally covered with a large and valuable growth of pine and oak timber, which was easily rafted to the mills on the River. The Commissioners of the Land Office had been for years vexed by the stealing of the timber from the lot, which they had been unable to prevent or to punish. This fact no doubt made the obtaining of the grant much easier than it would otherwise have been.

On securing the passage of the Act, and its signature by the Governor, Mr. B. returned with a certified copy; no one in Pompey knowing anything of it. He went immediately to the land, with the late Warren Scranton, and with his assistance, and that of Spencer Smith as surveyor, surveyed and subdivided the lot. Very soon, such portions were sold, that owners were settled on parts of the lot to watch the remainder, and prevent trespassing. The whole of the land was soon sold, producing a fund of about $4,000; the income of which tended very materially to promote the welfare and success of the school.—(See Clark's Onondaga, I: 245.)

All the older inhabitants of the town and the early scholars will well recollect the old Academy. It was a large building for that time and place, of wood, painted yellow, nearly square, being 50 feet by 40; its gable fronting the south; of two stories, and with a hall ten feet wide running through the middle of the first floor. On each side of this hall, at the front, was a study room, ten feet by fifteen. Behind each of these, and on each side of the hall was a long room extending to the rear of the building, forty feet by fifteen.

In the long room on the west side of the hall, the common school of the village was taught for many years; it being in fact a department of the Academy, long after the charter was granted. It had been so occupied even before the whole building was completed, and the charter obtained. In the room on the east of the hall, the Academy was taught. All the old pupils will recollect the long room; with its broad fire-place at the south end; the entrance from the hall, by the door about a third of the distance from the south end; the Preceptor's chair and table at the north end; the sloping desks, fastened to the wall, on either side; the long benches before the desks; both benches and desks of the finest white pine, and well whittled and marked. On the west side of the room, behind the door leading into the hall, and at the Master's right hand, sat the girls. On the other side, and below the hall door on the west side, sat the boys; the smallest of each sex being nearest the teacher, and rising by age, till the oldest scholars were trusted farthest from his eye. The favorite seats were those on each side of the massive walls of the projecting fire-place, with but a step between the seat and the boards that covered the bricks of the chimney. The seats could be seen and approached only from the side next the master. Here, many a game and trick were played; much fruit and many nuts eaten. From one of these secluded corners it was that about December, 1819, the live coal from the fire was dropped into the open hand of the new scholar who, on his first day at the school, stood before the fire, with closed eyes, and hands spread behind his back, during Mr. Leonard's morning prayer. That scholar recently died at a good old age; and he told the writer that he never knew or suspected whose sleight-of-hand had played the neat trick. If the perpetrator of it shall see these lines, he may now safely make due confession. Let him do so. "Better late than never."

In after years, when the District School-house had been built, the common school was removed thither. Then the west room became the chemical and philosophical laboratory and lecture room, which was so attractive on the Wednesday afternoons, when the routine of studying and reciting gave place to more enticing lectures and experiments. How pungent was the chlorine? How pronounced the odor of the sulphuretted hydrogen? How proud was the pupil chosen to stand with the teacher behind the table, to lend an occasional hand in helping an experiment through to success? Of what matter was even an extra breath of chlorine to one who was enjoying such a distinction?

The second story was the chapel. It occupied nearly the whole of the upper part of the building, and was forty feet square. The stairs leading to it were at the north, at the extreme rear end of the hall. At the south, or front of the chapel was "The stage," a broad platform raised just three feet from the floor. On each side of the stage, at the front corner of the building, was a small room for study, ten feet by fifteen. The roof was supported by four columns of carved or turned pine, at equal distance from the corners and centre of the room.

Church service was conducted here for years, and until the Congregational Church of the village was erected and dedicated, in 1817. Here also were held THE EXHIBITIONS which were the gala days of the town, when the pupils of Leonard and Littlejohn declaimed, and the laughing gas was administered, and the audience scattered before the steps of the happy but unconscious victim, whose brief delusion soon left him, to wonder what folly he had committed while under the influence of "the gas."

In 1833, the old Academy had become so dilapidated, and so unsuited to the wants of the school, as to require rebuilding. It was found necessary to have also a dwelling house for the Preceptor. A new subsciption was made, and money raised; the effort therefor commencing about the year 1831.

In 1834, the old building was vacated, and the new one commenced, which was finished and opened in the fall of

1835; the school being in the meantime taught in the District school house. The Preceptor's house was completed in May, 1836. The cost of the Academy was $3,000, with extras to the amount of $110. The cost of the Preceptor's house and extras, was $1,285.56. Timothy Butterfield was the builder.

Many curious entries appear in the minutes and among the files of the Academy.

On the 6th of October, 1815, the Prudential Committee order the Treasurer to pay "the bearer, the Captain of the band of musick, thirty-four dollars for the services of said band at the Exhibition of said Institution." This order is receipted by John Hoare who was therefore the "Captain of the band of musick."

There are, during several years, charges by, and payments to John Handy and Hezekiah Hopkins, (the two tavern keepers of the village,) for liquors, board and "horse bate," for the musicians.

During 1817, the scholars numbered 152; During 1818, 135; During 1822, 77; During 1824, 85.

It is difficult, if not impossible, to obtain a perfect list of the teachers who kept the common school, while it was held in the west room of the Academy. But the following list is believed to be nearly complete

James Robinson, kept a school in which he taught the classics and higher English branches, in 1805–6–7.

Abraham Plaunt, taught for some three or four winters.

Smith Dunham, taught, A. D. 1813–14.

Harvey Canfield in 1814.

Hugh Wallis, Dartmouth 1791; died 1848; aged 81, in 1814.

Miles Dunbar, Jr., in 1814–15.

Orange Butler, in 1815.

J. J. Deming, April 25, 1816, to Oct. 1, 1817.

Daniel Gott, 1817–18.

Daniel Munson Wakeley, 1818.

Manoah Pratt, (then Jr.) for three winters.

B. Franklin Chappell for one winter.

The list of teachers in the Academy proper, is believed to be more perfect.

The first teacher employed in the Academy was Ely Burchard; (Yale 1811, died 1866,) at a salary of $350. He taught from Dec. 5, 1811, to Oct. 5, 1813. Prior to the engagement of Mr. Burchard, three separate efforts had been made to engage other teachers; but all had for some reason proved unsuccessful.

On the 4th Sept. 1813, the trustees of the Academy approved of contracts made with Rev. Joshua Leonard* to take charge of the Academy as principal, at a salary of $500, and Smith Dunham to take charge of the common school, under the superintendence of the Academy, at a salary of $300. Mr. Leonard continued in charge of the Academy till 1822; being also most of the time pastor of the Congregational Church in the village.

On the 25th April, 1822, Rev. Eleazer S. Barrows, (Middlebury, 1811; and Tutor and Professor of Latin, in Hamilton College; died 1847,) and who had become pastor of the same church, took charge of the Academy under a written agreement, by which he was to take the interests of the Academy under his care and superintendence; to provide for its instruction by the employment of suitable teachers, and to superintend its government and general internal management. He continued in charge of the school till

*Rev. Joshua Leonard, born June 25, 1769. Graduated at Brown University, 1788, A. M. Yale, 1792. First settled in the ministry at Ellington, Conn., whence, about 1797 or 8, he removed to Cazenovia, N. Y. Here, on the 17th May, 1798, he organized a Presbyterian Church, of nine members, the first Church formed there. Continued pastor of that church for about 14 years, when he resigned his charge on account of impaired health; the church then numbering 127 members. From Cazenovia he removed to Pompey. He was Preceptor of Pompey Academy for about 8 years. He died at Auburn, N. Y. Dec. 18, 1843, aged 75 years.

April, 1828. But the actual teaching and management of the school were committed to others. Edward Aikin, (Middlebury, 1815; Died 1831,) came in May, 1822, and remained for about three years. Flavius Josephus Littlejohn, (Hamilton, 1827,) taught during part of 1825, infusing very great interest and life into the school. Henry Howe, (Middlebury, 1817,) succeeded; remaining till September, 1828, when he removed to Canandaigua, to take charge of the Academy there, and which he conducted with success for the next 15 years; dying in 1865.

Mr. Barrows, no doubt, made "a good thing" by this arrangement; as he received the Regents and tuition moneys, and $300 per annum out of the funds, with an annual allowance for repairs; making in all about $1,000 per annum, while he secured the services of the gentlemen who actually taught the school, for about half that sum, or less.

On the 25th October, 1828, Rev. Andrew Huntington, (Yale, 1815,) who still survives, took charge of the Academy, and taught it till July 14, 1834.

In October, 1834, Samuel S. Stebbins, (Yale, 1816; Died 1860,) and who like Mr. Huntington, was a fine scholar, became preceptor, continuing in charge until January, 1843.

Hon. Amos Westcott, lately mayor of Syracuse, now deceased, and a graduate of the Polytechnic Institute at Troy, N. Y., was assistant to Mr. Stebbins, from Sept. 1836, to Sept. 1838. Wm. E. Mason, succeeded him as assistant; teaching till August, 1839.

In September, 1843, Ensign Baker became preceptor, remaining so, till April, 1846. Harrison V. Miller, M. D., (Hamilton, 1851,) was assistant teacher in 1845–6. From Sept., 1846, to July, 1852, Truman K. Wright, (Middlebury, 1839,) was preceptor. Charles H. Payson, taught from Sept., 1852, to April, 1854. He was then succeeded by E. Delos Wells, (Williams, 1854,) who taught till August, 1855.

Rev. John F. Kendall, (Hamilton, 1855,) succeeded teaching till August, 1856. Wm. W. Waterman taught from, Sept., 1856, to April, 1857. S. Marshall Ingalls then taught till April, 1858. Theodore Beard, (Hamilton, 1856; Died 1860,) succeeded, teaching till Aug., 1859, with the exception of the latter part of 1858, when Daniel P. Baldwin, (Madison University,) supplied his place, during a sickness. George W. Kellogg, (Hamilton, 1859,) taught from October, 1859, to April, 1860; being then succeeded by Joseph Dow, (Dartmouth, 1833,) who remained two years. Lozenzo Fish succeeded him, teaching till August, 1864. He was succeeded by Orson G. Dibble, (Yale, 1864,) now the physician at Pompey, and the Secretary and Treasurer of the Academy. He taught till August, 1867, and was followed by Edwin S. Butterfield, (Yale, 1867,) and who taught till April, 1868, when Dr. Dibble returned for a term. P. V. N. Myers, (Williams, 1867,) taught from Sept., 1868, to July, 1869. Rev. Lemuel S. Pomeroy, (Hamilton, 1835,) for the next year. C. E. Havens, to March, 1871, and W. H. Avery, during the summer term of 1871. The first preceptress in the Academy, was the late Miss Lucretia Upham, who taught for six quarters in 1815–16. Miss A. M. Cufts, conducted a Female Department for six months, in 1825, under the administration of Mr. Barrows.

Upon the completion of the new school building, and the re-organization of the school, Miss Anne Hopkins became preceptress for the year 1835–6, assisted a part of the time by Miss Mary S. Hascall. Miss Margaret Sayles taught during 1836–7. Miss Eliza E. Randall being the music teacher. Miss Harriet N. Rand taught from October, 1837, to December, 1840. Miss Charlotte Buttrick, taught during 1841.

Miss Elizabeth H. Stone from January 1, 1842, to April, 1843. Miss Algenia Knox to April, 1844. Miss Giffing, Miss Hoskins and Miss Stella Whipple had charge of the ladies' school during the residue of 1844 and 1845, Miss Julia E. Reynolds during 1846–7. Miss Maria Doolittle in 1848. Mrs. T. K. Wright taught in this department much of the residue of the time while her husband was preceptor of the Academy.

Adelia M. Payson taught in 1853–4. Charlotte A. Birdseye, (Mrs. Harrison V. Miller,) to April, 1855; Ellen Hunt to April, 1856; Mary S. Griffith from Sept., 1856 to —— 1857; Pamelia Beard, from 1858 to April, 1860.

Minerva Adams taught from January, 1864, to April, 1864; Mary A. Birdseye, January to April, 1865; Laura J. Reddy for the same time in 1866; Elizabeth M. Hayden for the same time in 1867, and again in 1869; Annie Carroll from October to December, 1869; Clara Pomeroy from December, 1869, to April, 1870.

To make here any extended reference to the pupils of the Academy who have since become distinguished in the world, is impracticable, even if it were proper. It must suffice to say that the Academy left its stamp on almost all those who have gone forth from the town. Those who were here fitted for College, gained high honors in the institutions of the land. Here, Seabred Dodge became the great mathematician and engineer that he was. One of the pupils of this Academy laid here the foundations of scholarship which made him the first, and almost the only student at West Point, who was, throughout his entire course there, the first in every study, not excelled by any of his class in anything. Here future Governors learned to govern; and growing lawyers and clergymen, and congressmen and senators acquired that knowledge of books and things and men, that mastery of tongue and pen, and that discipline of mind, which fitted them for their places.

There can be but few among them who will not pay the tribute of grateful affection and respect to the wise and far-sighted men who founded and endowed this institution.

Consider what they did!

Within the first seven years from the settlement of this wilderness, while their own dwellings were but log huts, and their farms merely narrow clearings in a dense forest, where church and school were unknown; when the mill that ground their corn was fifty miles away through woods, threaded by a few paths, but without a road, and alive with wild beasts and more savage men; and, above all, in the midst of that terrible destitution of money, through which the new nation was struggling up from the abyss of bankruptcy into which it had been cast by the depreciated "Continental currency" of the Revolutionary War. Then it was that they, in a day of small things, put hands that faltered not, to a work so great, that its visible benefits have already outrun all record and all competition.

Lasting honor to their memory.

L. B.

APPENDIX NO. 1.

Whereas, the liberal disposed inhabitants of the town of Pompey, and other towns in the county of Onondaga, have generously contributed, and many others are disposed to contribute, considerable sums of money and other property towards erecting and instituting an academy in said Pompey, for the instruction of youth in the languages and other branches of useful learning. Of the necessity and utility of such an institution every individual is concerned. The rapid increase of the population and wealth of the county renders such an establishment highly necessary and important. The situation fixed upon for erecting the academy is nearly central, and for salubrity of air and accommodations for the students preferable to any other spot in the county. We, therefore, whose names are hereunto subscribed and seals affixed, having contributed more than one half in value of the real and personal property appropriated for the use and benefit of such academy, do request that an academy may be incorporated in said Pompey, to be called and distinguished by the name of Franklin Academy, subject to the visitation of the trustees in this instrument nominated and recommended, namely:

Ebenezer Butler, Junior, Timothy Jerome, William Stevens, Jeremiah Gould, Phineas Howell, Elihu Lewis, Dan Bradley, Comfort Tyler, James Knapp, John Lamb, Elijah Rust, Deodatus Clark, Hezekiah Olcott, David Williams, Walter Colton, Joseph Smith, James Beebee, John Kidder.

We, therefore, whose names are hereunto subscribed, do for ourselves and our legal representatives, promise to pay for the benefit of said academy, to any person whom the trustees shall appoint to receive the same, the several sums annexed to our respective names.

Pompey, January twenty-fifth, Eighteen hundred.

To the Regents of the University of the State of New York:

Eben Butler, Jr	$100	L. S.
Asahel Smith,	125	L. S.
John Kidder,	100	L. S.
Freeman Lewis,	50	L. S.
George Catlin,	50	L. S.
Walter Colton,	100	L. S.
Hezekiah Olcott	50	L. S.
Chancey Jerome,	50	L. S.
Joseph H. Smith,	30	L. S.
Timothy Jerome,	75	L. S.
John Jerome,	50	L. S.
Josiah Moore,	25	L. S.
Joseph Strong,	25	L. S.
Daniel C. Judd,	25	L. S.
Gad Loveland,	25	L. S.
James Beebee,	25	L. S.
Solomon Owen,	50	L. S.
Reuben Pixley, Jr	50	L. S.
Isaiah Olcott,	40	L. S.
Jonathan Eastman,	30	L. S.
John Fowler,	30	L. S.
David Williams,	30	L. S.
Thomas Mighells,	30	L. S.
Jesse Butler,	50	L. S.
Salmon Butler,	50	L. S.

(Endorsed.) "Petition Pompey Academy. To be laid before the Regents." 1800.

APPENDIX NO. 2.

Extracts from the minutes of the Regents of the University, relating to Pompey Academy:

At a meeting of the Regents of the University, held in the Senate Chamber on the 17th March, 1800. Present His Excellency, John Jay, Chancellor, Judge Benson, Judge Kent, Mr. DeWitt, Mr. Sylvester, Mr. Rupell, Mr. VanVechten, Mr. L'Hommedien.

"A Petition from Ebenezer Butler and others, praying for an incorporation of an Academy in the town of Pompey, in the county of Onondaga, was read and committed to Mr. Benson and Mr. DeWitt."

At a meeting held on the 31st day of March, 1800. Present His Excellency John Jay, Chancellor. His Honor, the Lieutenant Governor, Judge Benson, Judge Kent, General Schuyler, Mr. Russell, Mr. L'Hommedien.

"The Board proceeded to the consideration of the report of the committee to whom was referred the petition for the incorporation of an Academy at Pompey in the county of Onondaga. And whereas, it is uncertain whether that place is the most proper place for an Academy in the county of Onondaga, and there is reason to doubt the expediency of having more than one academy in one county. Resolved, That the Secretary do transmit a copy of said petition and this resolution to the Supervisors of Onondaga county, and request that they will at their next meeting inform the Regents whether in their opinion there be any and what objections to granting the prayer of said Petition."

At a meeting of the Regents, held February 16th, 1801.

"The Petition from the inhabitants of the town of Pompey, in the county of Onondaga, praying for an incorporation of Academy in said town, received at the last session, tegether with the proceedings of a meeting of the Supervisors of the said county, on the first Tuesday in October last, relative thereto, was read and referred to Mr. L'Hommedieu, Mr. Cochran and General Schuyler."

At a meeting of the Regents of the University, held pursuant to adjournment in the Senate Chamber, in the city of Albany, on Monday the twenty-third day of March, 1801.

Academies being intended to teach branches of literature superior to those which are taught in common schools, and requiring to that end a more extensive provision for the support of well qualified instructors, therefore,

Resolved, That in future, no Academy ought to be incorporated, unless it shall be made to appear by satisfactory evidence to this Board, that a proper building for the purpose hath been erected and finished and paid for, and that funds have been obtained and well secured, producing an annual net income of at least one hundred dollars. And, further, that there be a condition in the charter of incorporation that the principal or estate producing the said income shall never be diminished, or appropiiated; that the said income shall be applied only to the maintenance or salaries of the Professors or Tutors of the Academy.

An extract of the minutes.

FR. BLOODGOOD, Sec'y.

At a meeting of the Regents of the University, held pursuant to adjournment in the Senate Chamber, in the city of Albany, on Monday, the 15th day of March, 1802.

Resolved, That this Board approve of the application of sundry inhabitants of the county of Onondaga, for the incorporation of an Academy in the town of Pompey, in the said county, and that this Board will incorporate the same upon satisfactory evidence being given within a reasonable time, of a compliance with the resolution of this Board of the 23d day of March, 1801, and that a copy of the said resolution, together with a copy of this resolution, be certified by the Secretary, and delivered to the applicants.

An extract from the minutes.

FR. BLOODGOOD, Sec'y.

At a meeting of the Regents held in the Senate Chamber, March 11th, 1811. Present, His Excellency the Governor, Mr. Kent, Mr. Selden, Mr. VanVechten, Mr. Spencer, Mr. DeWitt, Mr. Clinton, Mr. Jenkins, Mr. Elmendorf, Mr. Taylor, Mr. Smith.

"The committee to whom were referred the application for the incorporation of an Academy at Pompey, in the county of Onondaga, by the name and style of Pompey Academy, reported that said application ought to be granted.

Whereupon, Resolved, That the same be approved of, and that the Secretary cause a charter to be made out for the said Academy."

APPENDIX NO. 3.

"At a meeting of the Supervisors of the county of Onondaga at Pompey, on the first Tuesday in October, Eighteen hundred.

The Board proceeded to consider the resolve of the Regents of the University, in which they requested the opinion of the Board whether there be any and what objections to granting the prayer of the petition of sundry inhabitants of the county of Onondaga, for the incorporation of an Academy at Pompey, in said county: Noted,

That in the opinion of this Board there exists no objection why the prayer of said petition should not be granted, and that the place mentioned in said petition is as suitable as any in the county."

A true extract from the minutes.

LEVI CURTIS, Clerk.

To the Regents of the University of the State of New York.

[Endorsed.]

"Vote of Supervisors of the county of Onondaga, where the Academy ought to be placed."

Committed to General Schuyler, Mr. L'Hommedien and Mr. Cochran."

APPENDIX NO. 4.

" *To the Honorable Board of Regents of the University of the State of New York.*

The inhabitants of the county of Onondaga, humbly sheweth, that we, being impressed with the belief of the importance of a literary establishment in said county of Onondaga, where the higher and more useful branches of literature are taught than in common schools, and being convinced also of Pompey in said county, being the most eligible situation in said county for such an institution: We, under these impressions and beliefs, did in the year 1800, present to your Honorable Board a petition praying the incorporation of an Academy in said Pompey, and we still being of the opinion and belief of the infinite importance and utility of an academy in the said county, and also that said Pompey is altogether the most proper place in the county for said Academy. We do, therefore, humbly pray that the Honorable Board will take into consideration our aforesaid petition, and grant the prayer thereof. And your petitioners, as in duty bound, will ever pray.

Ozias Burr, Daniel Wood, John Lamb, John Bowers, Reuben Pixley, Jr., Gad Loveland, Salmon Butler, Curtis Chappel, Joseph Jackson, Moses Lilly, Jr., Samuel Jones, Allen Butler, Amasa Wright, Elias Conklin, George Catlin, Josiah Holbrook, Timothy Cossett, Israel Mun, Salmon Squire, Selah Cook, Elijah Webb, Nathan Davis, Obed Handy, Haven Webster, Asher Frost, Ebenezer Hay, John Willard, Daniel Tibbals, Rupell Clark, Abel Bigelow, Orange King, Dix Hoar, Daniel C. Judd, John Baar, James Price, Ezra Hart, Meigs Brown, Ezekiel Webster, John Fowler, Jonas C. Leland, Harvey Luce,

POMPEY ACADEMY, DWELLING AND OLD BAPTIST CHURCH.

James Griffin, Jr., Joseph Mather, Benjamin Butler, Hezekiah Dodge, William Miller, Joseph Shattuck, Joseph Luce, Stephen Hayes, Levi Farnham, Isaac Higbee, Roderick Smith, Richard Crocker, William Howard, James Beebee, Epaphs. Emmons, Joseph H. Smith, Isaac Catlin, Isaac Hall, Artemas Bishop.

[Endorsed.]

"Petition for an Academy at Pompey, in Onondaga." "Recorded March 15th, 1802."

APPENDIX NO. 5.

This article of agreement, made and concluded this 20th day of July, in the year of our Lord, one thousand, eight hundred and seven, between William Lathrop and George W. Wood, parties of the first part, and Manoah Pratt, Henry Seymour and Samuel S. Baldwin, Committee to build the Academy in Pompey, parties of the second part, witnesseth: That the said party of the first part for and in consideration of the sums hereinafter specified, agree to lay all the floors on the lower story of said Academy; to make all the inside doors and hang them; to case the windows on said story; to make the bases and sur-bases in the several rooms; to lath the several rooms on said story; to make mantle-tree pieces when it is adjudged necessary by the Committee, and closets with shelves; to make the tables and benches which by said committee shall be adjudged necessary in the two large rooms designed for the public school; and to do all the joiner work on the lower floor which is necessary to finish the said story; the same to be done in a plain, neat, strong, workman-like manner. The making the outside doors are to be paid for independant of this contract. The said parties of the first part further agree to make the stairs and stair case in said building, which is to be done in a style and manner suitable to the other work done. The materials to be furnished by the parties of the second part. The work to be done in sufficient time, so that said story may be plastered this season, unless the said parties are materially delayed on account of materials. And the said parties of the second part, for and in consideration of the work covenanted to be done, agree to pay to the said parties of the first part, two hundred dollars, to be paid in obligations, which obligations are to be warranted collectable by the said parties of the second, and turned out to the said parties of the first part, when the above work is done; the said obligations to be due at the time they are turned out to the said parties of the second part.

In witness whereof, we have hereunto set our hands and seals, the day and year above written.

Sealed and delivered in the presence of Henry J. Baldwin.

Wm. Lathrop, [L. S.]
G. W. Wood, [L. S.]
For the Committee, S. S. Baldwin, [L. S.]

Agreed this 2d day of March, 1810, to relinquish the unfinished part of the within mentioned job, and to accept of one hundred and forty dollars, in full of what has been done.

$140. Wm. Lathrop.

APPENDIX NO. 6.

This indenture or article of agreement made between Henry Seymour, Samuel S. Baldwin and Manoah Pratt, of the one part, and the several other persons whose names are hereto subscribed, witnesseth, that the said Henry, Samuel S. and Manoah, do hereby agree to procure the Academy in Pompey to be finished and completed for the sum of four hundred and fifty dollars. And the said other persons whose names are hereto subscribed, hereby severally bind themselves, in consideration of the said undertaking, to pay the several sums annexed to our names respectively, to the said Henry, Samuel S. and Manoah, in our obligations for the said several sums, to be payable on demand, and to be given on or before the first day of October, 1810. Provided that no person shall be bound by this subscription, unless the said sum of four hundred and fifty dollars shall be subscribed hereto. Witness our hands and seals at Pompey; and we, the said Henry, Samuel S. and Manoah, do agree to pay the several sums annexed to our names, towards and as a part of the said sum of four hundred and fifty dollars.

Nathaniel Baker,------------------------$30------L. S.
Rec'd note for this. Cr. $5 in full of Mr. Baker.

James Wiggins, Jr. joiners' work,----------$20------
Paid by discount with D. Wood.

Ephraim Bond,---------------------------$25------L. S.
Rec'd note for $25.

Joseph Bennett,-------------------------$20------
Rec'd note for $20.

Marovia Marsh,--------------------------$15------L. S.
Rec'd note for $15.

Augustus Wheaton,-----------------------$30------L. S.
Rec'd note for $30.

V. Birdseye, ---------------------------$20------L. S.
Endorsed on Wood's contract with Committee.

Elisha Smith,---------------------------$10------L. S.
Rec'd note for $10.

Chester Coe,----------------------------$10------L. S.
Rec'd note for $10.

Timothy Hatch,--------------------------$10------L. S.
Rec'd note for $10.

Seymour Coe,----------------------------$10------
Rec'd note for $10.

Joseph M. Bostwick,---------------------$10------L. S.
Endorsed on Wood's Contract.

James Chappell,-------------------------$10------L. S.
Rec'd $5. Rec'd note for $5.

Leonard Hoar,---------------------------$10------L. S.
Rec'd note for $10.

James Carr,-----------------------------$10------
Charg'd J. Cowan, H. Seymour's Book.

Abr. Plaunt,----------------------------$10------L. S.
Rec'd note for $10.

Nathan Williams,------------------------$10------
Rec'd Cash in full. Cr. on H. Seymour's Books to Academy.

Titus Marsh,----------------------------$10------
Paid to Bald.

James Tolman,---------------------------$10------L. S.
Rec'd D. Wood's Receipt.

Chester Howard, in blacksmith work,------$10------L. S.

In Note.

David Hine,------------------------------$10------L. S.

Paid.

Luther Marsh,----------------------------$10------L. S.

Rec'd note for $10.

Aaron C. Hoar,---------------------------$20------

Aaron C. Hoar has paid D. W., ten dolls. same endorsed on Contract with E. W., the Committe, March 12, 1811. Attest, V. B. Remainder charg'd on H. Seymour's ac't.

Henry Seymour will advance one hundred dolls. on condition of collecting it on old subscription,-------L. S.

Samuel S. Baldwin will advance twenty-five dollars, on condition of collecting it on old subscription,------L. S.

Charg'd to S. S. B. in H. Seymour's Books, April, 1812.

Allen W. Heyden $10 in wood work to H. Seymour--L. S.

Stephen Hall has given his note for ten dollars, $10.---L. S.

Due on this subscription $5, March, 1811, including notes.

James Higgins,	$20 00
Victory Birdseye,	20 00
James Carr,	10 00
Nathan Williams,	10 00
Titus Marsh,	10 00
A. C. Hoar,	20 00
H. Seymour,	100 00
S. S. Baldwin,	25 00
A. W. Heyden,	10 00
Stephen Hall,	10 00
L. Marsh,	10 00
Chester Howard,	10 00
Abr. Plaunt,	10 00
Leonard Hoar, Jr.,	8 00
Seymour Coe,	10 00
Chester Coe,	10 00
Marovia Marsh,	15 00
Jasper Bennett,	20 00
Nath. Baker,	24 46
Dan. Wood rec't.	5 00
do do do	6 54

APPENDIX NO. 7.

Walter Colton, of the town and county of Onondaga and State of New York, being duly sworn, deposeth and saith, that he was an inhabitant of, and resided in the town of Pompey, in the county aforesaid, at the time a petition was in circulation addressed to the Regents of the University of the State of New York, purporting to be from the inhabitants of the county of Onondaga; that he saw John Kidder set the names of a considerable number of persons to said petition without their knowledge or consent, as the said Kidder then said. That the said Kidder then applied to this deponent to set the names of other persons to said petition, so that the names might not appear to be in one hand-writing; That this deponent declined setting the names of persons to said petition, believing it to be improper. That the said Kidder then applied to Hezekiah Olcott, who set the names of a number more to said petition, but the exact number set by the said Kidder or Olcott, this deponent does not recollect. And this deponent saith that he is acquainted with the persons who subscribed money to build an Academy in said Pompey. That several of the principal subscribers have since left the county. That Hezekiah Olcott has since died insolvent. That a considerable number more are in the opinion of this deponent wholly unable to pay the sums by them subscribed. And this deponent further saith, that he hath heard several of the subscribers who are able to pay, say that they were determined not to pay the sums by them subscribed, if they can avoid it. And this deponent, further saith not.

WALTER COLTON.

Sworn before me this 2d day of March, 1802.

MEDAD CURTIS,
Master in Chancery.

(Endorsed,)

"Aff't of Walter Colton, respecting the subscription for an Academy at Pompey." "Rec'd March 15, 1802."

APPENDIX NO. 8.

This Article of Agreement, made this 25th day of July, 1810, between Henry Seymour, Samuel S. Baldwin and Manoah Pratt, of the one part, and the several other persons whose names are hereunto subscribed,

Witnesseth, That the several other persons whose names are hereunto subscribed, do covenant, each for himself, with said Henry, Samuel S. and Manoah, that we, the said subscribers, within six months from the date hereof, will give and execute unto said Samuel, Henry and Manoah, our several bonds, conditioned to pay the several sums annexed to our names hereunto subscribed, in the penalty of double the said sums so subscribed, with interest on said conditions, payable annually at seven per cent., to be payable on demand; but with a proviso in said bond, that so long as the interest shall be perpetually paid, the principal shall not be sued for or collected, and that we also will give our separate mortgages to the said Henry, Samuel S. and Manoah, as collateral securities of the said bonds, on good real property, unencumbered, of at least double the value of the said several sums, situated within the County of Onondaga. And we, the said Henry, Samuel S. and Manoah, do hereby covenant with the said several subscribers separately, that we will hold this subscription and the said several bonds and mortgages, in trust for, and for the sole use, benefit and behoof of the Academy in Pompey; and that, so soon as the said Academy shall be incorporated, we, the said Samuel S., Henry and Manoah, will transfer, assign and set over to the said corporation this subscription and covenant, and also all mortgages and bonds that may or shall be given in pursuance hereof, and will also pay over to said corporation all sum or sums of money that may or shall be collected or received on this subscription, or on any bond or mortgage to be given in pursuance hereof. This subscription being for the purpose of raising and securing a fund for the support of said institution, and securing the same on real property. It is understood that interest is to be computed from July 28th, 1811.

Asa Wells, ---------------------- Fifty Dollars ---- L. S.
Manoah Pratt, ------------ One Hundred Dollars ---- L. S.
John Jerome, ---------------------- Fifty Dollars ---- L. S.
Henry Seymour, ---------- One Hundred Dollars ---- L. S.
Samuel S. Baldwin, --------------- Fifty Dollars ---- L. S.
Daniel Wood, ---------------------- Fifty Dollars ---- L. S.
Nathaniel Baker, ------------------ Fifty Dollars ---- L. S.
Chancey Jerome, ----------------- Fifty Dollars ---- L. S.
Daniel Tibbals, -------------------- Fifty Dollars ---- L. S.
Ebenezer Carr, -------------------- Fifty Dollars ---- L. S.
Charles Morris, ------------ Twenty-Five Dollars ---- L. S.
John Marsh, ---------------- Twenty-Five Dollars ---- L. S.
Marovia Marsh, ------------------- Fifty Dollars ---- L. S.
Stephen Tiffany, ----------- Twenty-Five Dollars ---- L. S.
Joseph Bennett, ------------------ Fifty Dollars ---- L. S.
Conrad Bush, --------------------- Fifty Dollars ---- L. S.
Timothy Hatch, ------------ Twenty-Five Dollars ---- L. S.
Elisha Smith, --------------------- Fifty Dollars ---- L. S.
Daniel Gillett, ------------- Twenty-Five Dollars ---- L. S.

I will give my bond according to the above subscription, but no mortgage, for Thirty Dollars.
V. Birdseye. } L. S.

Leonard Hoar, Jr., ---------- Twenty-Five Dollars ---- L. S.
Aaron C. Hoar, ------------- Twenty-Five Dollars ---- L. S.
Ozias Wright, -------------- Twenty-Five Dollars ---- L. S.
Isaac Hall, ------------------------ Fifty Dollars ---- L. S.
Silas Park, ----------------------- Fifty Dollars ---- L. S.
True W. Cook, -------------------- Fifty Dollars ---- L. S.
Lemuel Cook, -------------- Twenty-Five Dollars ---- L. S.
Hezekiah Dodge, ----------- Twenty-Five Dollars ---- L. S.
Amos Abbott, -------------- Twenty-Five Dollars ---- L. S.
Joseph Sacket, ------------- Twenty-Five Dollars ---- L. S.
Zadoc Seymour, ----------- Twenty-Five Dollars ---- L. S.
Jacobus DePuy, ----------- Twenty-Five Dollars ---- L. S.
Henry Tiffany, ------------- Twenty-Five Dollars ---- L. S.
Ithamer Coe, --------------------- Fifty Dollars ---- L. S.
Sylvanus Bishop, ---------- Twenty-Five Dollars ---- L. S.

Hezekiah Clark,--------------------Fifty Dollars----L. S.
Samuel Dunham, -----------Twenty-Five Dollars----L. S.
Artemas Bishop,-----------Twenty-Five Dollars----L. S.
Elijah Wells,---------------Twenty-Five Dollars----L. S.
Timothy Northrop, -------------Twenty Dollars----L. S.
Abraham Northrop,-------------Twenty Dollars----L. S.
Gideon Morley,-------------Twenty-Five Dollars----L. S.
Charles Sweet,----------------Twenty Dollars----L. S.
Samuel Johnson,-----------Twenty-Five Dollars----L. S.
Elijah Owen,---------------------Fifty Dollars----L. S.
Timothy Cossit,------------Twenty-Five Dollars----L. S.
William Cook,------------One Hundred Dollars----L. S.
Ozias Burr,---------------One Hundred Dollars----L. S.
James Lankton,------------Twenty-Five Dollars----L. S.
Samuel Wright,------------Twenty-Five Dollars----L. S.
Leonard Lincoln,-------------Twenty Dollars----L. S.
Ephriam Cleveland,--------Twenty-Five Dollars----L. S.
Lewis Rood,-------------------Twenty Dollars----L. S.

I agree to give my bond on the above condition, but no mortgage, for Twenty-Five Dollars.
Ephriam Bond. --L. S.

Levi Chase, ---------------Twenty-Five Dollars----L. S.
Titus Marsh,---------------------Forty Dollars----L. S.
James Carr,---------------Twenty-Five Dollars----L. S.
Josiah Holbrook,----------Twenty-Five Dollars----L. S.
Jonathan Stanley, Jr.,-------------Fifty Dollars----L. S.
Augustus Wheaton,--------------Fifty Dollars----L. S.
Joseph Bush,---------------------Fifty Dollars----L. S.

APPENDIX NO. 9.

To the Honorable, the Board of Regents of the University of the State of New York.

The petition of the several persons whose names are hereunto subscribed, inhabitants of the county of Onondaga, humbly sheweth: That being desirous to facilitate the education of youth in the languages and other branches of useful learning, and being convinced that the establishment of an Academy at Pompey in said county, would greatly promote so useful a design, your petitioners have at great expense procured a suitable site for an institution of that kind, consisting of two acres of land near the centre of said town, and erected a large and commodious building for that purpose; that the building is forty by fifty feet on the ground, two stories high and completely finished and painted, inside and out, and paid for. Your petitioners have also procured a fund of one thousand, four hundred and fifty dollars to be subscribed for the purpose of producing a net annual income for the support of the said institution, and that the same is well secured to Samuel S. Baldwin, Henry Seymour and Manoah Pratt, as trustees, for the sole use of said academy, at an annual interest of seven per cent; and that said Samuel S., Henry and Manoah have become obligated to transfer the said securities to the said academy when the same shall be incorporated.

Your petitioners further represent that they have been encouraged to go to so considerable an expense by a resolution of the Board of the Regents, of the 15th day of March, 1802, by which the Board were pleased to resolve that they approved of the applications of sundry inhabitants of the county of Onondaga, for the incorporation of an academy in the town of Pompey, and that the said Board would incorporate the same upon satisfacto y evidence being given within a reasonable time of a compliance with said resolution of said Board of the twenty-third day of March, 1801. Your petitioners believe that they have now complied with the above mentioned resolution of the twenty-third of March, 1801; and when the difficulties attending so considerable a public undertaking, in an interior part of the county, and in one so lately an entire wilderness, and when the general pecuniary embarrassments of the county for some time past, are duly considered, your petitioners believe that the compliance with that resolution has been as speedy as could reasonably have been expected.

Your petitioners further represent that the several persons whose names are hereto subscribed, have contributed more than one half in value of the real and personal estate collected and appropriated for the use and benefit of said institution.

Wherefore, your petitioners request that the said Academy may be incorporated, and be subject to the visitation of the Regents of the University of the State of New York, and they nominate for the first trustees of the said Academy, the following persons, to-wit: Henry Seymour, Senior Trustee, and Samuel S. Baldwin, Daniel Wood, Manoah Pratt, Ithamar Coe, Asa Wells, Hezekiah Clark, John Jerome, Silas Park, Jacobus DePuy, Daniel Allen, Chancy Jerome, Daniel Tibbals, Joshua Johnson, Derrick C. Lansing, Benjamin Sanford, Charles C. Moseley, William J. Wilcox, Johnathan Stanley, Junior, Levi Parsons, William Cook, Victory Birdseye, Jasper Hopper, James Geddes; which persons we pray may be incorporated by the name, style and description of "Pompey Academy," with a condition in the act of incorporation that the said principal sum of the said fund shall never be diminished or appropriated, and that the income of the said principal fund shall be applied only to the maintenance or salaries of the professors or tutors of the said Academy.

As, witness our hands and seals this 11th February, in the year of our Lord, one thousand, eight hundred and eleven.

Amasa Wright,------------------------------------ L. S.
Daniel Wood,------------------------------------ L. S.
Norris Case,------------------------------------ L. S.
Geo. Catlin,------------------------------------ L. S.
Hezekiah Clark,------------------------------------ L. S
Silvanus Bishop,------------------------------------ L. S.
Artemus Bishop,------------------------------------ L. S.
Henry Seymour,------------------------------------ L. S.
Victory Birdseye,------------------------------------ L. S.
Elijah Wells,------------------------------------ L. S.
Asa Wells------------------------------------ L. S.

Nathaniel Baker, ------------------------------ L. S.
Titus Rust, ------------------------------ L. S.
Daniel Tibbals, ------------------------------ L. S.
James Carr, ------------------------------ L. S.
Jeremiah Butler, ------------------------------ L. S.
Daniel C. Judd, ------------------------------ L. S.
John Jerome, ------------------------------ L. S.
Aaron C. Hoar, ------------------------------ L. S.
Timothy Northrup, ------------------------------ L. S.
Conrad Bush, ------------------------------ L. S.
Hezekiah Lathrop, ------------------------------ L. S.
Chancy Jerome, ------------------------------ L. S.
Jasper Bennett, ------------------------------ L. S.
Wm. Cook, ------------------------------ L. S.
Ebenezer Carr, ------------------------------ L. S.
Josiah Holbrook, ------------------------------ L. S.
Charles Morris, ------------------------------ L. S.
Allyn Hedges, ------------------------------ L. S.
Hezekiah Hopkins, ------------------------------ L. S.
John Marsh, ------------------------------ L. S.
Manoah Pratt, ------------------------------ L. S.
True W. Cook, ------------------------------ L. S.
Levi Jerome, ------------------------------ L. S.
Jesse Butler, ------------------------------ L. S.
Ezra Hart, ------------------------------ L. S.
Johnathan Stanley, Jun., ------------------------------ L. S.
Nathan Williams, ------------------------------ L. S.
Jos. W. Gould, ------------------------------ L. S.
Ithamer Coe, ------------------------------ L. S.
Lemuel Cook, ------------------------------ L. S.
Wm. Lathrop, ------------------------------ L. S.
Salmon Butler, ------------------------------ L. S.
Apollos King, ------------------------------ L. S.
Ichabod Lathrop, ------------------------------ L. S.
Stephen Tiffnay, ------------------------------ L. S.
Augustus Wheaton, ------------------------------ L. S.
Abel Olcott, ------------------------------ L. S.

Thomas Olcott, ---------- L. S.
Solomon Owen, ---------- L. S.
Enoch Wilcox, ---------- L. S.
Joseph Brush, ---------- L. S.
Jabesh Castle, ---------- L. S.
James Lankton, ---------- L. S.
James Higgins, ---------- L. S.
Joseph Mather, ---------- L. S.
Henry Tiffnay, ---------- L. S.
Levi Chase, ---------- L. S.
Robert Swartmont, ---------- L. S.
Daniel Hubbard, ---------- L. S.
Chester Coe, ---------- L. S.
Moses Lilly, ---------- L. S.
Samuel S. Baldwin, ---------- L. S.

Onondaga ss: Henry Seymour being duly sworn, saith, that he hath examined the statement of facts set forth in the above petition, and that he believes the same to be true, and further says 'not.

HENRY SEYMOUR.

Sworn before me this second day of March, A. D., 1811.

DANIEL WOOD, Justice Peace.

APPENDIX NO. 10.

Report of the trustees of Pompey Academy for 1817.

To the Regents of the University of the State of New York.

The Funds of the Academy consist of the Academy lot and building, estimated at $5,000

Personal Estate, "	2,500
Apparatus and Library, estimated at	150
Real Estate, being one lot in Camillus,	5,920
Amount,	$13,570

The teachers are Rev. Joshua Leonard with salary of $600
Gott " 300

The students number now 152; of whom 14 study the learned languages; of the higher branches of the Mathematics, and the others Reading, Writing, Arithmetic, English Grammar, Geography, Belles Lettres, &c.

REMARKS. 1. The building is of wood, 50 feet by 40; two stories high, and divided into seven rooms, viz: One 40 feet square for an Exhibition Room; two 40 by 15, for School Rooms, and four 10 by 15 for study rooms, all of which, except the Exhibition Room, have fire places. Besides which, each of the long rooms have stoves.

2. The Real Estate consists of one lot of land, which lies in Camillus, in the county of Onondaga. This lot has been contracted to be sold at different prices from 9 to 10 dollars per acre, and the contracts obligate the purchasers to pay the annual interest and instalments towards the principal, until one half of the principal shall be paid, then the purchasers to have a deed, and give a bond and mortgage.

3 The Personal Estate consists of Bonds aud Mortgages, and covenants to give bond and mortgages, on interest at 7 per cent., payable on the 28th of January, annually.

4. Prices of tuition are: For reading and writing, $1.50. English Grammar $2.50; Arithmetic, Geography, Logic, Rhetoric and Belles Lettres, $3; Mathematics, Natural and Moral Philosophy and other learned languages, $4 per quarter.

5. The Apparatus consisting of one pair of Globes, 12 inches in diameter, and two large stoves with pipe, and other articles of furniture for the school rooms.

6. Average price of board is $2.

7. The tuition is estimated at 600 dollars.

8. The benefits of the Institution are uniformly extended to families which are unable to pay the tuition.

Dated at Pompey, in the county of Onondaga, A. Dom. 1818.

HISTORY OF TOWN OF POMPEY.

Containing Account of Settlements and Improvements, its Geographical Features, a History of the Military Tract, &c., &c., Edited and Compiled by Ebenezer Butler, Member of Publication Committee.

GEOGRAPHIC FEATURES.

BY H. D. L. SWEET.

That portion of the State of New York, comprised in the original township of Pompey, lay between the parallels 42°, 51′, and 42°, 59′, 20″, north latitude, and between meridians 75°, 54′, 13″, and 76°, 11′, 58″, west longitude from Greenwich.

The present township lies between parallels 42°, 51′, 20″, and 42°, 59′, 20″, north latitude, and between meridians 75°, 54′, 13″, and 76°, 4′, 52″, west longitude. Pompey Academy being located 42°, 54′, 5″, north latitude, and 76°, 1′, 2″, west longitude from Greenwich.*

The name given by the Indians to this region was *Ote-ge-ga-ja-ke*, a place of much grass, openings or prairies. Another name given to this locality, not often repeated, and about which there is much superstitious resource, is *Ote-quch-sah-he-eh*, the field of blood, a place where many have been slain. (See State Gazetteer.)

Pompey is a part of the Military Tract, and was designated as township No. 10, on Surveyor-General's maps of surveys. On Saturday, 3d day of July, 1790, it received

*We are indebted to S. W. Clark, of Syracuse, who, from survey, has given us the degrees of latitude and longitude.

from the Commissioners of the Land Office, in New York City, the name it now bears. It was first given a municipal government as a part of Onondaga County, by Legislative enactment, in the year of 1794, in following words:—"All that part of the said County of Oncndaga, comprehending the townships of Pompey, Tully and Fabius, together with that part of the lands called 'The Onondaga Reservation,' bounded northerly by the road leading through the said Reservation, commonly called the Genesee road, and westerly by the Onondaga Creek, shall be and hereby is erected into a town by the name of Pompey." By subsequent Legislation, the boundaries of the township, as then fixed, have, (in the years 1798, in 1806 and in 1825,) been changed, its present boundaries being:—North by town of DeWitt and Manlius; east by the county of Madison; south by the town of Fabius; west by LaFayette.

The township is located upon the great dividing ridge, from which the waters flow north to the valley of the St. Lawrence, and south to the Chesapeake Bay.

This great ridge is divided within the township limits, by four great valleys. The first on the east, is on the east line of the township, cutting entirely across it, and with but very little inclination. The stream, the east branch of the Limestone Creek, which flows through it, has but few mill seats on its entire length.

The second valley lies about three miles west, and nearly parallel; has a greater inclination, and, although the valley extends entirely across the township, *a portion of the water flows to the south!* The stream which flows north, has at one place a fall of 137 feet, perpendicular, (Pratt's Falls,) and is quite rapid in all its course.

The third, or the Butternut Creek Valley, lies nine miles west of the east line, within the limits of the township, and has but little fall.

The fourth, or Onondaga Valley, lies about four miles east of the western boundary, and four miles from Butternut Creek Valley, and within the limits of the township has fall sufficient only for two or three water powers.

The greater portion of the township lies on three, a small portion however, on a fourth, of hills or ridges, the axis of which are nearly due north and south.

The first, or the one on the east, has an altitude of nearly 1,200 feet above tide water, or 800 feet above the level of the Erie Canal, at Syracuse.

The second attains an altitude of 1,743 feet above tide water. This point is in the cemetery at Pompey Hill.

The third attains, near the village of Lafayette, an elevation of from 1,400 to 1,500 feet.

The fourth, or Bear Mountain, is but little less in altitude than Pompey Hill.

The slopes of all these, except the last named, are not steep, and were originally covered with a heavy growth of timber—mostly deciduous trees.

Carpenter's Pond, which lies in the second valley, and from which the water flows south, is the only natural body of water.

Swamps are few and small; as also are gulfs and ravines. There are not, it is probable, 1,200 acres of the 60,000 in the original township, that may not be cultivated.

The soil is chiefly a clayey loam. Eighty years tillage has proved it of excellent quality.

In the northern part, a small quantity of limestone shows at the surface.

The surface, however, is generally underlaid by the Hamilton group of sholes, while upon the extreme highest portions, Genesee slate is found.

The climate is subject to sudden changes, and is particularized by high winds; the average temperature is lower by 3½ degrees, than the general average of the State. In the village of Pompey, on Pompey Hill, the wind often blows with terrific violence. The cool breezes of summer render this locality a remarkably pleasant one for those, who, through the warmest months of the year, seek relief from the oppressive heat of the city and valleys below. But the high winds of winter make it at times a situation most unfavorable for comfort or pleasure.

Although the annual temperature of this section is found to be lower than the general average of the State, and vegetation is uniformly backward, yet the robin appears here earlier, and the autumnal frosts are later than in many other sections.

This is one of the most healthy, as it is one of the *highest inhabitated portions of the State.*

The natural scenery is rarely equalled. The vision, from one stand point on Pompey Hill, is uninterrupted, being bounded by the horizon at every point of the compass, and embracing views in seven different counties.*

The landscape consists of hill and dale, placid lakes, dotted with sail, meandering streams, villages, forests, cultivated fields, beautiful farm houses, steam car, together with the beautiful city, and its hum of busy life.

Within the present limits of the town there are five villages containing Post Offices, viz:—Pompey Hill, Pompey Centre, Delphi, Oran and Watervale.

There are flouring mills at Pratt's Falls and at Watervale, two manufacturies of edge tools, one near Delphi, Sampson's on east branch of Limestone Creek, and one, Wood's, on west branch of Limestone; formerly there was, as will be remembered by many old residents, a woolen mill four miles north of Delphi, one-half the way between Oran and Delphi.

Population of the town in 1875, was three thousand, three hundred and sixty.

---

*Onondaga, Cortland, Herkimer, Madison, Oswego, Oneida and Cayuga.

SETTLEMENT AND IMPROVEMENTS.

POMPEY HILL AND VICINITY.

The township of Pompey obtained great celebrity abroad at a very early period, and was principally settled by people from New England, many of whom took up their residence here while the township was a part of the town of Mexico, Herkimer County.

The first white settler in the town of Pompey was Mr. John Wilcox; he came in 1789 from Oneida, in company with an Indian Chief, for the purpose of exploring the country. He made a settlement near an Indian orchard, which was located about two miles north of the present site of Lafayette village. (For these and further particulars relative to his settlement, see Clark's Onondaga, vol. 2d, page 241.)

The first settlement made within the limits of the present township, was made at Pompey Hill, by Ebenezer Butler, who originally came from Harwington, Conn., to Clinton, Oneida County, in the year 1788 or 9; remaining in Clinton till 1791, he left and came, guided by marked trees, to this place, and settled on lot 65, which tradition says, "he bought of a soldier for a horse, saddle and bridle." He erected his first, a log house, near where is now "the Stone Blacksmith Shop," and near to the spring which supplies the watering tub in the present village. Here in the same year, 1791, he moved his family, consisting of his wife, four children, his father and a maiden sister.

The following year, 1792, his brother, Jesse Butler, came from Connecticut, and buying 100 acres of him, on the north half of his lot, made a small clearing and put up a log house on a knoll about 30 rods north of the present site of the M. E. Church. He returned to Connecticut in the fall, and in the month of April, 1793, in company with George Catlin and their familes, on an ox sled, came back and made this his residence. Mr. Catlin, having bought of his brother-in-law, Ebenezer Butler, Jr., 100 acres, near the south side of his, (Butler's) section, settled on the same, and afterwards kept the first tavern that was opened in this vicinity. His house was located a little south of the one lately occupied by Judge Asa Wells.

Jacob Hoar came from Onondaga in the spring of 1793, and settled on lot 48; near a spring of water, at the first four corners on the road leading from the village of Pompey to Jamesville.

Here, afterwards, about 1800, was found something of a village, named *Log City*, which grew to contain ultimately, a store and ashery, owned by Justice Fowler, (uncle to O. S. Fowler, of New York,) a shoe shop and tannery, a turning lathe, a school house, together with a respectable number of settlers. Log City and the Hill were, for a time, rival settlements.

In the year 1794, Messrs. Jerome & Smith came from Massachusetts and settled on lot number 85, which is the lot first but one, south of that on which the Butlers had settled.

In 1797, Ebenezer Butler, Jr., or, as he was afterwards more familiarly known, Judge Butler, built the first *framed* house that was raised in the vicinity of Pompey Hill. This was located on the west side of what is now the public square, and on the present site of Hon. Manoah Pratt's dwelling, formerly Handy's tavern. The next year, 1798, he erected for his father a house, on the present site of the wagon shop so long owned and occupied by Joseph Beach. In the same year, his brother, Jesse Butler, built a frame house on the site where the M. E. Church now stands.

On the corner where the public house is now standing, Truman Lewis had, before 1800, built a small frame house and opened a tavern. From that day till this, there has been a house of entertainment kept in that place. A part of the house located near the Disciple's Church, and when taken down a few years since was owned by Mrs. Orr, was a part of the house built by Mr. Lewis, and, together with part of the frame of Mr. Pratt's house, (Handy's tavern,) and a barn situated on the place so long occupied by Calvin Dean, are the oldest frames recently standing in the village, or this locality.

North from the village, on the Pompey and Manlius road, near the barn on the land owned by David King, was located Nathan Davis. From him the farm passed to Victory Birdseye, Esq.; thence to Ansel Jones; thence to Mr. Geo. E. Wells; and thence to David King. A gentleman by the name of Mills, a tailor by trade, lived north of Davis, on the knoll by the "old thorn tree."

Farther north, and next neighbor, on a fifty acre lot, settled John Bars, a Hessian, one of the thousand taken prisoner by Washington, at Trenton, in 1776. Bars remained for a time; he sold to Mr. Anger, from whom the farm has passed successively, to Capt. Ebenezer Carr, to Messrs. Smith, Handy, Wicks, Wells and to its present owner, David King.

The next farm north was owned by the Lillys, who resided at the foot of the hill, near Mr. Wells' house. And, on the top of the hill they built a blacksmith shop, and were for a long time the only, as they were the first blacksmiths who carried on this business in the locality.

On the farm now owned by Randolph Beard, and where he resides, was located as early as 1800, Mr. Orsemus Bowers. Before this date it had been owned by one Bond, who also worked at blacksmithing. From Mr. Bond the farm passed to Capt. Carr, and to Beach Beard, father to present owner.

Mr. Orsborn, a carpenter, and the first in the place, settled on the farm formerly owned and occupied by Augustus W. Chappell. Mr. Orsborn sold to Mr. Fisher, who sold to Mr. Chappell's father, from whom it passed to the son. First north from Mr. Chappell, on hill opposite stone quarry, was one Foster. At the four corners, beyond, was first located

James and Samuel Curry. They sold to "The M'Keevers." Augustus Wheaton afterwards came into possession, buying, we think, of McKeever. Between Foster and Curry on west side of road, was Mr. White, who married a sister of Jacob Hoar.

At a later day than 1800, Morton Bostwick was settled, on corner opposite Augustus Wheaton. On the place now owned by Jas. VanBrocklin, first settled Mr. Sandiman Culver, who sold to Mr. Jakway, from whom it passed to Jasper Bennett, to Isaac Wicks and to Mr. Van Brocklin. Where Nicholas VanPatten now resides, Jacob Hoar settled. His first house however, was on the side west of the road, near to a spring of water, as it was the aim of the early settlers to locate at or near a spring, that water could easily be obtained. The first well that was dug in the village, was by Truman Lewis, and has since been filled.

Where now lives Messrs. Cramer Johnson and Eli Anderson, were located two brothers, Abel and Thos. Orcutt, and on the farm of Hiram Butts, lived Daniel Webster. Obed Handy lived on the farm of Ira Anderson, whose grandfather bought of Handy.

Mr. Timothy Cossitt, Sen., lived on the farm, so long owned by his son Calvin Cossett. Benjamin Butler and his son Salmon, settled opposite the farm so long owned by Rensselaer Johnson. They owned at first the farm of Mr. Johnson, and sold to his father, Rufus Johnson, who married Mary, sister of Judge Butler.

The Butlers sold to Ami Butler, son of Benjamin, a farm, which forms a part of that now owned by Mr. Doolett. Ami settled near where is now Mr. Doolett's house. Across from Butler's, Dea. Ezra Hart made a settlement. His house took fire from some cause, and burned to the ground, the Deacon loosing nearly every article of furniture and wearing apparel he possessed. He afterwards built another house, and after occupying it a few years, sold it to Jesse Butler, who occupied it till about 1847 or 8.

Dr. Walter Colton, the first resident physician, settled on the farm, and had at that time, a house situated a little north of the one now owned by Geo. Wells. He sold to Edward Boylston, a silver-smith, who for a time carried on his trade in that place; Boylston sold to Rev. Hugh Wallace, one of the first *settled* ministers of the Presbyterian church. It is just to remark, that Rev. Mr. Gilbert, who settled near where Mr. Albert Butterfield lived, and where Mr. Blair now lives, was at Pompey, and preached to the settlers before the settlement of Mr. Wallace, which occurred in 1801. So was also a Mr. Williston, 1798. Mr. Gilbert lies buried in the cemetery at Pompey Hill. Mr. Daniel Gillett settled and built a log house near where Mr. Seubal Knight lives. Samuel Johnson bought and made a clearing, where Daniel Marsh lived at the time of his death. In 1805, he sold to Asa Wells, who built a house and lived a little east, and back from the road. Mr. Wells sold to Judge Butler, or rather *exchanged* for 100 acres, the farm now owned by the Ryan estate, situated at the foot of the hill directly east from the village.

Mr. Wm. Lathrop resided where Frank Porter now lives. Mr. Lathrop drew the plan for, and framed the "Old Academy" building. Opposite Mr. Lathrop, lived one Titus Rust, a shoemaker, who afterwards sold to Mr. Marovia Marsh. Farther south, where Calvin Dean lived, was Nathaniel Brace; nearly opposite, lived Gad Loveland; farther south, (and where is now a few apple trees, beyond the Wells' house,) lived George, afterwards Maj. Catlin, who, as before stated, kept the first public house in the place.

Where Robert Ellis recently lived, Jas. Cravatt settled. He, very soon, sold to Chauncey Jerome, who lived upon the lot till his death. Next south, lived Jas. Lankland. Where Ira Ellis lately lived, Capt. Sely Castle made a clearing and built a house. Where Eli Pratt lives, was Jabez, afterwards Gen. Castle. Mr. Godfrey Williston settled where Mr. Guynn lived. Mr. Williston bought of one Doty, who first settled upon the farm. Mr. Urial Wilson was on the farm now owned by his son-in-law, Truman Woodford. Next, came Messrs. John Jerome and Joseph Smith, who came to Pompey, as before stated, in 1794. These lands are still owned by the Jeromes.

At the foot of the hill, on the road running east from the cemetery, where Mr. Elizur Seymour now lives, Sylvanius Bishop bought of Cravatt, and settled. Further east, where is "the Bliss place," Benjamin Hopkins settled. He bought of one Whitney, who had built on the site of the present dwelling. Isaac Frost settled where Maj. Berry now lives. Beyond the four corners east of where Frost resided, Mr. Curtis located, owning the farm on which is located No. 8 School house, the farm now owned by John VanBrocklin. Nearly opposite the old Curtis home is the VanBrocklin residence, where Nicholas Van Brocklin lived over fifty years. He purchased of one Campbell the father of Almira Campbell referred to in Mrs. Ostrander's letter. On this farm Wm. W. Van Brocklin was born. Next east lived Elijah Wallis for over fifty years, and next on the north side, Millard Robinson.

At and near the four corners, at the top of the hill east of Frost, were located Deodatus, Hezekiah and Thaddeus Clark. The first two, physicians. The last, father of Grace Greenwood, who was located on the farm next west of Van Brocklin's at the corners.

There were also in same locality, south, Berry Davis, the Judds, Samuel Dunham, Almer Pratt, Reuben Billings and Hanchett. Further east, at Wood's Corners, was Wood, and near by, were James, Noodiah and Epiphras Olcott.

North from Dr. Clark's was Rev. Mr. Gilbert; since Timothy Butterfield's home; then followed Samuel Flint, Elijah Wells and Artemus Bishop. At the foot of the hill, on road to Cazenovia, near the Pratt's saw mill, was Hooper Bishop, who only a few years since, was living in Michigan, at the advanced age of over a *hundred years*.

One Ackley lived west of the mill, and afterwards built the house occupied by Lewis Pratt.

On the farm now owned by Marshall R. Dyer, first lived Edward Hoar, who built a very substantial log house—the logs being hewn and made square, a circumstance quite unusual in those days. Mr. Hoar sold to Mr. Allen Hayden, who sold to Miles Dunbar. Elijah Howard bought of Dunbar. He sold to John Todd, from whom it has passed to Pitt, and now to Marshall R. Dyer. By Pratt's Falls, Manoah Pratt and the Smiths—Jared and Roderick—"took up" a lot of land one mile square, and settling, built a flour and saw mills. The first built in the present township of Pompey. These mills were erected in 1797 and 8.

In thus giving names of the original settlements made, we have taken a circuit about the village of Pompey, and named the settlers en route. By this review, we find there were, within the circle thus described, as early as about 1800, sixty or seventy families.

In Clark's Onondaga, we find that the entire population of the county at this time, was 1,036, and of this town, 309. Showing that nearly one-third of the entire population of Onondaga Co., (which then embraced Homer and Solon, now Cortland Co.,) was located in this vicinity.

At that time, what is now Onondaga Co., numbered only 885, Pompey containing nearly 50 more than one-third of the entire number. Clark further says, "At this time such a vehicle as a horse wagon was not in existence in this town or county; and the visiting was done mostly in winter on ox sleds, and happy and rich indeed was he who could yoke a pair of oxen of his own, make his way through the woods with wife and child or two on the sled, on an evening's visit to a neighbor's several miles distant—in fact, such a man was considered in rather opulent circumstances; and too, it was no disparagement for the belles and beaux of that day to attend singing school or spinning bee on the ox sled."

Within the next few years many changes took place; settlers came in rapidly; a very thriving community was established at what was then called Butler's Hill. Besides those already named we find named by Clark, the following parties who had settled in the town, "True Worthy and Selah Cook, the Holbrooks, Hibbards, Hinsdales, Messengers, Westerns, Allens and Burrs."

But, during the advancement of the community to this time, the trials attendant upon the emigration of the settlers, the deprivations necessary to be endured by them, in clearing the forests and commencing a settlement and a new home, were, by no means, light. Coming as many or nearly all of them did from Mass. and Conn., where they had enjoyed the comforts of a home in a comparatively old settled country; churches, schools, stores, mills, good roads, warm and comfortable dwellings, the social circle, and all of the comforts which a long established community enjoy; and breaking aloof from these, and either on foot, with axe across the shoulder, or with the family and family effects upon an ox-sled or cart, often bidding adieu to friends and kindred, they took up their line of march for this the then far West. To do this, and under circumstances so unfavorable, was not so pleasant a task as we, viewing it from our present stand-point, in days of rail roads and telegraphs, might suppose it to have been.

A journey then to "the West," was further than that of to-day, to California or to Oregon.

The "North River" then, was a distance so far from home, that the criminal who should escape to it, was safe from his pursuers. And New York and Albany were places farther, apparently, from them, than Pike's Peak or San-Francisco from us to-day!

When they were about to leave on their journey, the friends and neighbors for a great distance around, met at the homestead; prayers were said, psalms was sung, and those who were left behind, felt that those who had gone, were to them no better than buried. During the last 30 or 40 years, we have been accustomed to witness the departure of friends and neighbors who, by rail road, were to take their departure for Wisconsin, Minn. and California, but never with feelings such as saddened the hearts of those who bade adieu to those who were to be the first settlers of this, our native town.

Not unfrequently, the journey was performed by our grand-mothers in company with their husbands, sons and daughters, much of the way on foot, beside the cart or sled which carried the household goods!

As the young of to-day take a retrospect of those times and trials, and of the journeys performed by our grand-parents, may we not learn lessons of heroism, of self-denial and of devotion to the best interests of our descendants, which should they be acted upon, would somewhat improve our physical, and perhaps our social and moral condition? Then society could boast of men and women possessed with strong physical, and often strong mental abilities, to whose development we owe much of our present prosperity and happiness.

We can hardly realize the change since then. Fancy yourself surrounded by a number of little ones, cutting loose from the enjoyments of your present comfortable home, and all the blessings surrounding you, and wending your way, not by the comfortable and elegant rail road car, but by the slow, sure, tedious foot or sled-passage, over rough roads, across fords often deep and dangerous, over causeways, through swamps, through dense forests, the home of the panther, bear, wolf, deer and Indian; and, by the aid of marked trees, seeking your future home in a country which, because of these difficulties, is far from friends and the comforts you now enjoy; and in the lone wood, stopping to rear a log hut, commence a clearing and the settlement of a new country. Picture the gradual completion of your rude dwelling; the felling of the trees; the clearing of the land; its seeding and the growth of the little crop of corn or rye that is to become the bread of yourself and family; the hollow stump or mortar for cracking the same; and, in case of sickness, of the silent watch, the long lonely trip for the physician and medicine, in the absence of neighbors or the possession of the many comforts which make the sick room cheerful and the patient comfortable; the anxiety felt for the recovery of a dear friend, it may be wife or child; think of being now and then visited by the prowling wolf or bear, robbing you of stock whose flesh or wooly coat was to make your meat and clothing; of the trip on foot for miles through the forest, which on every side surrounds you, to the store, the shop or mill. In fine, if you can, think of being *alone in the wilderness*, with naught but trees, wild beasts and Indians for companions, and you may in some small degree realize the position and painful self-sacrifice of those who, eighty years ago, settled in Onondaga county, which to-day boasts so proudly of its thriving city and towns, its broad, well-tilled farms, its teeming graineries, its large and beautiful dwellings, and its *one hundred thousand* population.

It is to be hoped that this retrospect made by us, shall enable us fully to realize the debt of gratitude we owe to those who cleared our forests and left to us the benefits of their labors. And in so much as they labored for us, and at no great cost, have left so great an inheritance, let us guard well the homes they made, as well as the principles of government they established and secured to us. In spite of every difficulty, let us perpetuate, as far as in our power it lies to perpetuate, for those who shall come after us, the same homes and free institutions, unimpaired, to the end of time.

Clark says, "the earliest settlers were obliged to go to Whitestown, Oneida Co., a distance of 40 miles to mill. They, however, often used a stump as a mortar, and for a pessle a hard wood stick of proper dimentions attached to a spring pole, for the purpose of breaking corn, and other grain. Marketing and trade was mostly done at Whitestown, old Fort Schuyler and Herkimer, and the transportation was mostly done by ox teams, in the winter season."

The first grist mill built near the settlers, was that at

Jamesville, in 1794, called Jackson's mill. "The first mills erected in this town, were at Pratt's Falls, by Messrs. Pratt and Smith. A grist mill in 1798 and a saw mill a year or two earlier." Mr. Pratt brought the material used in erecting his mills, excepting the hewn timber, from Connecticut, hauling the same on an ox sled or cart. About the year 1810 or 12, Mr. Henry Seymour erected a windmill on Pompey Hill, near what is now the site of the Roman Catholic, formerly the Baptist church. It proved a failure. In a year or two after, he built near the site of the first, another windmill, which was used only in the preparation of grain for distilling. These mills stood for many years, and till about 1838.

The teams used by the earlier settlers were universally ox teams. There were no wagons in town. Only a single horse or two; these were used to work with the oxen, and to go to mill or to store. The first chaise was brought here by Judge Butler, from Philadelphia, where he had purchased it in exchange for cattle that he had driven thither from Central New York, to sell.

The plows used were what they called "The Bull Plow," made of wrought iron. The grain was covered by means of a crotch harrow with nine teeth; one such implement answered for a neighborhood. Scythes were brought from the East. The snath was a straight stick, found in the woods. Messrs. Abram and Timothy Northrop made the first bent snaths manufactured in town. Wooden forks were used for turning hay, Pitching forks were iron, with heavy tines. There being no barns, it was usual to stack the hay. This was done by means of a long handled fork, one answering for a community.

Other farming utensils were of the rudest fashion. Household furniture was very limited in quantity, and often rude in style. One table; the old chest with drawers; the cupboard in which were a few dishes; a few chairs; and one-half of a hollow log for a cradle would frequently complete the list.

At about the year 1800, the trading at stores was mostly done at Manlius Square. The first store, where a general assortment of goods was kept, was opened by John Meeker, about the year 1803 or 4, and in what was then Col. Hopkins' Tavern stand, at Pompey Hill. Before this, for a short time, Truman Lewis, who kept tavern, kept also a few goods. And, as before stated, at Log City, was a place where tea, sugar, coffee, &c., could be procured.

Mr. Meeker was soon followed by Clarke & Emmons, who built and used for a store, what was at the time it was taken down called "Dea. Baker's Old Red House." At about the time Clark & Emmons came, Henry Seymour and Orrin Stone opened a store. Clark & Emmons in a year or two left the place, and the firm of Seymour & Stone was the principal one doing a mercantile business in this village for a long period afterwards.

At this date, the cloth (flannel) which had been woven by our grandmothers, from wool they had carded and spun, was taken to Manlius to be colored and dressed—this making the full cloth worn by the settlers. Some of the families, it is related, wore deer skin breeches, the skins having been tanned by themselves; these when wet, would shrink, and instances are cited where "boys were obliged to wear them without taking off till they became dry." In time, other fulling mills were built; one in the hollow, near Mr. Conrad Bush's place; this mill, in the fall of the year, being well stored with cloth from the vicinity, took fire and burned, together with its contents, causing serious loss, and in many instances suffering, among the settlers.

Mr. Ezra Dodge, who lived on the farm so long occupied by his son, David F. Dodge, was a wheel-wright. He used to mend cart wheels, to make plows, &c.

The first blacksmiths after the Lillies, were Stewart & Smith; about 1804 or 5 they came from Vermont; they were brothers-in-law; one had a shop near the dwelling which Jesse Butler first built; the other one nearly opposite the present site of the M. E. Church.

Stewart moved to Ohio, and Chester Howard came and worked at the business. Merrit Butler and Harry Hopkins, who learned the trade of him, (Howard,) entered into partnership with him, and together they conducted the business for three years. Butler bought the shop, and afterwards worked at the trade in Pompey for forty years.

At about the time this partnership was dissolved, Harry Hopkins and George Merrill entered into co-partnership, for the purpose of manufacturing "thirty toothed harrows," a patent for which had been obtained by Jacob Pratt and Hopkins. They built the long shop which was located nearly opposite the site of the present Disciples' Church.

Joseph Beach worked at this trade on the Hill for many years. He also carried on wagon making extensively. Horace Butts and Merrit Butler at one time were somewhat extensively engaged in the manufacturing of wagons.

Mr. Hurlbut was the first cabinet maker; afterwards, Henry and Hezekiah Stevens settled in the village, and for many years conducted that business.

By reference to the laws of 1789, chapter 11, we find that authority was conferred on the General Sessions to organize townships; and accordingly, this township was organized by the General Court in session at Whitestown, in the same year. We believe, from the best information at hand, that for a period, Pompey embraced under this action of the Court, *all the Military Tract* bounded on the west by Preemption line, north by State line to McComb purchase, east by line south to mouth of Chittenango Creek, thence on line of military tract to Chenango River, on south by Pennsylvania State line. Settlements at or about this date, 1789, were made at Horsehead's, Morehouse Flatts, Cayuga Bridge, Chenango Point, at Manlius and at Pompey Hill. It is related that at the first town meeting held in 1794, after the formation of the town by direct legislative enactment, there were present settlers from many or all of the settlements above named.

"This first town meeting was held at Pompey Hill, at the house of Ebenezer Butler, Jr., April 1st, 1794. Moses DeWitt was chosen Supervisor, and Hezekiah Olcott, Town Clerk, Allen Beach, Wm. Haskins, George Catlin and Ebenezer Butler, Jr., Assessors, Thomas Olcott, Jeremiah Gould and John Lamb, Commissioners of Highways. A special town meeting was held 20th September, 1794, at the house of Ebenezer Butler, at which Wm. Haskins was chosen Supervisor, in place of Moses DeWitt, deceased." —(Clark.)

The first lawyer, or rather pettifogger, who came to Pompey Hill, was a Mr. Dunham, a man whose stay was of short duration. The first settled lawyer was John Keedar, who came here before or about the year 1800, and located near the site of Pompey Academy; he and his brother kept bachelors' hall; he was a first-class lawyer for his time; he was a German by birth, and because of a failure to receive some appointment at the hands of the State Government, he left the district and country. He was succeeded in 1806, by Daniel Wood, who bought the residence occupied by Keedar; Mr. Wood continued a resident of Pompey many years, and in the successful practice of his profession, till his death, which occurred in the year 1838. He was appointed the first Post Master at Pompey Hill, in 1811, (previous to this date the settlement went by the name of Butler's Hill,) and he was intimately connected with all the early history of the village. Almost simultaneously with Esq. Wood, came Samuel Baldwin; he was a man of great promise, and obtained an enviable notoriety as a lawyer; his office was near where is now located the watering tub, and in the north-east corner of what is now Mr. O. Jarvis Wheaton's door yard; afterwards it was removed to the site of what is familiarly known as "Esq. Gott's Office." Victory Birdseye, in 1809, settled in the place as a lawyer, and a partner of Mr. Wood. Daniel Gott afterwards came, taught school for a time, and then commenced the study of law with Wood & Birdseye. Then followed Chas. Bald-wind, Chas. B. and H. J. Sedgwick, Lucien Birdseye, LeRoy Morgan, Geo. H. Williams, R. H. Duell and others, whose name is legion—either as students at law or practitioners. Wm. W. VanBrocklin is the only lawyer at present located in Pompey; he is also Justice of the Peace.

The first physician in the town of Pompey, was Dr. Holbrook, who settled at Pompey Centre in 1793. The first resident physician at Pompey Hill, was Dr. Walter Coton. He was followed by Daniel Tibbals, who settled here in about the year 1800; he, Dr. Tibbals, spent in Pompey many years in the practice of his profession; he left the town about thirty or thirty-five years since, and moved to Erie, Pa., spending the residue of his life with his sons in that city.

Cotempory with Dr. Tibbals from the year 1814, Dr. Jehiel Stears has been a physician at Pompey Hill; he is still living at a good old age, and has not entirely given up the practice of medicine. Dr. Hezekiah Clark, in the year 1805 or 6, settled east of the village of Pompey, and practiced medicine in this locality for a great number of years. He was a surgeon, serving as such in the Revolutionary war. Dr. Rial Wright was a partner with Dr. Stevens for a number of years. Dr. L. B. Wells, during the first years of his practice, was a resident physician in this place. He was the first Homœpathic physician in Pompey.

Dr. J. Deblois Sherman settled at Pompey Hill about 1825. Resided opposite the old home of Marovia Marsh, where Frank Porter now (1875) lives. Office was on site of "Beard's stone store." He ranked high as a physician, went to the West or South Western States. Dr. Tibbals had a Drug store just south of Sherman's office.

The early settlers, with few exceptions, were young married people, or those with families of small children; and they early perceived the necessity of establishing schools. As early as 1794, do we find that a school was opened; and shortly after, a house was built for the purpose, and every

PRESBYTERIAN CHURCH, POMPEY HILL.

advantage possible was secured, that the children might be taught. Not that the facilities for obtaining a liberal education were then as available as now, but such advantages as were demanded by the times were procured, and the school was a leading feature or institution of the community.

The first school kept, was in a log house located near where Mr. Daniel Kellogg now lives. And among the first, if not the first teacher, was Miss Lucy Jerome, afterwards Mrs. James Geddes, mother of the Hon. Geo. Geddes, of Camillus.

The first house built for school purposes, was a frame one built in 1798, and located in the forks of the road on the village green; in the rear of which, was the first grave yard; afterwards, the house was moved north to near the present site of "Gott's office." There school was kept for a number of years, till the Academy building was erected. Then the "Common School" was kept for a number of years after, in a room of that building.

Among the early teachers, was Miss Hepsabah Beebee and Mr. Lyman Pitcher; as well as Mr. Jas. Robinson, who first taught English Grammar, a science that only the *oldest* and *most advanced* scholars aspired to study.

As the interest in education increased, the settlers conceived the idea of establishing an Academy. And as early as about 1800, the frame for such an institution was raised, and in the year 1811, was incorporated by the Regents of the University. And the trustees under the charter held their first meeting in the month of April, of the same year.

The educational interests of the people seemed to be among the more important, and whatever was done by them, it is evident, they meant should be well done, and that the benefits resulting from this institution be not for them and their children only, but for those who should come after them for generations to follow.

To this end, they saw the necessity of making it a funded institution. Citizens in the vicinity, and for miles around, owning real estate made contributions to it of from 50 to 100 dollars, and upwards, in mortgages on their farms. The interest accruing on the same to be paid annually. By this means there was accumulated, together with that received from the sale of Public lands and other sources, a fund of several thousand dollars, and the institution has been able, (though sometimes lacking a sufficient income from tuitions charged, to render it self-sustaining,) to support itself till the present time; and has ever, till Academies and Union as well as good district schools have become so numerous about it, ranked among the first Academies of the State.

Perhaps to this school, more than to any other one cause, do we owe the general intelligence of the people of this vicinity, which has won for the citizens of Pompey so fair a name abroad. And that has enabled her to send out so many sons to fill positions in councils of the State snd Nation, as well as to distinguish themselves in the law and other of the learned professions.

The men of those days seemed to believe that the interests of Education and Religion should go hand in hand, in a community! And that virtue and good morals, to be the result of the one, should be taught by the other. Consequently, we see springing up simultaneously with this institution, one being a part of the other, the church, where the gospel was to be preached,—the people taught their duties to their Maker.

The first organization of this kind was what is known as the Presbyterian Church, properly, "The First Congregational Church of Pompey.

This organization was effected, October 19, 1796, by Ameni R. Robbins, pastor of the church in Norfolk, Conn. The membership at first, consisted of the following twenty-two named persons:

MALES.	FEMALES.
Ebenezer Butler,	Desire Butler,
James Olcott,	Dorothy Butler,

Benjamin Butler,	Molly Jerome,
Joseph Shattuck,	Lucy Cook,
Ichabod Lathrop,	Freelove Cook,
John Jerome,	Amarilla Jerome,
Trueworthy Cook,	Lucy Jerome,
Selah Cook,	Susanna Carol,
Levi Jerome,	Hannah Griffis,
Moses Lilly,	Zeruiah Catlin,
Daniel McKeys,	Louisa Butler.

The last survivor of them, Mrs. Louisa Butler, died April 30, 1857. Having been for more than 60 years a communicant of the church.

The number of members increased from time to time, till in the year 1834, over 300 (305) persons were reported in good and regular standing in the connection.

The meetings were first held in the school house that stood in the fork of the road, near the centre of the green. When the old Academy was erected, meetings were held in that building in a room suited to the purpose.

At length, the congregation becoming too large to be accommodated there, the present church edifice was erected in the years 1817 and 18, and dedicated in the year 1819.

The number of ministers that have, since the date of its organization been settled over the church, has not been small. Among these, have been some of the best and most talented men of the country. The following is a list of names embracing all, or nearly all who have survived as pastors of this church.

Rev. Mr. Williston,---------------------------------- 1798
" Joseph Gilbert,--------------------------------- 1799
" Hugh Wallis,------------------------------------ 1801
" Jabez Chadwick,--------------------------------- 1812
" E. S. Barrows,---------------------------------- 1822
" B. B. Stockton,--------------------------------- 1829
" J. B. Shaw,-------------------------------------- 1833
" Ethan Smith,------------------------------------- 1835

" John Gridley,---------------------------------- 1836
" Asa Rand,------------------------------------- 1837
" Mr. Wheelock,--------------------------------- ——
" Clinton Clark.--------------------------------- 1845
" S. P. M. Hastings,----------------------------- 1848
" A. A. Graley,---------------------------------- 1856
" J. H. Morron,---------------------------------- 1862
" N. Bosworth,---------------------------------- 1863
" Mr. Eggleston,-------------------------------- 1866
" A. Cooper,------------------------------------ 1869
" J. Petrie,------------------------------------- 1872

The Baptist church was organized in the year 1817, and at one time was equally as thriving as the Congregational church. But owing to certain causes, the organization has ceased to exist, and most of the original members living ten years ago, were members of the Disciples', or Christ's church, an organization of comparatively recent date.

The Baptist congregation first held their meetings in barns and at the private dwellings of the members.

Among the early ministers, and the first who preached to them after their regular organization, was the Rev. Frederick Freeman, a resident of Fabius. They built the church which they subsequently occupied in the year 1819 or 20, immediately after the Presbyterian house was completed.

The Methodist church was organized at a later period. Rev. Mr. Torry or Father Torry as he was called, was among the first, if not the first, minister that had charge of this church. Since his day, the church being under the supervision of the Oneida Conference, has received its ministers by appointment, from the Bishops of the church, and has made changes regularly as per rule of the Itinerancy. No denomination can boast of more zealous or devoted pastors, than the M. E. church.

This society was first formed in the neighborhood west of the village; and they built a church which has stood till a recent day, opposite the dwelling of Mr. Nelson Hall.

About the year 1839, the house of worship in the village was erected; its membership may never have been very large, but it has embraced some of the pure and good men and women of the earth. Its early founders have gone to their reward and their works do follow them.

The Disciples of Christ's church was organized under circumstances which are fully given in the subjoined paper from the pen of the present pastor, Rev. A. S. Hale.

DISCIPLES OF CHRIST.

Early in the year 1833, the Baptist church at Pompey Hill was left without a pastor. During the Spring or early Summer of this year, the church formed an acquaintance with Elder J. I. Lowell, who preached before the church several times "on trial." Though a Baptist minister in regular standing, he was not fully in sympathy with all the doctrines of the Baptist creed, and he so distinctly informed the church. He was, however, nevertheless employed as the pastor of the Baptist church. At the time of his coming here, Mr. L. had recently had his attention called to certain ideas that he had once held as true, but which he was now firmly convinced were errors. Not being a man to hide any truth, or cover up any light he might possess, he began at once to declare "the whole counsel of God" as he had now come to understand it. Whatever his faults may have been, his great thought—the ruling idea indeed in his mind and life was—*God has spoken, let His word stand, and His will be done*, though all humanisms come to naught. It was then, perhaps, more dangerous than now, for any minister to advocate ideas not contained in "the creed."

But, regardless of creeds, Mr. L. was determined to follow truth wherever it might lead, or whatever might be the consequences. His ministry was popular for awhile, until it began to be whispered that he was a "Campbellite," whatever that might be. But the cry of "heresy" now raised with reference to his teaching, could not deter a goodly number from accepting the truths of God which he so forcibly set forth. Nicknames applied to truth, will not frighten the real truth-lover, who, like the noble Bereans of old, will for himself search the Scriptures to know what they really teach and require. Many persons accepted the views of Gospel truths presented by Mr. L., and many warmly opposed them.

Before the expiration of the first year of his labor in Pompey, the portion of the church which rejected these views, closed the meeting-house against the pastor. The church also, as its records shows, (on May 9th, 1834, and again May 17th,) excluded quite a number of its members, for no crime, immorality, or unchristian conduct, for no overt act committed in joining any other society, but simply for entertaining new, and as they thought, enlarged views of Gospel truth; or, as the record states it, "for embracing the Campbell or heretical principle."

Early in 1834, several persons were converted under Mr. Lowell's ministry. These, together with those who no longer found sympathy nor countenance in the Baptist church, desiring a home religiously, were necessarily led to the formation of a new religious society in the place. On May 3rd, 1834, as the records show, "The First Congregation of Disciples of Christ in Pompey" was organized, with twenty-eight members, whose names were as follows:

Calvin Peck,
Asa Wells,
Thos. M. King,
Alson Nearing,
Charles Little,
Malcom Bennett,
A. H. Squires,
Uriel Wilson, Jr.
Samuel Talbot,
Harry Knapp,
Willard Heydon,
Darius Wilson,
J. I. Lowell,
Mary P. Lowell,
Eliza Nearing,
Polly Wilson,
Mary A. Bush,
Temperance Wilson,
Paulina Talbot,
Mindwell Thomas,
Harriett Pratt,
Catherine Bennett,
Betsey Wright,
Rhoda Parsons,

Jacob Bush,	Polly Thomas,
Alvin Talbot,	Mary Knapp.

Seven of these persons still, (Aug., 1873,) remain members of the church. At the end of the year in which the church was organized, there were 50 members, and by the end of the next year (1835,) the number had reached 93.

In the year 1837 the society built the house in which they worshipped until 1868, when a new church was built, the old one having been sold for the use of the District school, in place of the school house which was burned down on the night of Feb. 11, 1868.

The first pastor of the church was J. I. Lowell. The first Elders were Calvin Peck, Asa Wells and Thomas M. King. Deacons, Alson Nearing and Charles Little. Treasurer, Malcom Bennett. Clerk, A. H. Squires.

The following ministers have served the church as pastors:—J. M. Bartlett, M. H. Clapp, M. H. Slosson, H. M. Selmser, J. M. Shepard, Andrew J. Smith, W. T. Horner, L. Southmayd, J. B. Marshall, J. C. Goodrich and A. S. Hale.

The present Elders are Harry Knapp, George Nearing and Lucius Crandall.

Deacons—U. Wilson, J. W. Garrett, Morris Bush and D. B. Knapp.

The church numbers now about 160 members.

The dead were first buried in a yard located on the public green, and back of the first school house. The first buried, were two children of Geo. Catlin, who died of scarlatina. The first adult buried there, was Mrs. Cravatt, wife of him who settled on farm recently owned and occupied by Robert Ellis. Col. Hezekiah Olcott, a resident of this town, an officer in the Revolution and a surveyor, while engaged in surveying the State Road, was taken ill of fever and died at Pompey West Hill; he was brought to this village and buried with military honors. He, it is said by those who remember him, was a very intelligent man, one of great influence, first among the first men of the country; a man much loved and whose loss was severely felt, not only at home but all through the county and central portion of the State.

About the year 1802 or 3, measures were taken to locate a new burial ground. The location selected was opposite Dr. Stearns' present residence, and the bodies that had been buried at the place before named, were desinterred and buried there. On reflection, however, it was determined that the locality was an unfavorable one, and the lot was abandoned as a burial place; and what is now the east or back part of the present beautiful cemetery was selected, to which place the dead were taken and buried. About the year 1823 the "new part" was purchased of Peter Smith, father of Hon. Garrett Smith of Peterborough. The first person buried in this new part, was Mr. Daniel Knapp, who died in the month of August of the same year in which the lot was fenced, 1823; he died suddenly, of Billious cholic, being ill only a few hours. A second "new part" situated north of the first, was recently added; and the whole yard under the direction of the present incorporate company, is kept in most pleasing order, with excellent fences, walks and shade trees.

A complete record of every burial is kept.

In speaking of Pompey Hill, Clark says: "This village was, within the memory of men still living, as prominent a place as any in the county. It gave more tone to the surrounding country and settlements, on account of its refinement and wealth, its intelligence and learning, than any place in the vicinity. People came here for legal advice, they came here for medical advice, to do their trading, and they came here for fashions, they came here for military parades, for political discussions and for general consultations of a public nature; they came here to engage in all the events incident of men in public life."

LA FAYETTE—(POMPEY WEST HILL.)

The first settler in this locality, was John Wilcox, before named as the first settler in the original township. He settled about two miles from the present village of La Fayette.

The first settlers in and near the village, were Joseph Rhoades, Apollos King, Zara D. Howe, Caleb Green, Joseph Smith, Dr. Silas W. Park, Mr. Owens and the Bakers, all or nearly all coming from Chesterfield, Hampshire Co., Mass., in or about the year 1801.

Rhoades built a log tavern and kept a public house on the site of the present one. He afterwards moved to Marcellus, where many of his descendents are now living. Mr. Apollos King did not remain any great length of time; he settled one-half mile south of "The Corners," moving from there to Otisco. Howe settled near an ashery on the Caleb Green farm, and put up a frame to a house. He did not complete the house, but selling his improvements to Dr. Silas W. Park, he moved to Otisco. Dr. Park finished the building and lived in the same, during the remainder of his life, a period of 24 years. The house was standing in 1870.

Joseph Smith settled near the site of Dr. Elijah Park's dwelling; he was a farmer, lived here about 20 years and till his death.

Erastus Baker, the first of the family by that name who settled in this locality, came in 1801, with Stephen ("Ensign") Cole and Rhoades, and settled on the hill just west of the village. In 1805 Seth made a settlement joining Erastus on the West, and Sydenham located to the north of him. Thomas, in 1803, settled one and one-half miles southwest of the Corners, in what is now called Sherman Hollow. The greater part of these lands remain in the hands of the Baker family to this day.

Joseph & Lemuel came in 1804, but made no permanent home; Joseph moving to Otisco, and died there. Lemuel went to the far West, and it is said, was finally killed by the Indians in Texas, when hunting for his cows.

Orange King and his brother, (if at all connected with Apollos King, it was a very distant connection,) came from Chesterfield, about 1800. They settled one mile north of the Corners. There was another brother who settled one mile west of the Corners.

About the same time Gen. Isaac Hall came from Great Barrington, Mass., and settled one mile south of Corners, on a soldier's claim. He purchased ten or twelve hundred acres, was the wealthy man of Pompey. It is said, that he brought into town with him half a bushel of silver dollars.

He gave his attention to the raising of stock. It was his custom to let to his neighbors, and to citizens elsewhere, cows, sheep, colts, &c., to double. He died about 1826 or 7, being worth, it was said, about 70,000 dollars.

Joseph S. Cole settled half mile south of Corners, came in at an early day, remained a short time, then went to Pennsylvania, afterwards returned to West Hill and died here.

The first and *only licensed* lawyer settling at West Hill, or village of La Fayette, was Samuel Baldwin, who had previously been located at Pompey Hill. He remained a number of years practicing his profession, afterwards went to Geneva and died, while living with his daughter.

The first resident physician at this village, was Dr. Silas W. Park, who settled as before stated on N. W. corner of Public Square. He cleared this Square of forest trees. He practiced medicine during his life-time. About 1814, Dr. Chauncey Williams became a partner of Dr. Park, which partnership continued for three years. In 1817, Elijah, brother of Dr. Silas W. Park, came and read medicine with him. Afterwards was his partner for three years. He then moved to Otisco, where he remained three or four years, then moved to Adrian, Mich., where he died. One Dr. Squires came and made a residence of two years, and then left.

After Dr. Silas W. Park's death, Dr. Ward Bassitt, of Salina, came and made a stay of one or two years. He then went to Cazenovia, Madison Co. In 1825, Dr. Rial Wright came and remained one and a half years. At this time Dr. Elijah Park, son of Dr. L. W. Park, who had previously studied medicine with his father and uncle, bought of Dr. Wright his ride, paying him $150.00 for the same. Dr. W. went to Pompey Hill, and, as a partner of Dr. Jehiel Stearn, practiced medicine in that village and vicinity for many years. Dr. Elijah Park has remained in the village and is to-day, (1872,) in the practice of his profession. Dr. Lyman Rose was a resident physician in the village for many years prior to his death, which occurred in 1867.

Lemuel Smith, father of Rev. Marcus Smith, was the first blacksmith settling at West Hill. Coming about year 1800, and remained till his death, 1817. His shop was located on site of the church. His anvil was situated near the spot where now stands the pulpit in the church.

Morris Clapp, brother of Mrs. Silas W. Park, came and settled as a blacksmith, in 1818. He worked here at his trade, 45 years. He died in 1870, aged 76.

Nathaniel Stearling, a carpenter and joiner, settled on farm now owned and occupied by Luther Baker. He built the Baptist church at Pompey Hill, and the church now standing in this village. The latter part of his life was spent upon a farm. He died in Connecticut. He was connected with, and was a leading man in the church, and in educational matters.

Before Stearling, James, Asa, and Joseph McMillin, brothers, carpenters and joiners, settled about one mile N. E. of Corners. Joseph and James built the first *framed* hotel, and the one now standing in the village; Stoughton Morse being landlord. The first hotel was built of logs, and James Higgins was landlord; this was in about 1808. The McMillens remained many years, finally selling, moved away and died in different localities West and South-west.

Dorus Porter, a cabinet maker, from 1820, lived in the village; was Deacon in church, now lives in Michigan.

Ansil King was a tanner and shoemaker at the Corners, for many years, a prominent man as a mechanic.

Caleb Green owned and gave half of the lot now used for a public square, Erastus Barker giving the other half.

Ansil Smith, Chas. Jackson, and General Hall were Justices of Peace. (The latter a number of years) before the division of the township. Col. Johnson Hall, son of Gen. Hall, was sheriff and member of State Legislature. He was a merchant at West Hill, carrying on a very extensive trade.

The first merchant was Stoughton Morse, the tavern keeper. Had a little store the first at the Corners, in connection with his hotel, in 1805. Then followed Ansil Smith as merchant, till 1812 or 14. During the war of 1812, Smith run a distillery, bought cattle for troops, sending stores of provision to Sackett Harbor, and to Granadier Island. After the war, Judge Hall was the merchant of the place.

Amos Palmeter settled one mile south of La Fayette Square, at about 1803. He had a pig pen covered with logs to protect the pigs from the bears. At a time when he had a lot of pigs in this pen, one of the logs happened to be moved so as to leave an opening; and in the night the squealing of the pigs aroused the family; but Amos was afraid to go out. His wife took an axe and went to the pen, and seeing a bear coming out of the opening, she gave him a blow, and pulled the log over the hole. She then took a fire-brand in her hands, and went south through the woods, three forths of a mile to a Mr. Johnson's, and had him come to help dispatch the bear. But, opening the pen, old Bruin was found dead from the blow she had already given him. This story illustrates the courage and pluck of our grandmothers in those days. Not, however, a very good story for Amos, we think.

In Sherman Hollow, the first settlements were made in 1793.

Among the first who located here were Solomon Owen and James Sherman.. They built, in 1795 or 8, grist and saw mills. The saw mill built by them is still in good working oider.

Mr. Sherman was father of Dr. J. De Blois and Joseph Sherman. The first was at one time a prominent physician at Pompey Hill. The latter a Justice of the Peace from 1830 to about 1840.

In 1794, Reuben Bryan, Amasa Wright, Samuel Hyatt, James Pierce and Amaziah Branch, settled in this hollow.

The last named, was the first school teacher at this place and at La Fayette Village. He died at Dr. S. W. Park's, of nightmare, in about 1818. He is said to have been one of the good men of the earth. He was poor, but well educated. He came from Massachusetts.

In the north part of Sherman Hollow, were John Houghtaling, William Haskins and Comfort Rounds, located as early as 1792.

The first white child born within the limits of the town, is said to have been Amy Wilcox. Born in 1791.

Chas. Johnson, a blacksmith, has carried on business at Sherman Hollow for about 50 years; and he is still at his forge working as industriously as ever.

DELPHI.

About six miles East and South from Pompey Hill, is located the beautiful valley of the Limestone Creek. A valley which became settled at an early day by a race of noble men and women, many of whose descendants to-day are filling positions of trust in State and Nation.

As early as about the year 1800, there were located within the present limits of the township of Pompey, and within this valley, a few settlers, who during the next five or ten years were joined by many others, and a settlement embracing fifteen or twenty families was [formed. At a later time a Post office was located there. At this time, when the settlers had met for the purpose of changing the name from "Pompey Four Corners," one of their number declared the valley and its surroundings, were similar to one with which he was familiar in Italy, and suggested that the name of a village in that valley be given to the village in this. The suggestion meeting the approval of the citizens, the Italian name "Delphi" was given to the settlement.

It is impossible for us to give the exact order in which the settlers came into this valley. Neither can we be sure that in every instance, correct dates are given. We are largely indebted for information to a gentleman who first settled in the township of Fabius; but who was in reality a member of this community; and who, to-day, (1873,) is a resident of the village. Mr. Elnathan Griffith, who, at 90 years of age, possesses a reliable memory; his statements corroborating the best information obtained from other sources.

Mr. Griffith came into the valley in the year 1806. And has since, without interruption, been associated with its history. He was intimately acquainted with those who had preceded him, and was made familiar with the date and the attendant circumstances of their settlement.

Samuel Sherwood was, probably, the first settler in this vicinity. He located in 1795 on lot No. 84, about one mile northwest from the present village, on a farm afterwards owned by Patrick Shields, who married Mr. Sherwood's widow. Samuel Sherwood was a Maj. Gen. of a regiment. He came from Saratoga county.

Rufus Sheldon, father of a very talented family, among whom is Harvey Sheldon, Esq., of New York, settled in March, 1800, near Maj. Sherwood's, one and one-half miles north-west from the village. In 1798 or 9, Elijah Hill, coming from Pittsfield, Mass., settled three miles down the valley, north from the village. In 1800, Col. Ensign Hill, brother to Elijah, came and settled a little south of the village. In 1802, James McClure settled one mile south of Elijah Hill. Samuel Draper came from Vermont, and settled in the vicinity, about 1803. Benjamin Coats and William Peas came with or near the time James McClure did. The three came from New Lebanon, Columbia Co., N. Y.

McClure and Coats settled on lands now occupied by their descendants. Mr. Peas settled one half mile north of Elijah Hill. Osias Burr and William Cook, also came from New Lebanon about this time, 1802. Burr was Justice of the Peace and Judge of Court of Common Pleas.

Elihue Barber came in 1801, and settled on the hill west of the valley, and about one and one-half miles from the creek. He was induced to settle out of the valley because the opinion prevailed that where the timber was off the bottom land, they would have little value, and "be too poor to raise beans."

Moses Blowers and Stutson Benson settled at an early day near Barber's, on lot 84.

Capt. Theopelas Tracy settled one-half mile S. E. on a farm now occupied by Henry Ryder. He built the *frame* of the first Grist mill on Limestone Creek. The same mill is now owned by Alex. Maxwell. This frame was erected by Capt. Tracy in about 1803 or 4. He sold to Moses Savage, who employed Mr. Elnethan Griffith, a mill-wright, to complete the mill.

The stone, "two run," were brought from Albany by teams that had taken wheat thither, to market. These stone are French Burr stone, and are still running in the mill. They cost $100.00.

Dea. Moses Savage settled on the east side of the Creek, and built the first carding mill that was erected in the valley. Also, in about 1825 or 30, he built the grist-mill now owned by Edgar Pratt.

Zebulon Edgerton, in 1806, had a good sized clearing one mile south of Delphi. The same farm is now occupied by Wm. H. Savage. His son, Mr. Reubin Edgerton, who came with his father, in 1802, is still living (1873) in Delphi, at the age of 92 years.

Dr. Joseph Ely kept an Inn on site of present hotel, and also practiced medicine in the locality. He bought, in 1804, of Peter Root or of Mr. Goodrich a Justice of the Peace. Mr. Ely found on the lot a "brush house," which some previous settler had left. This he occupied till fall of 1806. He then employed Mr. Elnethan Griffith, the only carpenter in the place, to put up a frame addition to this house. Dr. Ely came from Montgomery Co., N. Y.

At this time, 1806, there was a frame barn and several log houses in the vicinity. Salmon G. Willard and Daniel H. Hubbard had built a store in the fall of 1805, opposite, west of hotel. The wife of Mr. Hubbard, is still living at Delphi, aged 91 years.

In about the year 1808, William Shankland, father to Judge Shankland, of Cortland, settled in this valley, his house being located on the east side of the creek, and of the County line. He was a member of this community, although a resident of Madison county.

On what is called "the Hitchcock place," settled Walter Bates. This is near the old Indian Fort, on lot 99. This was, probably, the first settlement made on this lot. Robert Swarthout, son of the soldier (who drew the lot, was, verbally authorized by his father to come on and to sell out the lot. He was here for a short time for this purpose.

After selling the lot, or much of it, he moved to Ithaca. Hon. John M. Jaycox, is, we are assured, a descendant on the maternal side, from this family. Mr. Swarthout sold from this lot, in 1806, to Jasper Galliway, and, we believe, to Thos. Derbyshire. One of these sales embraced the land now occupied by Russel and Sheldon Strickland.

Horace Yates' name is also associated with this same farm.

Elisha Litchfield came in 1812. His dwelling was located on the site of Alanson N. Godfrey's house. He kept a store on the corner, near his house. His relative, Ephraim Cleaveland, came in 1810, and kept hotel on the site of the present one, for a year or two, when he died. His property fell into the hands of Maj. Litchfield, who continued for a short time to act as landlord. Hon. Elisha Litchfield was a prominent man among the prominent men of his day. Maj. of Regiment, Member of Assembly, Speaker of the House and Member of Congress.

Reuben Benton was an early settler and Justice of the Peace. Bela Cole lived at an early day where N. F. Potter has recently built a house, opposite the Baptist church.

The settlers at one time, did nearly all of their trading at Cazenovia, with John Lineland, who was agent for the Holland Purchase Co.

Messrs. Hubbard & Willard were the first parties who kept a full assortment of goods in Delphi, this was in 1805 and 6; they sold to Esli Squires. In 1810, Squires built and occupied a store on the corner, where Marble's store is now located; he then sold the building purchased of Hubbard and Willard, to Richard Taylor, father to Rev. Elisha L. Taylor, D. D., and to James M. Taylor, of New York.

Herrick Allen bought of Taylor; he was a leading merchant for many years, and became wealthy. His father, Daniel Allen, in 1802, settled two miles north of the village.

At an early day Schuyler Van Rensselaer was a merchant at Delphi. In 1818 he sold to Matthew B. Slocum, father to Maj. Gen. Henry B. Slocum, U. S. A.

Up to 1810, there was but one store.

Of the physicians, probably Dr. Joseph Ely was the first who settled in the valley; he remained about three years.

The following named physicians have practiced their profession, being at the time, residents of Delphi:

Doctor Frisby, Dr. Shipman, brother of A. B. Shipman, recently of Syracuse, was at Delphi, 45 years ago; he remained many years; he died in Rochester, in 1871. Dr. John L. King and Dr. Pettit, brother of Judge Pettit, of Fabius, were partners. Dr. Hiram Adams, so long a practicing physician in Fabius, was at one time connected with Dr. Pettit, in his office.

Dr. Goodell, succeeded Dr. Shipman. Others have followed; among them were Drs. Marsh, Hiram Wiggins, Eli Cook, Isaac Baker, Dr. Todd and Dr. Potter. The last named being the only resident physician living in the village at this date, 1873.

Amos Benedict had in 1806, two miles north from Delphi, a blacksmith's shop; the first shop of the kind in the village was owned and carried on by two brothers named Townsend.

Oliver Rogers was a wagon maker in 1816. Mr. Prinafore was a wheel-wright, and beside, made the "bull plow" as it was called, with wooden mould-board. Jabez Groudevant was cabinent maker in 1810, and worked here at his trade till his death, which occurred about the year 1850.

Deacon Abbott was the first tanner; as early as in 1807 or 8, he built all the vats belonging to the old tannery; he sold to James Reeves. About 1820, John and Michael Spencer, from England, came into possession of the yard and the business; they conducted the business for many years. Finally, it was determined that one should move to Cardiff, and continue the business there; to decide which should go they "*flipped coppers,*" John was elected to go; he became Judge of the Court. Afterwards, Member of Asssembly; he was much beloved by his fellow-townsmen, and his absence was a great loss to Delphi.

Caleb Perry, afterwards bought the tannery and worked at the tanning business till the building and yard was destroyed by a freshet.

One mile south-east from the village, Clark Rogers, in 1823, built an edge tool factory; this factory was afterwards owned and conducted by Holmes and Sampson, whose reputation as excellent workmen is wide-spread; their tools being known as of the best make in the country. This factory is now owned by John Sailsbury.

Henry TenEycke owned, till 1853, when it was destroyed by fire, a Woolen factory, which was established in 1812. It was located on the creek north from the village, and during the whole period of its existence did a heavy business.

To-day the village of Delphi is one of thrift. Two churches, a school, in which many celebrities have taught, among them are Jesse T. Peck, one of the Bishops of the M. E. church, Dr. Amos Wescott, recently of Syracuse, and Hon. D. G. Fort, of Oswego.

Several stores—among them a Drug store—a good hotel, shops, neat residences with beautiful yards, all contribute to render this village one of the most beautiful inland towns in Central New York.

From this valley and community, as descendants of the early settlers, whose names we have here recorded, have gone forth a Judge of the Supreme Court, a Maj. Gen. United States Army, a Doctor of Divinity, successful physicians, tradesmen, mechanics and lawyers.

WATERVALE.

FROM THE PEN OF WAKEMAN G. SPRAGUE, OF SYRACUSE.

Watervale, a village situated on West Branch or Limestone Creek, and about four miles north-east from Pompey Hill, was settled by Col. James Carr, about the year 1809. Mr. Carr built the first saw mill erected on the stream in this vicinity. He was soon followed, about the same year, or in 1810, by Willoughby Milliard, who almost simultaneously with Mr. Carr, erected the second saw mill. This place was first called Carr Hollow, then Hemlock Hollow, also Slab Hollow, on account of the great quantity of slabs made by those mills.

Ansil Judd, father to Solomon Judd, of Binghamton, and of Orvan R. Judd, of American Express Co., Buffalo, settled in the Hollow in 1812, and built the first wool-carding and cloth dressing establishment in the town.

The Post Office was established in 1820, and Ansil Judd was first Post-Master. He selected the name of Watervale, and published lines announcing the fact, viz :—

"The hemlocks are gone,
The Slabs are set sail,
And we'll call it Slab Hollow
No more, but Watervale."

George Ostrander settled about the year 1815, and built a distillery, using about ten bushels of grain a day, which amount in those days, was considered very large.

Benjamin F. Wheeler carried on the business of tanning and shoe making, for a long time.

Ira Curtis moved to Watervale at an early day, and opened the first store. He also built, and for many years kept the first hotel.

Wm. C. Fargo, O. Abbott, Benjamin Patten and V. R. Taylor, were among the first settlers.

Anson Sprague settled on a farm south of Watervale, in 1818. On this farm was found the celebrated Monumental stone, now in the State Agricultural and Historical rooms at Albany. The following description of this stone we take from Mather & Brockett's Geography of the State of New York, published in 1847, by J. H. Mather & Co., Hartford, Editor:

"In the town of Pompey, a stone was found some years since, about fourteen inches long, twelve broad, and eight thick. It had a figure of a serpent entwined about a tree, and this inscription.

Leo X De	tree &c	L. S.
VIx 1520–		† ∩

This inscription has been interpreted—Leo X. by the grace (or will) of God, sixth year of his pontificate, 1520. L. S. the initials of the person buried, (as it was undoubtedly a sepulchral monument,)—the cross, an indication that he was a Catholic, and the character ∩ perhaps a rude intimation that he belonged to the masonic fraternity. The date is correct, Leo X. having been elected Pope in 1513–14. It seems probable that some Spanish adventurers, in quest of silver or gold, lured by the report of the salt springs, and hoping to find there the object of their search, had wandered hither from Florida, which had been discovered and explored in 1502. One of the number dying here, his companions erected this simple memorial to mark the place of his burial."

Col. John Sprague and Ansil Judd built the grist-mill in 1830.

John Sprague and Anson Sweet, built the first two brick dwelling houses that were erected in the north part of the town, near the "Clapp Settlement." Capt. John Sprague, father to John and Anson, came from Milton, Saratoga Co., in 1798, and settled just out of Watervale, near the farm of the late Reuben Murray.

Wm. C. Fargo, father of Wm. C. of American Express Co., resided at Watervale at an early day; he had for a long time the contract for carrying the mail from Manlius via. Watervale, Fabius, Delphi and Pompey Center, three times a week. William G. Jerome and Chancellor Fargo for years rode the horse that carried the mail. North of Watervale prior to 1800, and about 1793, settled David Williams, Nathan Williams and another brother, all farmers, at what was called Williams' Corners. David Williams and wife at the age of 93 years, are still living in 1875.

HISTORY OF THE MILITARY TRACT.

[*Extract from the Journal of the Assembly of the State of New York, Dated March* 27, 1783.]

"A copy of certain resolutions of the Honorable the Senate, delivered by Mr. Duane, was read and in the words following, to-wit:

Whereas, Congress, by act of the 16th day of September, 1776, did resolve that the following quantity of Bounty

Lands should be given to officers, non-commissioned officers and privates, serving in the Continental Army, to-wit:

To a Colonel,	500	acres.
" Lieutenant Colonel,	450	"
" Major,	400	"
" Captain,	300	"
" Lieutenant,	200	"
" Ensign,	150	"
Each non-commissioned officer and private	100	"

And by an act of the 12th of August, 1780, did declare that a Major-General should have 1100 acres, and a Brigadier General 850.

"And, whereas, the Legislature of the State are willing not only to take upon themselves to discharge the said engagement of Congress, so far as it relates to the line of this State, but like as a gratuity to the said line, and to evince the just sense this legislature entertain of the patriotism and virtue of the troops of this State, serving in the army of the United States.

Resolved, Therefore, (if the Honorable the House of Assembly concur herein,) that besides the bounty of land so promised as aforesaid, this legislature will by law provide that the Maj. Generals and Brig. Generals now serving in the line of the army of the United States, and being citizens of this State, and the officers, non-commissioned officers and privates of the two regiments of infantry commanded by Colonels Van Schaick and Van Cortlandt, such officers of the regiment of artillery commanded by Col. Lamb, and of the corps of sappers and miners, as were, when they entered the services, inhabitants of this State, such of the non-commissioned officers and privates of the said last mentioned two corps as are credited to this State as part of the troops thereof, all officers designated by any acts of Congress subsequent to the 16th day of September, 1776, all officers recommended by Congress as persons whose depreciation on pay ought to be made good by this State, and who may hold military commissions in the line of the army at the close of the war, and the Reverend John Mason and John Gano, severally have granted to them the following quantities of land, to-wit:

To a Maj. General,	5500 acres.
" Brig. "	4250 "
" Col.	2500 "
" Lieut. Col	2250 "
" Major	2000 "
A Capt. and Regimental Surgeon, each	1500 "
Each of said Chaplains,	2000 "
Every Subaltern, and Surgeon's Mate,	1000 "
Every Non-Commissioned officer and private,	500 "

That the lands so to be granted as bounty from the United States, and as a gratuity from this State, shall be laid out in townships of six miles square; that each township shall be divided into 156 lots of 150 acres each, two lots whereof shall be reserved for the use of a minister or ministers of the gospel, and two lots for the use of a school or schools; that each person above described shall be entitled to as many such lots as his bounty and gratuity land as aforesaid, will admit of; that one-half of the lots each person shall be entitled to shall be improved at the rate of five acres for every hundred acres, within the term of five years after the grant, if such lots are sold by the original grantee, or within ten years from such grant, if the grantee shall retain the possession of such lots; and that the said bounty and gratuity lands be located in the district of this State reserved for the use of the troops by an act, entitled "An Act to prevent grants or locations of the lands therein mentioned; passed the 25th day of July, 1782.

Resolved, That His Excellency the Governor be requested to communicate these resolutions in such manner as he shall conceive most proper.

Resolved, That this house do concur with the Honorable, the Senate, in the last preceding resolutions.

Ordered, That Mr. J. Lawrence and Mr. Humfrey carry a copy of the preceding resolution of concurrence to the Honorable, the Senate."

Previous to the date of above extract, the Legislature of the State had by an act passed March 20, 1781, provided for the raising of two regiments for the defence of the State; and by an act passed March 23, 1782, had further provided for the raising ot troops to complete the line of this State in the service of the United States; and two regiments to be raised on *bounties* of lands, and for the *further defence of the frontiers of this State.* The land granted by these last mentioned acts being BOUNTY LANDS. Those granted, as provided for in extracts above made, being GRATUITY LANDS.

The original acts granting these lands, were subsequently, and from time to time, modified and amended, till finally, it was ordered by an act passed Feb. 28th, 1789, "That the commissioners of the land office shall be, and they are hereby authorized to direct the Surveyor-General to lay out as many townships in tracts of land set apart for such purpose as will contain land sufficient to satisfy the claims of all such persons who are or shall be entitled to grants of land by certain concurrent resolutions, and by the eleventh clause of the act entitled "An act for granting certain lands promised to be given as bounty lands, by the laws of this State, and for other purposes therein mentioned, passed the 11th day of May, 1784; which townships shall respectively contain 60,000 *acres of land*, and be laid out as nearly in squares as local circumstances will permit, and be numbered one progressively, to the last inclusive; and the *commissioners of the land office shall likewise designate every township by such name as they shall deem proper.*"

By same act, it was also ordered "that the surveyor general, as soon as may be, shall make a map of each of said townships, and each township shall be subdivided on such map into *one hundred lots*, as nearly square as may be, each lot to contain 600 acres, or as near that quantity as may be;

and the lots in every township shall be numbered from one to the last, inclusive in numerical order."

After such map had been made and deposited in the office of the Surveyor-General, and in the office of the Secretary of State, the commissioners were ordered "to advertise for six successive weeks, in one or more newspapers printed in each of the cities of New York and Albany, (whereof the newspaper published by the printer to this State, *if any such there be*, shall be one,) requiring all persons entitled to grants of bounty and gratuity lands, who had not already exhibited their claims, to exhibit the same to the commissioners on or before the first day of January, 1791."

By same act, it was further ordered, "that all persons to whom lands shall be granted by virtue of this act, and who are entitled thereto by any *act or resolution of Congress*, shall make an assignment of his, her or their proportion and claim of bounty and gratuity lands under any act or acts of Congress, to the Surveyor-General, for the use of the people of this State." This being done by the said parties, it was provided that for lands thus assigned, an equal number of acres were to be given by the State, and so far as possible in one tract, and under one patent, "provided the same does not exceed one-quarter of the quantity of a township."

It was also further provided that the lands to be granted by this act, be actually settled, for every six hundred acres which may be granted to any person or persons, within *seven years* from the first of January next, after the date of the patent by which such lands shall be granted; and on failure of such settlement, the unsettled lands shall revert to the people of this State." The letters patent were ordered "to be in such words and forms as the commissioners shall direct, and shall contain an *exception and reservation to the People of this State, of all the gold and silver mines*."

By an act passed April 6th, 1790, it was ordered "that the quantity of *fifty acres*, in one of the corners of the respective lots to be laid out in squares of 600 acres, shall be and are hereby subject to the payment of the sum of forty-eight (48) shillings to the Surveyor-General, as a compensation in full for his services and expenses in marking, numbering and surveying each of the said lots; and in every case where the said sum of 48 shillings, or any part thereof, shall remain unpaid for the term of two years next after the issuing of the respective patents, it shall and is hereby made the duty of the Surveyor-General to sell the same at public vendue; and the money arising from such sales, shall be applied in payment of expense of such survey." And in case a surplus of money was in hands of the Survey-General, after paying such expenses, it was to be applied to the payment of expense of laying out and making roads in the said tract."

By act of Feb. 28, 1789, six lots in each township were reserved and were to be assigned, "one for promoting the gospel, and a public school or schools, one other for promoting literature in this State, and the remaining four lots to satisfy the surplus share of commissioned officers not corresponding with the division of 600 acres, and to compensate such persons as may by chance draw any lot or lots, the greater part of which may be covered with water."

The act of 1780 provided "that whenever it appeared that persons applying for bounty or gratuity land, and had received from Congress the bounty promised by that body, or in case they failed to relinquish their claim to such lands, then the commissioners were to reserve for the use of the people of the State, one hundred acres in each lot to which such person was entitled; designating particularly in which part of such lot such reserved part was located. This gave rise to the term "*State's Hundred*" so frequently applied to sections of land on the Military Tract.

The Land Commissioners consisted of his Excellency, the Governor, or person administering the government of the State for the time being, the Lieutenant-Governor, the speaker of the Assembly, the Secretary of the State, the Attorney-General, the Treasurer and the Auditor thereof, the presence of three being necessary to form a quorum.

At a meeting of this Commission, held at the Secretary's office in the city of New York, on Saturday, the 3rd day of July, 1790, there were present,

His Excellency, GEO. CLINTON, Esq., *Governor.*
LEWIS A. SCOTT, Esq., *Secretary.*
GERARD BANCKER, Esq., *Treasurer.*
PETER T. CURTENIUS, Esq., *Auditor.*

The Secretary laid before the Board, maps of the surveys of twenty-five townships, made by the Surveyor-General—Simeon DeWitt. On each of which maps, the said townships respectively were sub-divided into one hundred lots, as nearly square as possible, each lot containing six hundred acres, whereupon the Board caused the townships and lots therein to be numbered according to the law and *designated them by the names they now bear*, to wit:—Lysander, Hannibal, Cato, Brutus, Camillus, Cicero, Manlius, POMPEY, etc.

The claims of persons entitled to land by virtue of law, were presented, and Lewis A. Scott and Robert Harpur were appointed to draw by ballot, (as had been provided by acts of Legislature) the lots of land to which they were entitled. It was resolved that for these lots of land thus drawn, Letters Patent should be made by the Secretary, signed by the Governor, to which should be affixed the seal of the State. The same to be delivered to the original proprietor, purchaser, attorney, heir, executor or administrator.

It was also resolved that the "States Hundred," when occurring in any lot, should be located in the South-east corner of said lot, and be laid out in a square, or as nearly so as may be. No resolution being passed or law providing for the location of the "Survey Fifty," it was variously located.

The balloting in Township No. 10, or Pompey, resulted as follows:

No. Lot	Patentee's Name and Rank.	No. Acres.	Date of Patent. 1790.	To Whom Delivered.
1	William Dunbar, pri	500	July 8	Isaac Brooks
2	Cornelius Woodmore, pri	600	" 6	Wm. J. Vredenburgh
3	Jas. Clinton, brig. gen.	600	" 3	Himself

No. Lot	Patentee's Name and Rank.	No Acres	Date of Patent.	To Whom Delivered.
4	Thos. Dixson, matross	600	July 7	Wm. DePeyster
5	Titus Underdunk, pri	500	" 8	Jas. B. Clark
6	Michael Leaster, pri	600	" 8	Jeremiah VanRensselaer
7	Jeremiah McGowen, pri	600	" 8	Robert Fowt
8	Nanning Vanderheyden, lieu	500	" 29	Gerrit VanSchoonhoven
9	John Wells, pri	600	" 7	Jeremiah VanRensselaer
10	Geo. Springsteen, pri	600	" 8	Wm. Henderson
11	Thos. Nellson, matross	600	" 9	John Quackenboss
12	Martin Waller, corp	600	" 8	Simon Veeder
13	John Snowden, pri	600	" 8	Patrick Shay
14	Abram Hyatt, lieut	600	" 7	Bernardus Swartwout
15	John List, pri	600	" 8	Major Connolly
16	Joseph Kitcham	600	" 8	Capt. Benj. Pelton
17	Stephen Powell, pri	600	" 8	Himself, by Order
18	Joseph Morgan, serg	600	" 8	Mr. Connolly
19	John Ramfier	600	" 8	Wm. Cockburn
20	Stephen McDougall, A-d-C maj.	500	" 3	John Lawrence
21	Mathew Colford, fifer	500	Sep. 13	J.B.Clark, per Mrs. Banker
22	John Chevalier, pri	600	July 8	Elisha Camp
23	Israel Coleman, corp	600	" 9	Ebenezer Clark
24	Elisha Harvey, lieu	600	" 9	Asa Spaulding
25	Reserved for Gospel, &c.			
26	John Brown, matross	600	" 8	Asa Spaulding
27	William Murray, pri	600	" 8	No Name
28	John Lambert, pri	600	" 8	Michael Connolly
29	Geo. Waggonman	600	" 8	John Quackenboss
30	Joseph Maroney, matross	600	" 9	David Quinton
31	Reserved for Literature			
32	Christopher Medler, matross	600	" 9	Philip Stout
33	Benjamin Kelso or Kely, pri	500	" 8	John Fisher
34	Philip Caldwell, pri	600	" 8	Jeremiah VanRensselaer
35	Nicnolas VanRensselaer, capt	600	" 9	Himself
36	Conrad Hilty, matross	600	" 9	Wm. J. Vredenburgh
37	Isaac Bogert, lieu	600	" 9	Michael Connolly
38	William Malcom, col	600	" 9	Himself
39	Henry Miller, pri	600	" 8	Cap. Cooper, for S'l Curray
40	Matthew Geeson, matross	500	" 9	Maj. Connolly
41	Christian Brandt, pri	600	" 8	Bartholomew Fisher
42	Cornelius T. Jansen, capt	600	" 9	Himself
43	Cornelius VanTassell, pri	500	Sep. 13	Augustus Sackett, Adm.
44	John Bateman, lieu	500	" 13	Elmer Cushing
45	Wm. Stevens, capt	600	July 9	Wm. Moore
46	Leonard Chapin, matross	600	" 9	Samuel Broome
47	Conradt Bush, matross	600	" 9	Gen. Clinton, for Bush
48	Wm. Stocker, pri	600	" 8	Maj. Connolly
49	John Neilson, fifer	500	" 9	Daniel Rodman
50	Chas. Kinney, pri	600	" 8	Ebenezer Clark
51	Abner Prior, surg'ns mate	400	" 9	John Mills, Esq.
52	Smith Wait, matross	600	" 6	No Name
53	Chas. Parsons, capt	600	" 9	David Noble, Esq.
54	Samuel Torrey, serg	600	Sep. 13	Lieut. Palmer Cady
55	John Uthest (al Han Jost Hess) p	600	July 8	Jeremiah VanRensselaer
56	John Dobson, pri	600	" 8	Jas. Hamilton
57	Fred Weisenfels, lieu. col. com	600	" 9	Himself
58	David Morrison, serg	500	" 8	Himself
59	Philip Burch, pri	600	" 8	Jer. VanRensselaer
60	Edward Wright, pri	600	" 8	" "

No. Lot	Patentee's Name and Rank.	No. Acres	Date of Patent.	To Whom Delivered.
61	Jonathan Briggs, pri	600	July 8	David Crosby, Jr.
62	Reserved for Gospel, &c.		--	
63	John Shaw	500	Sep.13	W. J. Vredenburgh
64	John Brown, matross	600	" 9	John Lawrence, Esq.
65	Hanjost Deymont	600	July 8	Peter Smith
66	Edward Curvin	500	" 8	Wm. Campbell
67	Reser'd for Gospel, Schools, &c.	--		
68	John Ryan	600	" 9	David Quinton
69	Christian Shantze, pri	600	" 8	Thos. Duncan
70	John Ackler, pri	600	" 3	Nicholas Fish
71	Thos. O'Bryan, Drummer	500	" 3	Mr. Connolly
72	Sam'l Townsend, paymaster,	500	Sep.13	Gen. Cortland and others
73	Reserved for Gospel, &c.		--	
74	Geo. Alkyser, cor	600	July 8	Isaac Stoutenburgh
75	Martin Rees, pri	600	" 8	Jas. Lowrey
76	Wm. F. Dougherty, maj	600	" 8	Lt. Col. VanDyck
77	John Lamb, col	600	" 7	Capt. Thompson
78	Samuel or Lurance Fletcher	500	Sep.13	W. J. Vredenburgh
79	Conradt Hyle	500	" 13	" "
80	Ashbel Dean, matross	500	July 9	No Name
81	John Tilliday, pri	600	" 8	Samuel Smith
82	John H. Devrance, pri	600	" 8	Jacob Clingman
83	John George Reamer	500	Sep.13	Rich. Edwards, Adm.
84	Samuel Lewis, lieut	600	Aug17	Himself
85	Daniel Loder, pri	600	July 7	Capt. Hagstaff
86	John Bogg, pri	600	" 8	John Quackenboss
87	Henry Elliott, pri	500	Aug24	Jacob Elliott
88	Othniel Preston, pri	600	July 8	Wm. Cockburn
89	John Thayer, matross	600	" 9	Jos. F. Sebor
90	Abijah Ward, pri	600	" 9	John Blanchard
91	John F. Hamtramck, capt	600	" 6	Michael Connolly
92	Thos. Willson, pri	500	" 8	Jno. Dill for Cor. Rose
93	Thos. Williams, lieu	600	" 9	John Bag
94	James Purdey, matross	500	" 9	Elias Newman
95	Jeremiah VanRensselaer, lieu	600	" 8	Himself
96	Reser'd for Gospel, Schools, &c.	--		
			1791.	
97	Hanyer Tewahangaraghkan, cap	600	Jan.29	Michael Connolly
98	Christopher Codwise, lieu	600	July 7	W. J. Vredenburgh
99	Barnardus Swartwout, ensign	600	" 7	Himself
100	James McCoy, pri	600	" 8	Elisha Camp

The following tabular statement shows the several owners of each lot of land in the township of Pompey, from 1790 to 1800, as recorded in County Clerk's Office, Onondago Co.

The Revolutionary soldier, Mr. Conrad Bush, relates "that at the time his regiment was discharged, so often had they been disappointed by the promises of Congress, that when their certificates were made out for their individual shares of land, a large majority had no confidence in the al lotment of these bounties, and many cried out, "who will give a pint of rum for mine? Who will give a blanket for mine?" A great many sold their shares for the merest trifle."—(Clark.)

It will be observed by this table, that the records confirm Mr. Bush's statement; at least circumstantially, for we see that soldiers sold or conveyed their titles, in many instances, more than once; and we are not sure that the consideration named in the deed was that actually received.

At so early a date as 1790, it was not possible for deeds to have been recorded, and no "searching the Records," could avail to assure purchasers as to the validity of their claims. Frauds were practiced in selling titles. In this town the soldiers themselves, did not, except in two or three instances, settle upon their lands.

It will be noticed that the dates of deeds and the time of actual settlement by the purchaser do not agree. The settlement dating anterior to the conveyance.

The reason for this, we have not been able to ascertain.

Date of Sale.	GRANTOR.	GRANTEE.	Acres.	Consd'n
		LOT ONE.		
July 8, 1790	State of New York	William Dunbar	500	Soldier
Sep. 12, 1791	William Dunbar	Isaac Brooks	500	25 pds.
Aug. 28, 1795	" "	Benjamin Wallace	500	60 pds.
" 31, 1796	Isaac Wells	" "	un. h'f	10s.
Sept. 5, 1797	Zebulon Mary	Zephaniah Platt	500	10s.
Nov. 17, 1798	Onon. Commissioners	Benj. Wallace	500	awarded
" 29, 1798	" "	Elkanah Watson	100	
		LOT TWO.		
July 6, 1790	State of New York	Cornelius Woodmore	600	Soldier
Feb'y 3, 1789	C. Woodmore	W. J. Vredenburgh	600	val. re'd
Mar. 18, 1796	W. J. Vredenburgh	Comfort Tyler	600	240 pds.
Oct'r 5, 1796	Comfort Tyler	Moses Carpenter	340	$1,250
Afterwards	" "	Jos. Bartholomew	200	
	" "	Stephen Angell	100	
	" "	Elijah Rust	20	
		LOT THREE.		
July 3, 1790	State of New York	Jos. Clinton, brig. gen.	600	Soldier
Mar. 27, 1792	Jos. Clinton	Moses DeWitt	600	600 pds.
	Subsequently divided among his heirs, who settled lot.			
		LOT FOUR.		
July 7, 1790	State of New York	Thomas Dixson	600	Soldier
		LOT FIVE.		
July 8, 1790	State of New York	Titus Underdunck	500	Soldier

Date of Sale.	GRANTOR.	GRANTEE.	Acres.	Consd'n
Mar. 3, 1796	Titus Underdunk	David Holbrook	450	150 pds.
Aug. 16, 1798	Com. Tyler, as Sheriff, sold D. Holbrook's int.	Benj. Grover	450	$6.00
“ 21, 1798	Benj. Grover	Nathaniel Weston	450	$15.00
Apr. 28, 1797	Surveyor-General	Jer. VanRensselaer	150	
	J. VanRensselaer	John Rogers	100	
	Jas. Caldwell	McGregor	100	
	Onon. Commissioners	Heirs of Rog. & McG	100	

LOT SIX.

Date of Sale.	GRANTOR.	GRANTEE.	Acres.	Consd'n
July 8, 1790	State of New York	Michael Leaster	600	Soldier
Nov. 25, 1790	Michael Leaster	Jer. VanRensselaer	600	20 pds.
Aug. 6, 1792	VanRensselaer	David Hibbard	600	200 pds.

LOT SEVEN.

Date of Sale.	GRANTOR.	GRANTEE.	Acres.	Consd'n
July 8, 1790	State of New York	Jer. McGowen	600	Soldier
Mar. 24, 1784	Jer. McGowen	Robert Towt	600	
June 20, 1793	Robt. Towt	Isaac Beekman	600	

LOT EIGHT.

Date of Sale.	GRANTOR.	GRANTEE.	Acres.	Consd'n
July 29, 1790	State of New York	Nan. Vanderheyden	500	Soldier

LOT NINE.

Date of Sale.	GRANTOR.	GRANTEE.	Acres.	Consd'n
July 7, 1790	State of New York	John Wells	600	Soldier
Dec. 11, 1783	John Wells	Edward Crompton	600	10 pds.
Feb. 26, 1785	“ “	Jos. Johnson	600	$20
Oct'r 7, 1790	Edward Crompton	Jer. VanRensselaer	600	20 pds.
Feb. 29, 1792	Jer. VanRensselaer & Abram TenEyck	Sam'l Messenger	300	120 pds.
“ 23, 1796	“ “	“ “	300	320 pds.
Mar. 1798	Abiathar Hull, as Sheriff, by virtue of exec'n ag'st Elias Jackson	Robert Jordan	600	
June 8, 1799	Onon. Commissioners	Sam'l Messenger	600	

LOT TEN.

Date of Sale.	GRANTOR.	GRANTEE.	Acres.	Consd'n
July 8, 1790	State of New York	Geo. Springsteen	600	Soldier
Nov. 8, 1783	Geo. Springsteen	Jonathan Owen	600	13 pds.
Apr. 4, 1789	“ “	W. J. Vredenburgh	600	
Nov. 3, 1791	Wm. Constable	Josiah O. Hoffman	600	
June 3, 1794	J. O. Hoffman	Wm. Cooper	600	
“ 3, 1794	Wm. Cooper	Thos. R. Gold	300	
“ 29, 1796	Thos. R. Gold	David Campbell	300	300 pds.
Mar. 31, 1801	Onon. Commissioners	Jonathan Owen	600	awarded

LOT ELEVEN.

Date of Sale.	GRANTOR.	GRANTEE.	Acres.	Consd'n
July 9, 1790	State of New York	Thos. Nellson	600	Soldier
Aug. 29, 1783	Thos. Nellson	Augustus Jones	600	13 pds.
Nov. 12, 1784	Augustus Jones	John Quackenboss, Garrett Patterson, Leonard Fishers	375	
Sep. 13, 1791	John Quackenboss	John Lawrence		

LOT TWELVE.

Date of Sale.	GRANTOR.	GRANTEE.	Acres.	Consd'n
July 8, 1790	State of New York	Martin Walker	600	Soldier
Apr. 5, 1785	Martin Walker	Lincoln Veeder		
Mar. 3, 1792	Lincoln Veeder	Jacob Judson	600	100 pds.
“ 29, 1792	Jacob Judson	David Tripp	100	5s.
May 30, 1792	“ “	Chas. Tripp	100	
Sep. 29, 1792	“ “	Elnathan Pickard	40	
Oct'r 8, 1794	Lewis Day	Asa Starkwather	100	72 pds.

Date of Sale.	GRANTOR.	GRANTEE.	Acres.	Consd'n
July 17, 1795	Jacob Judson	Sam'l Edwards	27	30 pds.
" 17, 1795	" "	Levi Jerome	244	195 pds.
Nov. 18, 1795	Jos. Annin	" "	156	90 pds.
		LOT THIRTEEN.		
July 8, 1790	State of New York	John Snowden	600	Soldier
	Jno. Snowden probably	Patrick Shay	600	
Aug. 24, 1790	Patrick Shay	W. J. Vredenburgh	600	30 pds.
May 30, 1797	W. J. Vredenburgh	Wm. Haskins	600	300 pds.
Apr. 4, 1798	Wm. Haskins	Reuben Hustis	150	450 pds.
		LOT FOURTEEN.		
July 7, 1790	State of New York	Abram Hyatt	600	Soldier
	Abram Hyatt probably	W. J. Vredenburgh		
May 16, 1795	W. J. Vredenburgh	Caleb Northrup	50	37 pds.
		LOT FIFTEEN.		
July 8, 1790	State of New York	John List	600	Soldier
" 29, 1789	John List	Isaac Bogert	600	12 pds.
Sept. 4, 1784	" "	Henry Plature	600	12 pds.
Aug. 14, 1792	Isaac Bogert	Jeremiah Gold	600	480 pds.
		LOT SIXTEEN.		
July 8, 1790	State of New York	Joseph Kitchum	600	Soldier
Aug. 16, 1791	Joseph Kitchum	Benj. Pelton	600	35 pds.
		LOT SEVENTEEN.		
July 8, 1790	State of New York	Stephen Powell	600	Soldier
Sep. 15, 1795	Stephen Powell	John Sprague	600	100 pds.
Mar. 1, 1796	John Sprague	Jno. D. Dickinson, Elijah Jones	600	$480
		LOT EIGHTEEN.		
July 8, 1790	State of New York	Joseph Morgan	600	Soldier
" 6, 1791	Joseph Morgan	Theodorous Fowler	600	40 pds.
Oct'r 4, 1791	Theo. Fowler	Nicholas Fish	600	
Sep. 10, 1800	Onon. Commissioners	" "	600	awarded
		LOT NINETEEN.		
July 8, 1790	State of New York	John Ransier	600	Soldier
Nov. 17, 1783	John Ransier	Thos. Tillotson	600	5 pds.&c
Aug. 18, 1790	" "	Isaac Davis	500	
Jan. 13, 1796	" "	Elkanah Watson	600	$105
Apr. 10, 1794	Thos. Tillotson	J. W. Gold	600	
Jan. 22, 1797	Elkanah Watson	" "	600	
May 23, 1800	Onon. Commissioners	" "	600	awarded
		LOT TWENTY.		
July 3, 1790	State of New York	Stephen McDougall	500	Soldier
Mar. 3, 1797	Robt. McClellen, claiming patent from State	Alex. Ellice	600	
		LOT TWENTY-ONE.		
Sep. 13, 1790	State of New York	Matthew Colford	500	Soldier
	Colford's heirs	Jas. B. Clark, Joshua Briggs	500	
Feb. 2, 1796	Joshua Briggs	Chas. Roys	225	
" 22, 1796	" "	Sam'l Messenger, Sam'l Edwards	225	224 pds.
		LOT TWENTY-TWO.		
July 8, 1790	State of New York	John Chevalier	600	Soldier
Feb. 8, 1785	John Chevalier	Elisha Camp	600	

Date of Sale.	GRANTOR.	GRANTEE.	Acres.	Consd'n
Apr. 15, 1791	Elisha Camp	Wm. Constable	600	
Nov. 3, 1791	Wm. Constable	Josiah O. Hoffman	600	

LOT TWENTY-THREE.

Date of Sale.	GRANTOR.	GRANTEE.	Acres.	Consd'n
July 9, 1790	State of New York	Israel Coleman	600	Soldier
Sep. 17, 1784	Israel Coleman	Rob't Shutes	300	30 pds.
Feb. 6, 1797	“ “	“ “	300	150 pds.
May 6, 1790	“ “	Ebenezer Clark	600	
“ 12, 1798	Ebenezer Clark	Enos Peck	600	525 pds.
Dec. 18, 1798	Onon. Commissioners	Ebenezer Clark	600	awarded

LOT TWENTY-FOUR.

Date of Sale.	GRANTOR.	GRANTEE.	Acres.	Consd'n
July 9, 1790	State of New York	Elisha Harvey	600	Soldier
Aug. 10, 1793	Elisha Harvey	Ebenezer Gay	600	45 pds.
“ 10, 1793	“ “	Asaph Drake	100	10s.
May 2, 1795	“ “	Joseph Hurst	180	
Dec. 6, 1800	Onon. Commissioners	Ebenezer Gay	600	awarded

LOT TWENTY-FIVE.

Reserved for Gospel.

LOT TWENTY-SIX.

Date of Sale.	GRANTOR.	GRANTEE.	Acres.	Consd'n
July 6, 1790	State of New York	John Brown	600	Soldier
“ 18, 1792	Asa Spaulding, Att'y for John Brown	Joseph Purdy	600	
Jan. 13, 1798	John Brown, person'y	Samuel Cobb	600	$600
July 18, 1792	Joseph Purdy	Ephriam Willard	600	
Sept. 8, 1792	Ephriam Willard	Samuel Beebee		
	Sam'l Beebee	Josiah Bigelow		
Mar. 1, 1802	Onon. Commissioners	Sam'l Beebee	600	awarded

LOT TWENTY-SEVEN.

Date of Sale.	GRANTOR.	GRANTEE.	Acres.	Consd'n
July 8, 1790	State of New York	Wm. Murray	600	Soldier
Jan'y 4, 1792	Wm. Murray	John Robinson		
Oct. 28, 1795	“ “	Daniel Hall	600	64 pds.
“ 28, 1795	“ “	Jeremiah Schuyler		
		John J. Cuyler	600	80 pds.
Jan'y 5, 1792	Daniel Hall	John Robinson	300	10 pds.
“ 6, 1792	John Robinson	Jer. VanRensselaer	600	53 pds.
Dec. 10, 1794	Asa Danforth	Richard Hiscock	100	130 pds.
June 10, 1795	“ “	Aaron Bellows	100	140 pds.

LOT TWENTY-EIGHT.

Date of Sale.	GRANTOR.	GRANTEE.	Acres.	Consd'n
July 8, 1790	State of New York	John Lambert	600	Soldier
Nov. 26, 1796	John Lambert	Nathan Williams	600	$500
Oct'r 3, 1797	Nathan Williams			

LOT TWENTY-NINE.

Date of Sale.	GRANTOR.	GRANTEE.	Acres.	Consd'n
July 8, 1790	State of New York	Geo. Waggonman	600	Soldier
Nov. 7, 1789	Geo. Waggonman	John Quackenboss	600	
April 1, 1792	“ “	Michael O'Brien	600	40 pds.
July 27, 1790	John Quackenboss	Henry TenBrooks	600	
	Joseph Annin	Levi Jerome	146	90 pds.

LOT THIRTY.

Date of Sale.	GRANTOR.	GRANTEE.	Acres.	Consd'n
July 9, 1790	State of New York	Joseph Maroney	600	Soldier
Feb'y 1, 1784	Joseph Maroney	Peter Nestell	600	8 pds.
Jan'y 2, 1793	Peter Nestell	Moses Phillips	600	
May 1, 1793	Moses Phillips	John Grant	600	100 pds.
June 3, 1791	David Quinlan, as assignee of J. Maroney	Wm. Dur	600	

LOT THIRTY-ONE.

Date of Sale.	GRANTOR.	GRANTEE.	Acres.	Consd'n
	Reser'd for Gospel, &c.			

LOT THIRTY-TWO.

Date of Sale.	GRANTOR.	GRANTEE.	Acres.	Consd'n
July 9, 1790	State of New York	Christopher Medler	600	Soldier
Aug. 10, 1793	Christopher Medler	Buckhart Livingston	600	40 pds.
Oct'r 1, 1794	B. Livingston	Thos. Cooper	600	
Jan. 22, 1796	Thos. Cooper	Geo. D. Wickham	600	
	Onon. Commissioners	Heirs of C. Medler	600	

LOT THIRTY-THREE.

Date of Sale.	GRANTOR.	GRANTEE.	Acres.	Consd'n
July 8, 1790	State of New York	Benjamin Kelso	500	Soldier
Feb. 27. 1784	Benj. Kelso	Geo. Bartholomew, John Fisher	500	
May 9, 1793	" "	Joshua Briggs	500	
Mar. 21, 1794	" "	Ephriam Marwin, Phil. VanCortland	500	$300.00
May 6, 1795	" "	Gideon Ball	500	80 pds.
" 6, 1796	Daniel Kelso, broth & heir of Benj. Kelso	Robert Smith	500	
Mar. 15, 1797	Daniel Kelso	Evander Childs, Luke Owens	500	40 pds.
Dec. 1794	Isaac Smith & others	Joshua Fisher	500	
July 22, 1794	Francis Warner	Chas. Tripp	100	$100
	Onon. Commissioners	John Fisher	333⅓	
		Eleanore Clark, Miron Clark	166⅔	

LOT THIRTY-FOUR.

Date of Sale.	GRANTOR.	GRANTEE.	Acres.	Consd'n
July 8, 1790	State of New York	Philip Cadwell	600	Soldier
Aug. 8, 1783	Philip Cadwell	Joseph Cadwell	600	
Jan. 11, 1796	" "	Geo. Pearson	600	400 pds.
May 19, 1796	Geo. Pearson	Joseph Cadwell	600	

LOT THIRTY-FIVE.

Date of Sale.	GRANTOR.	GRANTEE.	Acres.	Consd'n
July 9, 1790	State of New York	N. VanRensselaer	600	Soldier
Oct'r 4, 1794	Jeremiah Gold	Jabez Hull	a part	$400
May 30, 1796	Jabez Hull	Jas. Low	133	128 pds.
May 30, 1796	" "	Noah Hoyt	50	50 pds.

LOT THIRTY-SIX.

Date of Sale.	GRANTOR.	GRANTEE.	Acres.	Consd'n
July 9, 1790	State of New York	Conrad Hilty	600	Soldier
" 8, 1792	Conrad Hilty	Thos. Ruggles	600	110 pds.

LOT THIRTY-SEVEN.

Date of Sale.	GRANTOR.	GRANTEE.	Acres.	Consd'n
July 9, 1790	State of New York	Isaac Bogart	600	Soldier
Aug. 14, 1792	Isaac Bogart	Jeremiah Gold	600	480 pds.
May 4, 1795	Jeremiah Gold	I. Thos. Coe	600	360 pds.

LOT THIRTY-EIGHT.

Date of Sale.	GRANTOR.	GRANTEE.	Acres.	Consd'n
July 9, 1790	State of New York	Wm. Malcome	600	Soldier

LOT THIRTY-NINE.

Date of Sale.	GRANTOR.	GRANTEE.	Acres.	Consd'n
July 8, 1790	State of New York	Henry Miller	600	Soldier
June 21, 1783	Henry Miller	Samuel Cary	600	10 pds.
Nov. 4, 1873	" "	Edward Crampton	600	
Mar. 10, 1784	Edward Crampton	Nathaniel Platt	600	10 pds.

LOT FORTY.

Date of Sale.	GRANTOR.	GRANTEE.	Acres.	Consd'n
July 9, 1790	State of New York	Matthew Geeson	500	Soldier
	Matthew Geeson	Nehemiah Rockwell	500	10 pds.

Date of Sale.	GRANTOR.	GRANTEE.	Acres.	Consd'n.
Nov'r 2, 1790	Nehe. Rockwell	Mordecai Hall	500	43 pds.
July 2, 1791	Mordecai Hall	Theodosius Fowler	500	
Oct'r 4, 1792	Theo. Fowler	Nicholas Fish	500	
Mar. 3, 1796	Nicholas Fish	Abram Smith Manoah Pratt	500	300 pds.

LOT FORTY-ONE.

Date of Sale.	GRANTOR.	GRANTEE.	Acres.	Consd'n.
July 8, 1790	State of New York	Christian Brandt	600	Soldier
Sep'r 6, 1783	Christian Brandt	Bernard Bond	600	
Feb. 14, 1784	" "	G. B. & J. Fisher	600	
Aug. 30, 1784	" "	Isaac Smith	600	2 pds.
Apr. 27, 1795	Bernard Bond	Ithel Battle	600	40 pds.
Sep'r 2, 1795	Isaac Smith	John Fisher	600	
Dec'r 1, 1794	James Saidler & Isaac R. Smith	Robert Petit	600	
	Onon. Commissioners	John Fisher	600	awarded

LOT FORTY-TWO.

Date of Sale.	GRANTOR.	GRANTEE.	Acres.	Consd'n.
July 9, 1790	State of New York	Cornelius T. Jansen	600	Soldier
" 3, 1796	C. T. Jansen	David Green	300	180 pds.

LOT FORTY-THREE.

Date of Sale.	GRANTOR.	GRANTEE.	Acres.	Consd'n.
Sep. 13, 1790	State of New York	Cornelius VanTassell	500	Soldier
June 9, 1792	C. VanTassell's heirs	John Hagaman	500	300 pds.
Nov'r 4, 1799	Onon. Commissioners	Robert Troup	500	awarded

LOT FORTY-FOUR.

Date of Sale.	GRANTOR.	GRANTEE.	Acres.	Consd'n.
Sep. 13, 1790	State of New York	John Bateman	500	Soldier
	John Bateman's Att'y	John Jacob Astor Peter Smith	500	150 pds.

LOT FORTY-FIVE.

Date of Sale.	GRANTOR.	GRANTEE.	Acres.	Consd'n.
July 9, 1790	State of New York	Wm. Stevens	600	Soldier
Dec. 30, 1794	Wm. Stevens	Silas Holbrook Abiather Hull	600	360 pds.
Dec. 26, 1795	Silas Holbrook	Abiather Hull	300	160 pds.
July 22, 1796	Abiather Hull	Ambros Hull	100	
Dec. 8, 1797	" "	Betsey Leggett	500	$1100.00

LOT FORTY-SIX.

Date of Sale.	GRANTOR.	GRANTEE.	Acres.	Consd'n.
July 9, 1790	State of New York	Leonard Chapin	600	Soldier
" 7, 1784	Leonard Chapin	Samuel Broome	600	6 pds.
Jan'y 5, 1793	Samuel Broome	John Patterson W. J. Vredenburgh	600	

LOT FORTY-SEVEN.

Date of Sale.	GRANTOR.	GRANTEE.	Acres.	Consd'n.
July 9, 1790	State of New York	Conradt Bush	600	Soldier
Nov'r 1796	Conradt Bush	Elias Jackson	600	450 pds.

LOT FORTY-EIGHT.

Date of Sale.	GRANTOR.	GRANTEE.	Acres.	Consd'n.
July 8, 1790	State of New York	Wm. Stocker	600	Soldier
Sep'r 2, 1779	Wm. Stocker	Wm. Haskins	600	14 pds.
Mar. 23, 1792	Ebenezer Lowell	Jacob Hoar	50	10 pds.
" 1, 1796	Wm. Haskins	Jos. Griffins	100	$100.00

LOT FORTY-NINE.

Date of Sale.	GRANTOR.	GRANTEE.	Acres.	Consd'n.
July 9, 1790	State of New York	John Neilson	500	Soldier
Aug. 4, 1791	John Nielson	Dudley Woodbridge	500	20 pds.
Feb'y 1, 1793	Dudley Woodbridge	Moses DeWitt		$337.50

LOT FIFTY.

Date of Sale.	GRANTOR.	GRANTEE.	Acres.	Consd'n.
July 8, 1790	State of New York	Chas. Kinney	600	Soldier
Aug. 28, 1794	Chas. Kinney	Ebenezer Clark	600	Soldier
	Onon. Commissioners	" "	600	awarded

LOT FIFTY-ONE.

Date of Sale.	GRANTOR.	GRANTEE.	Acres.	Consd'n
July 9, 1790	State of New York	Abner Prior	400	Soldier
Oct'r 12, 1791	Abner Prior	Jacob Hallett	400	115 pds.
May 30, 1793	Jacob Hallett	Trueworthy Cook	400	$300
May 1, 1796	" "	Nicholas Low	200	

LOT FIFTY-TWO.

Date of Sale.	GRANTOR.	GRANTEE.	Acres.	Consd'n
July 6, 1790	State of New York	Smith Wait	600	Soldier
Mar. 14, 1784	Smith Wait	William Bell	600	
Apr. 16, 1791	" "	Isaac Miller	600	20 pds.
Oct'r 5, 1791	Isaac Miller	Frances M. Wickham	600	75 pds.
Apr. 18, 1795	Jonathan Bunnell	Geo. D. Wickham	600	100 pds.
June 9, 1796	William Bell	Walter Wood		
Aug. 5, 1796	Walter Wood	Deodatus Clark	600	709 pds.
Mar. 21, 1800	Onon. Commissioners	" "	600	awarded

LOT FIFTY-THREE.

Date of Sale.	GRANTOR.	GRANTEE.	Acres.	Consd'n
July 9, 1790	State of New York	Chas. Parsons	600	Soldier
May 1, 1792	Chas. Parson	Josiah Holbrook, Jr.	300	20 pds.
May 23, 1794	Josiah Holbrook	Baruch Holbrook	75	
Nov. 4, 1799	Onon. Commissioners	Robt. Troup	50	awarded

LOT FIFTY-FOUR.

Date of Sale.	GRANTOR.	GRANTEE.	Acres.	Consd'n
Sep. 13, 1790	State of New York	Samuel Torry	600	Soldier
Mar. 21, 1791	Samuel Torry	Elisha Gridley	600	
Oct'r 24, 1792	Palmer Cade Elisha Gridley	Ozias Burr	600	240 pds.
Nov. 10, 1792	Ozias Burr	William Cook	100	40 pds.
June 21, 1793	" "	David Allen	140	56 pds.
Oct'r 5, 1792	Nathaniel Meghell	" "	54	30 pds.
" 1, 1796	Ozias Burr	Nathaniel Meghill	160	

LOT FIFTY-FIVE.

Date of Sale.	GRANTOR.	GRANTEE.	Acres.	Consd'n
July 8, 1790	State of New York	John Uthest	600	Soldier
Jan. 15, 1791	Jno. Uthest alias Hass	Jer. VanRensselaer	600	5 shil.
Apr. 12, 1792	Jer. Van Rensselaer	Eleanor Bassitt	600	5 shil.
May 13, 1795	Eleanor Bassett	Jas. S. Tripp	600	

LOT FIFTY-SIX.

Date of Sale.	GRANTOR.	GRANTEE.	Acres.	Consd'n
July 8, 1791	State of New York	John Dobson	600	Soldier
" 2, 1796	John Dobson	Barney Connolly	600	250 pds.
Feb. 17, 1791	" "	Henry A. Tanner	600	10 pds.
Nov. 28, 1798	Onon. Commissioners	Henry A. Townsend	600	awarded
	" "	John Tayler	50	"

LOT FIFTY-SEVEN.

Date of Sale.	GRANTOR.	GRANTEE.	Acres.	Consd'n
July 9, 1790	State of New York	Fred Weisemfels	600	Soldier
" 11, 1789	Fred. Weisemfels	Richard Platt	600	10 pds.
" 2, 1795	" "	Jer. VanRensselaer	600	
May 3, 1795	Richard Platt	Sam'l Meradeth	600	
Dec. 6, 1800	Onon. Commissioners	" "	600	awarded

LOT FIFTY-EIGHT.

Date of Sale.	GRANTOR.	GRANTEE.	Acres.	Consd'n
July 8, 1790	State of New York	David Morrison	500	Soldier
Dec. 29, 1791	David Morrison	Simeon VanAntwerp	500	
	Robert McClellan	John Rogers	100	
Jan. 22, 1796	Jas .Cadwell	Call McGregor	100	
	Onon. Commissioners	John Rogers	100	awarded

LOT FIFTY-NINE.

Date of Sale.	GRANTOR.	GRANTEE.	Acres.	Consd'n
July 8, 1790	State of New York	Philip Burch	600	Soldier

Date of Sale.	GRANTOR.	GRANTEE.	Acres.	Consd'n
Dec. 15, 1783	Philip Burch	Edward Crampton	600	10 pds.
Oct. 2, 1790	Edward Crampton	Jer. VanRensselaer	600	20 pds.
Apr. 2, 1795	Jonas Stansbury	Isaac Nicoll Walter D. Nicoll	300	700 pds.
Nov. 2, 1796	Abram Ten Eyck	Joseph Rodes	300	----
Mar. 19, 1798	Asa Danforth	John Carpenter	600	----
Dec. 24, 1800	Onon. Commissioners	Daniel Pixley	300	awarded
" 24, 1800	" "	Abram TenEyck	300	"

LOT SIXTY.

Date of Sale.	GRANTOR.	GRANTEE.	Acres.	Consd'n
July 8, 1790	State of New York	Edward Wright	600	Soldier
May 30, 1794	Edward Wright	Eben. Willoughby ✓ Walter Wood	600	50 pds.
Mar. 3, 1789	" "	Jos. Shelden		
Nov. 4, 1794	Walter Wood	Abiather Hull	600	480 pds.
May 20, 1795	Jas. Shelden	Elkanah Watson	550	100 pds.
" 5, 1797	Abiather Hall	Walter Wood		
Jan. 10, 1798	Elkanah Watson	Asa Smith		
Dec. 23, 1800	Onon. Commissioners	John Tayler	50	awarded

LOT SIXTY-ONE.

Date of Sale.	GRANTOR.	GRANTEE.	Acres.	Consd'n
July 8, 1790	State of New York	Jonathan Briggs	600	Soldier
Feb'y 6, 1792	Timothy Titus & Wm. W. Morris assignees of David Crosby, Att'y of Jonathan Briggs	John Carpenter		

LOT SIXTY-TWO.

Date of Sale.	GRANTOR.	GRANTEE.	Acres.	Consd'n
	Reser'd for Gospel, &c.			
Aug. 12, 1800	Onon. Commissioners	Theo. V. W. Graham	50	awarded

LOT SIXTY-THREE.

Date of Sale.	GRANTOR.	GRANTEE.	Acres.	Consd'n
Sep. 12, 1790	State of New York	John Shaw	500	Soldier

LOT SIXTY-FOUR.

Date of Sale.	GRANTOR.	GRANTEE.	Acres.	Consd'n
Sept. 9, 1790	State of New York	John Brown	600	Soldier
Jan. 30, 1797	John Brown	Sam'l Cobb, Jr.	600	$100
Apr. 19, 1784	" "	Alex. McDougall		3 pds. 4s.
July 10, 1792	Ex. Alex. McDougall	John Lawrence	600	----
Dec. 27, 1796	Ebenezer Butler, Jr	Benj. Butler	50¼	30 pds.
Feb. 26, 1798	" "	Ezra Hart	100	$100

LOT SIXTY-FIVE.

Date of Sale.	GRANTOR.	GRANTEE.	Acres.	Consd'n
Sept. 9, 1790	State of New York	Hanjost Deymont	600	Soldier
Nov. 1, 1793	Deymont's Widow	Ezra Hull	600	50 pds.
Mar. 3, 1795	Ezra Hull	Ebenezer Butler, Jr.	600	40 pds.
Oct. 1798	Ebenezer Butler, Jr	Nathan Davis	100	$100
" 4, 1798	" "	John Willard	2	$129

LOT SIXTY-SIX.

Date of Sale.	GRANTOR.	GRANTEE.	Acres.	Consd'n
July 8, 1790	State of New York	Edwin Carvin	500	Soldier
May 20, 1792	Edwin Carvin	Eli. Kellogg, Jr.	500	25 pds.
Nov. 24, 1792	Eliphalet Kellogg, Jr.	Jas. B. Clark	500	----
Dec. 9, 1793	Edwin Carvin	Dan'l Delivan	500	2 pds.
Oct. 14, 1794	Daniel DeSavin	Philip VanCourtland	500	25 pds.
Mar. 2, 1796	Wm. Gilliland	John D. Dickinson	100	----
Apr. 13, 1795	Augustus Sackett	Jos. B. Clark		
May 6, 1796	Jos. B. Clark	Sam'l Sackett		
------- 1799	Onon. Commissioners	Philip VanCourtland	350	awarded
------- 1799	" "	Theo. V. W. Graham	50	"
------- 1799	" "	John D. Dickinson	100	"

LOT SIXTY-SEVEN.

Date of Sale	GRANTOR.	GRANTEE.	Acres.	Consd'n
	Reser'd for Gospel, &c.			

LOT SIXTY-EIGHT.

Date of Sale	GRANTOR.	GRANTEE.	Acres.	Consd'n
July 9, 1790	State of New York	John Ryan	600	Soldier
Mar. 3, 1791	John Ryan	Daniel Quinton	600	
July 14, 1783	" "	Anthony Maxwell	600	11 pds.
June 3, 1792	Daniel Quinton	Wm. Duer	600	
Nov. 15, 1792	Anthony Maxwell	Robert Affleek	600	
" 2, 1795	John Ryan	Jer. Schuyler John Cuyler	600	
" 12, 1794	Robert Affleek	Sam'l Beebee		
Jan. 3, 1795	C. Olbrath	Jas. Greenleaf	600	140 pds.
Dec. 14, 1799	Onon. Commissioners	Sam'l Beebee	600	awarded

LOT SIXTY-NINE.

Date of Sale	GRANTOR.	GRANTEE.	Acres.	Consd'n
July 8, 1790	State of New York	Christian Shantze	600	Soldier
Apr. 5, 1792	Christian Shantze	Wm. W. Gale		
Dec. 6, 1799	Onon. Commissioners	Geo. D. Wickham	600	awarded

LOT SEVENTY.

Date of Sale	GRANTOR.	GRANTEE.	Acres.	Consd'n
July 3, 1790	State of New York	John Ackler	600	Soldier
Aug. 24, 1784	John Ackler	Abram Freer	600	11 pds.
Oct. 24, 1790	Nicholas Fish	Jos. McCluer	600	
Sept. 20, 1792	Jos. McCluer	John Lamb	200	$200
Sept. 20, 1792	" "	Sam'l Draper	200	$200

LOT SEVENTY-ONE.

Date of Sale	GRANTOR.	GRANTEE.	Acres.	Consd'n
July 3, 1790	State of New York	Thos. O'Bryan	600	Soldier
Jan. 20, 1784	Thos. O'Bryan	Alex. McDougall	500	3 pds.
Dec. 20, 1796	" "	Jos. C. Yates John Prince	500	
July 1797	Jer. Van Rensselaer	John Rogers	100	
1799	Onon. Commissioners	John Taylor	50	awarded
1799	" "	Heirs of John Rogers	100	"

LOT SEVENTY-TWO.

Date of Sale	GRANTOR.	GRANTEE.	Acres.	Consd'n
Sept. 13, 1790	State of New York	Sam'l Townsend	500	Soldier
Dec. 10, 1790	Samuel Townsend	Elijah Hunter	500	60 pds.
Nov. 20, 1791	Elijah Hunter	Phil. VanCortland	500	
	Onon. Commissioners	" "	350	
	" "	Theo. V. W. Graham	100	awarded

LOT SEVENTY-THREE.

Date of Sale	GRANTOR.	GRANTEE.	Acres.	Consd'n
	Reser'd for Gospel, &c.			

LOT SEVENTY-FOUR.

Date of Sale	GRANTOR.	GRANTEE.	Acres.	Consd'n
July 8, 1790	State of New York	Geo. Alkyser	600	Soldier
May 5, 1793	Geo. Alkyser	Wm. Radcliff, Jr.	600	
	William Radcliff, Jr	Isaac Hall	300	
	Onon. Commissioners	Wm. Radcliff	H'f	awarded
	" "	Isaac Hall	H'f	"

LOT SEVENTY-FIVE.

Date of Sale	GRANTOR.	GRANTEE.	Acres.	Consd'n
July 8, 1790	State of New York	Martin Rees	600	Soldier
Sept. 10, 1783	Martin Rees	James Luvrey	600	10 Span.
Mar. 23, 1793	Cornelius Glen	Jos. Anning	600	

LOT SEVENTY-SIX.

Date of Sale	GRANTOR.	GRANTEE.	Acres.	Consd'n
July 8, 1790	State of New York	Wm. F. Dougherty	600	Major
Mar. 8, 1789	Wm. F. Dougherty	Robt. Dunlop	600	10 pds.
Feb. 19, 1790	Mathew Visscher	Albelower Stepentine	600	25 pds.

LOT SEVENTY-SEVEN.

Date of Sale.	GRANTOR.	GRANTEE.	Acres.	Consd'n
July 7, 1790	State of New York	John Lamb	600	Colonel.

LOT SEVENTY-EIGHT.

Date of Sale.	GRANTOR.	GRANTEE.	Acres.	Consd'n
Sept. 13, 1790	State of New York	Sam'l Fletcher	500	Major
	Heirs of Fletcher	W. J. Vredenburgh	500	$650
Feb. 8, 1796	Peter Elmendorf	Reuben Pixley	100	$400
Dec. 22, 1795	Wm. J. Vredenburgh	Jos. B. Clark	500	----
	Jos. B. Clark	Reuben Pixley	450	----
	Onon. Commissioners	Th. VanW. Graham	50	awarded
	" "	Peter Elmendorf	100	"

LOT SEVENTY-NINE.

Date of Sale.	GRANTOR.	GRANTEE.	Acres.	Consd'n
Sept. 13, 1790	State of New York	Conradt Hyle	500	Soldier
May 15, 1793	Conradt Hyle	Sam'l Hackett	500	$37
" 10, 1796	Samuel Hackett	Reuben Pixley	50	----
June 1, 1797	" "	Jas. B. Clark	200	----
July 1797	Jer. Van Rensselaer	John Rogers	100	----
June 21, 1796	Jas. Cadwell	Call McGregor	100	----
	Onon. Commissioners	Heirs of John Rogers	100	awarded

LOT EIGHTY.

Date of Sale.	GRANTOR.	GRANTEE.	Acres.	Consd'n
July 9, 1790	State of New York	Ashbel Dean	500	Soldier
Apr. 20, 1790	Ashbel Dean	Stephen Thorn	500	40 pds.
Mar. 14, 1790	Stephen Thorn	Charles Roe	500	200 pds.
Feb. 16, 1792	Timothy Benedict	Phil. VanCortland	500	45 pds.
1800	Onon. Commissioners	Peter E. Elmendorf	50	awarded

LOT EIGHTY-ONE.

Date of Sale.	GRANTOR.	GRANTEE.	Acres.	Consd'n
July 8, 1790	State of New York	John Tillday	600	Soldier
Oct. 14, 1789	John Tillday	Sam'l Smith	600	$3.
July 5, 1791	Samuel Smith	Chas. Platt Rogers	600	25 pds.

LOT EIGHTY-TWO.

Date of Sale.	GRANTOR.	GRANTEE.	Acres.	Consd'n
July 8, 1790	State of New York	John H. Deverance	600	Soldier
Jan. 10, 1799	John H. Deverance	Joshua Briggs	600	67 pds.
Apr. 10, 1793	John H. Deverance	Jacob Clingman	600	45 pds.
May 3, 1793	Jacob Clingman	Jos. B. Clark	600	----
Feb. 22,	Hugh Sackey			
	Joshua Briggs	D. & Smith Hibbard	450	495 pds.
Nov. 6, 1799	Onon. Commissioners	Th. VanW. Graham	50	awarded

LOT EIGHTY-THREE.

Date of Sale.	GRANTOR.	GRANTEE.	Acres.	Consd'n
Sept. 13, 1790	State of New York	John Geo. Reamer	500	Soldier
July 8, 1791	Elkanah Watson	Isaac Carpenter	500	47 pds.
June 5, 1797	Jer. Van Rensselaer	Elkanah Watson	100	----
" 10, 1798	Elkanah Watson	Asa Smith		
	Onon. Commissioners	Elkanah Watson	100	awarded

LOT EIGHTY-FOUR.

Date of Sale.	GRANTOR.	GRANTEE.	Acres.	Consd'n
Aug. 17, 1790	State of New York	Samuel Lewis	600	Soldier
July 4, 1792	Somuel Lewis	John Taylor	600	----
Nov. 1, 1791	Daniel Gould	Johathan Wood	600	300 pds.

LOT EIGHTY-FIVE.

Date of Sale.	GRANTOR.	GRANTEE.	Acres.	Consd'n
July 7, 1790	State of New York	Daniel Loder	600	Soldier
Dec. 10, 1791	Daniei Loder	Samuel Palmer	600	40 pds.

LOT EIGHTY-SIX.

Date of Sale.	GRANTOR.	GRANTEE.	Acres.	Consd'n
July 8, 1790	State of New York	John Boggs		
Jan. 17, 1784	John Boggs	Alex. McDougal		

Date of Sale.	GRANTOR.	GRANTEE.	Acres.	Consd'n
July 7, 1790	John Quackenboss	Henry TenBrook	600	
Mar. 1, 1802	Onon. Commissioners	" "	600	awarded

LOT EIGHTY-SEVEN.

Date of Sale.	GRANTOR.	GRANTEE.	Acres.	Consd'n
July 8, 1790	State of New York	Henry Elliott	500	Soldier
April 2, 1792	H. Elliott's heirs	Jasper Cropsey		
	" "	Augustus Sackett Jos. B. Clark	500	
	Onon. Commissioners	Heirs of H. Elliott Wm. Thompson		

LOT EIGHTY-EIGHT.

Date of Sale.	GRANTOR.	GRANTEE.	Acres.	Consd'n
July 8, 1790	State of New York	Othniel Preston	600	Soldier

LOT EIGHTY-NINE.

Date of Sale.	GRANTOR.	GRANTEE.	Acres.	Consd'n
July 9, 1790	State of New York	John Thayer	600	Soldier
May 25, 1790	John Thayer	Sam'l Bostwick	600	8 pds.
Oct'r 5, 1793	" "	Richard Rogers	600	31 pds.
June 20, 1794	" "	James Reed	600	100 pds.
Nov. 5, 1796	Jas. Reed	Isaac Reed		

LOT NINETY.

Date of Sale.	GRANTOR.	GRANTEE.	Acres.	Consd'n
July 9, 1790	State of New York	Abijah Ward	600	Soldier
Feb. 19, 1791	Abijah Ward	H. J. VanRensselaer Joseph Town	600	20 pds.
Jan. 6, 1796	Sybrant Bleeker	Stephen Raynard	100	$98.50
Apr. 8, 1795	H. J. VanRensselaer	Sam'l Forbes		
Feb. 20, 1796	Samuel Forbes	Thos. White	500	
Nov. 6, 1799	Onon. Commissioners	Stephen Raynard	100	awarded
" 6, 1799	" "	Thos. VanW. Graham	50	awarded

LOT NINETY-ONE.

Date of Sale.	GRANTOR.	GRANTEE.	Acres.	Consd'n
July 6, 1790	State of New York	John F. Hamtramck	600	Soldier
Apr. 14, 1791	John F. Hamtramck	Michael Connolly	600	$100
Oct. 4, 1790	Thos. Fowler	Nicholas Fish		
" 14, 1791	Michael Connelly	Thos. Fowler		

LOT NINETY-TWO.

Date of Sale.	GRANTOR.	GRANTEE.	Acres.	Consd'n
July 8, 1790	State of New York	Thos. Willson	500	Soldier
Jan. 3, 1792	Thos. Willson	Justus Banks	500	43 pds.
Mar. 4, 1787	Walter Wilson's heirs	Andrew White	500	
		Wm. Preston		
		Wm. Pool	500	$500
Dec. 7, 1798	Onon. Commissioners	White, Preston & Pool	500	awarded

LOT NINETY-THREE.

Date of Sale.	GRANTOR.	GRANTEE.	Acres.	Consd'n
July 9, 1790	State of New York	Thos. Williams	600	Soldier

LOT NINETY-FOUR.

Date of Sale.	GRANTOR.	GRANTEE.	Acres.	Consd'n
July 9, 1790	State of New York	James Purdey	500	Soldier
Jan. 26, 1784	James Purdey	Ebenezer Fitch	500	15 pds.
Nov. 16, 1785	" "	Elias Newman	500	8 pds.
Sep. 25, 1791	Timothy Benedict	John W. Watkins	500	45 pds.
June 28, 1793	John W. Watkins	Wm. Sprague	500	100 pds.
Mar. 25, 1801	Onon. Commissioners	David Hobby	100	awarded
	" "	Peter E. Elmendorf	100	awarded

LOT NINETY-FIVE.

Date of Sale.	GRANTOR.	GRANTEE.	Acres.	Consd'n
July 8, 1790	State of New York	Jer. VanRensselaer	600	Soldier
	J. Van Renssellaer	John Juan	600	36 pds.

LOT NINETY-SIX.

Reser'd for Gospel, &c.

LOT NINETY-SEVEN.

Date of Sale.	GRANTOR.	GRANTEE.	Acres.	Consd'n
Jan. 29, 1791	State of New York	Tewahangaraghkan	600	Soldier
Dec. 22, 1791	H. Tewahamgaraghkan	Cor. Van Slyck	600	20 pds.
" 7, 1792	Cornelius VanSlyck	John Atkinson	600	

LOT NINETY-EIGHT.

Date of Sale.	GRANTOR.	GRANTEE.	Acres.	Consd'n
July 7, 1791	State of New York	Chris. Codwise	600	Soldier
Sep. 2, 1790	Chris. Codwise	W. J. Vredenburgh	600	
May 17, 1786	Codwise' heirs	Abram Wilson	600	
Feb. 23, 1795	Geo. McCall	Abiathar Hull	600	
Nov. 14, 1797	Abiathar Hull	Geo. M'Call	600	
" 7, 1799	Onon. Commissioners	Penelope Hughson	200	awarded
		Catharine Remsen	200	awarded

LOT NINETY-NINE.

Date of Sale.	GRANTOR.	GRANTEE.	Acres.	Consd'n
July 7, 1791	State of New York	Barnardus Swarthout	600	Soldier

LOT ONE HUNDRED.

Date of Sale.	GRANTOR.	GRANTEE.	Acres.	Consd'n
July 8, 1791	State of New York	James McCay	600	Soldier
Oct. 11, 1791	James McCay	Elisha Camp	600	
Nov. 30, 1783	Elisha Camp	Goose VanSchaick	600	
Dec. 3, 1791	" "	Elisha Burdict	600	
Mar. 23, 1796	Zephaniah Platt, Nathaniel Platt	Jonas Platt	600	
Mar. 10, 1794	Ed. Crampton	Nathaniel Platt	600	
Feb. 6, 1795	Jos. Greenleaf	Samuel Wilcox	600	
Oct. 18, 1796	Samuel Wilcox	Jos. Greenleaf	600	
Nov. 16, 1798	Onon. Commissioners	Nathaniel Platt	600	awarded
Aug. 20, 1801	N. Platt	G. Platt	111	
Nov. 19, 1804	Chas. W. Goodrich	Joseph Ely	50	$1900
" 22, 1804	Joseph Ely	Chas. Ely	55	
Feb. 17, 1803	Theo. Platts	Jas. Foot	58	
July 2, 1805	Reuben Benton, Bela Cowles, Elijah Hall, Theophelas Tracy	Connected with this lot as owners of parts of it.		

We append a copy of a deed or bounty land warrant given by the State, as a specimen of the original deeds given for land. The deed is partly printed and partly written, on heavy parchment paper and reads as follows:

The People of the State of New York by the grace of God, free and independent:—To all to whom thefe prefents shall come, Greeting:—Know ye, that, in purfuance of an act of our legiflature, paffed the fixth day of April, one thoufand feven hundred and ninety; entitled "an act to carry into effect the concurrent refolutions and acts of the legiflature, for granting certain lands, promifed to be given as bounty lands, and for other purpofes therein mentioned." We Have Given, granted and Confirmed, and by thefe Prefents, Do Give, Grant and Confirm unto Abraham Tompkins, All that certain tract or lot of land, fituate, lying and being in the County of *Montgomery* and in the Township of Marcellus known and diftinguished on a map of the faid Township (filed by our Surveyor-General in our Secretary's Office, agreeable to law), by Lot number Twenty-four, containing six hundred acres; Together with all and fingular the rights, hereditaments and appurtenances to the fame belonging, or in any wife appertaining; excepting and referving to ourfelves all gold and filver mines, and also five acres of every hundred of faid tract or lot of land for highways; To Have and to Hold the above described and granted premifes, unto the faid Abraham Tompkins, his heirs and affigns, as a good and undefeafible eftate of inheritance for ever. On Condition nevertheless that within the term of feven years, to be computed from the firft day of January next enfuing the date hereof, there fhall be one actual fettlement made on the faid tract or lot of land hereby granted, otherwife thefe our Letters Patent and the eftate hereby granted fhall ceafe determine and become void. In teftimony whereof we have caufed thefe our Letters to be made Patent, and the Great Seal of our faid State, to be hereunto affixed. Witness our trufty and well beloved George Clinton, Efquire, Governor of our faid State, General and Commander-in-Chief of all the militia and Admiral of the navy of the fame, at our city of New York, this eighth day of July, in the year of our Lord one thoufand feven hundred and ninety and in the fifteenth of our independence. Approved of by the Commissioners of the Land-Office, and paffed the Secretary's office the 20th day of November, 1790.

GEO. CLINTON.

ROBT. HARTNER, D. Sec'y.

"Attached to the deed by white cord, is the pendant Great Seal of the State of New York, being a beeswax cast of the original seal, about four inches in diameter and three-eighths of an inch thick. On the obverse is a rising sun, and the motto "Excelsior;" and legend the "Great Seal of the

State of New York." On the reverse a rock in the ocean; legend, 'Frustra.'"

TOWN MEETINGS.

Copy of original records as found in Town Clerk's Office of Pompey, 1794.

At a meeting of the Freeholders and Inhabitants of the town of Pompey, in the county of Onondaga, as lately ordained by a law of New York, passed the 5th of March, 1794.

That the first town meeting be held at the House of Ebenezer Butler, Jun., Esq., in said town. April 1st, 1794, was chosen by a plurality of voices:

Moses DeWitt, Supervisor.

Hezekiah Olcott, Clerk.

Ozias Burr, Allen Beach, William Haskin, George Catlin, Ebenezer Butler, Jun., *Assessors.*

Thomas Olcott, Jeremiah Gould, John Lamb, *Commissioners of Highways.*

John Lamb, William Haskin, *Overseers of the Poor.*

John Wilcox, Samuel Draper, Joseph H. Smith, *Constables.*

Voted that the Constables shall be Collectors.

Joseph Atwell, Daniel Allen, Peter Messenger, Joseph Bartholomew, Samuel Sherman, William Rin, John Wilcox, Samuel Jerome, Trueworthy Cook, *Overseers of Highways.*

Timothy Sweet, Elisha Clark, *Fence Viewers.*

Elisha Clark, *Pound Keeper.*

Various by-laws were made, and among them one that there shall be a bounty of three pounds for every wolf killed within the bounds of this town. It was also

Voted, that the ensuing election be held at three different places, viz: At Moses DeWitt's on the fourth Tuesday in April.

At Ebenezer Butler Jun's., the Wednesday following.

At Daniel Allen's the Thursday following.

At an adjourned meeting of the inhabitants of the town of Pompey, legally assembled at the House of Ebenezer Butler, Jun., Esq., on the 20th September, 1794.

William Haskin was chosen Supervisor, in the room of Moses DeWitt, deceased.

Voted, that the sum of twelve pounds be raised for the purpose of purchasing books and paper, and other expenses of the town.

SECOND TOWN MEETING.

At the annual Town Meeting held at the House of Ebenezer Butler, Jun., Esq., in the town of Pompey and county of Onondaga, 7th April, 1795.

Voted that the mode of choosing Supervisor and Clerk be to speak and mark against his name, and the remainder of Town Officers by nomination.

The following persons were unanimously chosen to their respective offices:—

Ebenezer Butler, Jun., Supervisor.

Hezekiah Olcott, Clerk.

Thomas Gastin, George Catlin, Jeremiah Gould, John Wilcox, Josiah Holbrook, *Assessors.*

William Haskin, Samuel Messenger, Jun., Hezekiah Olcott, *Commissioners of Highways.*

Josiah Holbrook, William Haskin, *Overseers of the Poor.*

Daniel Allen, Ezra Hart, Jabez Hall, *Constables.*

Daniel Allen, Ezra Hart, *Collectors.*

James Olcott, Enos Peck, Adonijah Cowles, William Pease, Bariah Holbrook, Ebenezer Carr, Timothy Coleman, Hoar, John Jerome, Salmon Butler, John Vaughan,

Daniel Messenger, Timothy Sweet, Asa Barns, David Green Isaac Carpenter, Selah Cook, *Overseers of Highways.*

William Clark, Ozias Burr, *Fence Viewers.*

George Catlin, *Pound Keeper.*

Voted that a bounty of five dollars be given for the scalp of every full grown wolf killed within the limits of the town.

Voted that the next annual town meeting be held at this place.

THIRD TOWN MEETING.

At the annual town meeting of the freeholders and inhabitants of the town of Pompey, legally assembled at the house of Ebenezer Butler, Jun., Esq., on Tuesday, the 5th day of April, 1796.

The following persons were chosen to their respective offices:—

Ebenezer Butler, Jr., Supervisor.

Hezekiah Olcott, Clerk.

Jeremiah Gould, Timothy Coleman, William Cook, Henry Clark, Timothy Jerome, *Assessors.*

Hezekiah Olcott, Samuel Hyatt, Josiah Moore, *Commissers of Highways.*

John Lamb, David Williams, *Overseers of the Poor.*

Daniel Allen, Chancy Jerome, *Constables.*

Daniel Allen, *Collector.*

David Tripp, Samuel Chaffee, Samuel Messenger, Samuel Sherwood, Joshua Owen, David Porter, Henry Clark, David Williams, Hezekiah Wilcox, David Hibbard, John Bowers, Jacobus Depuy, Louden Priest, John Jerome, Joseph Tubbs, William Haskin, Joseph Smith, Henry White, Abel Olcott, Ichabod Lathrop, *Overseers of Highways.*

David Green, James Griffes, *Fence Viewers.*

Jeremiah Catlin, *Pound Keeper.*

Jeremiah Gould, David Williams, Ozias Burr, Thomas Olcott, Timothy Jerome, *Commissioners of Schools.*

Voted, that the next annual town meeting be at this place.

FOURTH TOWN MEETING.

At this meeting held April fourth, 1797, John Lamb, was chosen Supervisor, Walter Colton, Clerk, Five Assessors were chosen, Three Commissioners of Highways, Two Overseers of the Poor, Three Constables, Barriah Holbrook, Collector, Twenty-eight Overseers of Highways, Four Fence Viewers, George Catlin, Pound Keeper, and Five Commissioners of Schools.

It was also "Voted, that it is the wish of the town to have the township of Fabius and Tully incorporated into a town by the name of Fabius."

"Fifty dollars were also voted, to defray the expenses of the town."

School Commissioners were voted six shillings per day, for services.

At a meeting held December 25, 1794, it was again "voted that it is the wish of the town to have the townships of Fabius and Tully incorporated into a town by the name of Fabius, and that the first town meeting be held at the house of Joseph Tubbs.

Voted, that the Town Clerk be directed to forward the proceedings of this meeting to the Legislature, at their next meeting.

W. Colton, Clerk.

At the next town meeting held at the house of Ebenezer Butler, Jr., April 3, 1798, the following votes were passed:

Voted, that the mode of voting for Supervisor and Town Clerk be *viva voce.*

Voted, That John Lamb be Supervisor.

Voted, That first vote be reconsidered, and that the Town Clerk be chosen by uplifted hands.

Voted, That Walter Colton be Town Clerk.

Voted, That there be five Assessors.

Voted, That the last vote be reconsidered, and there be but four Assessors.

Three Commissioners of Highways were chosen, also three Constables, Jacobus DePuy, Collector, five Commissioners of Schools, two Overseers of the Poor, twenty-eight Overseers of Highways, three Fence Viewers, Jesse Butler, Pound Keeper: Deodatus Clark, Timothy Sweet, Levi Jerome, Commissioners of the Public Lots.

A bounty of five dollars was voted on wolves killed within the town.

This last vote was reconsidered.

Voted, That the next Town Meeting he at the house of Manoah Pratt.

At a Special Town Meeting held at the house of Manoah Pratt, on Thursday, the 29th day of Nov., 1798, agreeable to previous notice.

Voted, That Levi Jerome be Town Clerk.

After taking into consideration the Public Lot 67, designated for Gospel and Schools.

Voted, That the same be leased.

Voted, That the Commissioners of said land, lease the same discretionary.

Voted, to petition the Legislature for division of the County.

Voted, That one tier of lots be taken off the county of Onondaga and annexed to county of Chenango, to-wit: Cicero, Manlius, Pompey, Fabius, Solon and Cincinnatus.

Voted, That a committee be chosen to petition the Legislature for division of said county.

Voted, That Hezekiah Olcott, Levi Jerome and Deodatus Clark, compose said committee.

LEVI JEROME, Clerk.

The next Town Meeting was held April 2, 1799.

The meeting organized at house of Manoah Pratt, and by vote, "adjourned to the barn of said Manoah Pratt."

Voted, that the Supervisor and Town Clerk be chosen by ballot.

This last vote was reconsidered and it was "Voted, that Supervisor and Town Clerk be put in by *viva voce*."

John Lamb, chosen Supervisor, Levi Jerome, Town Clerk. The usual number of town officers were elected.

"Voted, That the next Annual Town Meeting be held at the *School House*, near Ebenezer Butler's and Truman Lewis'.

LEVI JEROME, Clerk.

At next Town Meeting held at the School House named above, on first Tuesday in April, 1800. The Supervisor and Clerk were for the first time chosen by ballot. The remaining officers were chosen by the uplifted hand.

John Lamb, chosen Supervisor, Levi Jerome, Clerk, Jesse Butler, Collector, Truman Lewis, Pound Keeper.

At next meeting held April 7, 1801, it was "voted that the Supervisor and Clerk be chosen by going round and mentioning to the Town Clerk. Voted that Supervisor and Clerk be put in by once going around.

John Lamb, chosen Supervisor, Levi Jerome, Clerk.

Voted that the Assessors be voted in by uplifted hands, and that there be three Assessors, one in the western district, one in the middle district and one in the eastern district.

Forty-three Overseers of the Highways, were chosen.

A bounty of five dollars was again voted to be paid for killing a full grown wolf, and two dollars and fifty cents for killing a young wolf.

It was "voted, that those who have taken leases on the Public Lot designated for Gospel and School be released setting out one half the number of Apple trees contained in said lease.

At next meeting held in School House near Truman Lewis', March 2d, 1802, the Supervisor and Clerk were chosen by ballot.

John Lamb, Supervisor.

Levi Jerome, Clerk.

Forty-six Overseers of Highways were chosen.

"Voted, That James Russel should have a lease of that part of the Public Lot that William Lilly had a year, for ten years from the time that he took possession of the same.

Next town meeting held March 1st, 1803.

Ozias Burr, chosen Supervisor.

Levi Jerome, Clerk.

Voted that there be a *Pound* and that it be built near John Osbourn's.

Voted that John Bowers be pound keeper.

Voted That the Supervisor build a Pound, of the first money coming into his hands.

A bounty of five dollars voted on wolves.

The total town expenses for year 1802, was......$123.85

For year 1803............................262.00

For 1804, expenses was.........................312.00

The meeting held 9th of March, 1804, was in School House near Hezekiah Hopkins.

It is the same School House occupied for this purpose from

1800 till 1809, in which year, the meeting was called at the Academy building. This School house was situated on what is now the Public Green in the village of Pompey.

At meeting held April 5, 1808.

It was "voted that hogs to run at large in the town be yoked and ringed, except within half mile of Col. Hopkins', and there not allowed to run."

(Up to this time hogs have been allowed to run without restraint.)

Voted that " Nathaniel Gillett be Pound keeper.

Voted that no man shall let Canada thistles go to seed on his land, or path-master on the highway, within his distrct, on forfeiture of $10.00.

Voted, That Nathaniel Baker and Jesse Butler be hog constables.

CHANCY JEROME, Clerk.

At the Town Meeting holden on the fourth day of April, 1809, at the Academy, Ozias Burr was chosen Supervisor, and Henry Seymour, Clerk.

Sixty-one Overseers of roads; Nathaniel Baker, Pound Master.

The meeting resolved that they will permit the Pound to be moved into the village, near the Academy.

Resolved, That all overseers of the roads in Pompey, shall be fence viewers.

Resolved, That the owner of every dog pay fifty cents.

Resolved, That hogs or cattle shall not be permitted hereafter to run at large within half a mile of Col. Hopkins', and that hogs shall not be permitted to run at large in other parts of the town, unless ringed and yoked. That hogs found running at large within the aforementioned limits shall subject the owner thereof to the payment of twelve and one half cents to the Supervisor, besides impounding fee to the Pound Master, who, with all other persons, are authorized to impound said hogs. And it shall be the duty of every person so impounding, to give public notice of the same, on pain of paying two dollars and fifty cents for every neglect to the Supervisor, for the use of the town.

HENRY SEYMOUR, Clerk.

At a meeting held April 3d, 1810, Ozias Burr was chosen Supervisor, and Victory Birdseye, Clerk.

Resolved, That this town remonstrate against the proposed division, and that the Supervisor and Town Clerk be appointed to remonstrate and do all other things necessary to prevent the said division taking effect.

Resolved, That it be left discretionary with the Commissioners of the Public Lots to lease them for such time as they shall think proper, not exceeding twenty-one years.

VICTORY BIRDSEYE, Clerk.

At next meeting, held April 2d, 1811, before the meeting proceeded to any business, the following notice was read to the meeting:

"Notice is hereby given to the Freeholders and Inhabitants of the town of Pompey, that a petition will be presented to the Legislature of the State of New York, at their session in the year 1812, praying a division of the said town of Pompey, and the town of Manlius, including in the town to be erected, the three south tiers of lots of Manlius, and three of the north tier lots of the town of Pompey."

March 11, 1811.

Signed, ELISHA BEEBEE,
JACOBUS DEPUY,
JOSEPH WILCOX,
ELNATHAN MARSH,
TIMOTHY COLEMAN.

At this meeting all of the town officers were chosen by ballot--Ozias Burr, Supervisor; Victory Birdseye, Clerk.

Resolved, unanimously, That this meeting disapprove of the proposed division of the town, and that a committee of three be appointed to remonstrate to the next Legislature against the said division, and that Samuel S. Baldwin, Ozias Burr and William Cook be that committee.

VICTORY BIRDSEYE, Clerk.

At the meeting April 7, 1812, Jacob R. DeWitt was chosen Supervisor, and Asa Wells, Clerk.

It was voted that $80.00 be raised for support of the Poor.

At next meeting April 6, 1813, William Cook was chosen Supervisor, and Chas. Baldwin, Clerk.

It was Resolved to raise $350, for support of the poor.

Resolved, That the Commissioners of the Public Lot apply to the Legislature for permit to sell the lot appropriated to the use of the gospel.

This year, April 29, Ebenezer H. Hale was appointed by Justices of the Peace in and for the County of Onondaga, a Constable in and for the town of Pompey, in the place of Philo Loveland, who refused to serve.

CHAS. BALDWIN, Clerk.

Town meetings were held at the Academy from 1809 to 1814.

At meeting held April 5, 1814, Asa Wells was chosen Supervisor, and Chas. T. Baldwin, Town Clerk.

It was resolved to raise the sum of fifteen dollars for support of Common Schools.

Also, that the proceeds from the Public Lot be devoted to the same use.

Resolved to raise $222, for support of the poor.

That one dollar and fifty cents per day be paid to Commissioners of Schools.

At a meeting held April 5, 1815, Asa Wells was chosen Supervisor, and Chas. Baldwin, Clerk.

Resolved, That any person having canada thistles on his land, shall cut them twice a year; once in June and once in September, on penalty of $5.00.

Resolved, That no cattle shall run at large within half a mile of any Tavern.

Resolved, That partition and all fences be four and one-half feet high.

April 2d, 1816, meeting met at the house of Hezekiah Hopkins, and adjourned to the house of John Handy. Asa Wells was chosen Supervisor and Charles Baldwin, clerk.

Resolved, That $300 be raised for support of the Poor the ensuing year; and also eighty-five dollars for the relief of Asa Cook.

At a meeting April 17th, 1817, it was resolved "to sell for keeping, at public auction to the lowest bidder, all paupers chargeable to the Town.

April 7th, 1817, it was resolved to apply to the Legislature to alter the time of holding Town Meetings to the Second Tuesday of March.

At a meeting held March 9th, 1819, Asa Wells was chosen Supervisor and Samuel Baker, Clerk.

Voted that there be a committee of five appointed to investigate the concerns of the Public Moneys, and how it be expended.

The following is a list of the names of persons elected to the office of Supervisors and Towns Clerks, in the Town of Pompey, from 1794 to 1875 inclusive, together with number of years they served:

Year.	Supervisor.	Clerk.
1794	Moses Dewitt and William Haskins.	Hezekiah Olcott.
1795	Ebenezer Butler, Jr.,	" "
1796	" "	" "
1797	John Lamb,	Walter Colton.
1798	" "	Walter Colton and Levi Jerome.
1799	" "	" "
1800	" "	" "
1801	" "	" "
1802	" "	" "
1803	Ozias Burr,	" "
1804	" "	" "
1805	" "	Asa Wells.
1806	" "	" "
1807	John Lamb,	" "
1808	Ozias Burr,	Chancy Jerome.
1809	" "	Henry Seymour.
1810	" "	Victory Birdseye.
1811	" "	" "
1812	Jacob R. DeWitt,	Asa Wells.
1813	William Cook,	Chas. Baldwin.
1814	Asa Wells,	" "
1815	" "	" "
1816	" "	" "
1817	" "	" "
1818	Asahel Smith,	James Chappell.
1819	Asa Wells,	Samuel Baker.
1820	Elisha Litchfield,	" "
1821	Asa Wells,	" "
1822	" "	" "
1823	John De LaMatter,	Moses S. Marsh.
1824	Charles Jackson,	" "
1825	" "	" "
1826	Elisha Litchfield,	" "
1827	Warren Scranton,	Nathan'l Andrews.
1828	John Smith,	" "

Year.	Supervisor.	Clerk.
1829	John Smith,	Nathan'l Andrews.
1830	Manoah Pratt, Jr.,	Rial Wright.
1831	John Smith,	David Mallory.
1832	" "	Calvin S. Ball.
1833	" "	" "
1834	" "	" "
1835	" "	" "
1836	" "	" "
1837	" "	" "
1838	" "	" "
1839	Horace Wheaton,	" "
1840	Levi Wells,	" "
1841	" "	" "
1842	Horace Wheaton,	William J. Curtis.
1843	Levi Wells,	" "
1844	Daniel Candee,	Calvin S. Ball.
1845	Levi Wells,	" "
1846	" "	Dan. W. Holbrook.
1847	Samuel Hart,	Levi S. Holbrook.
1848	" "	Calvin S. Ball.
1849	Manoah Pratt,	" "
1850	" "	" "
1851	Samuel Hart,	E. Henry Hill.
1852	Manoah Pratt,	Calvin S. Ball.
1853	Levi S. Holbrook,	" "
1854	" "	" "
1855	" "	" "
1856	" "	" "
1857	" "	" "
1858	Levi Wells,	" "
1859	" "	" "
1860	" "	" "
1861	" "	" "
1862	" "	" "
1863	" "	" "
1864	" "	" "
1865	" "	" "

Year.	Supervisor.	Clerk.
1866	Levi Wells,	Calvin S. Ball.
1867	" "	" "
1868	" "	" "
1869	" "	Frank L. Porter.
1870	" "	" "
1871	" "	" "
1872	Levi Wells and Julius Candee.	" "
1873	Marshall R. Dyer,	Orson G. Dibble.
1874	" "	" "
1875	" "	Wells M. Butler.

POMPEY, August 25th, 1828.

We, the undersigned, promise to pay to a building committee hereafter to be chosen from among ourselves, the several sums affixed to our names, for the purpose of erecting an Episcopal Church, at the four corners, formerly called Clapp's corners; one-fourth to be paid by the first of March next, and the remainder in November, 1829. This church when erected shall be under the care ot Wardens and Vestrymen and be governed according to the rules and regulations of the Protestant Episcopal Church in the United States. The sum subscribed by each individual may be applied on payment in the purchase of a pew.

Names.	Sums.	Names.	Sums.
John Sprague	$100	Milton Slosson	$25
Isaac V. V. Hibbard	100	Horace Sweet	25
Moses Hinsdale	125	Ansel Judd	32
John Clapp	100	Adolphus Sweet	50
Samuel Hibbard	100	Joel B. Hibbard	20
Carleton Clapp	40	Heman Murray	20
Marovia Marsh	50	Ira Curtis	20
Samuel Clement	75	James Carr	25
Chester Clapp	75	Lucius Cook, in labor on building	10
Chauncey Hinsdell	126	Reuben Murray	25
Anson Sweet	100		

Levi Wells.

Names.	Sums.	Names.	Sums.
James Lusk	100	Truman B. Stanton	10
Rhoda Gold, Lumber	20	Seymour Marsh	50
Philemon French	50	Joseph W. Bostwick	10
Kneeland Sweet	130	Ephraim Salmons	10
Anson Sprague	20	Jacob Hadley, 2 chairs for vestry room and Communion Table	10
Jacob R. DePuy	10		

A return of Mount Pleasant School, No. Three, in Pompey, taught by Levi Jerome from the fourth of December, 1799, till the fourth of March, A. D., 1800. Number of days of Instruction is 66.

Scholars' Names.	Days.	Scholars' Names.	Days.
Moses Hinsdell	63	Isaac Woodworth	42
Asahel Hinsdell	50	Adolphus Sweet	60
David Hinsdell	53	James Sweet	58
Sally Hinsdell	43	Charles Sweet	58
Elizabeth Hinsdell	56	Anna Sweet	60
Jonathan Hinsdell	66	Anson Sweet	23
Polly Hinsdell	38	Pamelia Sweet	19
Samuel Hibbard	54	Anson Cole	64
Robert Hibbard	6	Polly Cole	26
Rachael Hibbard	48	John Cole	54
Jacob Hibbard	51	Samuel Jerome	47
Isaac Hibbard	60	Electa Jerome	48
Sally Hibbard	62	John Jerome	64
Jonathan Hibbard	22	William Jerome	59
Nathaniel Hibbard	14	Cyrus Messenger	58
Desire Messenger	50	Chloe Messenger	61
John Kellers	63	Rebecca Messenger	49
Isaac Jerome	63	Stephen Messenger	50
Betsey Jerome	66	John Closs	64
Libbeus Jerome	65	Moses Soles	35
Jared Woodworth	53	Electa Jerome	61
Lewis Woodworth	54	Levi Jerome	65
Phebe Jerome	53	William Williams	28
Mary Jerome	36	David Williams	8

Scholars' Names.	Days.	Scholars' Names.	Days.
Sophia Jerome	27	John Williams	18
Daniel Williams	59	Solomon Baker	10
Nathaniel Williams	40	Andrew Guile	65
David Williams	38	Leman Pitcher	27
Jobe Williams	29	Amy Pitcher	50
Rebecca Williams	35	James Pitcher	47
Lavina Williams	27	Obadiah Williams	37
Elsa Williams	28	Anson Sprague	20
Charles Slocum	37	Isaac Higgins	13
Abel Brotherton	29	Achsah Messenger	12

Total, Seventy scholars, 2,995

The Instruction compensation for his services was $16 per month.

The above is a true return.

Attest, DANIEL MESSENGER, } Trustees.
DAVID HIBBARD }

Commissioners of School, Pompey.

BIOGRAPHICAL SKETCHES

OF

Pioneers & Early Residents of Pompey.

DR. EDWARD AIKEN, was born in Windham, Vermont, in October, 1796, and graduated at Middlebury College; he was preceptor of Pompey Academy soon after its organization; subsequently he practiced medicine in Utica up to the year 1829, when from failing health, he removed to Tallahasse, Florida, and died in the year 1831.

He was a gentleman of culture and fine sensibilities, and wherever he was located attracted a large circle of friends; as a teacher he was thorough and efficient; as a physician, he was kind and humane, one whose memory will not soon be forgotten by those whose pleasure it was to know him.

ANDERSON FAMILY.

Addy Anderson came to Pompey about the year 1803, and settled on fifty acres of land about half a mile west of the village of Pompey Hill, on the State road; he died soon after, leaving a wife and eight children, to wit: Margaret, John, William, Elizabeth, Samuel, George, James and Mary. John was about sixteen years old when his father died, and being the oldest son, his mother very naturally looked to him for aid in providing for so large a family, and in this she was not disappointed; for he filled the place of a father, assuming responsibilities,bearing heavy burdens and discharging obligations most faithfully. At the age of about twenty-seven, John married Miss Lydia Safford, and settled on the farm purchased by his father; they were blessed with nine children, to wit: Jane, James, Joseph, Juliet, Ira, Josiah, Harriet, Eli and Mary; as a farmer he was among the best in the town; he was a highly respected citizen and for many years a very valuable member of the Methodist Episcopal Church of Pompey Hill. He died of cancer in the face, at the age of fifty-six; his wife preceded him to the spirit world about two and a half years; only two are living of his father's family, Margaret and Mary, who reside in Palmyra now.

The former is well known in Pompey, having spent most of her life there; she never was married and is now (1873) nearly ninety years of age. Five of John Andersons children are deceased. Four, viz: Jane, James, Juliet and Harrie t, died before their father. Eli, who married Miss Hellen Baker,of LaFayette, and located on a farm purchased of Ely Beard, died at the age of thirty-two years on the Ely Beard farm. He was a member of the M. E. Church, loved and esteemed by all; he left a wife and two sons who reside in Wisconsin. Joseph, the oldest of the four living children, has for many years been a resident of the State of Wisconsin,and has been over twenty years in the work of the Christian Ministry and a member of the Wisconsin Annual Conference. Eight years he has served as Presiding Elder, and he is at present pastor of the Second M. E. Church of Oshkosh, Wis. Three years ago he was missionary in the Rocky Mountains and built the first Methodist Church in Wyoming Territory, at Cheyenne. He has been married twice, and has five sons living by his first wife.

Ira is settled upon the old homestead, thinking it doubtless the dearest spot on this green earth. He is still at the age of forty-five unmarried, strongly attached to Pompey, his native town, and an upright honest citizen. Josiah soon after reaching his majority married Miss Margaret Baker of

La Fayette, N. Y. Four or five years later he built a house on a part of the "old homestead" intending to make it a permanent home. His house scarcely completed is enveloped in flame and burns to the ground on a dark night. A little son two years old was burned to death while the other members of the family barely escaped with their lives. Instead of rebuilding he soon sold and moved with his family to Wisconsin, only to remain a few months, when he returned and settled on a farm in LaFayette. This he sold and purchased the "Morgan place" the early home of Judge LeRoy Morgan, which his father Lyman Morgan owned two miles north-west of Pompey Hill, where he now resides. He is a good farmer, having accumulated a handsome property. He has one son living, having lost a son and daughter. Mary married a Mr. Hall, a wealthy and respectable farmer of Wayne Co., N. Y., where she lived a number of years. At present she is living in Michigan, having a family of five children.

AVERY FAMILY.

Christopher Avery, a weaver, came from Salisbury, England, ~~about 1640,~~ and settled at Gloucester, Mass.; he was a Selectman of that town from 1646 to 1654; in 1658 he removed to Boston, and on August 8th, 1665, he purchased land in New London, Conn.; died in Groton, 1681. James Avery, the only son of the above, was born in England in 1620; he married Joanna Greenslade, in Boston, Nov. 10th, 1643; he removed to New London, in 1650; took an active part in the business affairs of the new plantation; he was chosen Townsman in 1660, and held the office for twenty years; he was captain in the only train band in the town, and was in active service in King Phillip's war; he was twelve times elected Deputy to the General Court, was one of the Commissioners of Peace, and an Assistant Judge; he died at Pequannock, in 1696. His four sons were James, Thomas, John and Samuel. The latter was born Aug. 14th, 1666, and married Susanna Palms, Oct. 27th, 1686; his sons were Samuel, Jonathan, William, Christopher, Humphrey, Nathan and Waitstill.

Humphrey, born July 4th, 1699, married Jerusha Morgan, Feb. 5, 1724; his sons were Humphrey, William, Solomon, James, Samuel, Christopher, Waitstill, Isaac and Nathan.

Solomon, born June 17th, 1729, married Hannah Punderson, Feb. 18th, 1751; his sons were Solomon, Miles, Stephen, Punderson, Henry, Cyrus and Humphrey.

Punderson Avery was born in Groton, Conn., May 21st, 1765; he consequently was not old enough to enter the war of the Revolution, but to show that he was of the right stock, we mention that at the massacre of Fort Griswold, on the 6th of Sept., 1781, nine of his uncles and cousins fell, and he waded in blood over his shoes to obtain their remains from the Fort. He married Lovina Barnes, daughter of Phineas Barnes and Phebe Bernent, Dec. 15th, 1786, at Great Barrington, Mass.; here he resided some time, and then removed to the then so called "Royal Grant," in Herkimer County; here he built and run a grist mill for a few years, and it was believed to be located farther west than any mill for grinding grain on the Continent. In 1796, he removed to Pompey, and settled on a farm a mile south of Oran; here he reared his large family, and died Sept. 10th, 1840.

Mr. Avery was peculiarly fitted by nature for a pioneer; he was among the first in any enterprise to improve the minds, the morals or condition of his fellow men; the church, the school and public library, always found in him an ardent supporter; his patriotism secured him a place as captain in the militia; and his integrity, as administrator for many a widow and orphan; his love of justice made him often the arbiter in his neighbors' quarrels, and his excellent judgment often turned the scale, for or against, many an incipient undertaking.

But he was most useful to his fellow men, perhaps, as a

mechanic; his trade properly was a mill-wright, but he often was employed on small machinery, and on one occasion, by a very wealthy man, to construct a perpetual motion; he had been taught to work by square rule, and a barn still standing next south of his old residence, is believed to be the first in the county framed by "square rule;" he was almost continually employed in building grist mills, saw mills, fulling mills, carding machines, tanneries, and later, cider mills and threshing machines. About 1820, he constructed a cast iron plow, which, for many years, was a general favorite in this locality; his inventive faculties were large, and he would probably have allowed them some little scope, and at some cost, had not prudence and the demands of a family of twelve children, kept him busy in labor that paid every day. His children were Hannah P., who became first Mrs. Samuel Willard, the mother of W. W. Willard, of Syracuse; her second husband was William Higgins, of Van Buren; Sally B., who married George Miller, of Tunkhannock, Pa.; Lucy, who married Belden Resseguie, VanBuren; William; Phebe, who married Colonel Reynolds, of Cazenovia: Candace, relict of Horace Sweet; Lucetta, who married William M. Wood, of Mishawaka, Ind.; Perlena, the wife of Abner Duell, Manlius; Perlina, the relict of Euroclyden Gerre, who resides in VanBuren; Cyrus; Nancy, the wife of Elam Thomas, Knowlesville, Orleans Co.; and Samuel.

William Avery, son of the preceding, was born in Herkimer county, August 16, 1793, married Eunice Hart, daughter of Comfort, October 24, 1815. He early manifested a disposition to be a mechanic, was continually contriving water mills and wind mills to drive other machinery, and long before he attained his majority he was employed in all parts of the country to repair machinery, and was considered the most skillful workman known in Central New York. His inventive faculties were of a high order, but often from a lack of books on mechanical subjects, he lost much valuable time in experiments that had long before been tried and exploded. His first invention of any importance, was a machine for making wire harness for looms in 1824. His other inventions were numerous, and hardly a year passed without a patent being granted to him. The one by which he is best known, was the rotary engine, believed to be still the simplest and cheapest in the world, and in a limited sphere has proved for about 40 years extremely valuable. The first steam saw mill at Centerville, this county, was run by one of these engines for many years, and did a vast amount of work.

In 1822 he built a small steamboat which was first launched on the mill pond at Buellville; it was afterwards taken to Cazenovia lake, and finally to the Erie canal. The Onondaga *Gazette* of October 1, 1823, says: "A steamboat built at Buellville, in Pompey, passed through this village last week." The engine from this boat was purchased by the late Henry Gifford, of Syracuse, who used it to pump salt water for many years.

Mr. Avery moved to Salina and carried on a large foundry and machine shop, and afterwards removed to Syracuse, where he was for a time in company with Elam Lynds; he built the machinery for the first steamboat on Lake Ontario, and was the first white man to navigate the St. Lawrence river, from Kingston to the head of the Long Sault Rapids, passing two considerable rapids before reaching that point. Travel on that route in those days was so inconsiderable that it did not pay, and the proprietors withdrew the boat in a year or two. In 1837 he removed to Chicago, which he then described as a little sickly sunken hole. He soon took a contract of the State of Illinois to make the rock cut on the summit of the Illinois and Michigan canal; the price was $1.49 per cubic yard, and the estimated cost $240,000; this was considered the largest contract that had ever been taken in this country at that time. While completing this great undertaking, by which the waters of Lake Michigan were calculated to be diverted to the Mississippi, he was attacked by a fatal disease, and died on the 16th of November, 1840, at Athens, and is buried at Rockport, Illinois. Some of his feats of walking when the country was new were considered very good; he walked on one occasion from Oran to Ithaca in a day and back the next.

Cyrus, the second son of Punderson, was born in Pompey, July 28th, 1807; married first, Calista Hibbard, February 3d, 1828; second, Lurinda Jones, February 3d, 1831; third, Sabra Vosburgh, January 3d, 1847. His early life was spent in Pompey and mostly at mechanical work. He removed to Tunkhannock, Pa., about 1840, where he has since resided, except for the last ten or twelve years, he has been in Europe selling his inventions, which are numerous, and some of them quite valuable. One winter he spent in Russia and threshed wheat for the Emperor several months; was on the most intimate terms with the Grand Duke, Constantine, and finally presented his machine to the Government. He has a large family of children—five sons, all mechanics, and five daughters.

Samuel Avery, youngest child of Punderson, was born in Pompey, February 18th, 1812; married first, Lucinda Jones, February 3d, 1831; second, Eliza Flynn. His natural bent was mechanics as with the others, but forced by circumstances to be a farmer, he came near being ruined for anything useful. Dr. Daniel Denison, who had had the credit of his misguidance, took him into his office as a student of medicine, and in 1844 he graduated at Castleton Medical College, Vermont. He removed to Rochester, and commenced the practice of medicine and surgery, his natural mechanical ability aiding him materially in the latter. He stayed here but a few years and finally removed to Phœnix, where, with the exception of a few months in Syracuse and a year in Baldwinsville, he has since resided. He gave up practice a few years since, and at present is the Secretary of the Oswego and Onondaga Insurance Company.

Grandentia H. and Florello P., sons of Cyrus, born in Pompey, reside at Tunkhannock, Pa., machinists. Henry

M., only living child of Samuel, resides at South Haven, Mich., a watchmaker and jeweler.

———

Rev. ELEAZER STORRS BARROWS

Was born January 18th, 1790, in Mannsfield, Conn.; in October, 1797, moved with his father's family, to Middlebury, Vt.; he prepared for College at the Addison County Grammar School, and entered Middlebury College, October, 1807, from which he graduated, October, 1811; he was in Castleton in 1811 and 1812; in the Carolinas from 1812 to 1815, where in 1815 he was ordained a minister of the Gospel; he finished his Theological studies at the Princeton Theological Seminary, 1815-16; was tutor in Middlebury College a portion of the year 1815; preached in Middletown N. Y., 1816 and 1817; December,1817,was appointed Tutor in Hamilton College,Clinton, N. Y., and in September,1818, Professor of Latin, which position he held for about three years; in April, 1822, he settled at Pompey Hill, and was soon after installed Pastor of the Congregational Church of Pompey; here he remained till 1828, and a portion of the time in addition to his duties as Pastor of the Church he had charge of the Pompey Academy. He edited the Christian Journal at Utica, N. Y., from 1828 to 1833, supplying the pulpit of the Waterville Presbyterian Church a portion of the time; from 1833 to 1842 he was Pastor of the Presbyterian Church at Cazenovia, N. Y., when his failing health compelled him to resign the position.

The remainder of his life was spent at his home in Utica, N. Y., performing such ministerial labors as his health permitted until his death, which occurred July 28th,1847.

He was married May 7th, 1822, to Miss Catharine C., daughter of Dr. Thomas Fuller, of Cooperstown,N.Y.,where she now resides enjoying a green old age and "her children arise up and call her blessed." Seven children were born to them, five of whom are now living; Mrs. M. F. Cooper, of Albany, N. Y., is the only one who can claim Pompey as the place of her nativity. Their two sons reside at Janesville, Wisconsin, and two daughters at Cooperstown, N. Y.

Such is a sketch of the life of one of Pompey's early ministers,furnished by one of the members of his family. How full of activity in good works from its commencement to its early close! Although only fifty-seven years of age when called to bid adieu to earthly friends, and enter into that rest which remains for the pure in heart, he had filled the measure of a long and useful life; he has ceased from his labors but his works follow him. Eternity can only reveal the extent of the influence he has exerted even as Pastor of the Church in Pompey and Preceptor of the Academy, not to speak of the other fields of labor in which he was engaged. The following letter written by his aged wife in response to a communication from Dr. L. B. Wells, of Utica, requesting the foregoing sketch for publication, will be of interest to those especially who knew her and who appreciated her many virtues.

COOPERSTOWN, Oct. 16th, 1871.

DR. L. B. WELLS.

Dear Sir:—Your favor requesting a history of my husband's life to be handed down to posterity with the worthies of Pompey, was duly received, and estimated as a mark of respect to myself and family; I sent it to my son, the Doctor, who has written the enclosed brief sketch which I hope may meet with your approbation,

Respectfully Yours,

CATHARINE F. BARROWS.

SYLVANUS AND ARTEMUS BISHOP.

Sylvanus Bishop was one of six brothers who settled in Pompey in 1793-94; he had previous to this served in the Revolutionary war; he came from Kinderhook, Columbia County, N. Y., in the year first mentioned, and bought land in the vicinity of Pompey Hill and began to clear and improve it; in the following year he brought his wife and eldest child, making the entire jorney on horse back and carrying their baby, then but six months old, in their arms. After about twenty years residence in Pompey they removed to Oswego; he lived to be over ninety-five years and died inJune 1860. During his early residence in Pompey, his second son, Artemas Bishop,was born December 30th, 1795, whose life has been one of marked success and usefulness in the profession of his choice; when but a child he manifested a love for study which induced his parents to give him the advantages offered by the towns people in the "Old Pompey Academy," under the tuition of Messrs.Burchard and Leonard. He entered Union College in 1815, with Orange Butler and others from Pompey, and was a class-mate of Hon. William H. Seward; having graduated,he studied Theology at Princeton, during which time he made a number of professional visits to the Chappel in the "OldAcademy"in Pompey; while at Princeton he decided to devote his life to the Missionary work, at the Sandwich Islands. In October,1822, he married Miss Elizabeth Edwards, of Boston ; they immediately joined the second company of Missionaries, then about to start from Hartford, Connecticut, in the ship Thames; after a voyage of over six months,they reached the Island in safety. Among the earlier labors of this faithful and eminent Missionary, were his translations of the Bible, and a Hymn Book into the Hawaiian language; he also made an excellent translation of Pilgrims Progress, in the same language. Later in life he was employed by the United States Government, in making Geological Surveys of the Island; he is now the Senior Missionary in that field; he has accomplished his half century of labor in that department. A son and daughter have both been sent to the United States to receive an education suitable to assist him in his arduous labors, both having returned some years ago.

REV. ARTEMAS BISHOP.

One after another, the venerable laborers, whose lives of faithful service have done so much for the people of the Sandwich Islands, are passing away. The death of Mr. Bishop, one of the second company who went as Missionaries to those islands, was mentioned in the "Herald" for February. The notice of his life is gathered from a sermon preached at Honolulu, on the Sabbath after he died, by Rev. Dr. Damon:—

"The Rev. Artemas Bishop was born in Pompey, N. Y., December 30th, 1705; hence, in a few days, he would have been seventy-seven years old. He graduated at Union College in 1819, and at Princeton Theological Seminary, in 1822. After marriage with Miss Elizabeth Edwards, of Boston, he embarked in November, 1822, at New Haven, with the first reinforcement of Missionaries destined for these islands. Among his associates were the Rev. Messrs. Richards and Stewart, Mr. Chamberlain, and several others. At his embarkation a large concourse assembled, and then was sung, for the first time, the hymn written by William B. Tappan, which has been so oft repeated:—

> "'Wake, Isles of the South! your redemption is near,
> No longer repose in the borders of gloom.'

"The company landed at Honolulu on the last Sabbath of April, 1823, and Mr. Bishop was stationed at Kailua, there to become the associate of the Rev. Asa Thurston. Having acquired the language, he became associated with Mr. Thurston in the work of translating the Bible. Together, they translated the books of Genesis, Numbers and Deuteronomy, and the Epistles of Paul to the Romans and Galations; while alone, he translated the 2d book of Samuel and the 1st of Chronicles.

"After remaining about twelve years at Kailua, he removed to Ewa, on the island of Oahu, where he labored for about twenty years with great usefulness and success. While residing at this station, he translated 'Pilgrim's Progress,' and many other books. His accurate knowledge of the Hawaiian language always gave him authority in all matters involving questions of criticism and translation. His fondness for study, reading, and literary pursuits was preserved to the very close of his career. He was wont to take cheerful views of life, ever looking on the bright side of all subjects. There was a golden thread of quiet humor interwoven into the texture of his mind. Solomon says, 'A man that hath friends, must show himself friendly.' He was one of those friendly, genial, and companionable men whose presence does not chill, but warms society.

"It is quite remarkable, that with the rapid tide of travel rushing past our islands, he never should have left them after his arrival, except on a visit as delegate to the Marquesas Mission, in 1858. He never rode upon or saw a railroad, or witnessed the operation of the telegraph. Few men, however, were better acquainted with the progress of scientific discovery. Emphatically might Goldsmith's description of the Vicar, in the 'Deserted Village,' apply to him, while officiating, for nearly forty years, as a missionary at Kailua and Ewa:—

"'A man he was to all the country dear,
And passing rich with forty pounds a year;
Remote from town he ran his godly race,
Nor e'er had changed, nor wished to change his place.
Unskillful he to fawn, or seek for power,
By doctrines fashioned to the varying hour;
Far other aims his heart had learn'd to prize,
More bent to raise the wretched than to rise.'

"It is quite impossible not to admire the life of such a veteran Missionary, who left his country fifty years ago, and after voyaging around Cape Horn, settled down among the Hawaiians to learn their language, assist in reducing it to a written form, and then spend a long lifetime in preaching and laboring among this people. His thoughts have become their thoughts. By means of the sermons which he preached, books and hymns which he wrote and translated, and above all, by the life which he led, his own life-thoughts have become interwoven and intertwined with the life-thoughts and literature of Hawaiians.

"As a minister of the gospel, he necessarily made the whole Bible his life-study, but when he ceased from the active duties of the ministry, and enjoyed time for calm reflection and meditation, his mind dwelt almost exclusively upon the prophetic parts of Scripture, and especially upon the Book of Revelation. It afforded him unspeakable satisfaction to contemplate the future triumphs of the gospel as unfolded in these prophetic portions. He had no doubts and misgivings upon the subject, but from his extensive reading of history, and the progress of the nations in science, art, religion and civilization, he confidently anticipated the universal spread of Christianity over the whole earth."

ELIZUR BRACE,

BY HIS SON, REV. SAMUEL W. BRACE, OF UTICA, N. Y.

In opening Mr. J. V. H. Clarke's reminiscences of Onondaga County, I find that he has set down Pompey as one of the original towns formed at the first organization of the County in 1794, and that it comprised at that time the townships of Pompey (as it now is), Fabius and Tully, and a part of the Onondaga Reservation, including LaFayette; he informs us farther, that the township obtained great celebrity at a very early period, and was principally settled by people from New England, many of whom took up their residence in it while it was a part of the township of Mexico, Herkimer County. The first settlers, he says, in the present town of Pompey, were Ebenezer Butler, from Harwinton, Connecticut, who located on Lot number 65, in 1792. His brother, Jesse Butler, and Jacob Hoar, and Mr. Clarke might have added his brother-in-law, Nathan Davis, and others, came on in the spring of the same year. My father, Captain Elizur Brace, was a native of the same town of Harwinton, in Litchfield County, and a neighbor of those adventurous pioneers to the then far west, but did not move to Pompey until four years afterwards, that is in 1796. In the spring of that year he made a journey, mainly on foot, to the wilderness settlement of his former neighbors, and purchased of Ebenezer Butler a portion of land south of the present village and covering entirely the summit of the hill. On this he commenced the erection of a log house, after the fashion of others who had preceded him in the new and far off settlement; this house, however, he did not finish until after his removal there with his family, in the latter part of October of the same year; hence our accommodations, as I well remember, for I was then six and a half years of age, were scant and uncomfortable, until our famous log house, with two rooms, and a linter, as it was then called, was fit for occupancy. We located, by the kindly consent of our old neighbors, in the first school house ever built on Pompey Hill, and this, of course, was a log structure of but one room, and at that time, for a few weeks, unoccupied. On its split-out, hewed and uneven floor, we spread our beds, for our bedsteads had been left in the country where they were made; here, also, we cooked and ate our homely meals, sat upon our rough benches and hoped for a day of better things. Such a day at length arrived, for before the setting in of winter, we found ourselves comfortably located in our new and highly elevated dwelling, as it was not only like a city set upon a hill, but probably the second best in the settlement. Our neighbors were munificently mindful of us in their offerings of vegetables and other materials of an edible character, as they had them to spare. In the meantime, or before leaving our pent up quarters in the school house, my father had manufactured a table from cherry planks, split from a log given him by Esq. Butler, as this gentleman was then beginning to be called. To her great sorrow, my mother's fine table, the only one we attempted to bring with us, got completely shipwrecked on the way. According to the custom of olden times, a house warming was expected when we were fully settled in our log palace. With its two windows, of twelve lights each, which my father had been careful to bring with him; beside these and other things which might be named, an excellent split and hewed basswood floor—two doors of like material, with latches and latch-strings hanging out, a chimney in the middle, partly of stone, and topped out with rift-sticks and plastered, were some of the leading characteristics of our new dwelling; and as to the house-warming, so much desired and talked of by our friends and neighbors, that was deferred till mid-winter, when the marriage ceremony of my oldest sister was to take place. She had early on our arrival, become affianced to Dr. Walter Colton, the young physician of the town, and the first that ever settled in it for practice, though Mr. Clarke, in his reminiscences of Pompey, states the case entirely different, informing us that Dr. Samuel Beach was the first physician in this town, having come there in 1798, and that Dr. Josiah Colton settled two miles east of Pompey Hill in 1801. This statement, with sundry other mistakes of Mr. Clarke, is too palpable to need refutation. Dr. Tibbals, of whom he speaks in after years, became a resident of the place, and a co-practitioner with Dr. Colton, as the ride of the latter became very extensive, hardly circumscribed by the limits of the whole large county. Dr. Colton early entered into the politics of the day, although such a thing as a newspaper was unknown, except as fugitive copies of the Albany papers were obtained from the postoffice at Onondaga Hollow. This was the only postoffice in the County, and all the region round about. Daniel Wood, Esq., was the first postmaster at Pompey Hill in 1811; previous to that time, the Hollow was the principal postoffice tor the town, and to it, the writer, in the days of his early youth, often went as the post-boy for the neighbors, sometimes on horse-back, but oftener on foot. At that period there was no Syracuse, but a miserable drunken place, known as Cossit's Corners, and approached by roads of corduroy construction, and as the Irishmen of Salt Point used to say, a plentiful variety of mud holes. In those days, slavery was rife in all parts of the Empire State, nor did it entirely cease until 1828, when it came to an end by gradual emancipation. Pompey had its slaves; a number were held on the Hill by some of the most respectable families, but treated not as slaves in the south were said to be, but with much lenity and kindness. They were, however, quite nu merous in the northwestern part of the town, near what is now Jamesville; sundry families there as the DeWitts and DePuys, of Dutch extraction, held numbers of them, and with their labor entered largely into the cultivation of tobacco; hence it was that Pompey became the first town in all Central and Western New York that was defiled with the raising of this filthy and poisonous plant. I do not remember to have seen a one, or even a two-horse wagon on Pompey Hill earlier than 1804; indeed, horses were scarce and riding vehicles drawn by them were things of after consideration. The saddle, Dr. Franklin's seat of health, was in vogue for getting about, when the use of feet was relinquished; my mother, of course, had her down country pillion, like sundry others who had immigrated from the land of steady habits with their husbands and families. Ox teams were the order of the day, both in summer and winter, when the feet or saddle were not used; hence, carts and sleds, and those often of a clumsey character, were the modes of swiftest conveyance. The earliest school that I attended was taught by Miss Lucy Jerome, afterwards the mother of the Hon. George Geddes, a lady of distinguished talents and high mental culture. Mr. Merrit Butler, of Pompey, and myself, are probably the only persons living who attended that school, which was kept two summers in succession, but as Mr. Butler is twenty days in advance of me on life's rugged and eventful journey, he is allowed to speak for himself and to correct me, if wrong in this matter of more than seventy years memory. As descendants of Puritans, the early inhabitants of Pompey were strict observers of the Sabbath, keeping themselves and their children at home, except when they were favored with some kind of public religious services on that holy day. If no Missionary or regular minister of the gospel was among them, a prayer meeting was usually held, or a sermon read, and for attendance on Sabbath service, not men only, but women, (ladies, indeed,) would walk two or three miles or more. They used to meet in barns, private houses and school houses. The Rev.

Joseph Gilbert, from Harwinton, Conn., a nephew of my father, a hatter by trade, settled about two miles east from the Hill in 1793, and then quietly pursued his early vocation of hat making, in connection with farming, on a limited scale; wool hats and these usually exchanged for such commodities as the inhabitants had to spare, were the main production of his log shop. Mr. Gilbert was an uneducated man, but a man of fine natural talents, and of rare Christian character; in him the word of Christ dwelt richly in all wisdom; his example and influence in attending funerals, visiting the sick and meeting with the brethren on the Sabbath, were of the most salutary kind, and though dead, he yet speaketh. At the time of the Re-Union, June 29th, 1871, I visited his grave, and the graves of many others whom I well recollected from my boyhood, and found myself irresistably impressed with the solemn fact that the fashion of this world passeth away.

THE BALL FAMILY.

Stebbins Ball, Jr., who came to Pompey in the winter of 1799, from Saratoga County, was born in Granville, Conn., in 1775; his father was Maj. Stebbins Ball, who served seven years in the revolutionary army, and was wounded; at the close of the war, he was honorably discharged, with the rank of major. Stebbins Ball, Jr., settled on lot num-29 Pompey, on the farm now owned and occupied by Benjamin F. Wheeler; he was a carpenter and joiner, an excellent mechanic, and gave promise of great usefulness in the new country where house-builders were so much needed; but death early closed his career, in the year 1802, at the age of twenty-seven years; his children surviving him were Stephen C.,and the twins, Alvin M., and Calvin S., also two daughters, Betsey and Charlotte; Betsey married William J. Millard, of Watervale, in Pompey, and Charlotte married, Manoah Pratt, Jr., of Pompey.

Stephen C. Ball, son of Stebbins Ball, Jr., was born in

Charlton, Saratoga County, N. Y., in 1797, and came to Pompey with his parents; he served in the war of 1812, and was in the battle of Niagara; he died in Homer, Cortland County, N. Y., February 22d, 1871, leaving nine children, —one son and eight daughters; he was a tailor by trade.

Alvin M. Ball, (twin with Calvin S.) was born in Charlton, N. Y., October 11th, 1798, married Miss Lucretia Vickery, of Pompey, and settled on the farm now occupied by his son Frederick, two miles north east of Pompey Hill. He raised a family of ten children—one son and nine daughters.

Calvin S. Ball, (twin with Alvin M.) was born in Charlton, N. Y., October 11th, 1798; lived in Pompey about seventy years; was a silversmith, and taught school several years in Watervale and Pompey Hill; was Town Clerk of Pompey, from about the year 1837 to 1862, excepting one year; he also held the office of School Commissioner, and that of Inspector of Schools for several years. He was twice married; first to Miss Adaline M. Wood, of Watervale, by whom he had four children--three sons and one daughte,who are now living. His second wife was Miss Sarah H. Hungerford, of Watertown, N. Y., by whom he had two daughters, twins, one of whom lived to the age of seven years; both wives, and the twins lie burried in the grave yard at Pompey Hill.

Mr. Ball, moved from Pompey in 1869, and now resides at Milo Center, Yates County, N. Y., in the enjoyment of good health, having outlived the expectation of everyone who knew him in early manhood. About 1822, when at Trenton Falls, he was attacked with pleurisy, which left him with a severe cough. From Trenton Falls, he was brought on a litter to his home inPompey,and with him a coffin and shroud, as the doctor declared it was very doubtful whether he could survive the journey; but he arrived in safety, and finally after fo ur years of suffering, he recovered from what all supposed to be an incurable consumption, and entered upon the active duties of life. The coffin is still in existence, but long ago the shroud was used for other purposes; his son Calvin S. Ball, Jr., is a dealer in Watches, Silver Ware, Jewelry, &c., a prosperous business man, and resides in Syracuse.

JOSEPH BAKER,

Was born at Chesterfield, Mass., November 21st, 1778; at the age of twenty-six years, he moved, following his brothers, Erastus, Lemuel and Thomas, to Pompey, west Hill, now LaFayette, where he settled on a farm near his brothers, where he remained till 1810, when he removed to Otisco, where he died June 8th, 1855, aged 77 years; he was married March 23d, 1802, to Betsey Danforth, by whom he had eleven children; she died April 4th, 1840, aged sixty-two years; he was again married to Mrs. Hannah, widow of Captain Timothy Pomeroy, of Otisco; he is described as a very tall and straight man, with lungs of unusual size, possessing a strong loud voice, a robust constitution, never sick, and scarcely knew how to sympathize with those who were; at last without a moments warning, while at work fixing some brine in the pork barrel, he was stricken down, and in an instant fell upon the floor from the effects of a paralytic stroke. He was a farmer, and spent the greater part of his early life in clearing the forest; he in company with Lewis Billings, used to take land to clear at $10 per acre; they would go out in the morning and each strive to be the first to fall a tree, which was no sooner down, than the sturdy pioneer was cutting it into logs; the first finished, they would run to the next, and all day long the strife was continued. The logs were drawn into heaps by the neighbors, every man owning a team participating in the bee; on these occasions, song and mirth, strife and victory, made all joyous and happy.

Mr. Baker was in the habit of calling his boys, seven in number, in the morning, saying in his stentorian voice, "come boys, shoulder arms," and suiting the action to the word, would swing his axe on his shoulder, the boys following in single file to the woods. He was a very hard working man, and often when working and sweating in the field,he would say to one of his boys, "go to the well and get me a drink from the bottom, and out of the north west corner."

He survived two years and a half after one side was paralyzed and his mind gone; then as of old he would call his boys, and when they failed to come, he would say, " I have brought up a large family of boys, and not one will now come at my call!" When in health he was fond of music and fun, and was a leader in the sports of the day; his tenacity to life was strong, and not till one foot had decayed from the body, did he yield to the fell destroyer.

BENSON.

Peter Benson came to Pompey about the year 1793, being then thirteen years of age; he came to assist his older brother in building a barn, for Samuel Sherwood, on lot number 84; the compensation for building which paid for 100 acres of land on the same lot.

This farm is located about one mile north-west from the village of Delphi, and was afterwards owned by Peter Benson. The father of Mr. Benson, came a few years later; his name was Stutson Benson, was a farmer, and resided in Pompey till his death, which occurred in 1820. One incident of his life is worthy of note. At the time of his marriage, he was unable to read or write; like Andrew Johnson, he learned his alphabet of his wife; he became a well read man, particularly in the Bible, and occasionally engaged in preaching the Gospel; much of his writing is now in possession of A. P. Benson, of Pompey, and is a neat legible hand with correct orthography. Peter was the eighth child and fifth son, in a family of ten children; he was five feet and ten inches in height, with broad shoulders and firmly knit frame, and weighed in the prime of manhood, 200 pounds; he had a firm, quick step, and never would allow his children to move at a slow pace, or as he termed it, "as though they were pulling stakes out of the ground;" he was of a jovial turn, was never morose or austere in his family, though his rule with his children, was instant obedience, and they found it the part of wisdom to pay strict attention to this inflexible rule. He was a farmer, and acquired a fair competence in his calling; he died in 1864, at the age of eighty-four years; at the time of his death, he was a resident of Fabius.

EBENEZER BUTLER, Sr.

Ebenezer Butler, Sr., who accompanied his son, Ebenezer, in making the first white settlement at Pompey Hill, was born December, 1733. He was grand-son to Jonathan Butler, one of two Irish adventurers who came to Connecticut about the year 1710; he served with the Connecticut troops against the French during the French and Indian War; he was with Washington in the revolution; and also, in a detachment called out to suppress "The Shay's Rebellion" in 1787. Although a farmer by occupation, after locating in Pompey he took little part in business life; he was a religious man, and took a very active part in organizing the first church established in Pompey, being chosen one of its trustees. This church or religious society was formed June 16th, 1794, and was called "The First Presbyterian Society of Pompey." This was not only the first religious association in Pompey, but in Onondaga County, when it embraced the whole military tract; he was also a member of the church subsequently organized by Rev. Ami Robbins, in 1800, under the name of the "First Congregational Church of the Town of Pompey." He lived in Pompey till his death, which occurred in 1829, enjoying in an unusual degree that choicest of Heaven's temporal blessings—good health. He never was ill, and died at the age of ninety-six years, falling dead with a quantity of wood in his arms which he had just been preparing for the fire.

Ebenezer Butler, Jr., the first white settler at Pompey

Hill, and within the limits of the present township, was born at Harwinton, Conn., in 1761. He served, as did his father, in the Revolutionary War. He was taken prisoner and suffered all the hardships and cruelties imposed by the British upon those unfortunates who were confined on board "The Prison Ships" in New York harbor. After his release, and at the close of the war, he returned to his native town; married Miss Rebecca Davis, and moved to Clinton, Oneida County, N. Y. When located there, he bought a soldier's claim to Lot No. 65, of the town of Pompey, and in 1791 or 1792, moved with his family, consisting of his wife and four daughters, his father, aged about sixty years, and a maiden sister, to, and made a settlement upon this Lot, at what is now Pompey Hill. He built a log house for himself near where is now the ruins of the old stone blacksmith shop; another for his father and sister, near the corner by the wagon shop. He afterwards bought Lot No. 64, and in 1797, put up the first frame building in this vicinity; this was a house located on the present site of Hon. Manoah Pratt's residence. Here he kept a hotel for a number of years; he was largely engaged in buying and selling real estate, and for many years also bought cattle in Central New York, and drove them to the Philadelphia market. Before he came to Pompey, in 1791, he was Collector of the District of Whitestown; he was Supervisor of the town of Pompey, Justice of the Peace, a Member of the State Legislature in 1799 and 1800, Judge of the County Court, and one of the first Trustees of Pompey Academy before its incorporation by the Regents; he was associated with the first company formed for the manufacture of salt at Salina. He left Pompey in 1802 or 3, and moved to Manlius. His wife died in 1808, and her remains lie buried in the cemetery at Pompey Hill. He lived in Manlius till 1811, and then moved to Central Ohio, where he died in 1829, aged sixty-eight years; he has descendants living near Columbus, Circleville and Chillicothe, Ohio, many of whom rank among the first families of the State.

Yours
Victory Birdseye

VICTORY BIRDSEYE.

Victory, eldest child of Ebenezer and Eunice (Tomlinson) Birdseye, was born at Cornwall, Conn., December 25th, 1782.

Through each of his parents he came of the best stock of his native State. His paternal grandfather was the Rev. Nathan Birdseye, who was born August 19th, 1714, graduated at Yale College, 1736; was settled as pastor of the Congregational Church, at Westhaven, Conn., in 1742; remained in that pastorate for 16 years; in 1759, removed to Oronoque, in the town of Stratford, Conn., where he resided till his death on the 28th day of January, 1818, at the age of 103 years, 5 months and 9 days. A single fact will show of what stuff, both of body and mind, this man was made, who, born in the first month of the reign of George I, lived to within two years of the end of the reign of George III. After he was more than 100 years old, he rode on horse-back one Sunday, to and from the Church, in the village of Stratford, a distance of some five miles; went into the pulpit, and conducted all the exercises of the worship; and, being too near-sighted to read, repeated from memory, the chapter and psalms which were read and sung, and preached the sermon, much to the pleasure and edification of the audience.

The maternal grandfather was Beach Tomlinson, of Huntington, Conn., a man of uncommon strength, both of body and mind, and who died early in the present century, at a very great age.

Among the objects most early sought, obtained at great sacrifice, and cherished during his whole life by the subject of the present sketch, were the portraits of his grandparents Tomlinson. Many of the residents of the town have seen these portraits in his dwelling; and all the older inhabitants will remember the pride and affection with which he regarded them.

The unusual name of "Victory," came into the family by

an incident so singular as to be not unworthy of mention here. It was first given to the infant son of Captain Tomlinson, under the following circumstances:—The child had been born in the early fall of 1759, in what was then one of the outer and most exposed settlements of the Colony of New Haven. It was during the "Seven Years' War," as it was called in Europe; but known in America by the name, implying so much, of the "French and Indian War." Wolfe had gone up the St. Lawrence with his fleet and army, to attack the French in their strong-hold of Quebec. On his success seemed to depend the safety of almost every family in all the Colonies; especially those in the backwoods—on the edges of the wilderness. For the defeat of the English army would let loose on the Colonies the French, with their murderous allies, the Indians.

On a Sunday morning, late in the fall of 1759, as this infant was being carried to the church to be baptised, and to receive some name that had been borne by older members of his family, and just as pastor and people were gathered at the Church, an outcry was heard in the distance. A Courier from the back settlements on the Hudson came riding up, waving a white flag, and shouting "victory, victory, victory!" For a moment he drew rein at the steps of the Church, to give breath to his horse, while he told to pastor and people the story of the battle of the Heights of Abraham, on the 13th of September, the death of Wolfe, and the great victory of the English. To every one who heard, the tidings seemed as of life from the dead. For the power of the French and Indians was broken; and now the Colonists could lie down and rise up, without fear of rifle or tomahawk, or scalping knife. After a short halt, and repeating his glorious news, the messenger departed, bearing the glad tidings to the eastern towns; still, as he went, waving his flag, and shouting "victory." When he had vanished, the congregation gathered in the Church for worship and thanksgiving; but before they could proceed, the child must be christened. As he was brought forward for baptism, the minister, an aged man, dipping his hand in the water, and placing it on the forehead of the child, and apparently forgetting the family name which it was intended he should bear, said:—"Victory, I baptize thee, in the name of the Father, and of the Son, and the Holy Ghost."

Such a name, so given, became so dear to the family, that when at the successful close of another great war, the first child of a new generation was born to them, it was, as a matter of course, given to him.

This second Victory early displayed great aptness, as well as fondness, for learning. He was fitted for college, partly at the Grammar School at Cornwall, and partly at Lansingburgh, N. Y., where one of his uncles, Tomlinson, then resided. Entering Williams College, Massachusetts, in September, 1800, he graduated there September 5, 1804, in the same class with Luther Bradish, Robert and Henry D. Sedgwick, and others, and preceding only by a year, Daniel Moseley and Samuel R. Betts, subsequently so prominent in the judicial history of this State. Returning to Lansingburgh, he pursued the study of the law with his uncle, Gideon Tomlinson, and Cornelius Allen. There, as at school and in college, he was noted for the thoroughness of his studies. Mr. Allen said of him many years after, that he was the most industrious student he had ever known.

Mr. Birdseye was admitted an Attorney of the Supreme Court of New York, Feb. 12, 1807, and as Counsel, Feb. 15, 1810. He removed to Pompey in June, 1807. On the 14th of October, 1813, at Onondaga Hill, he married Electa, daughter of Capt. James Beebee, of the Revolutionary Army. He early took high rank, and obtained decided success as a lawyer, commanding, at the same time, the respect and good will of his neighbors and the whole community, and receiving, during his whole life, many tokens of public confidence, both private, political and professional.

In November, 1814, he was elected to the Fourteenth

Congress, in which he served from March 4th, 1815, to March 4th, 1817.

He was a delegate to the Constitutional Convention of 1821, which formed the second Constitution of New York.

He was a Member of the Assembly for 1823, and of the Senate during 1827 and 1828. He there took a leading part in the perfecting and passing of the Revised Statutes of the State.

He was also a member of the Assembly in 1838 and 1840, and in Nov., 1840, was elected to the Twenty-Seventh Congress, in which he sat from March, 1841, to March, 1843.

At the extra session, held in the summer of 1841, perhaps the most exciting question presented arose out of the proposed Bankrupt Law, which was very strongly pressed. The Whig party was then in power for the first time. Mr. Birdseye was a Whig. The Bankrupt Law was proposed and passed as a party measure; but he deemed it so impracticable, as to be unworthy of his support; and, after striving in vain to perfect it, he voted against it with the warning that it would prove unsatisfactory to the country, and dangerous to the party.

The soundness of his judgment was vindicated by the repeal of the law by a large majority of the very Congress which had enacted it.

But, while thus made known to the public at large by these offices, he was best known at home and among his immediate neighbors, by the services which he rendered them in their own affairs.

Soon after his removal to Pompey, he was appointed a Justice of the Peace, and held that office for the term of four years. On the 8th of April, 1811, he was appointed a Commissioner in Insolvency, under the Act of April 3, 1811. He was appointed Postmaster at Pompey, April 25, 1817, and held that office for about twenty-one years. On the 13th of April, 1818, he was appointed Master in Chancery, serving a term of four years. On the 20th of June, 1818, he was appointed District Attorney of Onondaga County, and held the office for about fifteen years.

On the 26th of May, 1830, he was appointed Special Counsel, in place of John C. Spencer, resigned, to conduct the prosecution of the persons accused of the abduction and murder of William Morgan.

Within the town of Pompey, and in its vicinity, Mr. Birdseye was as well known and as greatly esteemed and beloved for his services in connection with the founding and putting in operation of the Academy at Pompey, as for any other services ever rendered by him. Up to the time when he became a resident of Pompey in 1807, all the efforts for the obtaining of the necessary endowment of the Academy and the erection of its building, though vigorously prosecuted, had failed of success; but, shortly after his settling in the town, he devoted himself to the establishment and endowment of the Academy. From that time forth, nearly every paper connected with its history was prepared by him, and many of them are still in existence, in his well known and peculiar handwriting.

Within less than three years after his removal to the town, a sufficient endowment had been raised. Within another year, the building was completed; and directly thereafter the Academy was put in operation.

Until his death, he remained closely connected with it; being for many years Secretary, Treasurer or President of the Board of Trustees, and at times holding all these offices, and performing their duties. He prepared the reports; he invested and made available its funds; he procured for it the grant of the lot of land (number 15, in the Township of Camillus,) which formed a large part of its property; and during the last 30 years of his life, while he was carrying on a very large professional business, was weighed down by political cares and labors, and was rearing and educating his large family, he gave the same attention to the interests of the Academy, conducting its affairs, investing and collecting the income of its property, collecting the tuition bills, and giving personal attention to the course of instruction in the School, with apparently the same zeal and interest and affection with which he had assisted in laying the foundation of the Institution, in his earliest manhood.

Besides this active political and professional life, and his zealous labors in behalf ot the Academy, he was the common adviser and friend of the people of the town, and of many in the surrounding towns for long distances. The natural kindness of his heart, the fairness and openness of his mind, his love of truth and justice, and fair dealing, his dislike of strife, and his hatred of litigiousness, made him the general arbitrator and peace-maker of the neighborhood; he brought and defended no suits which could be avoided by any efforts at peace-making, short of most serious sacrifices; and, with all his other occupations, he superintended the large farm he had acquired, giving much care and no little time to its management. He seemed rarely happier than when he could turn his back upon the Courts and his law office and give himself up to the care of his farm. He often said that in the hay field, in the harvest, and the care of his sheep, he was again a child on his fathers' farm and in his fathers' family, and that such occupations alone had made possible his professional labors.

His life, filled with such labors, drew gradually, and in fact imperceptibly, to its close. On Christmas day, 1852, he attained the age of three score and ten; but he was apparently in the enjoyment of as good health, and nearly as great vigor, as he had ever known; he had, years before, had several serious attacks of disease of the lungs; but they had all passed off, leaving few, if any, visible traces behind. For months, he continued to perform all his accumstomed labors in the office, on the farm and about the Courts; he was as full of interest as ever in public affairs, and in all that claimed the thoughts of those around him. He conducted his cases, and attended the trials in which he was engaged, with undiminished vigor; there were, certainly, occasional symptoms and indications of advancing age and approaching weakness; and late in August, 1853, when some such sign had attracted attention and caused remark, he said: "It is of little moment; merely something to remind me "that I grow old; I must not forget, and I am not allowed "to forget, that I am a mere tenant at will of this frail "tenement of a body;—that I may be called away to leave "it at any time; lest I forget it, my Great Landlord gives "me occasionally a notice to quit."

Scarcely any words could better indicate his temper and the tone of his mind. Early in the last week of his life, he had kept an appointment, made sometime before, to try a case in a neighboring town. He returned in the middle of the week, apparently well; Thursday and Friday were spent as usual; a part of each day in his law office, and at his usual labors, and the afternoon upon his farm; on Friday evening, he received his mail matter, and looked it over as usual, conversing of the news of the day; he retired early, remarking that he must rise early, in order to visit the county town on the morrow.

After retiring, he was seen to be sleeping with the natural easy breathing of a healthy old age; when sought to be aroused at the dawn of the next day, he was found cold in death! Not a limb had moved; not a pang had been felt; nor had even the fingers been clasped! The machinery of life had simply stopped,—the Great Landlord had merely repeated His notice,—the tenant had obeyed, and gone without a struggle, whither he was summoned! Thus peacefully ended this long, laborious, useful, peaceful life in the night of Friday, or on the morning of Saturday, the 16th and 17th of September, 1853.

Mr. Birdseye was a kind husband, a fond father, a good neighbor, a faithful friend, a wise counsellor, a public spirited citizen, an incorruptible servant of his fellow-citizens in every office and in every trust. He loved children ardently—in fact he loved all his fellowmen. His aim in life was to make all his fellowmen wiser and better; his aim in his business life was to make all with whom he had to do, honest, true and just. He was an unerring judge of men and their character; he knew whom to trust and whom not to trust. In fact, it may be doubted whether this profound knowledge of men, and this sagacity in weighing and measuring them, and their motives and actions and character, was not his most remarkable endowment; but he possessed also a singular knowledge of affairs and events, both of his own time and of the past; he continued all his life to read largely, and he seemed never to forget anything he had read; every fact in history, science, philosophy and politics seemed to be assimilated with, or made a part of his own thoughts; he preserved to the last his fondness for the classical studies of his youth, and Tidd and Blackstone never drove from his memory Virgil, Horace, Tacitus and Homer.

As a lawyer, he had few superiors in those parts of his profession to which he devoted himself.

His knowledge of men and things, his full mastery of the principles of the science of the law, his sagacity, his patience, his industry in preparing, and his coolness in the trial and argument of causes, secured for him a success in his cases that was indeed remarkable. Not that the first success—that before a jury—was always his; for his tastes and habits, the very frame of his mind, fitted him rather for the arguments at the bar of the Court than for captivating juries; but he seemed ever to try his causes for the ultimate triumphs and success of the final judgment; hence it was, no doubt, that it was truly said of him, that although he was sometimes beaten in the Courts below, he was almost uniformly successful in the Appellate Courts.

Of this soundness of judgment, this accuracy of knowledge, this thoroughness of mental action, it will not be easy to speak too strongly; he used ever to inculcate them, as he ever inculcated kindness and honesty and truth. Once, in answering an objection that such accuracy could not possibly be secured in the great majority of cases, and was, therefore, scarcely to be expected or striven for, he replied that that was not so. And, among other things, he said he would venture to cite his own experience, and he went on and stated that experience. He said that, during the four years of his acting as Justice of the Peace, he rendered about 4,000 judgments, being, on an average, 1,000 per year. That only four of them were ever sought to be reviewed in the higher Courts; that three of the four were affirmed in the Common Pleas, (the first Appellate Court,) and no further appeal was ever taken; that, in the fourth case, his judgment was reversed in the Common Pleas; but that that reversal was itself reversed in the Supreme Court, and his original judgment was affirmed. So that not one of his judgments was ever in fact set aside. He stated also, that, during the fifteen years of his service as District Attorney of Onondaga County, (then the fourth or fifth County of the State in population and wealth and standing, perhaps even higher than that in the extent, variety and importance of its criminal business,) he had with his own hand drafted, he believed, every indictment found in the County, and had tried every one that was tried; and that, during the whole period, he did not remember that a single indictment was quashed, or found defective on a demurrer, or a single prisoner was ever acquitted by reason of any technical failure or flaw in an indictment; of course, he had not convicted all the criminals indicted and brought to trial during his long term of office; but none of them had escaped, so far as he could recollect, by reason of any fault or flaw of his in preparing the indictment. When he was told that this implied an accuracy, a care and a patience that were almost super-human, and which it was therefore useless to try to equal, he replied: Not at all; it was simply the result of carefully applying ordinary powers to the faithful discharge of ordinary duties; that another could do all that he had done and more; and that probably he owed as much of his success in the discharge of these important duties, to the good will and confidence of the public, and of the members of his own profession towards himself, as to anything else; that they believed he meant to do his duty fairly and honestly, and so failed to look for, and of course to see, the errors he must no doubt have committed—that it was not human to avoid every error or mistake; and that there was the best authority for saying, "*Loquando dormitat bonus Homerus.*'

The wife of Mr. Birdseye, who was almost eleven years younger than himself, survived him more than seven years, dying on the 5th day of October, 1860.

They reared a family of twelve children, viz:

Victory James, married Betsey Anne, second daughter of Daniel and Anne Marsh, of Pompey, now residing in Pompey.

Ellen, married Charles A. Wheaton, then of Pompey and subsequently of Syracuse.

Ebenezer, died in New York City, May 12, 1846.

Emma Rawson, resides in Syracuse.

Lucien, graduated at Yale College, August 16, 1841, married Catharine Mary, daughter of Samuel and Philena Baker, of Pompey, resides in Brooklyn, N. Y.

Henry Clay, graduated at Yale College, July, 1844; died at Albany, N. Y., Feb. 18, 1847.

John Clarence, Lowell, Mass.

Albert Franklin, married Mary Catharine, daughter of Elias and Hannah Post, who died Sept. 4, 1875. Resides in Pompey.

Charlotte Amelia, married to Harrison V. Miller, M. D., of Syracuse.

Horatio, married to Laura Amelia Chapman, resides in Pompey.

Julia Catharine, married to Rev. John F. Kendall, D. D., then of Baldwinsville, N. Y., and now of LaPorte, Ind.

Eunice Electa, resides in Syracuse.

BARBER FAMILY.

Elihu Barber was born at Hebron, Conn., March 17th, 1768, and was the seventh and youngest son of David Barber, who at that time was a rich merchant, buying his dry goods in Boston, but shipping potash, beef and horses, from New London, Conn., to the West Indies in exchange for rum, sugar and molasses for his trade; like most younger sons of rich men, Elihu was a petted, indulged and I might say, poiled boy, thinking his father rich enough to supply his every want, without any exertion of his own; and this state ot things continued till the close of the Revolutionary War; when in consequence of a forced payment of a bill for several thousand dollars due a Boston house, for goods bought just at the commencement of the war, (the parties going to England during its continuance as they were Tories) he was irretrievably ruined; having armfuls of Continential money which at that time however was of very triffling value, as we read that Thomas Jefferson gave $6,000.00 of it for an overcoat.

A little farm of thirty acres, in the sterile town of Hebron, and a tract of two hundred and fifty acres of wild land in the extreme northern part of Vermont, was all that was left of his father's large fortune, and a life of toil and privation was before him, where before, was ease and plenty. January 25th, 1791, he married Hannah Gott, and together they toiled on; her busy hands, ripe judgment and sterling good sense, helping to cheer and direct him, until in the early part of 1801, they sold out for $700, and started for Pompey, having all their worldly goods upon an ox sled drawn by two yoke of steers, all their own.

In the latter part of February they reached Pompey and moved into a log-house, on lot 84, and the property of Maj.

Sherwood, where they lived three weeks; buying in the meantime one-hundred acres out the north-west corner of lot 69, from Stutson Benson, paying therefore his hard earned seven hundred dollars, the deed bearing date March 7th, 1801. They almost immediately moved into their new home, and the ringing of his axe as he labored to increase his three acre clearing, and the clang of her loom as she wove woolen and linen cloth for the neighbors at the rate of ten yards a day, and doing her own work, soon began to tell in the way of bettering their circumstances, the clearing steadily enlargening, a fruit orchard of all kinds suitable to the climate soon in bearing, with thrift and plenty everywhere. In a short time a large frame barn was built, and in 1810, a thirty by forty house after the pattern so common in dear old Connecticut is furnished, and moved into—that busy *loom* having paid for the brick in the chimney, the sawing of all the lumber, and the carpenters'wages for the labor in shingling and clap-boarding the house.

About this time, they began to enlarge their boundaries, adding piece after piece, until they had paid for, and owned, over five hundred acres; the request the active house-wife making when told from time to time, I can buy a hundred acres of Mr. ——; "can we pay for it?"always was "get me fifteen more cows and you may buy it."

This *butter business* was carried on until Elihu Barber was as *well* known by the name of "Butter Barber;" for during the war of 1812, it was his custom to carry, on certain days of every week, three pails of golden rolls of butter to market; one in each end of a bag across the saddle, and one in front of him, thus riding into Manlius, nine miles distant, and arousing the proprietor of the hotel from his slumber with his customary call of "halloo the house," and by nine o'clock he was back on his farm.

At intervals of a few years, now that want was no longer probable, they made their pilgrimage to the land of their birth, toward which, notwithstanding its roughnesss and sterility, their hearts turned as faithfully as the needle to the pole. When the First Baptist Church of Pompey was organized, and a house of worship erected, Elihu Barber took an active part in its construction, and gave liberally toward it, and his wife was one of its most zealous and influential members; showing her faith by her works, and being a constant attendant and worshiper until old age prevented—and truly it may be said of her, "she did what she could" for the glory of God.

This long walk together was sundered March 27th, 1848, by his death at the homestead, four score years of age. In 1857 she died at the house of their youngest son, David Barber, at Manlius, aged over eighty-eight years. The *early* years of their married life, were years of toil and privation; but industry, economy and an indomitable energy that knew no such word as *failure*, brought them while yet they were middle aged, to comfort and plenty. And although the monumental marble that marks their resting place records no victories won on tented field, still when in early life, grim want and pinching poverty threatened to assail and overcome them, they, by steady advances, utterly routed them. The forest that encircled their home, at first, echoed the howling of wild beasts; but soon was heard the looing of cattle and bleating of sheep, whose wool the humming spindle and clanging loom, transformed into clothing; and the forest *itself* melted away before the continuous strokes of the axe, and in place of it came luxuriant harvests. Plain and assuming people were they, in the front rank of pioneers, whose onward tread has carried civilization from ocean to ocean; by whose industry, the desert now blossoms like the rose; and by whose examples of stern integrity, unbending principle and Christian faith, towering temples and modest churches dot the land, spreading the gospel of peace. Truly their victory has proven greater than any record written in blood.

Four children were born to this couple, viz: Henry Barber, born February 13th, 1792, died in 1850; Lydia Barber, born June 6th, 1797, died in 1804; Hannah Barber, born October 14th, 1799, died April, 1872; David Barber, born September 8, 1802, died January 21, 1867. Henry Barber was some nine years of age when his parents moved into Pompey, and being a strong, vigorous boy, soon bore a hand in the labors of the period. About 1819, he married Sarah Shields, and lived about one mile from the old homestead until his death, which occurred in 1850, leaving four sons and two daughters. Hannah Barber was married about 1816, to Daniel W. Carver, living for a long period in the Valley, two miles north of Delphi, afterward removing to Saratoga Springs, where Carver died in 1857, and Mrs. Carver died at the home of her son in Illinois in 1872. They had three children, two sons and one daughter. David Barber was married to Harriet Hinsdell, Oct. 6th, 1828, and settled close to the homestead, where he lived until 1852, when he moved near Fayetteville, living there until his death, which occurred Jan. 21st, 1867. His wife is still living, as also are their two sons and one daughter. Being possessed of a strong constitution, great energy and perseverance, and a farsightedness and good judgment, that would have made him successful in *any occupation* or profession, it is not strange that David Barber succeeded as a *farmer*. Earnest in purpose, when his decision was once made, nothing turned him aside from the prosecution of his plan, and he was often successful in an undertaking, in which a weaker man would have met with a disastrous defeat. He was proud of his occupation, and stood in the front rank of agriculturists. Firm and unyielding in what he thought right, still his social qualities were of a high order, his integrity unquestioned and his word as good as his bond.

REUBEN BILLINGS' FAMILY.

The oldest living couple (residents of the Town) who were present at the Re-Union, at Pompey, held June 29th, 1871, were probably Reuben and Sally Billings; the former being in his 83d, and the latter in the 86th year of her age; and while making mention of this fact, it may not be deemed a miss to give a brief synoposis of their history, as follows: Reuben Billings' was born in the Township of Longmeadow, Hampshire (now Hamden)County, Mass., February 13th, A. D., 1789; he was the second son of a large family, (12 in all) and has survived them all, except his youngest sister, who lives at Warehouse Point, Conn., and is upwards of 73 years of age. On April 30th, 1809, he was married to Sally Denio, eldest daughter of Joseph Denio, of Delhi, Delaware County, N. Y.; she was born on George Washington's birthday, February 22d, 1786; she has also outlived all the members of her father's family, (8 in all) the last one having died over 20 years ago. From Delhi they first went to Longmeadow, Mass.; but in June, 1812, they moved to Pompey, N. Y., arriving there the 23d of the same month, after a tiresome journey of thirteen days, being hauled the whole distance by an ox team. They first moved into a house on the "Cape" as it was called in School District, Number 8, a few rods south of where Dr. Hezekiah Clark formerly lived, and is now owned and occupied by John H. Clark, Esq.; he had not been in town three hours before Peter Ostrander,the path master,warned him to work on the road. In the winter of 1812 and 1813, he taught the School in District Number 8, but a few rods from the place where Grace Greenwood was subsequently born. In 1813 he moved on to a part of lot number 96, one mile south, where he has ever since resided. In those early days of our town's history, he taught singing school at Pompey Hill and various places, and was leader of the Choir at the Dedication of the Presbyterian Church, in 1818, and when Rev. Jabez Chadwick was ordained its pastor. He also vividly remembers about the sale of pews and the little incident that led little Horatio Seymour to afterward become a noble friend of temperance.

In those early times, a tailoress was deemed of as much use to society, perhaps, as a tailor, and Mrs. Billings was considered an expert as a tailoress, dress and cloak maker, and also milliner; she used to make all sorts of wearing apparel; besides she could cut coats, vests and pants, equal to the best of tailors. She used to keep apprentices to the trade, while she, day after day, was kept busy in cutting "mens' clothes;" and people from the adjoining Counties of Madison and Cortland were generous patrons of Mrs. Billings, or "Aunt Sally" as she was frequently called. Many a tailor in those days en vied Aunt Sally her skill and reputation. Reuben and Sally Billings, had but two children—a daughter and a son; Amanda M. Billings, was born May 19th, 1811; married, May 13th, 1832, to Pierce Ellis, who died December 9th, 1864; consequently she is now a widow and lives with her aged parents. Her brother Homer Augustus Billings, was born in Pompey, N. Y., on the old place September 4th, 1826; consequently is a native citizen of old Pompey. On Nov. 9th, 1835, he commenced the profession of School Teacher, and has taught fifteen terms of four and five months each; he also traveled for several years in several States as Agent for the sale of Patent Medicines. On April 14th, 1862, he married Helen M. Smith, of Dublin, Wayne County, Indiana; he brought his wife to Pompey shortly after, and has since resided with his parents and sister, on the farm where he was born.

ELIAS CONKLIN.

Elias Conklin, one of the pioneer settlers of Pompey, came from Long Island and settled in Pompey in 1797. He cut his way through the forest from Pompey Hill, making the first road to the place where he built the first saw and grist mills in the town, which then covered a large territory, if not the first in the County. These mills are still known as the Conklin Mills, now in LaFayette, and are owned by Conklin Brothers. Mr. Conklin married Rachael Haight, and they reared a family of five children. Betsey, the oldest daughter, was born January, 1801; Harriet, February, 1803;

Daniel N., October, 1807; Sarah A., February, 1810; Josiah D., June, 1812. Daniel N. died September, 1836; Mrs. Elias Conklin died in August, 1840. The subject of this sketch died April, 1854. Harriet Conklin married Publius V. Woodford, and died February 14, 1872; Betsey Conklin married Warren Butts, and died April 15, 1872; Sarah Ann Conklin married Samuel P. Hayden, and died May 7, 1872. The three sisters all dying within less than three months. Mr. Elias Conklin, commonly known as "Boss Conklin," a carpenter and joiner by trade, was a large and successful farmer, as well as miller. He employed a large number of workmen, and built houses and barns and did other mechanical work for his neighbors, such as making wagons, sleighs, carts, ploughs, &c.; at an early day he made very many coffins, sometimes for pay, sometimes when persons were poor, without pay, and would assist in digging graves without charge, so great was his sympathy for the unfortunate. He was a very active and prominent man in society and church matters, being Trustee, and very effective and liberal in building the "First Congregational" and Baptist churches at Pompey Hill. He was a very benevolent man, giving very many bushels of grain to the poor, and never turning any away empty from his tables or his mills.

SAMUEL CLEMENT.

Samuel Clement was born in the town of Northbridge, Worcester County, Mass., January 1st, 1772. At the age of three years, his parents emigrated to Croydon, Sullivan County, N. H., a newly opened region, where they were exposed to, and encountered the trials and hardships of pioneer life. Their situation was rendered more embarrassing by the distracted state of the country, placed as they were upon the border of civilization, between the demands of their friends on the one hand and the encroachments of foes on the other. The aggressions and treacherous warfare of the Tories and Indians were particularly distressing at this period, and the border settlements were often thrown into consternation and danger at the sudden and stealthy approach of the savage enemy. Many in this little settlement were the atrocious murders committed, and the dwellings plundered and consumed by the torch of the incendiary. Thus early was Mr. Clement schooled in the hardships of frontier life and to face danger and death in its most appalling form. The lack of educational advantages was severely felt by the rising generation at this Revolutionary period; but Clement, not daunted by the want of teachers or the scarcity of books, availed himself ot all the means in his power. While his hands were employed with the axe or hoe, his brain was busy with reflections upon what little science he had acquired; at the age of twenty he was considered competent to teach a district school, and he commenced teaching at Milton, Saratoga County, N. Y. In the autumn of 1793, in company with Timothy Sweet, he visited Pompey, and concluded to make it his future home. He spent the winter of 1793 and 4, teaching in Westmoreland, Oneida County, and early in March came with his axe on his shoulder to his forest home, by the aid of marked trees, (there being no roads laid out) and built himself a log cabin and covered it with the bark of trees. Early in April, he lent his aid to organize the town of Pompey and acted as clerk of the meeting which effected that object. In the fall of 1794 he married Ruth Hibbard, daughter of David Hibbard, who battled with him in life's stern necessities for thirty years, when she died leaving eleven children. Mr. Clement taught school in the winter of 1794 and 5, on Lot No. 28, Pompey, about a mile from his residence. This is believed to have been the first school taught in the County; Major Danforth sent his brother's son, and in the summer of 1795, his own daughter; some of the scholars who attended that school are still alive. He continued to teach in that district for some time, till the growing cares of the farm and a rising family, compelled him to relinquish the occupation. He died in Pompey, May 29th, 1856, in the 85th year of his age. Five of his children are still living; Polly, Diantha, Lucy, Elihu, Jacob and Charles, are dead. Of those living, John Clement resides in Cold Water, Mich.; David, in Darlington, Wisconsin; Hiram, in Pompey, N. Y.; Julia and Charlotte, in DeRuyter, Madison County, N. Y.

HENRY CLARKE.

Henry Clarke, the oldest son of Dr. Hezekiah Clarke, was born January 25th, 1789, in Lanesboro, Berkshire Co., Mass., and came with his father to Pompey in 1805. He entered the law office of Wood & Birdseye, as a student under them. While there, in 1812 or '13, he was drafted as Sergeant-Major in the army, with quarters at Oswego, N.Y. At the close of his term he was offered a Captaincy in the Regular Army; but he declined the flattering offer, and resumed his studies. When Wood & Birdseye dissolved their partnership, he continued and finished his course with Victory Birdseye, Esq., and was admitted to the Bar of the Supreme Court in February, 1814, then in session at Albany.

In March of that year he formed a co-partnership with Caleb B. Drake, Esq., in Ithaca, N. Y., where he closed his life February 19th, 1817. Few young men in so short a time have acquired so flattering a reputation for ability in his profession and moral worth, as he. It is believed that he was the first student at law in Pompey.

At the same time that Henry Clarke was in Wood & Birdseye's office, Daniel Gilbert, (son of Rev. Joseph Gilbert, a Congregational Clergyman, who lived and died on the farm now owned by Albert H. Butterfield, on lot No. 66, Pompey,) was a student at law in Cazenovia. He established himself in his profession in 1813, in the village of Salina, now First Ward of Syracuse.

CLARKE FAMILY.

As all, or nearly all, of the early settlers of the town of

Pompey have passed away, the responsibility of rescuing their names from forgetfulness, especially those of them who, by their intelligence, thrift, skill or moral worth, have been prominent in their generation, devolves upon, and is the imperative duty of their descendants who have the knowledge of their worth.

Of the Clarkes, there were seven brothers; six of them were professional men, and one of them a farmer; and five of them had special interest in Pompey.

Dr. Deodatus Clarke was born July 27th, 1762, and died January 10th, 1847; he settled on lot 66 in 1795, and owned the whole of lot 52. He moved thence to Oswego, in 1807, where he died. Two of his sons are now living, Edwin W., (a lawyer, retired from practice) now lives in Oswego, N.Y., and Ossian, his youngest son, a physician and surgeon, in Neosho, Wis.

Henry Clarke, farmer, settled in Pompey about 1795, and moved to Manlius prior to 1805, where he died in 1810. None of his children are now living.

Thaddeus Clarke was born February 12th, 1770; he settled on lot 81 in 1820, and moved thence to Fabius, about the year 1830; thence to Rochester, and thence to New Brighton, Pa., where he died February 15th, 1854. His widow now lives in Dowagiac, Mich. His children now living, are Joseph B., Attorney, Dowagiac, Mich., Frederick J., Merchant, Ottumwa, Iowa, Charles E., Colonel in the Regular Army, Rufus L. B., Attorney, Dr. William E., Chicago, Ill., Lucy C., wife of Rev. Amory D. Mayo, Sarah I., (Grace Greenwood,) Washington, D. C., and Albert Henry.

Erastus Clarke was born May 11th, 1768, attorney, another brother, settled in Utica, N. Y., in its infancy, of whom the Hon. Ambrose Spencer said:—"He is the only man I ever knew who could split a hair, and then show the difference ot the parts."

He owned the whole of lots 81 and 54, and about 200 acres

of lot 37, Pompey. It is said that he took a petition to Albany, for the incorporation of Pompey Academy, and a bill prepared for that object, the passage of which through the Legislature he procured, with an appropriation of a military lot for the benefit of the Academy. He died November 6th, 1825.

Dr. Hezekiah Clarke, the eldest brother of the five, was born December 19th, 1757, in Lebanon, Conn, and was the son of Dr. John Clarke, grandson of Moses Clarke, great-grandson of Dr. Daniel Clarke, Jr., and great-great-grandson of Daniel Clarke, who emigrated to America in the year 1640, and settled at Hartford, Conn. His maternal grandmother, was Elizabeth Edwards, daughter of Timothy Edwards, and sister of President Jonathan Edwards.

He studied Medicine and Surgery under his father; was appointed by Governor Trumbull, Surgeon's Mate in the Third Connecticut Regiment, in the army of the Revolution, commanded by Colonel Samuel Wyllis, General Parsons' Brigade. Subsequently, on the re-organization of the army, denominated the First Connecticut Regiment.

He was in the regular service two years, when, by reason of protracted sickness he left the army.

Afterward, when Fort Griswold, on the river Thames, opposite New London, was captured by the British under the traitor Arnold, he repaired to the scene which might put savages to the blush, and gave his professional aid.

When he arrived at New London, he found a large number of men who could not pass over, the enemy having destroyed all the craft on the river, but by searching he found a rickety skiff, utterly unseaworthy. Here he found himself in a dilemma; for he could not cross in it alone, and they who were standing there refused to accompany him, concluding that, if it could not carry *one*, *two* must inevitably go down with it. After much effort, he prevailed on one man to row the skiff, while himself bailed the water out of it, and thus, by their united effort, they arrived safely on the opposite side.

He immediately repaired to the scene of murder, (for it was nothing less,) and assiduously devoted himself to the relief of the unfortunate victims, by dressing their wounds, and rendering any other assistance of which they stood in need. Thirty years after, three of the sufferers called on him in Pompey, to express to him their gratitude for his timely and kindly aid.

Soon after the close of the war, he settled in Pittsfield, Mass., where he remained one year. He then (June 2d, 1786) married Miss Lucy Bliss, daughter of Hon. Moses Bliss, of Springfield, Mass., and grand-daughter of Timothy Edwards, and settled in Lanesborough, Berkshire County, Mass. There he pursued his profession about eighteen years, then moved with his family to Pompey, where he arrived November 3d, 1805; he lived in the house then owned by Daniel Wood, Esq., near the Academy, one year, and then settled on the farm on lot 66, where his son John H. Clarke now lives. Here he continued to labor in his profession till infirmities incident to old age terminated his labors, and he closed his useful life in Pompey, March 4th, 1826.

Dr. Clarke's reputation as a Physician and Surgeon, stood high; but his reputation as a Surgeon did not consist so much in the number of limbs amputated, as in their preservation; but when it became necessary to resort to the tourniquet and knife, he knew how to use them. He was a skillful operator.

His children were:—

First—Henry, who studied law with Hon. Victory Birdseye, served as an officer in the war of 1812, and died at Ithaca, February 19th, 1817.

Second—Harriet, married Hon. Daniel Gilbert, and died at Coldwater, Mich., November 27th, 1864.

Third—Charles, died at Dowagiac, Michigan, April 22d, 1874.

Fourth—Lucy, died July 29th, 1846.

Fifth—John H., now lives on lot 66, Pompey.

Sixth—William M., now lives in Onondaga, near Syracuse.

Seventh—Moses B., died November 20th, 1865.

Eighth—Theodore E , died October 26th, 1853.

PAUL CLAPP.

Paul Clapp, the father of John, Chester and Carlton, was born in the year 1752, at Chesterfield, Mass., and when the youngest son, Carlton, was two years old, he immigrated to Pompey, in the year 1798. His family then consisted of his wife, whose maiden name was Hepsibah Guilford, and nine children, to-wit:—Paul, Jr., Sally, Electa, Hadessa, Patty, Philena, John, Chester and Carlton. Electa lives in George County, Ohio, and is the only surviving member of the family. Paul Clapp was a soldier in the war of the Revolution, and at the time of his death was a recipient of a pension; he was a member of an expedition through the northern wilderness, which made an aggressive war upon the Indians and Tories, and was taken prisoner, carried to Canada, and suffered great hardship. After coming to Pompey, he took up a large tract of land, to which he afterwards added largely; being engaged in agricultural pursuits till his death, which occurred in 1845, upon the land which he reclaimed from its wilderness state. Three of his sons settled on his land in Pompey—John, Chester and Carlton. Paul Clapp, Jr., went to Ohio, being one of the pioneer settlers in that State. John Clapp married a daughter of David Hinsdell; his children now living are Addison Clapp, of Pompey, Edmund O. Clapp, of Syracuse, Therissa, wife of Chester Baker, of LaFayette, N. Y., Mary Clapp, of Manlius, N. Y., Rhoda, wife of Dr. Tollman, of Onondaga Valley, and Flora, Mrs. Reed, of Manlius Village.

Chester married Sally Hinman about the year 1819; their living children are Morris H. Clapp, of Urbanna, Ohio, and Esther, Mrs. Dorwin, of Syracuse.

Carlton Clapp married Harriet Foote, of Manlius; their surviving children are Mary A., Mrs. Hervey Jerome, of Lincoln, Nebraska, Guilford C. Clapp, of Pompey, N. Y., and DeLancy Clapp, of DeWitt, N. Y.

Edmund O. Clapp, named above, died in Syracuse since writing this sketch.

JOHN J. DEMING.

Sacred to the memory of John J. Deming, whose biography it has been impossible to obtain. He was an accomplished gentleman, a profound scholar and favorite teacher. He was one of the early teachers in Pompey, and taught in the west room of the old Pompey Academy.

> "Full many a flower is born to blush unseen,
> And waste its sweetness on the desert air."

DODGE FAMILY.

Hezekiah Dodge came to Pompey with his brother, Ezra, in 1795, and settled on the same tract of land on Lot No. 50. He owned that portion of the land subsequently known as the John Wells' farm. Like his brothers, his life was devoted to agriculture. He, too, was one of the early contributors to building and endowing the Pompey Academy. He removed from Pompey in 1842, and went to live with his son, Oren, who moved to Lysander, Onondaga County, in 1826. With him he lived till his death, which occurred in 1844, at the age of sixty-five. He was married in Connecticut, to Hannah Roberts, whose father was a Revolutionary soldier; by her he had six children; in the order of their ages, they were Nehemiah, Oren, Charles, Julia, Joanna and William. Nehemiah went to Oswego, and died at about the age of fifty-two. He was married to Fannie Beebe, and left four children who live in Wisconsin, except one who resides at Grand Rapids, Michigan.

Oren, who was seventy-five years old Jan. 3d, 1875, married Almira Russ, by whom he had three children, Caroline,

Sarah and Julia, two of whom only, Caroline and Julia, are living and both married. They reside in Schroppel, Oswego County, N. Y. His first wife died, and he married Almira Lyboult, who died in 1868. He now lives with his third wife, who was Mrs. Susan Smith, at Plainville, in Lysander. Two years ago, at the age of seventy years, she wove eleven hundred yards of carpeting, manufactured twenty pounds of wool and did her own house work, her husband and herself constituting the family.

Julia, the fourth child of Hezekiah, married Dr. George Morley, who lived on the farm now owned by Joseph Wallis. She died leaving no children.

Charles, the third son of Hezekiah, married Nancy Wells, of Cazenovia. At first they went to Lysander, and thence to Michigan, stopping a short time near Rochester, N. Y. From St. Joseph, Mich., they moved to near Austin, Texas, Dec. 3d, 1853, where they now reside. He is a farmer and largely engaged in raising cattle. One child, a son, died in Michigan, and he has remaining one daughter, Helen, who married Judge Turner, of Texas. He, on account of his Union sentiments, was obliged to leave his State and come north. During the campaign which resulted in the second election of Lincoln, he advocated the Republican cause upon the stump, in various places through the North.

Joanna Dodge married Jerome Sweet, a nephew of Horace Sweet, late of Pompey. They went to Indiana, near Albion, where he engaged in farming. They have four children, having lost one son in the late war; three daughters and one son are living near their parents; they are all married.

William Dodge moved to Michigan and engaged in lumbering; he was married to Juliette Dunham, of Little Utica, N. Y. He met a violent and sudden death while at work in the saw mill which he built. He left a widow and five children.

Ezra Dodge came to Pompey from Litchfield, Conn.,

about the year 1795, and located on Lot No. 50, where Thomas Cox now resides, the farm still being known as "The Dodge Farm." He was a farmer, and changed from its wilderness condition the land upon which he settled, and which his son, David F., subsequently owned. He, in common with the pioneer settlers, was subjected to the toils, privations and hardships incident to pioneer life; and yet, in common with the early settlers of Pompey, he found time to devote his attention to the early establishment of schools and churches. He was among the subscribers to the endowment fund of the Pompey Academy. He was old enough to remember the Revolutionary struggle, and believed and acted upon the principle that the general diffusion of knowledge and virtue is essential to the perpetuity of the system of government which the patriots of '76 fought to establish. Before he came to Pompey, he had married Polly Foote, and six children were the fruits of that union; they were, in the order of their ages, David F., Ira, Clarissa, Hezekiah, Seabred and Ezra, Jr. His family were of more than ordinary intellectual ability. He and his wife lived and died upon the land they reclaimed from its wilderness state.

David F. Dodge, his eldest son, married Ada D. Roberts in 1824, and inherited a part of the farm of his father, upon which he lived till 1854, when he purchased the village house and lot, now the Catholic pastoral residence, and subsequently the Daniel Wood residence in the village of Pompey Hill, together with the farm attached, where he lived till his death, which occurred in 1869. His widow still survives, living in the family of her daughter, Mrs. Daniel G. Wheaton, upon the farm where her husband died. In early life Mr. Dodge was, for eighteen winters, a successful teacher, and he and his wife were Protestants, but about the year 1835 they renounced the faith of their fathers and embraced the Catholic faith, and Mr. Dodge was largely instrumental in establishing the Catholic Church at Pompey Hill. He was a man of extensive reading and of strong intellectual power, and although devoted to agricultural pursuits during his active life, was always fond of debate, and was accustomed to attend and participate in the discussions at the Lyceum of the Academy. Their children were Diane, Mary, Hobart and Cynthia.

Diane died in 1856, and though young, she had acquired among a circle of choice friends, an enviable reputation for intellectual and moral worth. She gave early promise of authorship of a high grade of excellence. Mary became the wife of Daniel G. Wheaton, of Pompey, and resides on the farm her father left, surrounded by a large family of children.

Hobart is a lawyer, and resides in Perrysburg, Ohio; he married Sarah, a daughter of Capt. Wilkinson, of Lake Erie; they have three children—two daughters and a son.

Cynthia has chosen to devote her life to the service of the Church; she is Sister of Charity at Mount St. Vincent, on the Hudson.

Ira Dodge, the second son of Ezra Dodge, commenced life with little inheritance but his strong arm and strong common sense; these he has made the most of, and now at a ripe old age resides in LaFayette, which was originally a part of Pompey, enjoying the fruits of his labors. His sons Harvey, Daniel and Homer, all in affluent circumstances and devoted to farming, live in his immediate neighborhood.

Clarissa is the wife of Nelson Hall, of LaFayette.

Clarissa, the third child of Ezra, died at an early age unmarried.

Hezekiah Dodge was a practicing Physician and Surgeon; he went south, and in Georgia married a Planter's daughter: here he lived about twenty years; from Georgia, he moved with his family to Mount Pleasant, Ill. They are both dead, leaving them surviving a large family of children, who are residents of Illinois.

Seabred Dodge was the intellectual giant of the family, and with the assistance of his eldest brother, David F., acquired a thorough classical education; he graduated at Hamilton College, and took high rank as a scholar; espepecially did he excel in mathematics, being, in his day, one of the best mathematicians in the United States. He chose engineering for a vocation, and went to Ohio in 1826, and at first located at Cleveland; he was the chief engineer of the Ohio Canals, and had the supervision of their construction. Late in life he married Jane Town, and they located at Acron, Ohio. His arduous labors and exposures incident to his calling, among the miasmatic swamps and lowlands, engendered disease which took him prematurely from this world, and he died in 1849, leaving his widow but no children to survive him. He was a man of the highest integrity, always guarding with exact justice, the interests of the State. One circumstance in his life illustrates this truth:—Water lime was an article much used in the construction of the canals, and the Ohio lime seemed not to be suited for the purpose; a limited contract was made for a supply from Onondaga County, N. Y., and his brother David F. was chosen to negotiate for what should be needed; making a position for him which promised weath, at what was supposed at the time, a necessary expense to Ohio; the brothers very soon ascertained how to make the Ohio lime answer the purpose, and his brother's rich prospects were quickly ended, to the great saving of the people of Ohio. It would be refreshing for officials and contractors in these days to imitate an example of integrity thus manifested by these two brothers. His widow now resides in the city of Cleveland.

Ezra Dodge, Jr., married Miss Armena Hendricks, and they went to Ohio, but remained but a short time, and finally settled at Mount Pleasant, Ill.

Here he remained till his death, which occurred about the year 1865, leaving a large family, who reside in the vicinity of Mount Pleasant.

THE DUNHAM FAMILY.

Deacon Daniel Dunham, emigrated from Windham, Connecticut, in the year 1795, and established the clothiers' trade, at the old mills in Manlius; he also bought a wild lot of land, of about one-hundred and thirty acres, three miles south-east of Pompey Hill. Captain Samuel Dunham, his son, was born in Windham, Conn., in the year 1780. When he was seventeen years of age, his father sent him alone to work and clear up his new lot of land in Pompey. He boarded at the four corners near the old residence of Dr. Hezekiah Clarke, about two miles south-east of Pompey Hill, also near the place where "Grace Greenwood" was born. From here he went daily to his work, one mile south by marked trees, for two years clearing the land, and he put up a log house. Then his two sisters came, and kept house for him, for five years longer. He then at the age of twenty-five, married a Miss Parmerlee, of Cazenovia; he continued to reside on this farm up to his death, at the age of sixty-nine years; his wife survived him, and he left a large family of children. His son Samuel Mosley Dunham, was born on the old farm in Pompey, September 17th, 1805, and lived with his father until he was twenty-five years of age. He then married and lived for five years on the farm which was the birthplace of Grace Greenwood, and next west of the farm then and till his death, owned by Nicholas Van Brocklin. When at the age of thirty years, the winter of "the deep snow," March 10th, he moved to the town of Clay, where he still resides. The following are the remaining children of Captain Samuel Dunham: General Albert Tyler Dunham, who resided many years at Chittenango, married the daughter of Colonel Sage, of that place, and subsequently removed to Troy, N. Y. He has been engaged on Public Works for many years, and acquired a handsome fortune; he now lives in New York City with his second wife, his first wife having died several years ago; Mary Ann Dunham, now Mrs. Clute, resides in Syracuse; Charlotte Sophia, now Mrs. St. John, now resides in Orange,

New Jersey; Nancy Maria, now Mrs. Knight, resides in Collins, Erie County, N. Y.; Susan Amelia, now Mrs. Abbott, now resides in Fort Dodge, Iowa; Charles Parmerle, the youngest son lived and died on the old homestead, which is now owned by Lewis H. Robinson, married a daughter of Deacon Asa H. Wells, Doxanna, by whom he had two children—Luella and Harriet; his widow and daughters now reside at Pompey Hill.

THE FENNER FAMILY.

James L. Fenner, the father of Frederick W. Fenner, who, it will be remembered very happily responded to a sentiment "to any body," on the occasion of the Pompey re-union, was born in Rhode Island, May 2d, 1777. His wife, Betsey Perry, was born in Dighton, Bristol Co., Mass., June 18th, 1780. They were married February 22d, 1801, and in the Spring following moved to the State of New York, and temporarily settled in the vicinity of Manlius village. But after looking for a favorable locality for his business (being a Millwright,) he resolved to locate on the farm now occupied by Charles Carr, but was unsuccessful in obtaining a good title. It became the property of James Carr, (afterwards Col. Jas. Carr.) Mr. Fenner then located on the farm next west. Soon after saw mills were built and the pioneer settlers became active in lumbering and building dwellings and barns. Slabs became plenty, and the pioneer flourishing village was named Slab Hollow. Mr. Fenner was active in erecting the saw mills, and was one of the proprietors who erected the first grist mill in Slab Hollow. It was built on the creek nearly north of his residence on the road running west to the Murray neighborhood. Mr. Fenner permanently settled in Slab Hollow, in Pompey, as early as 1804. Their second child, a son, was born in Pompey. So early did he come that he had to cut his road from Manlius to his residence in Slab Hollow. He and his family continued to reside in Pompey until March 20th, 1818, when he moved to Lysander, Onondaga Co., where he owned over three hundred acres of wild timbered land, nearly all of which he lived to see under a state of cultivation. During the war of 1812 he was a volunteer in the service of his country. His wife died at Lysander, March 16, 1849, being at the time of her death nearly sixty-nine years of age. Mr. Fenner survived her till January 16th, 1851, being then nearly seventy-four years of age.

Nine children were born unto them, six of whom claim Pompey as the place of their birth: Betsey Fenner was born in Manlius, July 25th, 1803; James L. Fenner, Jr., was born in Pompey, Sept. 14th, 1805; John L. Fenner was born in Pompey, Dec. 1st, 1807; Darius P. Fenner was born in Pompey, Oct. 12th, 1809; Frederick W. Fenner was born in Pompey, Sept. 9th, 1811; Russel B. Fenner was born in Pompey, Feb. 9th, 1814; Harriet J. Fenner was born in Pompey, Sept. 21st, 1816; Luther W. Fenner was born in Lysander, May 14th, 1820; Ethalannah Fenner was born in Lysander, July 21st, 1822. Of these, three have died; Betsey Washburn died in Granby, Oswego County, N. Y., March 20th, 1847; James L. Fenner, Jr., died May 11th, 1856, in Lysander, Onondaga County, N. Y., and Ethalannah Blackman died January 20th, 1862, in Northfield, Minnesota.

Frederick W. Fenner, whose son, James R. Fenner, now resides in Delphi, in Pompey, after living in Lysander four years, came back to Pompey and lived with his aunt, Anna Allen, with whom he lived at the time the name of Slab Hollow was changed to Watervale. It seems that about the year 1823, the citizens of Slab Hollow became dissatisfied with the name of their village; one of two things must be done they said, either to move out or change its name. So they resolved, in a public meeting called for that purpose, to change its name to Watervale, that name being suggested by Ansel Judd, who was always consulted at that day upon all important matters touching the interests of the village. It was also resolved, that Mr. Judd, who was somewhat given to the muses, should originate some lines appropriate to the occasion. Of much that was written, the following lines are given from memory:

> "The timber's all gone, of the Slabs we've made sale,
> We've no more now Slab Hollow, but we've now Watervale."

THE FLINT AND RICE FAMILIES.

Thomas Flint and his brother, Henry, emigrated from England in 1635, where they and their ancestors had dwelt for eight hundred years, as appears by the record. It was Matlock in Derbyshire, by the river Darrow, which place Thomas sold for forty thousand pounds. Thomas came to Boston and settled there, and in 1637 removed to Concord. His property was chiefly expended in improving the town of Concord. For three years he was a representative of the General Court of Massachusetts and Assistant until his death, which occurred Oct. 8th, 1653. Henry was a minister of the gospel and was ordained at Braintree (now called Quincy), March 17th, 1640. He married a sister of President Hoar, and died April 27th, 1668. The eldest son of Henry Flint graduated at Harvard College in 1673, and afterwards became a Professor in that institution. John Flint, son of Thomas, was Lieutenant and Representative in 1677 and 1679. He married a sister of President Oaks, of Harvard College, in 1677, and died in 1687. His children were Mary, Thomas, John, Abigail and Edward.

John Flint, son of the above John, settled in Concord as did his father. His children were Ephraim, Abigail, Mary, Sarah, John, Hannah and Jane.

The next list includes the children of the last named John Flint, who was born May 12th, 1722, was married to Hipsibah Brown, Jan. 12th, 1744. Their children were born and died as follows: Hepsibah, born Nov. 1st, 1747, and died June 4th, 1790; Edward, born Aug. 14th, 1749, died March 25th, 1812; John, born Aug. 11th, 1751, died Oct., 1822; Nathan, born Feb. 11th, 1755, died March 2d, 1824; Ephraim, born April 17th, 1757, died Aug. 22d, 1769;

Thomas, born May 6th, 1759, died Nov. 6th, 1839; Eleazer, born Aug. 9th, 1761, no date of his death; Cumming, born Sept. 11th, 1763, died July 1st, 1831; Abisha, born Oct. 20th, 1766, died April, 1807.

Samuel Rice married Hepsibah Flint, daughter of John Flint and Hepsibah Brown, named in the last foregoing list. Their children were Hepsibah Rice, born Aug. 15th, 1766; John, born March 18th, 1768; Samuel, born Jan. 5th, 1770; Abigail, born May 6th, 1776; Elizabeth, born April 18th, 1778; Ephraim, born May 26th, 1780; Sarah, born March 4th, 1784; Abisha, born March 20th, 1786; Eleazer, born May 20th, 1790.

Shortly after the birth of Eleazer, June 4th, Mrs. Rice died, and her husband, Samuel, married Mrs. Davis about 1792, and they had two children; Thomas, who was born July 30th, 1794, and Amos, born Feb. 5th, 1797. All of Samuel Rice's children were born in Ashby, Middlesex County, Mass.

Thomas Rice, the youngest but one of Samuel Rice's children, married Charlotte Flint, daughter of Edward Flint, named hereafter in the next list of Flints, Jan. 25th, 1814.

Their children were Elizabeth F., who was born in Ashby, Mass., December 16th, 1814; Thomas was born in Ashby, September 17th, 1817.

The following four children were born in Pompey:

Samuel F., born February 3d, 1820; Elmira C., born June 20th, 1822; Amos, born June 27th, 1824; Edward F., born July 2d, 1831.

Thomas Rice and wife, with two children, Elizabeth and Thomas, moved from Ashby to Pompey, and settled on a farm half a mile east of Oran, in March, 1818; he lived on the farm for several years, and then moved into the village of Oran, where he died March 25th, 1843. Elizabeth F. Rice, daughter of the above Thomas, married Erastus P. Williams, of Pompey, July 31st, 1842, and died without children, November 23d, 1844. Thomas Rice who is a resident of Syracuse, and engaged in the grocery trade, married Mary Dorsey, of Geneva, September 2d, 1846; their children were all born in Syracuse, and are all living except the eldest, who died September 12th, 1852.

The following are their names and date of birth:

Eva Mary, born August 26th, 1848; Ella Elizabeth, January 12th, 1854; Thomas Dorsey, March 29th, 1858; Paran Flint, September 11th, 1759; Ernest, September 11th, 1860; Arthur Cleveland, June 7th, 1866; Mary Sera, November 14th, 1872.

Samuel F. Rice, son of the elder Thomas, died September 25th, 1840, and was not married.

Elmira C. died March 29th, 1843, and was never married.

Amos married Mary Gilbert, October 24th, 1854, in Lyons, N. Y.; they had one child—Charles Edward, who died, and Amos died, February 19th, 1858.

Edward F. Rice married Ellen A. Eaton, in Fayetteville, August 31st, 1854; they reside in Syracuse, and he is engaged in the dry goods trade.

The following are the names and date of birth of their children:

Nellie, born June 30th, 1857; Lizzie Elmira, May 25th, 1860; Edward Eaton, June 11th, 1866, and died August 22d, 1866; Edward Irving, born July 12th, 1868. They were all born in Syracuse.

Amos Rice, who was born in Ashby, Middlesex County, Massachusetts, February 5th, 1797, married Betsey Fairbank, of Ashburnham, Mass., April 3d, 1817. They moved to Pompey in the fall of 1821, and remained about twenty-two years, when they moved to Tecumseh, Michigan. They both died in 1859; the wife January 1st, and the husband August 15th; they had five children—the first two born in Mass., and three in Pompey, as follows: Samuel Leonard

Rice, January 27th, 1819; Mary Ann, Aug. 30th, 1821; Elizabeth F., August 31st, 1829; Artemus F. January 24th, 1831; Ellen M., May 7th, 1837; the youngest died May 8th, 1839.

Samuel Leonard Rice married Charlotte H. Tracy, March 31st, 1844; and the following are their children: Joseph E., born July 29th, 1845; George W., September 8th, 1851; Charles H., November 25th, 1854; John T., August 23d, 1856; Frank T., May 13th, 1859; Herbert E., November 13th, 1863.

Elizabeth F. Rice married Henry B. Wier, of La Porte, Iowa, November 27th, 1850.

Mary Ann Rice married Charles Strong, of Tecumseh, Michigan, March 7th, 1841, and died April 12th, 1845, leaving one child—Mary E., who was born February 23d, 1843, and lives in Tecumseh.

Artemus F. Rice married Eugenia H. Chaplin, of Tecumseh, April 24th, 1860; they have one child, Alice; Frances, born January 28th, 1868; they reside in Tecumseh, Mich.

Of the children of Samuel Leonard Rice, who was born January 27th, 1819, two are married; Josephine E. Rice married Lucius W. Parish, October 1st, 1868.

George W. Rice married Francis L. McGregor, November 2d, 1871, but in a few months, death severed the tie—the bride only living till February 14th, 1872.

We will now return to the Flint family, and conclude this extended record. The Edward Flint who was born as before related, August 14th, 1749, married Hepsibah Fletcher, February 28th, 1770; their children were as follows:

Ephraim, born September 14th, 1770, and died September 9th, 1774; Rebecca, born February 2d, 1773, and died September 13th, 1774; Hepsibah, born February 22d, 1775, and died June 21st, 1851; Rebecca, born June 22d, 1777, and died April 6th, 1861; Samuel, born March 16th, 1780, died March 18th, 1855; Ephraim, born August 5th, 1782, died September 21st, 1868; Elizabeth, born April 22d,1785; Abigail, born December 6th, 1787, died October 12th, 1859; Edward, born March 30th, 1790: Charlotte, wife of Thomas Rice above named, born December 22d, 1793; John, born February 20th, 1797, and died October 14th, 1844.

Samuel Flint, named in the last family above, was born at Concord, and as before stated March 16th, 1780. He obtained a liberal education, and was an excellent mathematician; many of the years of his early manhood were spent in teaching, and for several years in New York City. In 1819 he came to Pompey, and engaged in farming, having purchased and settled on the farm north of the one so long owned by Timothy Butterfield.

On the 27th of January, 1825, at Pompey, he was married to Betsey McKnight, who was born Sept 11th, 1802, at Oxford, Chenango Co., N. Y. Mr. Flint continued the pursuit of agriculture till his failing health prevented him, and he continued to occupy his farm till his death, which occurred March 18, 1855. His wife survived him only a few years. They left only one child, Charlotte, who was born June 16th, 1826, and was married to John Soule, July 12th, 1843. Mr. Soule and his wife retain the Flint farm to which they have made additions more than doubling the area.

Their children are as follows: Edward F. Soule, born May 24th, 1844, and died January 14th, 1850.

Samuel Fletcher Soule, born November 2d, 1847. He resides in Pompey, and is agent for the American Sewing Machine.

Ida Elizabeth Soule was born May 2d, 1851, became a teacher, was married to Mr. Clark, June 16th, 1875, and resides in Fabius.

John Flint, born May 12th, 1855, and resides with his parents in Pompey.

Delia A. Soule, born February 23 1858. Is a teacher, resides with her parents during vacations.

Eudora Josephine Soule, born June 24th, 1862, and lives with her parents.

Edward Lawrence, born May 8th, 1865, and died June 14th, 1872.

JOSEPH W. GOLD AND MRS. RHODA GOLD.

Mrs. Rhoda Gold was born in Harwinton, Litchfield Co., Connecticut, in the year 1777. At the early age of thirteen she commenced teaching in her native town, and although the opportunities for acquiring knowledge where not what they are now, she possessing a studious and enquiring mind, dignified and pleasing manners, soon became a successful teacher. At the age of eighteen she was confirmed by the venerable Bishop Seabury. At twenty-five she was married by the late Bishop Griswold, then her beloved pastor and predecessor in the Parish school. Soon after her marriage to J. W. Gold they removed to the then almost wilderness of Pompey, where the fifteen years of her married life were passed. Mrs. Gold was one of the members of Christ's Church in Manlius, from its first organization, and although she lived at a distance of four miles towards Pompey Hill, neither storm nor sunshine detained her from her accustomed place in the church. Waited on by her faithful negro Prince, Sunday morning always found her at her post of duty.

She was always interested in the advancement of education and was one of the original subscribers to the fund for founding Hobart College. She was a constant reader of the Gospel Messenger from its first publication, and when age and infirmities prevented her hearing the word preached in church she solaced herseif with her paper, her prayer-book and her Bible. The last years of her life were spent in Milwaukee, Wisconsin, having survived her husband nearly fifty years.

Joseph Wakeman Gold left his paternal inheritance in Cornwell, Connecticut, to endure the hardships of frontier life in the wilderness of Pompey, in 1796. He was in prosperous circumstances but afflicted with the asthma for thirteen years, which he bore with fortitude, and closed his life at about the age of forty with resignation.

DAVID GREEN.

The early citizens of Pompey will remember David Green. He was born in New Milford, Connecticut, in 1760, and with his wife, whose maiden name was Hannah Pease, immigrated to Pompey in 1796. He took up three hundred acres of land around the Corners which still bear his name. Physically he was a man of large size, weighing three hundred and twenty pounds. As a citizen he was held in high esteem by his neighbors. He was an exemplary christian and a member of the Protestant Episcopal church. He has long since gone to rest with his fathers. Two daughters were the fruits of his marriage, Ellinor and Hannah. The latter of whom married Benj. F. Freeman, of Ray, Michigan. She is dead having left a large family. Ellinor married David Southard, and she also is dead, having left one child living, David Green Southard who is a resident of Pompey, owning and occupying the same land his grandfather, as a pioneer, reclaimed eighty years ago.

CALEB GREEN.

Caleb Green, son of Jedediah Green, was born in the State of Rhode Island, in 1753. Arriving at the age of manhood he married Miss Elizabeth Moon, and moved to Dutchess county, N. Y., just before the outbreak of the war of the Revolution. From information in possession of the family, it is probable that he was with one of the expeditions which marched to the relief of Fort Schuyler in the valley of the Mohawk, in the Summer of 1777, and that he did mueh other service during the continuance of the war. A few years after the conclusion of peace he removed to Easton, Washington Co., where he engaged in farming. In 1806 he came to LaFayette, then a part of the town of Pompey, and purchased a farm of Joseph Rhoades. Here he built the homestead which is now occupied by his grandson, Mr. George H. Green. One acre of the farm was donated for church and school purposes, and on it now stands the Presbyterian church.

Mr. Green died March 29th, 1817, aged 63 years. His wife died Feb. 6, 1828, aged 73 years.

The following were the names of the children of Caleb and Elizabeth Green:—Zilpha, wife of Johnson Babcock, of Tully, (born in 1774); James who died in Bridgeport, Ct.; Comfort, wife of Job Andrews, of LaFayette; Russel, late of Cardiff, (died Nov. 1871, aged 86 years;) Griffin, of New York city; Betsey, wife of John Norton, of Ellery, Chautauque Co., N. Y.; Sally, wite of Minot Hoyt, of Harmony, Chautauque Co., N.Y.; Turpin, who succeeded to his father's estate in LaFayette, and where he died Dec. 20, 1851; and Ransom, the only surviving member of the family, now in the 76th year of his age, who resides in Cleveland, Ohio.

HON. DANIEL GILBERT.

Daniel Gilbert was born in Sheffield, Mass., Sept. 12th, 1786. He was the youngest son of Rev. Joseph Gilbert, who was at that time pastor of the Congregational Church in that place. In 1790, he moved with his father's family to Waybridge, Vt., and thence, in 1799, to Pompey, Onondaga County, N. Y., and settled on Lot No. 66, on the farm lately owned by Albert H. Butterfield, where his father died in 1806, and was buried in Pompey Hill Cemetery. Of his childhood we can learn but little; but very likely he was reared in the industrious and christian manner of such families in those times, and hence the virtue and stability of his riper years. He studied law in Cazenovia, N. Y., and in 1812 was admitted to practice, at which time he moved to

Salina, now the First Ward of Syracuse. He was soon appointed Justice of the Peace, which office he held for twelve years in Salina, and afterwards for about the same length of time elsewhere. In September, 1817, he was married to Miss Harriet Clarke, eldest daughter of the late Dr. Hezekiah Clarke.

In 1832 he removed to Fayetteville, N. Y., where he remained only one year, moving then to Gaines, Orleans County, N. Y. While there, he was appointed Associate Judge of the Court of Common Pleas for that County, which office he held for five years, being at the same time Justice of the Peace and Postmaster.

In 1844, he moved to Coldwater, Mich., whither his sons had preceded him. There his infirmities were such as to prevent his engaging actively in business; the only office which he held there was that of Circuit Court Commissioner.

He was a patriot as well as a christian. When traitorous hands sought to rend the country, to destroy the glorious unity of a nation born in the agony of his fathers, and paptized in the blood sweat of his brothers, old political lines and shibboleths were of but little note in the presence of the question, *whether we shall be, or shall not be, as a nation;* whether we shall have and maintain a national government or not.

Too old and infirm to bear arms, he gave his first-born, (Henry Clarke Gilbert, Colonel of the Nineteenth Michigan Regiment, who fell at the battle of Resaca, gallantly leading a successful charge upon a battery); and when that son was borne home and laid in the tomb, leaving him sonless, he calmly said: "He was dear to me, but our country is worth the life of many such."

He died at the city of Coldwater, Mich., Feb. 15th, 1865. Having faithfully "served his generation, by the will of God he fell asleep," and was laid by the side of kindred dust, to rest until the morning of the resurrection.

ALLEN WILLARD HAYDEN.

HAYDEN FAMILY.

Allen Willard Hayden, a direct lineal descendant of the English baronet, William Hayden, (who came to this country in 1630 and settled in Dorchester, Mass., and who served in the early Pequot Indian War with some little distinction and notoriety,) was born at Harrington, Litchfield County, Conn., in June, 1783, and, together with his father, Allen Hayden, and his three brothers, Zora, Harvey and Allen, Jr., came to Pompey, Onondaga County, N. Y., in Sept., 1800, and settled on what was since called the Todd Farm, about one mile east of Pompey Academy. They cleared about three acres of land and sowed it to wheat that fall. The spring following they cleared the land and set out the orchard west of the house, where it now stands. Four years after, Allen Willard married Abigail Castle, sister of Gen. Jabez and Philo B. Castle, and with his father bought Lot No. 94, situate about two and one-half miles south of the village of Pompey, on which he lived about fifty years. In personal appearance he was commanding, standing six feet in height and very heavily built, being well calculated to bear his part in the hardships of those early times, and many stories are told of his great strength and courage. A man well liked by his neighbors and of a kind and genial disposition. By profession a farmer, he did his work well and was successful, having a large and fine tract of land under good cultivation. He reared a family of eleven children, seven boys and four girls, who all lived to a good age, and to see both father and mother close their earthly career. When the father died, in June, 1858, in his seventy-fifth year, and the mother in January, 1864, in her seventy-ninth year, the whole family, in an unbroken circle, gathered around their remains as the last few words were said before depositing them away from sight forever. Then that united circle of brothers and sisters, all of whom had reached the years of maturity, and some of whom were verging upon old age, and were themselves the heads of families, could feel, as perhaps they had never before felt, that in each they had lost a parent indeed—one who had reared them in the paths of sobriety, honesty and rectitude. Having but little fortune to bestow upon their children, they left them the noble example of a moral and religious life—a heritage which the subsequent history of their descendants has shown that they knew how to appreciate and to profit by.

The first child of Allen Willard Hayden was born in 1806, and lived only a short time.

Rowena, the next child, was born on July 4th, 1807, and was married to Archibald H. Colby, and reared a family of five children, Helen, Henry, Caroline, Spencer and Imogene, all of whom are now living. Rowena died in Rochester, N. Y., in March, 1872.

Samuel P., the third child, was born in July, 1809, and was married to Sarah A., the youngest daughter of Elias Conklin, a short sketch of whose life may be found in this volume. Samuel P. Hayden was a successful farmer, and also a carpenter and joiner, and carried on that business for about thirty years. He lived on the farm adjoining his father's till 1855; he then sold his farm and bought the Wheaton and Jesse Butler farms adjoining, and also the stone store at the village of Pompey Hill, built by Beach Beard, and there carried on the mercantile business successfully for sixteen years. He held prominent positions in society and church, and was a very active member of the Board of Trustees of the Pompey Academy, being one of the executive committee and its President for fifteen years. He was well known, and was often appointed to town offices and filled them with satisfaction to all; he was also appointed Postmaster in 1860 and held the position for six years. He reared a family of six children: Sabra A., born in 1834, and now married to Homer J. Crandall, and living in Syracuse, N. Y.; Ellen L., born in 1837; Elizabeth M., born in 1839; Daniel E., in 1844; Elma D., in 1847, and George, in 1854, Daniel E. served in the Union army during the late rebellion, and is now (1876) residing in Syracuse. In 1869, Samuel P. Hayden left Pompey with his family and moved to Syracuse and engaged in the lumber business. The family all remained together, an unbroken circle, until the spring of 1872, when Mrs. S. P. Hayden, a very amiable, Christian lady, a good mother and an ornament to society, died at the age of sixty-two years, and was buried in the beautiful cemetery at Oakwood. Samuel P. Hayden died in 1874.

The fourth child of Allen Willard Hayden was born in January, 1811, and died in March of the same year.

Seymour, the fifth child, was born in 1812. He was a successful farmer, and lived both in Pompey and Cazenovia, N. Y., and afterwards moved to Syracuse and there died, the first of an unbroken chain of brothers and sisters so long united and without a missing link. Seymour Hayden married Mary Ann Coburn, of Cazenovia, in 1837. They had two children—Loren C., and Sarah A.

Willard, the sixth child of Allen Willard Hayden, was born in 1813, and married Almira Hanchett, of Pompey; he was an active and hard-working farmer, and lived on the old homestead for a long time. In 1870, he with his family moved to Iowa, where he is now living and engaged in carrying on a large farm. His oldest son, Wilson, died when about two years old; Cora J. is married to L. B. Curtis, of Pompey; Oscar E., the third child, now resides in Rochester, N. Y., and is engaged extensively in the manufacture and sale of furniture. William is with his father.

Charles J., the seventh child of Allen Willard Hayden, was born in 1816. He married Esther Dannals, of Fabius, and removed to Rochester early, and there engaged extensively in the furniture trade and manufacture. He was, in 1855–6, mayor of Rochester, and has held other prominent positions. He has been very successful in business, establishing large warehouses and manufactories of furniture, and has amassed a large fortune. His family consisted of Frances J., Oscar E., Omar D., Ella and Charles, Jr. Oscar E. died when quite young, and Omar D. when about twenty-two years old.

Carmi, and a twin brother, who died, the eighth and ninth

children of Allen Willard Hayden, were born in 1818. Carmi Hayden married, in 1847, Ellen Butler, who was a daughter of Merritt Butler, one of the first settlers and at the date of this sketch the oldest resident of Pompey. Carmi is a farmer, keeps a summer boarding house, is also a carpenter and joiner, and is at present (1876) post-master of the village. He is now the only one of the family left in Pompey. He has but one child, Nellie.

Angeline, the tenth child of Allen Willard Hayden, was born in 1819, married Solomon G. Chesebro, of Manlius, in 1842, and removed from there to Syracuse. They reared a family of three daughters—M. Dorleska, Anna L. and Frances M.

James E., the eleventh child, was born in 1822, and married Catharine Ives, of Oswego, in 1848, and settled early in Rochester, where he has since carried on very extensively and successfully the furniture trade. He too has succeeded in establishing a large manufactory and warerooms, and has amassed a large fortune. He has had five children, of whom only three are living, Eloine, Alexander and Aggie.

A. Louisa, the twelfth child of Allen Willard Hayden, was born in 1825, married Salmon P. Bishop, of Pompey, in 1859, and lived with her mother on the old homestead until the latter's death. She then, being broken down in health, removed to Syracuse, where she died in 1867, at the age of forty-two years. She left no children.

Mary Ann, the thirteenth child, was born in 1826, married Lucius A. Nearing, of Pompey, in 1851, and now lives in Syracuse, where Dr. Nearing is a successful and prominent dentist. They have two children—Jennie and George.

Sely C., the fourteenth child of Allen Willard Hayden, was born in 1830, married Anna J. Coburn, of Cazenovia, in 1855, and the same year located in Syracuse, where he has since been extensively engaged manufacturing and dealing in furniture, has established a large business and amassed a good fortune.

This is, in brief, the record of one of the largest and oldest, as well as one of the most successful families of Pompey.

PELATIAH HAYDEN AND DESCENDANTS.

Pelatiah Hayden was born in Newington, Connecticut, moved into Pompey from Kingsboro, N. Y., with his wife Hepsibah and three children, Almira, Lucy and David Ellsworth. This was in February, 1816. He settled two miles south of the present village of Pompey, on a farm partially cleared, joining the farms of John C. and Ira Jerome. Here he remained till his death. His father was a soldier of the Revolution. Almira married Erastus Colton, of Pompey, and died without heirs, November 13, 1838. Lucy married James H. Child, of Sullivan, Chenango county, whom she still survives, also without issue, but the foster mother of two or three, making her home with her brother in the village of Pompey Hill.

David E. was eight years of age, when the family moved from Kingsboro. Arriving at suitable age he married Lucinda Cooley, and continued on the old homestead more than fifty years, bringing up a family of four children—Hiram C., Caroline, Hector and Lucy. Two others died in infancy.

Hiram C. became a minister of the gospel, having graduated at Amherst College, and Union Theological Seminary of New York. At the time of this writing, (1874,) he has preached at Montville, Conn., a year and a half, four years as pastor of the First Congregational church, of Meriden, Conn. Four years as pastor of the First Congregational church, Painesville, Ohio, and is now pastor of the First Presbyterian church of Cleaveland, Ohio. At intervals of labor he has traveled in Europe, Egypt, Palestine, Sinai and California. He has been twice married, first to Elizabeth R. Coit, of Norwich, Conn., May 1st, 1861, who died thirteen months thereafter, leaving an infant daughter who is still living. His second wife was Sarah J. Merriman, of Meridan, Conn., who is the mother of two children.

Caroline Hayden gave herself to the vocation of a teacher of music, and is now located at Lester, Michigan. Hector, married Amelia Jones, of Pompey, after serving his country in a cavalry regiment during the civil war of 1861 to 1865, and settled in Meriden, Conn., pursuing the calling of a carpenter and builder. They have one child. Lucy married Richard Bishop, of Pompey, a farmer, and now resides in Lester, Michigan. They have four children.

HINSDELL FAMILY.

In writing a history of the first settlers of Pompey, the writer has to bear in mind; first, that but little space can be allowed for each family; and secondly, that he must not paint the bravery, honor and virtue of "a long line of noble ancestors," but confine his history to those only who actually settled in Pompey.

Among the above named was David Hinsdell, who was born at Salisbury, Conn., June 30th, 1854; but soon after his birth, his parents were compelled by the hostility of the Indians, to move to Lenox, Berkshire County, Mass., where they had formerly lived. Here David Hinsdell grew to manhood, was married to Farozina Remus, and in due time became the father of five children, removing in 1787 to Galway, Saratoga County, N. Y.

At this place five *more* children were born; when he came to the conclusion that in order to support his growing family, he must remove to some more fertile locality, and Pompey seemed to him the modern Canaan for which he longed. The purchase of one-fourth of lot 6 was made 1794, and preparations made to move and occupy it the next season; but his house taking fire in the night, the family escaped with but little save what clothing they chanced to have on, thus rendering their migration impossible for a time. However, in September, 1795, he sent Moses, his oldest son, then eighteen years of age, to Pompey to build a house and make such preparations as would enable the family to follow the coming winter: once arrived upon the scene of his future labors, the youthful Moses found that he had no resources to draw upon, but his brawn and muscle; therefore, he drew upon them, and his *draft was honored*, for he first cut, logged, and burnt over two acres, which he sowed to wheat; then from the logs he had sawed for the purpose, he built a log house, covering it with bark and having it completed ready for the occupancy of the family who came in February, 1796. Here David Hinsdell had two *more* children born, and from a school roll now in possession of the family, it appears that in the winter of 1799 and 1800, six of his children attended a school taught by Levi Jerome.

David Hinsdell died in 1822, and his wife some years later, the homestead passing into the possession of Chauncy Hinsdell, who lived on it until his death, which occured a few years since, and his children still own it. All the sons except Chauncy and Moses,sought homes in other localities; Moses buying fifteen acres on lot 17, in 1801, of Mr. Sweet, giving therefor his note, as he had nothing else to give—adding however, in the course of time, five hundred acres to the first purchase. In order to follow out in detail my sketch of Moses Hinsdell, I must go back to 1798, when being twenty years of age,he bargained with his father for his *time*, cutting off therefor, a certain piece of timber, which being duly finished, he stepped out into the world to make his own furtune, being possessed of good vigorous constitution, the clothes he had on, two pairs of shoes and his good axe. In 1800 he joined hands and fortunes with Rachael Hibbard, marrying her in November of that year; her worldly possessions being one cow, eight sheep, and I think a little crockery; she also was possessed of good common sense, a kind loving heart full of noble impulses and good will to all, and a self sacrificing disposition, which stood the test of more than forty years of married life; helping over the rough places, cheering the despondent, restraining the wayward and volatile, developing into a pure Christian mode of life which enabled her to say "thy will be done," when she was called to her reward in 1841. There were born unto this couple ten children—six sons and four daughters, viz: Eli B. Hinsdell, who died at Salina, in 1856. Harriet Hinsdell, (Mrs. David Barber,) now living in Syracuse. Polly Hinsdell, (Mrs. John S. Wells,) who died in 1863. Eliza Hinsdell, (Mrs. L. B. Pitcher,) living in the town of Salina. Samuel Hinsdell, living at Fairmount, N. Y.

David H. Hinsdell living at Manlius, N. Y., Stephen Hinsdell living at Syracuse. Myraette Hinsdell, (Mrs. D. Fairbank,) living at Kalamazoo, Mich. Perry H. Hinsdell living in the town of Salina, and Moses B. Hinsdell who died in Lyons, Mich. In 1843, he was again married to Mrs. Phebe Underwood, who is still living at Forrestville, N. Y., but in 1857 he died in Pompey, at the age of seventy-eight years. I have remarked that Moses Hinsdell started out in life at twenty years; and he so started determined to *succeed*, if truth, integrity and industry *could* succeed—as he knew they *must*. Following firmly in the path he marked out, he soon was a man of influence among his fellows, and during his long life, no man could accuse him of extortion, fraud or untruth. In his later years, he often remarked with pride, that no note he ever gave came to maturity unpaid, except in one instance, when an $100 note given on demand to the holder's order, came back to him after "many days," having passed current from one man to another in the usual first of April payments, until over twenty endorsements graced its back, having passed through over a score of hands, and paid over $2,000 of indebtedness. A *very positive* man, and one accustomed to think and act quickly, he was often wrong, and clung to that wrong with a tenacity worthy of a better cause; but no man was more willing to accept the truth than he, when it was shown to him. He was generous to a fault in a cause he deemed *worthy*, but no man, or set of men, ever caused him to swerve from a position his judgment told him was well taken. He was just the kind of a man to settle in a new country, and help to develop it, and there are too few of them in this present day. He never mixed much in politics, always refused office, and really accomplished what he said ought to be every man's mission, viz: "to make the world some better for having lived in it."

DAVID HIBBARD.

The reader will recognize the above as a Pompey name. The subject of this sketch was a revolutionary soldier, like many other pioneer residents of Pompey. He settled in Pompey on lot No. 6, in 1794. In addition to agricultural pursuits, he was a carpenter and joiner. During his early residence in Pompey, his son John was killed by the falling of a tree. This left him four sons and five daughters. The names of the four remaining sons were Samuel, Robert, Jacob and Isaac V.V. Hibbard, the latter of whom was a member of the N. Y. Assembly in 1853. Samuel M. Hibbard, a son of Isaac V. V., now occupies the old homestead of his grandfather, David. Samuel Hibbard, son of David, has two sons resident in Pompey; one bears the name of his grandfather, David Hibbard; the name of the other is Charles Hibbard.

HEZEKIAH HOPKINS.

Col. Hezekiah Hopkins was born in Harwinton, Litchfield Co., Conn., and moved thence with his family in 1800 to Clinton, Oneida Co., N. Y. Here he remained about two years, and then came to Pompey Hill. He was married to Eunice Hubbell, by whom he had nine children; five of them were sons and four daughters—Sheldon, Milton, Harry, Hezekiah, Jr., Richard, Fanny, Laura, Dothy and Charlotte, the latter being born about a year after their arrival in Pompey. Col. Hopkins kept the hotel on the site now (1874,) occupied by Peter Oley, some twenty-four years, very much to the satisfaction of the public, keeping a very temperate, quiet and orderly place. He sold to his son Harry and purchased a small farm near the village, where he and his wife lived with his son Hezekiah until their death, being at the time of their decease about seventy-eight years of age. Soon after purchasing the hotel, Harry built an addition and continued to keep the hotel about three years, when he leased it to Capt. Pitt Dyer, for a term of years.

He was Deputy Sheriff under Doctor Granger, and a very faithful and efficient officer. He also held the office of Commissioner of Highways. In 1837 he sold his real estate in Pompey, and moved to Cleveland, Ohio, leaving his oldest son Jerome and daughter Caroline behind, both being employed in Manlius village, Jerome as a clerk in the store of Azariah Smith, and Caroline as a teacher. His wife, (Theodocia Jerome,) died of consumption, in Cleveland, in 1839. In 1841 he married Mrs. Theodocia Hamilton, near Medina, Ohio, where he lived on a farm with her for thirty years, when she died. And now being eighty-one years old and in failing health, he came to live with his son Jerome, in Cleveland, where he continued till his death in 1872. He was present at the Re-Union, June 29th, 1871. Mrs. Beardslee, of Syracuse, is now the only surviving member of the old Col. Hopkins' family. Harry Hopkins' surviving children are Jerome, George and Sophia, all living in and near Cleveland, Ohio.

ENSIGN HILL.

Colonel Ensign Hill, who was one of the pioneer settlers of the east part of Pompey, near Delphi, was born in Washington, Berkshire County, Mass., May 28th, 1772; his wife Polly H. Kellogg, was born in Dalton, Berkshire County, Mass., February 29th, 1776; they were married September 29th, 1801, and moved to Pompey in the fall of that year. Mr. Hill had been to Pompey the year before, had purchased fifty acres of land and cleared enough to put up a pioneer house, near where the watering trough now is, about one hundred rods south of Delphi village. All he had when coming to Pompey, was a horse, saddle and bridle, which he sold to Judge Platt near Utica; the avails were paid towards his land; although possessed of the usual amount of energy and pluck characteristic of early settlers, the toil and hardships incident to pioneer life caused him occasionally to feel despondent. When one day indulging in a melancholy mood, a stranger rode up to where he was clearing the forest and entering into conversation, finally offered him fifty dollars for his bargain in the purchase of his land; he thought if the stranger could see fifty dollars in it, he could find it, and so he still toiled on, never more indulging the wish to return permanently to the home of his childhood. He added largely to his first purchase, and became one of the leading farmers in his neighborhood; and although his pursuit was the tilling of the soil, he always manifested a lively interest in public affairs. Descended from revolutionary ancestors, he early formed an attachment to the military service, and became colonel of a regiment of militia. He was a New England Democrat, and an ardent admirer of Andrew Jackson. He was an earnest supporter of the administration of Madison, during the war of 1812. He lived to see Pompey, the home of his adoption, a populous and thriving town; his first wife died December 20th, 1818, after which he married a widow lady, Mrs. Humphreyville. Mr. Hill died December 4th, 1832, having lived to see his favorite general and statesman elevated to the Presidency of the United States a second time. All his children were born in Pompey. Ensign W., the eldest, was born June 20th, 1802, was a farmer and merchant, an excellent penman and book-keeper; he resided in Pompey the whole of his life, which terminated September 7th, 1870. Three children, Orange, Lydia S. and Charlotte, died in childhood.

A second son, Orange, was born February 21st, 1806, and now lives in Delphi, and is a farmer.

Charles R. K. Hill was born January 3d, 1810, and now lives on the old homestead in the elegant mansion erected by his father; he is now an acting Justice of the Peace in Pompey, elected as a democrat, although his party is in a large minority in the town.

William Hull Hill was born July 4th, 1812, and was

named in honor of Hull's victory over the English. He retains the patriotism of his childhood, born as he was upon the nation's birthday; he it is of whom Luther R. Marsh said, upon the occasion of the Re-union of Pompey's children, June 29th, 1871: "that he came from New York with one Hull Hill, who had since acted as though he owned the whole Hill.

Mary Ann Hill was married to Dr. Rocius Morse, and lived in Elmira; died January 6th, 1870.

James L. Hill was the only child by his second wife; he married an only daughter of Hamilton Allen, of Pompey Valley, and now resides near Syracuse.

JOSIAH HOLBROOK.

Josiah Holbrook was one of the early settlers of Pompey. He was born in the year 1757, in Adams, Mass., and married Rachel Wright. They resided in Adams, where some of their children were born, till 1792, when they commenced their journey to Pompey. Mr. Holbrook had purchased of a soldier a wood-land farm in Pompey, which he had never seen. Equipped as pioneer settlers usually were, with all their household goods loaded upon a cart drawn by a yoke of oxen and a single horse for a leader, in 1792 they came to Springfield, Otsego Co., N. Y. Here they tarried with his sister till the spring of 1793, when in March they finished their pilgrimage to their future home located on Lot No. 53, the farm recently owned by Mr. Hubbard, east of Pompey Center. The family at that time consisted of Josiah Holbrook, his wife, father and mother and six children—Abigal, Silas W., Patty, Frestus, Rachel and Electa. After they came to Pompey four more children were born unto them, who, in the order of their ages, were Adolphus, Josiah G., Amanda and Samuel. Adolphus was born in 1793, and is said to be the third white child born in Pompey. Few were then the conveniences of life, and many hardships were encountered. There were no roads or bridges; by marked trees they came; they pounded their corn in a mortar or went to Whitestown, near Utica, to mill.

It is true that Surveyors, the pioneers of civilization, had come before them and marked the trees, but before the golden harvests could be reaped, the majestic forests must yield to days of constant toil. How many of our generation are fitted for the obstacles which they manfully met, and heroically overcome? About this time, over in Pompey Hollow came Ozias Burr, Samuel Draper and Mr. Lamb. David Green, too, came the same year and settled on what has since been called "Green's Corners." Soon after came Barak Holbrook and Luke Holbrook, who married Wm. Duguid's sisters. William Duguid, another of Pompey's pioneers, who is the ancestor of the Duguid family.

Notwithstanding the limited resources at command, Mr. Holbrook, in common with his town's people, early became interested in public improvements. He was one of the first subscribers to the Pompey Academy fund. As we look over the individual history of Pompey's pioneers, and note the personal sacrifices they made from their small and toilsome gains to the establishment of schools and churches and the interests of society, and make comparison with the present public spirit manifested, we may well pause and ask ourselves whether this is an age of progress in Pompey or of retrogression. Mr. Holbrook was a Christian, and attended the Presbyterian church.

Only two of his children are living. Festus, at the age of eighty-six years, resides in Michigan, having raised a large family who are all dead. Josiah G. resides south of Cold Water, Michigan, and has a large family. These two sons left Pompey and went west in the spring of 1815. All of his children were married while living in Pompey. He died in November, 1831, at the age of seventy-five years, and he and his wife, his father, mother, two sons and three daughters, all lie beneath the green sod of the old hill town which they assisted to make rich with golden harvests.

Silas W. Holbrook, the eldest son of the pioneer Josiah,

married Thankful Skinner, whose father was also a Pompey pioneer, having settled on Lot No. 22, near Oran, in 1794. Their children were Silas L. Holbrook, Levi S. Holbrook, Aurelia Holbrook, Chapin M. Holbrook and Josiah E. Holbrook. Of these Silas L. married Nancy Hubbard, by whom he had three children, Henry L., B. Franklin and Dwight. They all live in Pompey.

Levi S. Holbrook married Fidelia Woodward, September 1, 1831; they have no children. He now resides in Syracuse, having left Pompey a few years ago. He has been honored by his fellow citizens with various public trusts. From 1853 to 1858 inclusive, he represented Pompey in the Board of Supervisors, and the latter year was a member of the State Legislature. From 1862 to 1869 he was a revenue officer of the general government.

Aurelia Holbrook married Samuel E. Tarbell, and they reside in Wisconsin.

Chapin M. Holbrook married Malinda Safford, and they and their only child live in Pompey.

Josiah E. Holbrook married Alcemena Smith, daughter of John Smith, a Pompey pioneer, and they reside in DeWitt, N. Y. They have no children.

Daniel W. Holbrook, another grandchild of the old pioneer, married Martha Porter, of Pompey, and moved to Michigan, where he died. His wife now resides in Syracuse, and her son, Levi, with her. Their only remaining son, Daniel, is a resident of California.

Adolphus Holbrook was twice married, and Josiah G. Holbrook, of Jamesville, N. Y., was one of his children by his first wife. By his second wife he had two children, Maria and Henry H., the son only being now living, making his home in Jamesville, N. Y. His widow lives in Pompey with Lucien Northrup, who was the husband of Maria, who died several years ago. Thus have we traced an imperfect record of another Pompey family, and the reason why we have not made mention of them all, is because our information is not sufficient to make any further record authentic.

JONAS HINMAN.

Jonas and Esther Hinman settled in Pompey in the year 1796 or 1797; he was one of the earliest pioneers of the wilderness of Onondaga County.

It is not necessary in this sketch, to give in detail, nor delineate particularly the hardships and sufferings of those times of which the surviving children and grand-children of those strong souls are conversant; therefore, I pass to the time when Mr. and Mrs. Hinman were two of nine persons who organized the first Baptist Church of Pompey, which, at a later period, moved to Manlius village.

Mr. Hinman's family consisted of twelve children, and while the youngest child was an infant, by trusting too implicitly in human nature, he lost his property, since known as the Hubbard farm. He transplanted the apple orchard, still standing—nearly three-fourths of a century ago, when his oldest children were so small that with difficulty they carried water in little bottles to water and keep alive the trees. At the time he met with his reverse fortune, he was past his prime in life, and broken in health; still, with his hopeful temperament and natural energy, he divided his family, and boldly entered on his second pilgrimage as pioneer in the wilds of Lysander.

When he had there completed his log-cabin, he removed his wife and the younger children to the new home, to share the privations attending a new settlement, with this difference between the first and the last—in the last instance he had eight children to suffer with him, instead of two.

Mr. Hinman was generous to a fault, and his benevolence, supported by a deep-seated sense of christian piety and honor, and a full trust in Providence, and his natural firmness, all working together on his active nervous brain, set the ball in motion which should abolish imprisonment for debt. He looked upon that law as oppressive, unjust and wicked. He was bondsman for the poor, unfortunate men, till at last he released a villain, St. John, who was not a poor man, but secreted his property, and absconded; consequently Mr. Hinman was obliged to sell his farm to pay the bond, and beggared his family, for which they suffered, as only natural pride and a preponderance of inherited sensitiveness can be made to feel, where poverty was looked upon as low and degrading by those who were more fortunate in possessing material wealth.

I will say to the mothers of the present young generation of Pompey's children—instruct your children that ignorance is far more degrading in every position or department in life to which they may be called, than honest poverty.

Nearly twenty years later Mr. and Mrs. Hinman returned to Pompey to die among their brethren; their married life was sixty-two years, and in death they were not long separated. Mrs. Hinman died aged seventy-eight; Mr. Hinman survived his wife but one year, aged eighty-six; they were buried in the cemetery at Manlius village.

The names of Mr. Hinman's children, and where located, are as follows: Mary W. Symonds, Watertown, N. Y.; Electa Drake, Yonkers, N. Y.; Sarah Clapp, dead; Hervey, dead; Betsey, dead; Hiram, dead; Horace, Lapeer City, Mich.; Lydia M. Wisner, Mahattan, Kansas; Charlotte N. Clement, Pompey, N. Y.; Heman, St. Catharines, Canada West; Samuel Hayden, unknown; Emily H. Robinson, New York City.

DANIEL KNAPP.

The subject of this notice was Daniel Knapp, who emigrated from Orange County, N. Y., to Pompey, Onondaga County, N. Y., about the year 1800; he located on a farm one mile north from Pompey Academy; his wife's maiden name was Christianna Phelps, with whom he settled on the above mentioned farm in 1803; they lived together on that farm till 1823, enduring the hardships and engaged in the active labor of pioneer life. During this period, six sons were born unto them. He died August 6th, 1823, and was

Joshua Leonard

the first one buried in the Pompey Hill Cemetery as it is now located. His wife assumed the responsibility of settling the estate and managing the farm, exhibiting great energy and tact in her arduous duties; she paid off the heirs as they became of age, which left her full control of the whole farm, which she managed for over forty years; at the age of eighty-three years, having become incapacitated to continue the management of her farm, she went to reside with her son, Harry Knapp, who still continues to reside in Pompey, where she died January 1st, 1869, at the advanced age of eighty-seven years, leaving her children to inherit a second time the same estate upon which she and her husband had settled sixty-six years before. The value of her estate at the time of her death, was about eight thousand dollars. Such in brief is the history of one of the early settlers of Pompey and his faithful wife, furnished by one of their children. It is refreshing in these days of indolence and ease to notice the energy and pluck of such pioneer settlers as these, and it is eminently proper to rescue their memory from forgetfulness and present them as examples to the rising generation.

REV. JOSHUA LEONARD.

COMPILED BY LUTHER R. MARSH.

Rev. Joshua Leonard was a conspicuous feature in the early history of this town; he came of English stock; through the unvaluable records published by the New England Historic-Genealogical Society of Boston, we are enabled to trace his ancestry. Rev. Peres Fobes, L. L. D., pastor of the Congregational Church in Raynham, Mass., furnished, some seventy years ago, an account of the Leonard family, which is believed to be the first family genealogy of any considerable extent printed in New England; and, in 1851, William R. Deane, a member of the Society, brought the memoir down two generations later. From these records, it appears that the progenitor of Rev. Joshua Leonard was James Leonard, who, with his brother Henry, son of Thomas

Leonard, came from Pontypool, in the maritime English County of Monmouthshire, bordering on South Wales; a region rich with collieries and blazing with furnaces, penetrated by the fertile vales of the Usk and the Wye—the scene of important historical events; where Owen Glendower was defeated, and where, long after, Cromwell triumphed. The brothers, James and Henry Leonard, came to Taunton, Mass., in 1652, and James established there the first iron-works in the United States, and died, 1691, aged seventy-three years. The manufacture of iron seems to have been an inheritance of the Leonards—not only before they came, but afterwards; both in New Jersey, where Henry settled and established that business—followed there by successive generations—and in Massachusetts, where, at Lynn, Braintree, Rowley village, and Taunton, and at a later date at Canton, they set up their mills; so that it came to be said that, "where you can find Iron Works, there you will find a Leonard."

"They were probably interested in most, if not all of the iron works established in this country within the first century after its settlement, and it is a remarkable fact," says Mr. Deane, in 1851, "that the iron manufacture has continued successively, and generally very successfully, in the hands of the Leonards or their descendants, down to the present day. Their old forge, though it has been many times remodelled, has been in constant use for nearly two hundred years, and is now in the full tide of successful operation."

"James and his sons," says the same authority, "often treated with the Indians, and were on such terms of friendship with them, that when the war broke out, King Philip gave strict orders to his men never to hurt the Leonards. Philip resided in winter at Mount Hope; but his summer residence was at Raynham, about a mile from the forge."

Tradition says he was buried there under the front porch of the old Leonard mansion—a mansion which sheltered the heads of six generations of the name—the brick used in its construction having been brought from England.

James Leonard, (son of above James,) and his son James, were both Captains, and each lived to be more than eighty years old. Stephen Leonard was a son of the latter, and was a justice of the Peace, and a Judge of the Court of Common Pleas. His oldest son, Major Zephaniah Leonard, born March 18th, 1704, of Taunton, died on the same day his wife, 23d April, 1776; he in his sixty-third, she in her sixty-second year, and were both buried in the same grave; the inscription on the monument is historical.

He was a man of enterprise and energy, possessing great native dignity of character, and filled with honor the distinguished station in society which he attained. In 1761 he was appointed a Judge of the Court of Common Pleas, which office he held until his death. Their oldest son, Captain Joshua Leonard, was born January 5th, 1724, and died 27th November, 1816, aged 92 years.

His oldest son was the Rev. Joshua Leonard, (of the sixth generation from the progenitor James,) the subject of this notice, who was born June 25th, 1769. He graduated at Brown University, 1788; was first settled in Ellington, Conn., whence, about the year 1797 or 1798, he went to Cazenovia, Madison county, N. Y., then in its infancy; stationing himself on the rim of civilization as it advanced westward across the continent. At this place, on the 17th of May, 1799, he formed a Presbyterian Church—the first one there, consisting of only nine members; he continued the pastor of this church about fourteen years, when, on account of impaired health, he resigned his charge; the church then numbering 127 members. In a theological work published by him at Cazenovia in 1834, "The Unity of God," he says: "I was the first pastor who settled in this wide region of country; my church was a single, independent, Congregational Church; I was a single, independent, Congregational Minister. From Cazenovia to the Pacific Ocean, there was not one Congregational or Presbyterian pastor; not one in this State to the north or south of me; not one to the east, nearer than Mr. Steele, of Paris, in Oneida county." On leaving the Cazenovia church, he moved to Pompey, and, in 1814, became preceptor of the Pompey Academy; occupying that position for eight years. Under his administration that Institution flourished, and had a wide influence.

He still continued to accept the frequent invitations to fill the neighboring pulpits. He was a man of sterling integrity, untiring industry, of a fetterless independence and boldness, of very extensive reading, large and accurate acquirements, and a singular power of condensed expression.

As, robed in a long flowing morning gown, with high hose and knee-buckles, staff in hand, he used to take his rapid morning walks through the village, he left an impression of dignity and goodness on the minds of the youth so vivid, that it has yet scarcely been dimmed by the half century intervening.

He died at Auburn, at his daughter's, Mrs. Helen L. Williams, December 18th, 1843, aged 75 with faculties unimpaired, retaining his undiminished interest in all the literary and scientific progress of the day; Mrs. Leonard having died at Lincklaen, Chenango county, nineteen years previous. Of their nine children, six survive, and reside at Chicago, Ill. the youngest of whom is sixty-three years old; longevity being one of their characteristics, as if some of the iron of their manufacture had entered into their composition; a sister still surviving, at Raynham of the age of ninety-nine.

LUTHER MARSH

Must have come to Pompey sometime prior to 1812. Born, Walpole, N. H., October 14, 1782; died, Chicago, November 14, 1859, aged 77. He was son of Captain Elisha Marsh, (who subsequently removed from Walpole to Guilford, Vermont,) and grandson of Rev. Elisha Marsh, a graduate of Harvard, and the first minister at Westminster, Mass., from 1742 to 1757.

LUTHER MARSH.

This clergyman was arraigned for heresy, for saying that "obedience is the condition of salvation;" and that "he would as soon worship the devil as worship such a being as requires more from his creatures than they are able to perform;" for saying that "if all that was required of a man was to believe, then the condition of salvation was easy and pleasant to fools." He was a spicy character. One morning, on meeting the sheriff from a neighboring town, who was on his way to sue the town, and who, pursuant to the custom to serve writ on some one of the citizens, served it on him; saying in a pleasant manner as he handed him the writ; "The grace of God, Mr. Marsh." "Yes, by the hands of the Devil," was the quick retort. He moved to Walpole, Cheshire Co., N. H., and became Judge of the Court of Common Pleas.

Luther Marsh was the fifth, in direct line, from *John Marsh*, one of the first settlers of Hadley, Mass., and afterwards, 1639, of Hartford, Conn., where he married Anne, daughter of John Webster, Governor of Connecticut. Luther Marsh, June 24th, 1812, married *Emma Rawson*, daughter of Doctor Thomas Hooker Rawson, of Canandaigua, N. Y. She was the fourth from Rev. Grindal Rawson, of Mendon, Mass., the friend and classmate at Harvard, of Cotton Mather; who, in preaching his funeral sermon, (1715,) said, "We honored him for his doing the work of an *Evangelist* among our Judeans, of whose language he was a *master* that had scarce an equal, and for whose welfare his projection and performances were such as to render our loss herein hardly to be repaired. Such services are Pyramids." Grindal Rawson was the twelfth child of Edward Rawson, of Boston, who came over from England in 1636, and was, for thirty-six years, 1651-1686, Secretary of the colony of Massachusetts. Emma Rawson was also the sixth from Rev. Charles Chauncey, the second President of Harvard College. She died at Pompey, April 4th, 1820. By this marriage there were four children, of whom two survive; Luther Rawson Marsh, lawyer, New York city, and Elisha Azro Marsh, dealer in mines, California.

Luther Marsh married, for second wife, Margaret Leonard, daughter of Rev. Joshua Leonard, of Pompey. She resides at Chicago. By this marriage there were two children, Alexander Marsh, lumber merchant, and Joshua Leonard Marsh, lawyer, both of Chicago, Ill.

Luther Marsh was High-Sheriff of Onondaga county for two terms, 1823-6.

NOAH PALMER, Sr.

Was born in Brantford, Conn.,in the year 1764. When he was seven years old his father died in Connecticut,about the beginning of the Revolutionary War. As early as 1790 he came from Brantford to Cazenovia, and bought a place with Col. Linclaen, in 1797, in Pompey, near Oran, now owned by his grand-son Daniel D. Palmer. Upon this farm he lived thirty-eight years. After he died his son Noah owned it thirty-six years. He was a nail maker, and worked for old Col. Linclaen at that business for five or six years. It is said he made the first nails that were used in building in the town of Pompey. He died in the year 1835, upon the land which he purchased in 1797, in Pompey; his son Noah succeeding him in the title to the estate. Two of his children, Noah and Martha, were born in Pompey, and these are both now (1874) dead. One daughter Mrs. Edmund Thomas, is living. Mr. Palmer was of that type of manhood whose stern and unyielding integrity bears fruit, in the years when his form lies silent in the grave, of whom it may be justly said, "Tho' dead he yet speaks."

DR. SILAS PARK.

Silas Park was born in Litchfield, Conn., December 1st, 1778. Having acquired a good education, he commenced the study of medicine with his uncle, Dr. Robt. Starkweather in Chesterfield, Mass. He moved to Pompey West Hill, in 1800, and commenced the practice of his profession,his ride extending from Liverpool, on the north, to Port Watson, (Cortland village,) on the south, and from Skaneateles on the west, to Cazenovia on the east. This area then contained less than 3,000 white settlers whose population is now over 200,000 people. In 1802, he returned to Massachusetts and married Miss Dolly Clapp, of Chesterfield, daughter of Col. Amasa Clapp, of Chesterfield, a soldier of the Revolution. On his return to Pompey, crossing the Hudson river at Albany in a sleigh, the ice broke, letting sleigh, horses, baggage, wife and all into the water. They narrowly escaped drowning. They were rescued by citizens of Albany, who by chance saw them in their danger. This accident compelled them to remain in Albany a day or more. Nothing unusual occurred during the remainder of their journey. In 1803 their first child and only son, Dr. Elijah Park was born. In the war of 1812, Dr. Silas Park went as a surgeon with the soldiers who were called from this section to Smith's Mills and Sackett's Harbor. There he met surgeons of the regular army, and he took a high position among them as a skillful physician and surgeon. He died in 1824. His wife survived him, living at the old home till she reached the age of 95 years, and died in the year 1867. When we ask what can be said of her, the answer is, "Anything and all that is good."

Their only son, Dr. Elijah Park was born in Pompey, now LaFayette, April 1st, 1803, and he studied with his father, and also with Doctors Beach and Davis of Marcellus, and his uncle Dr. Elijah Park, of Otisco, He graduated at the Berkshire Medical Institute, December 26, 1826. He was at the time he graduated and has continued to be a practicing Physician up to the time of his death, his home being in LaFayette village. He was married twice, the first time August 24, 1824, to Miss Catharine Parent, of Otisco. By her he had ten children, four sons and six daughters; seven of them, two sons and five daughters are married and living within three hours ride of the old home. One married a carpenter and joiner, the others are farmers or farmers' wives. He was married a second time, April 14, 1843, to Betsey Parent, his first wife's sister, by whom he had two children, both of whom are dead. Both his wives are also dead, Catharine died September 20, 1842, and Betsey December 4, 1867. Dr. Park held the office of Supervisor of the town of LaFayette, three years 1861–2 and 3, and was a Justice of the Peace one, 1869. His medical practice extended over the county of Onondaga, and often in the neighboring counties. For nearly fifty years he rode over the hills and through the valleys of his native county, kindly administering to the wants and necessities of the afflicted. His life was too busy in dispensing the healing art, to allow him time to make collections, and like Dr. Wm. Taylor, of Manlius, although he did a business that would have yielded a large fortune, he died June 17, 1873, leaving but a moderate share of worldly possessions, but rich in the kind wishes of his many friends, and richer still in the smiles of his beneficent Redeemer.

The following notice of his death appeared in a Syracuse paper, the day after his decease.

Death of Dr. Elijah Park of LaFayette.—Dr. Elijah Park, one of the oldest and most respected residents of this county, died at his residence in LaFayette, on Tuesday morning, aged 71 years. Dr. Park was born in the town of LaFayette, and was the son of Silas Park, an eminent physician, who resided in that town. The son followed the footsteps of his father, attended medical lectures at Berkshire Medical College in Pittsfield, Mass., in 1827, and became one of the most popular physicians in this section of the State. He had a very extensive practice in his immediate neighborhood, and was frequently called as counsel to other localities. The deceased was always an active politician and popular citizen, and represented his town for several terms in the Board of Supervisors, and held other responsible town offices. He was elected Justice of the Peace three terms in succession at a period when the party with which he acted was in a large minority in the town, but his well known integrity and capacity carried him over party lines and elected him to the office. He was always among the foremost in village or town enterprises, and his judgment, sagacity, and proved integrity and honesty, placed him in the front rank among his fellow citizens on all occasions where intelligence, prudence, and sagacity, were needed to direct the councils of the people. He had a wide circle of relatives and acquaintances, and his loss will be sincerely mourned by all who knew him. The funeral will take place on Thursday afternoon at 2 o'clock, under the direction of the order of Odd Fellows, of which the deceased was a prominent member, and of the order of Free and Accepted Masons of which he was also a member.

LEMAN HARMON PITCHER.

COMPILED BY LEMAM BAKER PITCHER.

Leman H. Pitcher was born in Rutland, Vermont, November 26th, 1781; he was the son of Reuben, the son of Ebenezer, the son of Samuel, Jr., the son of Samuel, Sr., the son of Andrew, who came of Somerset County, England, in 1633, and settled in Dorcester, Mass., where he died in 1660.

Leman H. Pitcher went to school about six months before he was eight years old, and about three more between the age of twelve and thirteen. From eight to twelve he lived with his uncle Harmon, who was too poor to send him to school, yet rich enough to send his own son of like age, summer and winter. At one time he asked his uncle if he might go to school, and the reply was "that it cost money," and "that it was not expected that everybody would go." This caused him to cry, for which he was called a "booby," and ordered off to bed. In later years, he has often told his children, that this circumstance caused him to form a resolution, "that he would know something if he had to steal it." While young Oliver, his cousin, played and slept, Leman H., as opportunities offered, read his books, and at twelve he was the better scholar. The next year he lived with his mother, and the two succeeding years worked out for $50 and $65 per year. In 1796, he and the family moved to Pompey, and settled where Adison H. Clapp now resides. In the winter of 1797 or 1798, he and John Sprague studied arithmetic during the evenings with an old surveyor, who lived near Watervale, to whom they gave a bushel of oats, then of the value of fifteen cents, for each evening.

In November, 1798, his right foot was nearly severed just below the ankle joint. When climbing a well post to assist in adjusting the well sweep, his step-father Starkweather, attempted to strike the axe in the post, to assist him in climbing, but his foot slipping just as the axe fell, received the full force of the blow, and his foot was held only by the skin of the heel. A council of Doctors was held, and all advised amputation; one said, "it might possibly get well;" to this he replied, "I am without education, trade or money, and I had rather go to the grave with my foot, than to live a poor cripple all my life;" "do the best you can, I am resolved to live or die with my foot." During the following year while the wound was healing, he studied hard to prepare himself for teaching schoool and for business. In 1800 he taught his first school in a school house that stood near the corners about a mile north-westerly from the Hill towards Jamesville. In 1801 and afterwards he taught on the Hill as related by Mrs. Miller in her paper, June 29, 1871. He continued to teach five or six years, winters, and sometimes summers. Between 1801 and 1808 he was constable and deputy sheriff, and about this time he became a free mason. In the Spring of 1808 he married Hannah Baker, aunt of Dea. Samuel Baker, of Pompey Hill, and moved to Camillus, N. Y.

Leman B. Pitcher was in Camillus January 30th, 1809. Mr. Pitcher was engaged in the fall of 1810, and the winter and summer following in preparing and rafting hewn timber for the Montreal market. Going down the Oswego river he ventured too near the falls and was carried over with a broken raft with two other men one of whom was drowned. All he had (about $4,000) and something more, was embarked in the business. After some loss of timbers and many delays he sailed from Oswego with his re-collected raft and was again damaged in running the rapids of the St. Lawrence river, and finally when about fifty miles above Montreal the news of the declaration of war reached him. This news was unexpected. Two days later his timber in Montreal was worth only half price, and the next only a third and no cash at that, and to make bad worse he was notified to take the oath of allegiance or leave in three days. If he left his timber, it would be confiscated. He therefore sold it for dry goods, being the best he could do, and as non-intercourse was declared, his only chance was to smuggle the goods home. This he attempted, but when near Ogdensburgh, his goods were seized and he arrested. His excuse was that the circumstances compelled him to do as he had done, and through the influence of his masonic brothers he was allowed or enabled to escape. He reached Oswego with sixteen cents and a roll of coarse cloth. All else was gone. When he left home he expected to return in five or six weeks with $6,000 or $7,000. He was gone from June to January, and came back with almost nothing. In the Spring of 1812, he took a farm on the ridge road two miles east of Lewiston on the Niagara frontier, where he raised vegetables which he sold to the soldiers stationed at Lewiston. He also bought of others and sold. In this way he accumulated over $2,000, before the 19th of December, 1813. Then the British and Indians who had crossed the river about three miles below the night previous, surrounded his house and took him and his family prisoners, plundered them of every thing they thought worth carrying away, and burned the remainder with the buildings. Mr. Pitcher was taken by one party who had charge of the men prisoners destined for Halifax. On the road half way to the river, this party was attacked by the Tuscarora friendly Indians, and while the skirmish was going on he escaped. The mother and her three children, Leman B., Sally and Nancy were stripped of every garment that could tempt the cupidity of a savage. The last garment was an old red cloak. This an Indian demanded and an officer told him he "must not have it," for which the Indian shot him. The snow was about six inches deep, and Mrs. Pitcher with a babe in her arms, a sick boy on her back, and a little girl walking by her side, half naked with other prisoners was driven on by a drunken and uncontrollable rabble of Indians and a few British soldiers. On the road they saw one child tomahawked, another gun-clubbed, and still another empaled upon the stake of a fence. The number of women and children prisoners from Mr. Pitcher's neighborhood, was nineteen. They had rations for three days, and after that they were turned adrift to live and sleep in the woods near Queenstown, without fire, food or clothing. For nearly three weeks they lived on what the soldiers and indians threw away, and slept close together to keep warm in a rude cabin made of poles and brush. They were put over the river and set at liberty at Lewiston, without food, the snow nearly 10 inches deep. They followed the ridge road east by the ruins of their home, and coming to an old house they covered the blood-stained floor with straw, and nestled down to rest. About 11 o'clock at night, they were startled by the cry of "who comes there," and "I have a flag of truce." It was Mr. Pitcher who had that day been to Forts Niagara and George, and up to Queenstown, where he learned that his wife, children and others had been set at liberty. When he found them he was returning to get horses to go to Buffalo that night. The sleigh he procured was soon filled with nineteen happy souls, women and children, while he, his brother James and a friend, ran by their side, thirteen miles, when they all found food and rest. A few days after, in the early part of January, 1814, Mr. Pitcher and his family arrived safely in Pompey. Thus twice was Mr. Pitcher ruined by the war. In the following fall he commenced keeping a hotel five miles east of Buffalo, where in sixteen months he cleared $1,800.00, with which in the Spring of 1816, he moved into Chautauque county on a branch of the Allegany river.

The cold seasons of 1816,17 and 18, were unproductive, and in 1821 he moved poor and discouraged to the Cataraugus creek, and ever after only tried to "bring the year about." Here he acted as Justice of the Peace for thirty-six years, noted as a peace-maker, and no judicial decision of his was ever reversed. In 1826, while traveling on a journey in Genesee county, a heavy shower coming up he stopped and finally remained over night with a farmer, and there found "The old family Bible," which was taken in 1813, carried to Canada, retaken by the U. S. soldiers, brought back and sold at Black Rock for whiskey, and afterwards bought by the farmer for half a bushel of potatoes. The last eight years of his life Mr. Pitcher spent with his son Leman B. Pitcher, and he died April 14, 1867. His brother James P. Pitcher will be remembered by the early residents of Pompey as a successful school teacher from 1805 to 1810. He married Anna Brewer, and went with his brother to Buffalo and Chautauque County, and about forty years ago, to Oakland County, Michigan, where he and his wife died in 1868, respected by all who knew them.

MANOAH PRATT, Sr.

Manoah Pratt, Sr. was born in 1754, in Glastenbury, Connecticut, and in 1796 he came to Pompey. He and Abraham Smith purchased five hundred acres of land on Lots No. 39 and 40, obtaining title thereto through General Fish, of New York city. Pratt's Falls are upon this land. At this time but few settlers were located in this part of the town. Murry had settled on Lot No. 28, and Hezekiah and Ezra Dodge on Lot No. 50. Messrs. Pratt and Smith commenced immediately to reclaim their wilderness farms, and a beautiful creek running through that of Mr. Pratt, he erected a saw mill and a flouring mill in 1796, being among the first mills built in Onondaga County. These mills were built upon the rock overlooking the falls, where the miller attending to his accustomed labor was in constant communion with the magnificent natural scenery of the place, viewing at will objects of grandeur and sublimity, that the lover of nature would travel miles to witness.

Mr. Pratt, had married a Miss Elizabeth Loveland, daughter of Solomon Loveland, of Glastenbury, and all his children were born in Connecticut, except the youngest, Manoah Pratt, Jr., who was among the earliest of the sons of Pompey. Having procured a frontier home his family came to Pompey in February, 1797, and with them came his father-in-law, Solomon Loveland, who was a miller, and who for some twenty years attended the mill. At the age of eighty-five years he would take a bag of two bushels of wheat from the back of a horse and carry it into the mill. He died at the age of ninety-seven years, and was buried in the cemetery near what was known as "Dodge's school house," near the center of the present town of Pompey. Mr. Pratt, in addition to carrying on his saw and flouring mills, engaged in agriculture, making large additions to his first purchase. He was active in the early improvements of the town, and contributed freely to the establishment of schools and churches. He was one of the first to organize the Pompey Academy, was a member of the building committee and spent much time and money in assisting to bring the enterprise to a successful termination. He finally donated one hundred dollars to the institution, for which he gave a mortgage on his land, which his son Manoah Pratt, Jr., finally paid after his father's death. He closed busy life in death at the age of eighty-seven years, in the year 1841. His wife survived him only one year, and died at the age ef eighty-eight years, and the memory of their heroic labor and constant toil remains a rich legacy to their descendants.

Their children in the order of their ages, were Lucretia, Joseph, Betsey, Daniel, Jared, Onor and Manoah, Jr. Lucretia, the eldest, married Chester Howard, and they in turn became pioneers, moving to Ohio in 1836, and settled in Westfield, about thirty miles from Columbus. At ages above eighty years both have gone beyond the final river, leaving them surviving four sons. Two of these have since died. One lives in Ohio, and the residence of the other is unknown to the writer. So runs the stream of life until it is lost in eternity. Joseph Pratt was a farmer, and lived and died upon the land inherited from his father. He married Eunice Smith, who is also dead, and three children survive them, one son, Joseph, resides upon a part of the old homestead. Two daughters are also living.

Betsey Pratt married Henry Cook, a son of Truworthy Cook, who was a pioneer of Pompey. When her father's family came to Pompey a severe accident happened to Betsey on the journey. It was near Schenectady, where they had stopped for refreshments. Active as children will be, she was on the street engaged in play, when a loaded sleigh came down a hill with such speed as to prevent her getting out of the way. She was thrown down and the loaded sleigh passed over her leg grinding it to a jelly. The limb was amputated and yet the accident only detained them three days. Although thus crippled she would dance with ease. They moved to a place near three river point and settled near the Seneca river. They too, are both dead, and their daughter Jerusha also. Freelove lives with her aunt Onor, and of the remaining two, Henry lives in Antwerp, and Munson in Philadelphia, Jefferson County, N. Y.

Both of the sons are wealthy farmers, engaged extensively in dairying and dealing in cattle.

Daniel Pratt married Mary Morgan, and they lived in Pompey till their death, engaged in farming. They left five children, of whom Mrs. Hodge, widow of the late John Hodge, of Fayetteville, and Eugene D. Pratt, reside in Fayetteville, N. Y., S. D. Pratt, in Penn Yan, N. Y., Edward Pratt, at Oran, in Pompey, and Homer D. Pratt, at Manlius Center, N. Y.

Jared Pratt, resided in Pompey till about the year 1830, when he moved to Jeffersen County, N. Y. After a residence there about five years he moved to Michigan, upon the territory in dispute between Michigan and Ohio. The dispute terminated in favor of Ohio, and this left him in the latter State, where he remained engaged in farming till his failing strength obliged him to abandon that vocation. He died in Ohio, and only one grand-child now remains of his family.

Onor Pratt married Joseph Chase, a wealthy farmer who resided in Jefferson Co., N. Y., till his death. His widow survived him and is still living on the farm at the age of eighty-one years. Although blind, in which condition she has been for several years, she carries on a dairy farm of three hundred acres, with sixty to seventy cows. A sister's daughter, Freelove Cook, lives with her, giving the old lady the benefit of her sight in the management of the farm. Mrs. Chase has no children.

Manoah Pratt, Jr. was born in Pompey, in 1798. He early showed an interest in books, and was sent to the Academy, where he received a liberal education under the tuition of Burchard and Leonard. After he had completed his Academical course he entered the law office of Daniel Wood, Esq., the father of Senator D. P. Wood, of Syracuse. With him, and subsequently with Samuel Baldwin and Victory Birdseye in succession, he finished his legal studies and was admitted to practice in 1823. Before this, in 1819, he had engaged in teaching school in connection with his studies. He taught in the common schools and the Academy, and among his pupils were Governor Seymour and other Pompey boys of his age, who cherish the remembrance of their school boy days when he was their teacher, with the greatest pleasure.

About the time he was admitted to the practice of law his father's advanced age incapacitated him to attend to his farming and other duties. His older brothers were mostly settled and he was pursuaded to abandon the law and embark in agriculture. Accordingly, having married Miss Charlotte Ball, he became a farmer, and settled upon the old homestead, taking care of his aged parents for nearly the remainder of their lives. His fellow citizens, however, would not allow him to remain entirely in retirement upon his farm, and for four years he representeed Pompey in the Board of Supervisors, and for one year was a Member of the State Legislature. In all his public official duties he manifested capacity and integrity that would be refreshing in these days of venality and corruption.

His first wife lived only ten years after their marriage, and she left five children who were in the order of their ages— Othello C., Calvin B., Helen C., Mary E. and Leonidas E. A few years after the death of his first wife, he married Miss Pamelia Slauson, by whom he had one child, Marcus M. Pratt. With her he lived twenty-two years and she died. It was during this latter married life that a severe affliction came upon him, the nerve in his right leg became diseased to such an extent that he was obliged to submit to a painful surgical operation by which a part of the nerve was taken out, and he became again comparatively strong but to some extent lame.

After the death of his second wife, he married a Mrs. Adams with whom he is now living in the village of Pompey Hill, having sold his farm some twenty years ago. By his third wife he has one child, Carrie D. Pratt, now eleven years of age, the pride and comfort of her parents. During the past few years the nervous affection of his leg returned to trouble him, if possible, with redoubled fury. This time the attack was in the lower extremity of the limb, and the excrutiating torture which he suffered was beyond the endurance of any ordinary man. Although he had the most skilful medical aid and the best of care, his limb finally began to mortify and a counsel of Physicians gave him up to die. It was, however, determined to amputate the lower part of the leg, that it might be endurable to nurse him. This being done, to the surprise of all, his unconquerable tenacity for life mastered the difficulty, and he became well again. He manages to get about with the aid of a chair, refusing to use crutches.

But his suffering did not end. Last winter as he was going home from Capt. Taylor's store, he fell and injured the unlucky limb and received a great shock to his nervous system. Again his life is in iminent danger, but again that iron will and tenacious clinging to life overcomes the difficulty, and to-day, (Summer of 1875,) having a full head of black hair and black whiskers with a sound limb to help his locomotion, he would pass for a man of forty-five. Physically incapacitated as he is, he cultivates his garden, saws his own fire-wood, takes an interest in public affairs and keeps posted on all the current topics of the day. His mind is vigorous, and his memory retentive. In politics he has always been a democrat, and hopes to see the day when the people will wake up to the necessity of demanding of their public servants honesty in the administration of government, or if otherwise, to require them to step down and out. He is, probably, the oldest living person who was born in Pompey, and nothwithstanding his physical afflictions, is quietly passing down the declivity of life with apparently as much enjoyment as falls to the lot of man. Othello C. Pratt his eldest son, like his father, received a liberal education at the Pompey Academy, as did all Mr. Pratt's children. He was in 1849 a pioneer Californian, and knows much of the hardships of pioneer life. Having seen the golden State arise from infancy to a condition of wealth and influence, and having himself acquired a competency, he returned in 1857 to his native town, and married Lucinda, eldest daughter of O. J. Wheaton, of Pompey, and he is now a resident of the healthful village of Pompey Hill.

Helen C. Pratt married E. Beard, of Pompey, and they reside in Syracuse, N. Y. He is engaged in the furniture trade with Seley Hayden, also a son of Pompey.

Calvin B. Pratt went to California among the early adventurers, and died in Nevada.

Mary Pratt married Orville Slauson, of Pompey, a farmer, and resides on the old Slauson homestead, about two miles north of Pompey Hill.

Leonidas Pratt, a lawyer, and married, resides in San Francisco, California. He has acquired some distinction in the golden State, having held the office of District Attorney, Supreme Court Judge and State Senator.

M. M. Pratt resides in Phœnix, Oswego Co., N. Y. He is adjuster of claims, and assistant Secretary of the Onondaga and Oswego Insurance Company.

Carrie D. Pratt, the youngest child, remains with her parents. So closes an imperfect record of a family that has kept the ancestral name untarnished. So should it be with all the families of our land.

MILLARD ROBINSON.

The old residents of Pompey will remember the earnest and impressive singer at the Methodist Camp Meetings. That singer was Millard Robinson. His father, Isaac Robinson, was a soldier in the revolutionary war, and died in Otisco, Onondaga Co., having early come to that town from Saratoga Co., N. Y. Millard was born in the town of Edinbury, Saratoga Co., Nov. 13th, 1792. At the age of 16 he became converted, and united with the Methodist Episcopal church, of which he was an earnest and prominent member till death called him away. October 10th, 1810, he was married to Electa Grimes, a daughter of Thomas Grimes, Esq., and in 1811, moved to Pompey, and settled two and a half miles south of Pompey Hill. He served as a musician in the war of 1812. Built a section of the Erie canal, and afterwards purchased a farm of one hundred acres, three miles east of Pompey Hill, about the year 1825, on Lot No. 65. Here he raised a large family of children and remained on this farm till his death, which occurred in 1867.

JOHN SMITH.

Almost every community has its John Smith. The list of the pioneers of Pompey would be incomplete without a

John Smith, but of him who was among the first settlers of Pompey there is more than simply the name John Smith. Pompey's John Smith was born in Buckland, Hampshire Co., Massachusetts, July 20th, 1787, and died in Pompey, September 15th, 1872, in the 86th year of his age. His father having heard a good report of the country in central New York, resolved to send his son John on a tour of inspection, that he might know from him what advantages the new country offered. Accordingly, there being no public conveyance, he came all the way on horseback to Pompey, through the wilderness, oft times having no companions but the wild denizens of the forest. Having explored the country to his satisfaction, he returned to his eastern home on foot, having sold his horse. His report fully corroborated all that had been before related of Pompey's healthful clime and fertile soil. His father then resolved to find a home in the "western world," and called to his aid some neighbors, who assisted him to make a "sled." Soon they were on their way, his father with the other members of the family, and he, with a "yoke of stags," and the "sled," with their household goods. There was a gathering of neighbors, the farewells were spoken, and they were off. Scarcely had they started when the sled broke down. It was quickly repaired again, kind wishes were exchanged and very soon the "old homestead" was lost to view. The route they pursued lay over the Hoosac mountains to Williamstown, when they came upon bare ground. Here they purchased a cart, unloaded and repacked their goods, and left the "sled" at the hotel at Williamstown, where, long years after, the subject of this notice saw it in the same yard where it was left.

Before they got to Litchfield the axletree of the cart was broken. Again the goods were unloaded, and while the repairing was going on, some unruly swine made a raid upon their commissary department, and the good things prepared for their journey as was the custom in those days, were either consumed or greatly disarranged. When they came to Litchfield, snow again appeared, and they were obliged to

JOHN SMITH ESQR.

change from wheels to runners. With such incidents as usually happen to persons traveling in a forest region, they continued to the end of their journey upon runners, and arrived in Pompey early in 1804, having been upon the road fifteen days. They moved into a log house about one mile northwest of Butler Hill, now Pompey Hill, on the road towards Syracuse, near where Baxter Knapp now resides. Mr. Smith was a resident of Pompey from that time up to the day of his death. He was twice married—first to Alcemena Anable, of Aurelius, Cayuga county, N. Y., by whom he had eight children, and secondly to Mrs. Betsey Wright, by whom he had three children. He was a man of sterling integrity, and enjoyed in a large degree the confidence of his fellow citizens. He was elected and held the office of Justice of the Peace for fifteen years, and was appointed Associate Judge of the Common Pleas, which position he held five years, when the courts were held in Onondaga Valley, and about the time of the removal of the Court House to Syracuse. He was a member of the Board of Supervisors several years, and gave the casting vote to locate the "old Court House," between Syracuse and Salina. He held the offices of Associate Judge, Supervisor, Justice of the Peace, and was a member of the Court House building commission all at the same time; and when the Court House was finished he resigned all his official positions and devoted the remainder of his active life to the pursuit of agriculture. His father, Elisha Smith, Sr., was a revolutionary soldier, and was in the army of Gen. Gates, and at the capture of Burgoyne. His father-in-law, Edward Anable, was also a soldier of the revolution, and fought in the battle of Bunker Hill. He continued in the service till the close of the war, and was one of six men who attempted to blow up a British frigate in the North river, barely escaping with their lives.

John Smith's children, eleven in number, were Ansel A., Calvin E., Isabella, Alcemena Holbrook, Angelina Ellis, Cleopatra Ellis, John Q., Andrew, Dexter, Hesley and Frank.

The names of those living can be found in the directory near the close of this volume.

THOMAS D. SAFFORD

Was born at Preston, Conn., and at the age of 18 years he came to Pompey, and worked at the carpenter and joiners trade for some time. In 1807 he purchased a farm of 80 acres, only four of which was cleared. The same year he married Huldah Palmer, daughter of Rev. Nehemiah Palmer, of Brookfield. He served in the war of 1812, having been drafted. Their children numbered twelve, two of whom died quite young. In September, 1832, the eldest son was taken with typhoid fever, and the whole family one after another, were taken down with the fever except the mother and one daughter. Three of the family, the husband and two daughters, died with the fever, and the family was afflicted from September till the last of February. Five years later, a daughter died with consumption. Seven children and the mother are yet living, and Mrs. Safford attended the re-union of Pompey's children June 29, 1871. She was 84 years old the 18th of March previous. The eldest son, Barnard C., married Laura A. Palmer, and they reside in Wayne, Erie Co., Pa. He is a farmer. Charles P. married Lorinda Bently, in Michigan. Warren D. married Irene Bogardus, of DeWitt, N. Y. They live near Janesville, Wis., and are both farmers.

One daughter, Harriet S., married Rev. Geo. M. Jenks, and resides at Centreville, Iowa. He is the pastor of the Congregational church at that place. Malinda A. married Chapin M. Holbrook, and resides in Pompey. He is a farmer. Alonzo T. married Miss Lydia Peet, of Conn., is a farmer. His mother and youngest sister Sarah L., live with him a short distance west of Pompey Centre.

JOSEPH SHATTUCK.

Joseph Shattuck with nine sons, "grown up men," came

to Pompey at an early day, and settled on the lot Conrad Bush had drawn. He bought his land of some person who had no legal title, and paid eleven shillings per acre. Soon with the help of his sons he cleared sixty acres and put up a double log house, but was ejected from the land by Conrad Bush when he came to settle on his section. And he refused to remunerate Mr. Shattuck for the improvements made. He then bought and settled on what was known as the Mory farm from which he was also ejected. Feeling that there was no security in purchasing on the Military tract, he with six of his sons, Sabina, Joseph, Alfred, Truman, Eli and another, left Pompey and went to the town of Cohocton, Genesee Co., on "The Holland Purchase," and there they made a settlement. The misfortune of Mr. Shattuck was that of many others who purchased "Soldier claims." The government had so often failed to keep faith with the soldier, that they ceased to have faith in it, and believing the titles to lands which were promised at the time of enlistment, were likely never to be given, they would offer them for sale at a nominal price. Speculators bought these claims in great numbers. Often the soldier repeatedly sold his claim. After the war the lands having been surveyed, were drawn and awarded to the soldier, who having been honorably discharged from the service could present a valid claim. They found the previous sales and transfers were not binding, and in many instances sold again. Parties who bought these lands were subject to great annoyance and often loss.

This fact for a time retarded the settlement of this portion of the State. The Legislature finally made a law establishing a commission called "The Onondaga Commission," whose duty it was to settle the conflicting interests of the claimants. After this work was accomplished, settlers feeling they could be secured in their purchases, and allured by the richness of the soil, healthy climate, and central location came on rapidly,and the "Military tract" was in a short time fully settled.

Three of Mr. Shattuck's sons, Stephen, Chester and Ansel remained in Pompey, declaring "they were determined to fight it out." The last named of these brothers, Ansel, and others, Thomas Eldridge being one, settled upon the lot upon which Col. Henry Tiffany had located. Each buying of the Colonel a fourth of the section. They built and located each on a corner of the lot. The other two brothers located on farms south of Pompey Hill, where they lived long, exerting a salutary influence upon the society in which their lot was cast. Stephen lived to be 90 and Chester 70 years of age.

SWEETS.

Mary Sweet, the widow of Isaac, came to Salem, Mass., in 1631, with her three children, John, James and Meribah. She removed to Rhode Island in 1636; had land granted to her in 1637. For a second husband she married Ezekiel Holliman, the first minister of the colony under Roger Williams.

John Sweet, son of the above, born in England, followed the fortunes of his mother. He settled about three and a half miles south-east of Greenwich village, on Warwick Neck. He built a mill on the Kingston side of the stream. In 1638 he received land of Roger Williams, was a commissioner of Warwick in 1653, a Freeman in 1655, had permission to buy land of the Indians in 1663. In 1675 his mill was burnt by the Indians, and descendants of the family say the stones still remain, showing the site of the mill. His children were John, Daniel, James, Henry, Richard, Benjamin, William, Jeremiah and a daughter. His wife was named Eliza.

James Sweet, son of Mary, born in England, settled in Warwick, near his brother. He was a commissioner of Warwick, in 1653, purchased land of the Indians in 1662, was a commissioner from Providence in 1657, and was called General in 1658. He married Mary Green, the daughter of the 1st John Green. Their children were Phillip, James, Mary, Benoni, Valentine, Samuel, Jeremiah, Renewed and Sylvester.

From some one of these seventeen Sweet families that existed in 1690, the Sweets of Pompey claim to be descendants.

Joseph Sweet, the son ot Henry and Mary, was born March 7, 1687. He married Rachel. His eldest son Henry, born August 9, 1710; and 2d son Timothy, May 27, 1713; he married Alice, the daughter of William and Thankful Sweet. She was born February 18, 1721. Her first husband was Thomas Mitchell, married November 20, 1739; and children, George, Dorcas and Deborah; married Timothy, about 1750, children: Charles, who was killed in the Revolution, Timothy and Oliver. He removed to Virginia, on the forks of the Potomac, was killed by the Indians, when Alice returned to Rhode Island, with her two children, on horseback, Oliver unborn, a nine day's journey in 1757. For her third husband, she married Sherwood, and had one son Seth, who was an early settler in Wyoming county. She died in Pompey, May 6, 1814, aged 93 years three months.

Timothy Sweet was born in East Greenwich, R. I., Oct. 24, 1753. Of his early life we know nothing, but at the dawn of the revolution, he enlisted under Col Seth Warren, and was at the taking of Forts Ticonderoga and Crown Point. In the autumn of 1775, he was captured at "the cedars," in the expedition against St. Johns, Canada, and was taken to Halifax, and afterwards to New York, and placed in the Sugar House Prison. Here he lay for years, and in the fear of death from the inhumanity of his keepers, he enlisted into the British army as a servant to Captain Miles. As soon as health and strength permitted, he escaped from Long Island to the Connecticut shore, but not daring to join the Continental army for fear of a recapture, he visited Salisbury, Conn., where in September, 1780, he married Eunice Woodworth. They emigrated to Saratoga, were within the sound of the great battle, and Eunice personally saw the surrender of Burgoyne. They emigrated to Pompey in 1794, reaching what is now the "Old Homestead," on the 28th of January, where within eight days, Kneeland Sweet, was born.

Within three months after his arrival, he was elected to the office of fence viewer, and at the next town meeting to the office of Commissioner of Highways. In this capacity he labored for many years, and assisted in laying out most of the roads in the original township.

He soon became a prominent if not the leading farmer in the town, and one of the first in the county. In 1803, he purchased of Dr. Mordecai Hale, of New York city, two cows of Mr. Livingston's importation. These were of the best short-horned stock of that day; one came to Pompey in calf, which proved to be a male; Mr. S. paid $500 for the cow and calf, an emormous sum for that day. The other cow, equally good when she started, was injured on the passage, and she was sold for $60. She entirely recovered, and from these three sprang the celebrated "Sweet breed." The "dam" of the bull was red and he the same, the other was spotted. The bull was sold in 1808 to Israel Chapin, of Canandaigua, for $350, where he founded the "Norton breed."

The cows of this stock were remarkable milkers, Mr. Geddes said in 1857, "there are persons now living who attest that the mother of the bull gave 40 quarts of milk in a day." Mr. Sweet originally took up the 600 acre lot No. 18, he also had No. 86 in Fabius, and 10 in Camillus, at the same time. No. 18 was about half sold, a fair sized farm given to his eldest son, and the remainder retained under his own control till 1817. No. 86 Fabius, was sold, and No. 10 Camillus was partitioned among his sons and sons-in-law. He afterwards purchased the most of Lot 17, a part of this was sold, and the remainder distributed among his sons and sons-in-law. From 1800 to 1817, he was the most prominent farmer in the country, tilling more land, and producing the most grain, cattle and horses and sheep. About this time he distributed his land among his children, and retired from active life at 65, in full health and active faculties. The giving up of all activity and responsibility in worldly affairs, was a sudden start in the down-hill of life, which he descended rapidly, and twenty years that might have been usefully spent, was absolutely squandered, and the last few of them in mental darkness. He died March 7, 1837.

His children were Adolphus, Aurel, who married John Sprague, Charles, James, Anson, Anna, who married Nathan Williams, Pamelia who married Jest C. Finck, Kneeland and Horace.

Eunice Woodworth, daughter of Abner Woodworth, and Hannah Dyer, wife of Timothy Sweet, was born in Canaan, Conn., November 22, 1762. Being deprived of educational advantages in her early years, she learned to read after her marriage, and acquired a decent education for those days. About 1800, at the earnest solicitation of Dr. White, of Cooperstown, she commenced the study and practice of obstetrics, he furnishing her books and instruction gratis. She was peculiarly adapted for the profession by nature, and made a most successful practitioner for about 45 years. In the sparsely settled country where she first commenced practice, her " ride" was often extensive, but professional calls few, but in later times, her ride was not so distant, and the calls more numerous; in the aggregate some hundreds. She was present also on hundreds of occasions, when not called professionally. She closed a long, honored and useful life, January 25, 1845.

Adolphus Sweet, born in Milton, Saratoga Co., married Obedience Johnson, June 17, 1811. He was a farmer on the farm next north of the old Homestead. He was crippled for many years, and died April 10, 1839. Obedience died in Michigan, January 11, 1862.

Their children were Andalucia, who married Edgar A. Brown, widow, resides at Covington, Kentucky. Timothy, the only bachelor in the tribe resides at Rhonersville, Cal. Henry, a farmer at Dover, Lenawe Co., Michigan. Harriet who married George A. Wright, died in Michigan, 1858, and George who is a farmer and resides at Dover, Lenawe Co., Michigan.

Aurel Sweet, born in Milton, Saratoga County, married John Sprague, August, 1803. They resided on the farm now owned by Guilford C. Clapp, until 1834. Their children were Anna, who married John Morley, resides in Cayuga Co. Belinda, who married Harry Weed, and resides at Forestport, Oneida Co. Mary, who married Hiram Wood, and Aurilla, who married Alonzo Wood, Clarissa, who married H. V. S. McMechan, widow, Trenton, N. J., and Charlotte, who married W. D. Stewart, Northville, Minn. They removed to Fayetteville in 1834, where she died April 19, 1835.

Charles Sweet, born in Milton, Saratoga county, married Theodosia Clapp, Nov. 12, 1805. He was a carpenter and joiner and bridge builder. He removed in 1811 to the Holland Purchase, and built a saw and grist mill, he went to Greenupsburgh, Ky., about 1820,and has never been heard of since. He left two children in Pompey, with his relatives, Charles, who removed to Chicago, in 1835, and Philura,who married the Hon. Alvin Raymond, of Racine, Wisconsin.

James Sweet, born in Milton, Saratoga county, married Betsey Jerome, October 28, 1806, and a second wife Laura Clark, 1821. He was a cabinet maker, and specimens of his handicraft are in the houses of most of the relatives.

In the war of 1812, he enlisted into the Navy, on board the Brig Argus, was in an engagement with a British vessel, took a prize, six boxes of gold. The firing of cannon made him deaf forever after. He returned from the war and went on to a farm, on Lot 10, Camillus, where he resided till November 25, 1828, when he died. By his first wife he had one son, Jerome.

Jerome Sweet, son of James, born in Pompey August 11, 1806. On the enlistment of his father in the Navy, he went to reside with his uncle Anson, with whom he remained until he reached his majority. He married Joanna Dodge in 1827, and soon after went to reside on a part of the farm given his father, on Lot No. 10, Camillus. Here he remained several years, and then removed to Ohio. In 1842 he removed to Noble county, Indiana. The country was new, and from the first he took a leading position in all that pertained to the welfare of the country. He was a representative man in the church, school, agriculture and politics. In 1851 he was chosen to the Legislature of that State, and upon that body at that time devolved the labor of revising the Statutory code, and a new and complete code of Jurisprudence. He discharged his duties to the entire satisfaction of his constituents. He died August 24, 1869.

Anson Sweet, born in Saratoga county, Oct. 23, 1788, married Charlotte Seeley, January 18, 1810. He resided on the farm now owned by Ezra Casler, on Lot 17, until 1834, when he removed to Fayetteville, then to the Old Homestead and finally to Manlius.

As early as 1818, he practiced under-draining on Lot 17, bringing into cultivation quite an extensive swale. The drains were dug very deep and stoned like a cellar drain in those days—a sound stone on each side, and a flat one on top clincked tight, and the drain filled above with moist earth. These drains work well to this day.

He was a successful farmer and laid up a competence, which he still enjoys. He resides with his only daughter in Rochester.

Mrs. Sweet died at Manlius, February 18, 1861. His children were Charles, who for a time managed the old homestead, but removed to Wisconsin in 1850, and now resides at Granby, Missouri; James B., who owned the old homestead for some years, removed to Manlius, then to Syracuse, back to Manlius, then to Fayetteville, Skaneateles, and finally to Syracuse; his life was a checkered one, sometimes on a farm, sometimes in a public house, but always cheerful to the last few months of his life, when he became deranged, and died Sept. 2, 1871; and Charlotte L., who married the Hon. George G. Munger, of Rochester, where she now resides surrounded by a happy family of girls.

Anna Sweet, born in Milton, Saratoga county, a twin with Anson, was married to Hon. Nathan Williams, March 14, 1805. Her husband was a merchant and had a store on the Four Corners, north of the old homestead, opposite of Charles' Hotel. She died Aug. 22, 1807, leaving two children, Luna, who married John R. Wright, and Miphry, who died young.

Pamelia Sweet, born in Saratoga Co., married Jost C. Finck, a lineal descendant of General Andrew Finck, of revolutionary fame, and of German origin, in 1808. He was the lawyer of the family; removed to Johnstown, Montgomery county, then back to Pompey, then on a farm which his father-in-law gave him in Camillus, on No. 10, where he remained till 1832, then to Cato, then to Weedsport, then to Allegany county, where she died January 18, 1839. Her children were Mariah, who married Asoph Kinne, Anna, who married Orlando Galt, Jacintha, who married Lewis P. Roode, Edmund A., Amelia, who married Rev. A. J. Crandall, Eliza, who married Rev. Walter Hare, Lucy, who married B. Brooks Joslin and Hulbert. Amelia resides at Cazenovia, all the remainder are west.

Kneeland Sweet was born in Pompey February 5, 1794, we think the oldest person born in town, at this writing.

He received the best education attainable in that day, being sent by his father to Johnstown Academy for the polish. In 1820 he came in possession of the Old Homestead, about 300 acres of land, and heavily stocked with horses, sheep and cattle, and implements of every kind, the most complete in town.

He married Julia Ann Kennedy, of Marcellus, in 1819; they removed to Manlius about 1833, and to Mason, Mich., 1842, previous to the war he removed to Granby, Mo., where Mrs. Sweet died 1866. Their children were Warren G., a farmer at Granby, Mo., Loren, a farmer and merchant at Mason, Mich., J. Frances, who married the Hon. James A. Chase and resides at Buffalo, William G., a farmer at Mason, Mich., Isabel, who maried the Hon. Jerome B. Fitzgerald, Edgar B. and Andalusia, who died young, and Frederick K., the youngest grand-child of Timothy, a Druggist at Lockport, N. Y. Kneeland resides with his daughter Isabel at Niles, Mich.

Horace Sweet, born in Pompey April 1, 1796, was never calculated for anything but a farmer, it was his glory, his pride and the height of his ambition to be called a "good farmer." His earley education was on the farm, and that continually, it being thought worse than useless to expend time and money on any one who expected to be a farmer. He lived in the expectation of having the "Old Homestead" all his early life, and by diligence and industry fitted himself for the responsible situation. In 1817 he married Candace Avery, and for two years managed the farm. In 1819 his father gave him a small farm where Hiram Clement now resides. In 1823 he removed to the farm two and one-half miles north of the Hill, where he added to his acres and his family in about equal proportion.

His experiments in farming were continual and always too extensive, for when a failure, the loss was too great He tried all sorts of grain and all kinds of implements. He purchased the second cast-iron plow in town, and used the first. He had the first threshing machine, the second horse-rake, the second mowing machine, the first drill, the first roller, the first sub-soil plow, one of the first of the Michigan sub-soil plows, and among the minor implements, was ever ready to try for a better one.

In the cultivation of his farm he always desired to be in advance. He purchased stone for the front fence in 1834 at quite a cost, and had drains in every low place as early as 1840. He always wanted to "plow deep" and in many of the fields every stone that the plow hit in the bottom of the furrow was taken out. Foul stuff was his abomination, and many a day was spent in pulling charlick and daisies with corresponding backache. He always wanted to do things so much better than was absolutely necessary, that he needed a fortune to back him. As we said at the commencement his ambition was to be called a "good farmer." This distinction he achieved "if he did not make a cent."

His back was injured by a fall about four years previous to his death, and he suffered long, but finally like a shook of corn cut by an early frost, he departed August 4, 1858 aged 62. His children are Clarence H., mechanic, who resides at Knowlesville, Anson A., mechanic, Syracuse, Homer D. L., Genius of the "Claud Melnot school," resides at Syracuse, Wheaton B., the only representative of the fifty grand-children of Timothy remaining in town, William A., mechanical engineer at Syracuse, John E., Professor of Applied Mathematics at Cornell University, Helen L., who died 1842, and Anna E., widow of Charles C. Bates, resides at Syracuse.

JOHN TODD.

John Todd was one of the early settlers of Pompey, and owned and occupied the farm now occupied by M. R. Dyer. He and his wife will be remembered as good, honest christian people—members of the Bapt'st church. Mrs. Todd was decidedly opposed to instrumental music in church, and when Mr. John Talbert assisted the choir with his bass viol, she left the church, for she said, "having introduced fiddling in church, the next thing would be dancing."

Mr. Todd died about the year 1830, and Mrs. Todd lived several years thereafter—a member of the family of the late Pitt Dyer. They left no children.

SAMUEL TALBOT.

Samuel Talbot, one of the early pioneers and settlers of the old township of Pompey, was born in the town of Stoughton, Mass., August 15, 1778. Young Talbot when about twenty years of age, started with his wife, together with the families of Asa Drake, and —— Holmes to seek heir fortunes in (what was then considered) the far west, amidst the wilds and uncultivated regions of "York State." Their means for transporting their families and household goods were very primitive and simple, yet their perseverance and courage overcame the many perplexing annoyances they met with on their journey. Their course was pursued through the unbroken country and forests, fording streams and rivers, frequently being delayed in making rafts upon which the latter were crossed. Their furniture and provisions were drawn by two yokes of oxen, hitched to each sled. On arriving at the Hudson near the city of Albany, they crossed upon the ice. Here it was found necessary to make a halt long enough to put new wooden shoes upon two of the sleds which had completely worn off; the third sled proved equal to the task, and did not receive any repairs until they arrived at Pompey. Talbot settled in the north-west part of the town, where he remained about ten years; he then removed to Cleveland Mills, Steuben county. The house he occupied in that place caught fire and was consumed together with nearly all its furniture. He then removed to the Cohocton River, one and a half miles from Liberty Corners, and purchased a farm of 108 acres, exchanged that land with one Sexton, of Poultney, but the title of the property proving spurious, he lost everything he paid on it, and was left with only a few articles of household goods, besides a pair of young cattle, with which he removed back to Pompey and worked the Grimes' farm upon shares for two years. He then purchased a small farm of fifty acres, paying for it from a dowry his wife received from her father. The same farm is now occupied and owned by his only living daughter, Mrs. Morse. He died with small-pox in 1859, aged eighty-one years; his wife also died from the same disease the same year, being one or two years his senior.

Mr. Talbot was a descendant of the Talbots of Strafford-shire, England, whose history, both civil and military, are well known to many historical readers of the present day. The first American Talbot was impressed upon a British man-of-war vessel, while bathing with other boys of about his own age on the English coast. His name was Peter, son of the Earl of Shrewsbury. He escaped from the vessel in 1662, and swam to the Rhode Island shore. From thence he proceeded to Stoughton, Mass. He left a son George, who left Peter, who was father of the subject of this sketch. Samuel, not unlike his progenitors, was six feet and five inches in height, large bony frame, muscular and was possessed of an enduring constitution. There are many incidents told of his remarkable strength and endurance, among the number we will relate the following: Talbot had acquired considerable skill in the use of carpenter's tools, and in those days he was often called upon to assist the early settlers in building their cabins and houses. He had occasion to work at house building in Ohio, soon after the Erie canal was opened for business; on his return from that State in the fall, he came from Buffalo in a boat, landing at Syracuse with his large tool chest which was left upon the bank of the canal, while he sought for some means to transport it to Pompey Hill. He could find no farmer or neighbor of his in town, and it being Saturday in the afternoon, he concluded to carry it upon his back, which he did by the aid of straps and cords, arriving at his home about midnight. He did not remove the chest from his back until he arrived home, only stopping occasionally and resting by leaning the chest upon a stump or by the side of a tree on the route through the forests. As a wood-chopper he had but few equals in this section of the State. An incident is frequently told by residents of Pompey, who are now living and can vouch for the facts.

Talbot's wife wanted a pair of *andirons* or "fire dogs" for their huge fire place, which were already decorated with "cranes" and "hooks," but not complete without the articles above mentioned. Young Talbot with his axe upon his shoulder started for Mickles' Furnace, which was located about two miles south of Syracuse, near the junction of the two roads leading from Onondaga Hill and Onondaga Hollow; he saw Mr. Mickles and made a bargain for the fire dogs, he (Talbot,) agreeing to chop and pile up *seven and a half cords of maple wood* for them. He returned home put his axe in excellent order, and on the following day a little after day-break he commenced his work felling the trees, chopping, splitting and piling up the wood; about sunset Mr. Mickles went into the woods to see what progress Talbot was making, and found him cording up what he had chopped, which measured a *little over seven cords.* Mr. Mickles was surprised to see the result of the day's work, and said to Talbot, " you need not chop any more I am satisfied and you can come to the furnace and make your selection of "fire dogs," which he did, taking them, together with his axe, upon his shoulders and started for home.

Mr. Talbot was a devoted member of the Disciples church, and a consistent temperance man, honest and square in all his dealings with the world. He left a son (Alvin, since deceased,) and a daughter, (Mrs. Morse,) who is now living on the old homestead in Pompey, on the road leading to the Hollow and Jamesville.

ELIJAH WELLS.

Among the pioneers of the town of Pompey may be numbered Elijah Wells, who was born in the town of Wethersfield, Hartford County, Conn., February 27, 1775; he was married January 16, 1800, to Lucy Sellew, of Glastonbury, of the same county; he came to Pompey in the fall of 1799, and purchased a forest farm of one-hundred acres, on Lot No. 51; after making his purchase, he returned east to spend the winter. In the spring of 1800, he returned to Pompey, and applied himself to clearing up his land. During the summer he cleared ten acres and also built a log house for his future residence. In the fall he returned east and prepared to remove his family to what might be regarded his wilderness home. In February, 1801, he left the home of his childhood for his chosen residence in the then far west. The journey was performed at this inclement season of the year in an open sleigh with the additional responsibility of caring for an infant child of a little more than three months old. Deacon Asa H. Wells, who, till 1874, resided a half mile north of Pompey Hill, was that little child whose familiar voice in the choir of the Congregational Church at Pompey, for nearly a half century has been heard nearly every Sabbath, singing praises to the God who then preserved him. Thus they came into this western wild, bringing with them their effects to commence the battle of life. Often has the writer of this little sketch been thrilled in listening to the recital of the perils and trials of those pioneer days. Elijah Wells and his wife were both for many years active members of the "First Congregational Church," in Pompey, and for many years he was one of the Deacons of the Church. Their children feel that they owe very much to them, and cherish their memory with feelings of veneration. Those early days in the history of our fathers, were days of severe struggle and privation; and this was peculiarly so with the subject of this sketch. In order to dispose of the heavy timber of the dense forest, and get his logging done—not having a team of his own, he was obliged to depend upon a neighbor who had an ox team, giving two days of his own labor, for the services of his neighbor with his team one day. In this way he accomplished the clearing of the first ten acres. In the fall of the same season, he sowed it to winter wheat, which gave him an abundant crop the following season. The nearest market to him at this time was Utica, fifty miles away, and in the winter of 1801 and 1802, he hired another neighbor, Artemus Bishop, who was always actuated by a high sense of honor and ready to accommodate as are pioneer settlers generally, and who had a horse team to carry his crop to market; for it when delivered at Utica, he received forty cents per bushel. From this he had to pay for the transportation to market. This was the manner of beginning to build up the town of Pompey, and from such small beginnings, they contributed by mortgaging their farms to build up Pompey Academy. From this, let the present generation learn a lesson and show a little public spirit by stopping the decline of that venerable institution, by contributing out of their abundance sufficient to place it financially upon a firm basis.

To them were born five sons and two daughters; four of the sons are yet living; one son and the daughters have passed away. Elijah Wells, the subject of this sketch, died in the fall of1830. Lucy Wells, his companion, died in the fall of 1857. Of their family Asa H., the eldest son, now resides in Manlius, and George, the youngest, still remains in Pompey. John S., the second son who married Polly, a daughter of Moses Hinsdale, died at his residence near the old homestead in 1854. Russell, the third son, is a resident of Manlius village. Elijah, Jr., the fourth son, resides in Naples, Ontario County, N. Y.; he alone chose a mercantile life, while all the others have made agriculture their pursuit for life. Of the daughters one died in infancy, the other at the age of twenty-five unmarried. The sons have all been married, and have long enjoyed the society of their respective families.

EDWARD WICKS

Was born at East Hampton, Long Island, in 1752, and died in the year 1834, aged 74 years. His father, Capt. Edward Wicks, was a sailor, and having charge of a schooner which sailed between Connecticut and the West Indies, took his son, the subject of this sketch, with him. He was thus taught the rudiments of a sea faring life, till he was about fourteen years old; then he was bound to a tailor; but being ill used he ran away from his master, and in company with his younger brother, Capt. John Wicks, father of the late E. B. Wicks, of Syracuse, took charge of a vessel making voyages to the West Indies, until the war of the revolution. He was then obliged to return to his trade for support, and worked in Providence, R. I., from house to house for fifty cents per day, taking pay in Continental money, of which he paid $210.00 for a pair of shoes; these, however, he said were a "good pair." He married Elizabeth Conklin, of East Hampton, daughter of Lineas Conklin, and aunt of Judge Conklin, formerly of Auburn, who was the father of Hon. Roscoe Conklin, of Utica, and of Frederick Conklin, of New York. During the revolution, his father had moved to Guilford, Conn., with his family, and remained there till 1800, and then emigrated to Oneida Co., N. Y., between Clinton and Paris Hill. In 1816 he came to Pompey, and bought of Mr. Handy the farm which Barrs the Hessian, one of the thousand taken prisoner by Gen. Washington at Trenton, had settled. The farm was lately owned by Dea. Asa H. Wells, and now by David King. Here he remained till his death, which occurred in 1834. His wife died at the age of sixty-four years, in the year 1826, in Pompey. They left four children. Harriet, the eldest, married Augustus W. Chappell; Marvin died in 1848; Isaac C. now lives at the age of seventy-five years, in Pompey Hill village; Eliza, who was six years younger than Isaac C., married John Clark, and settled in Brunswick, Medina Co., Ohio, and died in 1850. Mrs. Chappell died in 1829 in Pompey, of a malignant fever then prevailing, as did also her son, Edward F. Chappell. She left surviving three other children—Helen, Sylvia and Byron.

DANIEL WRIGHT.

The subject of this sketch was born September 9th, 1794, in Hebron, Conn., and from there emigrated to Pompey, arriving February 29, 1799, with his parents, who settled on Lot No. 16. His father died Nov. 13, 1805, and his mother March 13, 1806, the year of the great eclipse. Then young Daniel went to live with his brother-in-law, and remained with him two years. He then commenced to work by the month and day for different persons, always strictly fulfilling his contracts, till 1812, when he bought a farm and paid for it with the money that years of toil had secured. But the title to his land failed and he lost it. Again he went to work by the month and day, and when over thirty years of age he married Miss Eva Helmer, of Manlius, April 21st, 1826. Their children were ten in number, and were raised to become men and women. To support his large family he continued to work by the month and by the day. His wife died July 17th, 1866, since which time he has lived with his sons. The 18th of February, 1869, his leg was broken by a fall and the broken limb was cared for by Dr. Knapp, of Jamesville, under whose skillful treatment aided by the strong vitality of his patient, he was enabled to be about in a short time. At the age of 78 years he could chop and pile two cords of wood in a day, and although the vigor of his younger days is departing, he can walk ten miles in a day. His life spent among the farmers of Pompey, has demonstrated that though poor a man may be honest. But his life's labor is nearly done, and he is now only waiting to join the pioneers of Pompey, who have gone before him over the river. In conversation he shows that though young when he came to Pompey, he well remembers the scenes and hardships of pioneer life. He remembers of families suffering for the want of food, and so reduced as to eat beach leaves. In a mortar they pounded their corn and baked their corn cakes in the ashes, rolling them up in cabbage leaves and covering them up with coals. But they thanked God and were contented, looking for a better day.

AUGUSTUS WHEATON.

Augustus Wheaton was born in the year 1775, at New Milford, Conn., and died at the age of seventy-seven years, and was buried within a mile of the place of his birth. Four brothers emigrated from Scotland and settled in Connecticut. Their names were Esuek, Orange, Sylvester and Joseph Wheaton, the last named being the father of Augustus, who came to Pompey in 1810. He had purchased land in Pompey in 1807, but did not move his family till 1810. Three sisters, Lydia, Sylvia and Loraine had preceded him. All of them were married and were older than Augustus, who was an only son.

Lydia married Jasper Bennet, of Connecticut, and settled in 1806, on the farm now owned by James VanBrocklin, about a half a mile north-westerly from Pompey Hill. They had one son Malcomb and four daughters—Orphia, Oladine, Lurianne and Jane, of whom Oladine married Ozias Wright, late of Pompey. Sylvia married James Chappell, of Mass., and settled on the farm now owned by Geo. Kenyon, in 1808. Their children were Lydia Ann, Augustus W. and Franklin. Augustus W. inherited his father's farm. Franklin was first a teacher and subsequently a lawyer. He went to Kentucky and married a daughter of Gov. Metcalf. Augustus W. married Harriet Wicks, and lived most of his life upon the farm inherited from his father. Their children were Helen, Sylvia and Byron, the former of whom married Henry Baker, son of Dea. Samuel Baker, late of Pompey. She died and Henry Baker now lives on his father's farm with his second wife. Sylvia Chappell married Dr. John Clark, of Brunswick, Ohio; Byron married Delia Bowles, and they reside in Jasper Co., Indiana. Loraine Wheaton married Joseph M. Bostwick, and came to Pompey about 1806, and settled on the farm now occupied by Watson Watkins. She died in 1829 and left four children, Nancy, Laura, Wheaton and Bennet. Nancy married Myron Wheaton, of Conn. Laura married Albro Leach, Wheaton Bostwick married a Miss Bennet, of Conn., and now resides in DeWitt, Onondaga Co., N. Y. Bennet moved west, married and still resides west.

Augustus Wheaton married Hannah Givens, of Conn. Their children were Orlin J. and Flora, both born in Connecticut, and Julia, Horace, Homer, Louisa, and Charles A., all of the latter born in Dutchess Co., N. Y., to where Augustus moved after the birth of the first two children. After moving to Pompey, four more children were born unto them, whose names were Sheldon, Elvira, Caroline and Harriet.

Augustus purchased a farm of 410 acres and lived on the east side of the road south of where A. C. Sloan now resides, from 1810 to about 1823. While in Pompey, he engaged in the pursuit of agriculture and droving, and about the latter date, he disposed of his farm and moved to Syracuse, and became inspector of salt. After a residence in Syracuse of five years, he returned to Pompey, and remained till about the year 1833, when he returned to the place of his birth, and died about the year 1852, and as before related, was buried within a mile of his birth place. His wife died in 1825, and her remains repose in the cemetery at Pompey Hill. Mr. Wheaton was a man of energy and public spirit, always interested to advance and better the condition of his town. He was a leading man in building the first Congregational church in Pompey.

Orlin J. Weaton, the eldest son of Augustus, married Sophronia Stone, of New Milford, Conn., in 1821. They have reared a large family, all of whom were born in Pompey. These are Lucinda, wife of O. C. Pratt, of Pompey. Leman S., who died at the age of six years; Daniel G., who married Mary, second daughter of David F. Dodge, late of Pempey, Delia, wife of the late Geo. B. Senter, of Cleveland, Ohio, Ellen M. wife ot H. B. Dodge, of Skaneateles, N. Y. Flora, wife of John C. Grannis, a lawyer of Cleveland, Ohio; Francis, wife of Dr. O. G. Dibble, of Pompey, and Garret S., of Cleveland, Ohio. Mr. Orlin J. Wheaton has led a very active life. He has mostly been engaged in agricultural pursuits, but for many years was a drover, and as such has traveled over very much of the western country, and especially Ohio.

Flora Wheaton, the second child of Augustus, married Moses Seymour Marsh, who came to Pompey, in 1816. Mr. Marsh was a clerk for his uncle, Henry Seymour, the father ot Gov. Seymour, and he subsequently owned the store which he purchased of his uncle, and Horace Wheaton became his clerk, and in turn became the purchaser of the store, which he continued to occupy till 1846 or 1847.

Seymour Marsh built the stone store now owned and occupied by Capt. John J. Taylor, upon the site of the old Henry Seymour store. The children of Seymour and Flora Marsh, were Henry S. Marsh, now of New York, Clarissa, wife of E. S. Dawson, Treasurer of Onondago Co. Savings Bank, of Syracuse; Richard Marsh, of New York; Flora Marsh and Charles Marsh, of Cleveland, Ohio; and George Marsh, of New York.

Julia Wheaton, the third child of Augustus, married Richard Cuyler, of Aurora, N. Y., who went into business at Vienna, N. Y., and there died. Their children were Mary, wife of Hon. R. H. Duell, of Cortland, N. Y. Louisa wife of Giles Lawrence, of Philadelphia, Pa. Jane, wife of Hon. Chas. Foster, of Cortland, N. Y. Julia and Glenn, the latter being a resident of New York, and engaged in the insurance business. Mrs. Cuyler, now Mrs. Lawrence, is again married and resides in Cortland, N. Y.

Horace Wheaton married Helen Webb, of Syracuse, a daughter of James Webb, who had been County Judge and member of the State Legislature. Their children are James, Helen, Edward and George. Helen is married to Mr. Turner, a merchant of Chicago; Edward resides in New York; George is a traveling agent. Mr. Wheaton has been a leading democrat and represented the town of Pompey for a number of terms in the Board of Supervisors; was for two terms a representative in Congress, having been first elected in the fall of 1842. As before stated he purchased the store at Pompey Hill, of Moses S. Marsh, and there continued the mercantile business till about 1846, when he removed to Syracuse, and there he has since resided. For a time since his residence in Syracuse, he engaged with his brother Chas. A., in the hardware trade. More recently, he has been a Justice of the Peace, which office he now holds.

Homer Wheaton is a graduate of Hamilton College. In 1826 and 7 he studied law with the late Victory Birdseye, and afterwards with Judge Nehemiah H. Earll; was admitted to practice and opened an office in Syracuse with Henry Davis, Jr., son of Dr. H. Davis, president of Hamilton College. Subsequently pursuing the practice of law, but a short time he became an Episcopal clergyman, which vocation he followed many years. He is now extensively engaged in agricultural pursuits, and devoted to the production of fine stock. He married Louisa, daughter of Judge Isaac Smith, of Dutchess County. Judge Charles Wheaton of Poughkeepsie, is his son.

Louisa Wheaton, married John Flemming, late of Manlius, N. Y. He was a lawyer, Surrogate of Onondaga County, Indian agent and Master in Chancery. Their children were John, Louisa and Mary, who are dead, and Elizabeth who is married and resides in Tennessee, and Flora who resides in Washington, D. C.

Charles A. Wheaton married Ellen Birdseye, daughter of Hon. Victory Birdseye, late of Pompey. They had twelve children, as follows: Cornelia, wife of Frederick Ayer, of Lowell, Mass., Ellen L. wife of Dr. A. R. Morgan, late of Syracuse, now of Astoria, Long Island; Edward of San Francisco, Cal., in the Express and Banking business of Wells, Fargo & Co. Homer, who is dead. Emma C., principal of the St. Paul, Minn., Young Ladies' Seminary. Clara who is in San Francisco, Cal., teaching. Florence B. Wheaton, Lucia C., a teacher at St. Paul. Henry B. Wheaton, a student at law, Boston, Mass. Mary H., wife of Mr. Kittridge, a lawyer of Boston, Mass. Charles A., now of Harvard University, and Mabel F. who is at her fathers, Northfield, Minn.

Mr. Wheaton married a second time, his first wife having died Dec. 1858. His second wife was a Mrs. Wagoner, whose maiden name was Archibald. By her he has five children, all living at home with their parents. Mr. Wheaton, while a resident of Syracuse, was a successful merchant at first in the dry goods and subsequently in the hardware trade. Several years ago, he went south and engaged in the construction of a railroad. In this enterprise he was unfortunate. Subsequently he went to Minnesota, where he now resides. He has held many positions of public trust, and is now editor of the Rice County Journal.

Sheldon Wheaton, the first child of Augustus, born in Pompey, died from being scalded, at the age of two years.

Elvira Wheaton, married, being the second wife of John Flemming, by whom she had two children, Caroline and William. Caroline is the wife of John A. Baker, of Seneca Falls, William is in the express business at Coxsackie, N. Y.

Caroline Wheaton, married a Mr. Clark, of Montezuma, who is now dead. She resides in New York, and has two children, James and Caroline Clark; James is a merchant in New York, and Caroline is with her mother.

Harriet Wheaton, married Geo. B. Walter, late of Syracuse, but now residing at Astoria, Long Island. He is a lawyer, doing business in New York. They have three boys one of whom is at the Cornell University.

TABOR D. WILLIAMS.

Mr. Williams was not among the Pioneer settlers of Pompey, having emigrated to Pompey in 1831. His family consisted of his wife, whose maiden name was Miss Lydia Goodrich, formerly of Lenox, Berkshire Co., Mass., and his two sons George H., and Charles T. Williams, aged respectively nine and six years. Mr. Williams was a shoemaker, and followed that occupation for several years, after he came to Pompey. His eldest son George H. Williams, entered Pompey Academy at the age of 14 years, and remained there four years under the tuition, of the late Samuel S. Stebbins, an accomplished teacher, scholar and gentleman. At the close of his academic course, he entered the law office of the late Hon. Daniel Gott, of Pompey. Three years thereafter and in the year 1844, he was admitted to the bar at Syracuse; in September of the same year, he went to Iowa and entered the office of Hon. D. F. Miller, at Fort Madison; in 1846 he was elected to the convention which framed the constitution of Iowa, serving on the committee which reported that instrument. On the admission of the State into the Union, he was elected Chief Justice of tne Supreme Court; in 1852 he was elected presidential elector, on the democratic ticket and cast his vote for Pierce, carrying the vote of the State to Washington as messenger of the Electoral College. On his way home he received intelligence, of his appointment to the Chief Justiceship of Oregon Territory, by the new President. In 1857 he was re-appointed to this office, by President Buchanan; he was also elected delegate to the convention, which framed the constitution of Oregon, two years thereafter, he resigned the Judgeship and resumed, the practice of law at Portland. In 1864 he was elected United States Senator, from Oregon and served the full term. At the expiration of his Senatorial term, he was appointed by President Grant, to serve as a member of the Joint High Commission, which convened at Washington for the settlement of the Alabama Claims, his last appointment, recently received from President Grant, being to fill the office of Attorney General of the United States. In 1850 he was married to the daughter, of General V. P. Van Antwerp, of Keokuk, Iowa, who died in 1863, and he contracted a second matrimonial alliance, with Mrs. Kate George, of Oregon in 1867. Mr. Williams second son Charles F., is by occupation a harness-maker and resides at Honeoye, Monroe Co., N. Y. Mr Tabor D. Williams and his wife, are still living in Pompey and are very proud, of the high position their son George has attained

---

THE FARGO FAMILY.

William C. Fargo.

The biography of no family identified with the history of old Pompey more clearly illustrates the advantages of a republican form of government, than that of William C. Fargo. His father, whose surname was also William, was a descendant of Moses Fargo (or Firgo as it was often written), who emigrated from England to Connecticut, about the year 1670, and settled in New London. The history of New London by Frances Manwaring Caulkins, published in 1852, has the following statement: "With other new inhabitants that appear between the years 1670 and 1700, and to whom house lots were granted is Moses Fargo in the year 1680. He had nine children of whom the five youngest were sons, Moses, Ralph, Robert, Thomas and Aaron."

The histories of New London and Norwich contain frequent reference to members of this family in connection with the annals of the revolutionary war. William C., at the age of seventeen, was among the first to enlist, and he served faithfully during the whole of the memorable struggle for independence. At the close of the war he engaged in commercial pursuits, his principal business being the shipping of cattle and horses to the West Indies. For a time this enterprise proved successful; but the loss of two ships during a stormy voyage brought a reverse from which he never recovered financially. He died about the year 1800, leaving a widow and several children, one of whom was William C. Fargo, who was born in New London, Connecticut, March 20th, 1791. Left thus early without inheritance, he was thrown upon his own resources. In those days, as now, fortune was to be sought in the west, and having learned the trade of a distiller, on the 23d of January, 1807, he left Connecticut with his uncle John Ames, emigrated to Plymouth, Chenango County, N. Y., where he worked as a laborer, until the November following, when he moved to Jamesville, Onondaga county, N. Y., and found employment in the distillery of Benjamin Sandford.

He remained in this position until the latter part of the summer of 1809, when he made his first visit to his uncle Chappell, who married his father's sister and resided in Pompey. His visit over, he continued his westward journey, and in September commenced work in Ontario Co., about seven miles north of Geneva, for a Mr. Smith. His term of service expiring the following April, he resumed his westward route, working by the day or week as he traveled, and reached Buffalo in September. It was his intention to find employment in a distillery at Eleven Mile Creek; but Buffalo offered what he regarded a more lucrative position, and he engaged as a bar-tender for Robert Cook. Buffalo was not a populous city at that time, but it gave him employment until May, 1812, when he was drafted in company with James Ellis, William Adams and John Coon, as a soldier in the United States army in the pending war with Great Britain. John O'Connor, of New York, was then recruiting in Buffalo, and preferring to be voluntary rather than drafted soldiers, Mr. Fargo and his three associates enlisted for the war in the third regiment of heavy artillery, under command of Col. Alexander Macomb, who was afterwards promoted to the rank of General, when the command of the regiment devolved on Col. George E. Mitchell.

The recruits were first ordered to Canandaigua, but the 4th day of July, 1812, found them at Fort Niagara. On or about the first of October, fifty picked men of whom Mr. Fargo was one, were detailed to open communication with the Canadian side of the river, so that the troops could be safely crossed over. It was a hazardous undertaking at the best, and as the enemy was informed of the enterprise by sympathizing rebels on this side, the fifty were compelled to return. On the 12th of October, the attempt was renewed, only fifty soldiers at first embarking. One boat load was carried down by the current and taken prisoners. On the morning of the 13th, under cover of the darkness that then prevailed, the rest of the fifty were able to land, the boats returned, and as soon as possible the militia under Gen. Van Rensselaer, were conducted to Canadian soil. About sunrise, Mr. Fargo was one of the number who forced their way up the steep acclivity and captured the enemy's battery on the heights which by this time was being actively used against the Americans who were crossing the river. A second engagement occurred about eleven o'clock, during which the British General Brock was killed. Mr. Fargo was wounded in his right thigh, just before the Americans won possession of the ground. When reinforcements arrived from Fort George, Mr. Fargo, with other wounded Americans, was brought back to the American side, and placed in a barn with a Mr. Bennett, the log-house hospital being full. They remained here all night before their wounds could be dressed. Mr. Fargo's wound was very painful, and his leg so much swollen that a council of physicians decided that the limb must be amputated. Dr. Brown of Cherry Valley, N. Y., obtained permission to make an effort to save the limb, and resorted to a poultice of beach-leaves and new milk boiled together. No material improvement was manifested at the expiration of the first twenty-four hours; but on the day following the beneficial influence of the treatment was apparent, and Dr. Brown was permitted to take charge of the patient until the following April, when Mr. Fargo was removed to Fort Niagara. His wound, however, did not heal until June. On his recovery, Mr. Fargo had charge of the artillery in what was known as the Block House. From this station in August, 1813, he kept up an incessant firing on Fort George, for four days. Soon after this, orders were received for the discharge of invalid soldiers, and Col. Mitchell gave Mr. Fargo his choice, to be discharged, or accept an unlimited furlough and engage in recruiting and apprehending deserters. He chose the latter and was so engaged until the close of the war. It was while recruiting that in February, 1814, he again visited Pompey, and from there went to Albany where he received orders to enlist no more soldiers. He immediately repaired to Sackett's Harbor, and was placed in charge of the Ordnance Department. In 1815, after peace was established, still continuing in the army service, he went to the Island of Mackinaw with Capt. Benjamin Pierce, who died about 1871. Here he was sergeant-major of the garrison, under command of Col. John McNeal. In 1816, orders came to construct a fort at Green Bay, at the mouth of Little Fox River. This work was designed for the protection of explorers and others against the Indians who were then very hostile. Mr. Fargo was detailed with twenty picked men to protect the workmen who were building the fort. Having accomplished the purpose of the expedition, he returned to Mackinaw in July, 1816, and remained there until the expiration of his term of service, on the 7th of May, 1817.

No longer a soldier, he commenced his journey to Pompey. To Detroit he came by water, and thence on foot. To Norwalk, Ohio, he had the company of James Gates. From there twenty-one miles towards Cleveland, there was no human habitation, and Cleveland, then, could boast of only two families and two houses, one of them a public one. From Cleveland his fellow-footman was a Mr. Fellows, and together they trudged on to Pompey, where they arrived in June, 1817. Mr. Fargo made a visit to his uncle Ames in Chenango County, shortly after, and returned in July. On the 10th of August, 1817, he was married to Tacy Strong, who was born September 14, 1799, in Hebron, Conn. They remained in Pompey until 1819, when they went to Jamesville, and for the first time commenced house-keeping. At the expiration of a year, they returned to Pompey, where they resided, in and near the village of Watervale, until the spring of 1848.

All their children were born in Pompey, and Dr. Jehial Stearns who now, at the age of eighty-four years, resides at Pompey Hill, attended at the birth of each of them. The following are the names and dates of the birth of their children:

William G. Fargo .... May 20th, 1818.
Jerome F. Fargo .... February 6th, 1820.
Rufus Fargo .... December 26th, 1821.
Chancellor L. Fargo .... January 12th, 1824.
Sarah Ann Fargo .... March 24th, 1826.
Maryette Fargo .... December 18th, 1827.
James C. Fargo .... May 5th, 1829.

Charles Fargo........................April 15th, 1831.
Thomas B. Fargo........................May 7th, 1833.
Emeline Fargo........................May 17th, 1836.
Willett H. Fargo....................February 15th, 1840.
Mortimer H. Fargo..................September 27th, 1843.

While in Pompey, Mr. Fargo was engaged in distilling and farming. When the office of constable was held in higher public estimation than at present, he held the postion for six years. From Pompey, he removed to Cicero Corners and bought nine acres of land of John Van Bramer. Here he resided from April 1, 1848, until November, and then removed to Manlius near what is known as the High Bridge, and lived there for fifteen years, when he consented with his wife to accept the gift from his children of a substantial and comfortable home in the city of Syracuse where he has resided for the past ten years, surrounded with all the accessories of a life of ease and repose. His wife died November 9th, 1870, and was buried in Forest Lawn Cemetery, at Buffalo, in the lot of W. G. Fargo. Her resting place is marked by a beautiful monument inscribed "Mother." Mr. Fargo was acquainted with many of the pioneers of Pompey and his retentive memory of incidents and his correct and clear narrative of facts, which came under his obsevation, renders it very interesting to spend an hour or a day with the veteran. At one time he knew personally every resident from Marcellus to the east boundary of Onondaga county, and can still name many of them from memory. He still retains much of the vivacity and humor of his earlier years, and preserves the quiet and unobtrusive manner which always characterized him and which always won him friends.

William G. Fargo, the eldest son of William C. Fargo, as may be inferred from the statements above, commenced life financially at the bottom of the ladder, and he commenced it practically at a very early period. His childhood was that of the son of a laboring-man, who was struggling under adverse circumstances to make his expenses meet his income. He had the advantages of the country school in the winter months, and made ordinary proficiency in the elemental English branches. He learned to read, write and cipher, and, at the age of thirteen, was employed by Daniel Butts, farmer and mail contractor, to carry the mail on horseback, twice a week from Pompey Hill by way of Watervale, Manlius, Oran, Delphi, Fabius and Apulia, back to Pompey Hill, a circuit of about forty miles. This Post-office business compelled him to promptness and persistence. The circuit must be rode and the mail delivered in all weathers, and under all circumstances, and in this service he was grounded in the idea that when a contract is made it must be performed to the letter.

From this time until 1835, he worked as opportunity offered for different persons; but for the most part, for Mr. Ira Curtis, of Watervale, who kept a country tavern and a store. In this employment he learned something of the routine of business, and refreshed his arithmetic in the way of keeping accounts. He was permitted to attend the district school occasionally during the winter months. But young Fargo's ambition was not to be restrained in these narrow limits, and his father encouraged him in enlarging his sphere of action. In the winter of 1835, he made an engagement with Messrs. Hough & Gilbert, grocers, of Syracuse, which was continued for about one year, when he obtained a better situation with Messrs. Roswell and Willett Hinman, grocery merchants, with whom he remained three years, perfecting himself constantly in business habits.

Next, we find him a clerk in the forwarding house of Messrs. Durnford & Co., of Syracuse, where he remained about a year. He was steadily climbing the financial ladder, and began to think of embarking in business on his own account. In January, 1840, he married Miss Anna H. Williams, daughter of Nathan Williams, one of the pioneers of Pompey. Eight children have been born to them, only two of whom—Georgiana and Helen—are living. Georgiana in

1866 married Mr. Charles W. M'Cune, who is now a resident of Buffalo.

Soon after his marriage, Mr. Fargo removed to Weedsport, and, in company with his brother Jerome, started a grocery and provision store and a bakery. The business did not prove successful, and at the end of the first year the balance was on the wrong side of the ledger.

In 1841, Mr. Fargo removed to Auburn, to accept the freight agency of the Auburn and Syracuse Railroad Company, then just completed, and in 1842, he resigned this position to accept that of messenger for Pomroy & Co., who had established an express line between Albany and Buffalo. At this time, the rails were laid to Batavia, and express packages were carried by stage from Batavia to Buffalo, until the completion of the Buffalo and Attica Railroad. After a year's experience as a messenger, Mr. Fargo was appointed agent for the company at Buffalo, to which city he removed in November, 1843. The Express business was in its infancy then, but Mr. Fargo recognized in it the elements of indefinite growth and expansion. In January, 1844, in company with Mr. Henry Wells and Mr. Daniel Dunning, he organized an Express Line from Buffalo to Detroit, by way of Cleveland, under the firm name of Wells & Co. The capital these partners possessed, was principally industry, energy and determination. The one who was able to borrow $200 on a short note was regarded by the firm as a financial success. At this time, the only railroads west of Buffalo was the one in Ohio, from Sandusky City to Monroeville, and the one in Michigan from Detroit to Ypsilanti. These expressmen employed the steamers on the lakes in the season of navigation, and stages and express wagons in winter. They did not do a very heavy business, but it was a growing one, and they pushed it forward as rapidly as practicable. They extended the line to Chicago, Milwaukee, Cincinnati and St. Louis and westward to Galena.

After a year's experience, Mr. Dunning withdrew from

the partnership, and, in 1846, Mr. Henry Wells sold his interest to Mr. William A. Livingston, and the firm name was changed to Livingston & Fargo. About this time, Mr. Wells removed to New York, Mr. Livingston came to Buffalo, aud Mr. Fargo was located in Detroit, where he remained about one year, returning to Buffalo in 1848, when Mr. Livingston took up his residence in Cincinnati.

The express business west of Buffalo was managed in this way until March, 1850, when the American Express Company was organized, consolidating the interests of Johnston Livingston and Henry Wells and the firm of Livingston, Wells & Co., proprietors of the line between New York and Buffalo; those of Butterfield, Wasson & Co., proprietors of a rival line between these cities, and those of Livingston & Fargo, who owned the lines west of Buffalo. Henry Wells was the first president, and William G. Fargo the first secretary; these positions were held by these gentlemen respectively, until the consolidation with the Merchants' Union Express Company, in December 1868, when Mr. Fargo was elected the president and remains such. This company has a capital of $18,000,000; maintains two thousand and seven hundred offices and gives employment to more than five thousand men, of whom six hundred are messengers.

At the time the western lines were established, the whole number of offices, between New York and the most remote western station, did not exceed thirty, and the number of men employed, from seventy-five to one hundred. This simple statement illustrates the growth of the express business, and is of itself proof of the energy, executive ability and the perfect system of the gentlemen who have made it the magnificent success it is.

In 1851, Mr. Fargo, Henry Wells and their associates organized a company, under the firm name of Wells, Fargo & Co., and commenced to do an express business, between New York and San Francisco by way of the Isthmus, and to operate interior lines on the Pacific coast. This enterprise proved successful, and was continued over this route until the completion of the Union and Central Pacific railroads, when the water was abandoned for the rail, and the management of the company transferred to San Francisco. While the control was in New York, Mr. Fargo was director and vice-president, and he still continues a director. This company has a capital, of $5,000,000, and is doing a lucrative and constantly increasing business.

In 1857, the several express companies in the United States, were requested by the government to make proposals for the transportation of the mail overland from St. Louis, by way of what was known as the Southern route, through El Paso, Texas, Fort Yuma and San Diego, to San Francisco. A contract having been made, the companies organized for this service under the name of the Overland Mail Company. The mails were carried by this route until the outbreak of the rebellion. The company had been at large expense for outfit, the construction of roads, the sinking of wells, and the erection of buildings, all of which was a total loss. The government ordered the company upon the middle route, substantially that of the present railroad, and a new contract was made for daily service, for the sum of $1,000,000 a year. At this price, however, it was not remunerative. The government paid in greenbacks and the company was compelled to pay all its expenses in gold. The business was done at a great risk. Property to the value of hundreds of thousands of dollars was destroyed, and many murders committed by the Indians. The company could not protect life or treasure, the passenger business ceased almost entirely, and when the company disbanded upon the completion of the Pacific Railroad, it had lost directly and indirectly fully, $10,000,000, and for this investment its stockholders have never received a dollar.

Mr. Fargo was for some time a director and vice-president of the New York Central Railroad Company; was connected with and a large contributor to the enterprise of the

Northern Pacific Railroad, and for several years a director. He is now a director of the Buffalo, New York and Philadelphia Railroad Company, and is largely interested in the Buffalo Coal Company, and the McKean and Buffalo Railroad Company, all of which are enterprises undertaken to advance the manufacturing interests of Buffalo. Mr. Fargo is also a stockholder in several of the large manufacturing establishments of Buffalo, and thoroughly identified with the growth and progress of the city of his residence.

Mr. Fargo was Mayor of Buffalo for four years, from 1862 to 1866, and distinguished himself for his courtesy, impartiality and executive ability. He has been a large and constant contributor to charitable, religious and, in fact, all public enterprises. He is a man of remarkable decision of character, an instinctive judge of men with the rare power of organization and control, and of unflinching resoluteness and determination. His success has been in no sense accidental. He has trod with a purpose all the rounds of the ladder of his fortune, and at no step has the faintest breath of suspicion attached to his integrity.

Jerome F. Fargo, now a resident of Buffalo, led as a child the life of all his brothers. He worked on a farm in the summers, attended school in the winters, until he was fourteen years of age, when he hired out to a farmer with the understanding that he was to remain until he became twenty-one. Farm-life, however, did not agree with his health, and, in 1835, he engaged as a clerk in Curtis' store on Pompey Hill. In 1836, he found employment in the grocery store of Polley & Goetchius, at Syracuse, where he remained a few months, and then hired to John Stone, as an apprentice to the baker's trade. He remained here until 1838, when he removed to Weedsport, and engaged as a journeyman baker with Peter Sampson. After a years service in this capacity, he was clerk in the grocery and dry goods store of Baylis & Mills, in whose employ he remained something more than a year. Then in company with William G. Fargo, he commenced business in Weedsport as a merchant and baker. Upon the termination of this partnership, he continued the bakery until 1841, when he removed to Auburn, in the employ of the Auburn and Syracuse Railroad Company. For two years he acted as local freight conductor, and ran the first through freight train from Rochester to Albany without transfer, in the winter of 1846. In 1847, he was promoted to a passenger conductorship; removed to Syracuse in 1849, and had charge of the train from Auburn to Syracuse, and, upon the consolidation of the Auburn and Syracuse and Auburn and Rochester railroads, continued in this capacity until the organization of the New York Central Railroad Company. He served the Central road until June, 1856, when he removed to Buffalo. He was one of the proprietors of the Corn Dock Elevator, had charge of its construction and was engaged in its management until its destruction by fire in 1865. For five years, he was one of the lessees of the City Elevator, and continued in this business until the Spring of 1872. In July of the year following, he was appointed to the position of superintendent of the real estate and personal property of the American Express company on all the lines west of Buffalo, which position he still holds.

On the first of July, 1839, he married Miss Hannah Watson, of Weedsport, N. Y. They have been the parents of seven children, of whom only two are living. George W. Fargo, of Buffalo, and a daughter named Bessie.

Rufus Fargo died at the age of two years, and his remains lie in the cemetery at Pompey Hill.

Chancellor L. Fargo learned the trade of a carriage maker, at Auburn, N. Y. He conducted that business for about five years at Watervale, and subsequently engaged in the Express business. His first wife was Phœbe Williams, a daughter of Nathan Williams, of Pompey, who died soon after marriage, and his second wife Rebecca Winchester. He died while a resident of Manlius, and was buried at Watervale. Three sons survive him, Samuel W., of Auburn; Orrin, of Buffalo, and Fayette, of Chicago, Ill.

Yours &c
W C Hays

MRS. WILLIAM C. FARGO.

Sarah Ann Fargo, married Harvey S. Reed, a brother of Col. Ralph T. Reed, late of Watervale. They reside at Detroit, Mich., and have two children, Charles F., and Fannie, who reside with their parents.

Maryette Fargo, married Samuel P. Wormley, formerly of Ontario County, but now a resident of Marshall, Michigan. They have three sons--Frank, George and James.

James C. Fargo came to Buffalo, as clerk in the office of Wells & Co's Express, in 1844, and advancing step by step in the Express business, now occupies one of the most responsible positions in connection with the American Express Company. He was made agent of the company in Detroit, in 1848, and was afterwards agent and manager of the lines which center at Chicago. He remained here until 1866, when he removed to New York city, to accept the position of General Superintendent and Manager of all the business of the company, which he still holds, to the satisfaction of all parties. He is, also, President of The Merchants' Despatch Transportation Company, an organization which has a capital of $3,000,000, and owns and operates more than three thousand freight cars. He is, also, one of the directors of the National Express Company. He has mastered the Express business as thoroughly as any man in the country, and possesses in a marked degree the family characteristics of energy, promptness and decision.

James married Fannie Stuart, of Battle Creek, Mich., and his family consists of three children—William and James, now students in Williams College, and Anna.

Charles Fargo commenced his express education in the Detroit office under the charge of his brother James, and worked his way steadily up. After several years of experience in the Detroit office, he was appointed agent at Toledo. When James C. was transferred to Chicago, Charles took his place at Detroit, and upon the transfer of James to New York, he removed to Chicago, where he still resides, holding the important position of Assistant General Superintendent of the Western Division of the American Express Company, and, also, that of director in the company.

He married Mary Jane Bradford, of Cooperstown, N. Y. They have four children—Irene, Livingston, Ada and Florence.

It should be said of the brothers James C., and Charles, that they have grown up in the Express business, and have given it their close and undivided attention. In its general scope and in the most minute details, they are equally at home. They deserve and have won the confidence and respect of all the Express managers in the country, as gentlemen of marked ability and conspicuous exactness and trustworthiness. Their relations with the railroad companies and other transportation lines extend over a period of nearly thirty years, and they are probably acquainted with a greater number of railroad officials and business men in the country, than any other two men of their years. To these brothers may justly be given a large share of credit for the perfect organization and successful working of the American Express Company.

Thomas B. Fargo, married Miss Lou Winfield. They reside in Detroit, Michigan, and have one daughter.

Emeline Fargo, married Frederick Deese, of Syracuse, who was for fourteen years passenger conductor on the New York Central Railroad, and is now engaged in the Express business. They have two daughters, who reside with their parents.

Willett H. Fargo died at Decatur, Ill., on Monday, Feb. 14th, and was buried in Detroit. He married Emeline Caldwell, of Chapinville, N. Y. They have nochildren.

Mortimer H. Fargo, the youngest son, married Mary Drake, of Painsville, Ohio. He is now agent for the American Express Company, at Green Bay, Wisconsin, where his father nearly sixty years ago guarded the construction of a fort to protect the pioneers of civilization. During the summer of 1875, the veteran Fargo, at the ripe old age of eighty-four years, visited his son at Green Bay.

This is a hasty and condensed biography of a family that, as much as any other from Pompey, has been and is identified with the growth and progress of the present century.

THE VAN BROCKLIN FAMILY.

Nicholas Van Brocklin, late of Pompey, although not a pioneer, resided in Pompey over fifty years, and mostly reclaimed the land on which he settled in 1821. He was born May 26th, 1786, in Johnstown, Montgomery county, N. Y.. at a place called Sammon's Hollow, about four miles west of the village of Johnstown. A brief mention of his ancestors will show that his father's name was Gilbert Van Brocklin, and he had three brothers, Malachi, Nicholas and Harpet, all of them patriots in the revolutionary war, and engaged in the cruel contest which occurred in that eventful period, upon the borders of civilization, with the remorseless tories and Indians. One of the brothers, Nicholas, was taken prisoner by the tories and Indians, transported into the wilderness and was never heard of more. This vicinity was the theatre of the operations of Brant and the Johnsons whose baronial mansion was near Johnstown.

The grand-father of the subject of this sketch, emigrated from Holland about the year 1730, with two brothers and a sister. The names of two of the brothers were Nicholas and Alexander, the other is thought to have been Harpet and the sister Barbara. Only two of the brothers who came from Holland were married and from them have sprung probably all the Van Brocklins in the United States. The maternal ancestry of Mr. Van Brocklin was Scotch and his mother's ancestral name was Wilson.

In early life he was surrounded by a settlement remarkable for its independence and patriotism, including the Sammons, the Fondas, the Vedders and others of revolutionary fame. The political contests in the early days of the Republic waged in his native county, which but a few years before had been the witness of a ferocious savage warfare by patriots on the one hand and tories and Indians on the other, made a lasting impression on his mind and closely allied him to that party which opposed the Federalist, and always through the subsequent years of his life, he was a zealous supporter of the Democratic party.

At about the age of twenty-four he married Margaret, a daughter of John and Mary Shields, who with their family one son and seven daughters emigrated from Ireland about the year 1800. Mrs. John Shield's maiden name was Mary White and three of her brothers were Presbyterian ministers. Mr. Shields first landed in Delaware, but soon came north to Montgomery county, and in 1820 to Pompey, where he resided till his death. Of his children, Mary married a Mr. Newkirk and after his death a Mr. Dawson. Jane married Bela Farr, late of Norwich, N. Y.

Isabella married Jeremiah Van Epps, late of Homer, N.Y. Martha married James Gilmore, late of Manlius, N. Y. Elizabeth married a Mr. Frazier and her husband died soon after, and she ever after lived with her sister Sarah, who married Henry Barber a son of Elihu mentioned on another page of this volume. Patrick Shields, the only son, married Mrs. Sherwood a widow of one of the Pompey pioneers, and lived near Delphi in Pompey, till his death. As before stated Margaret married Nicholas Van Brocklin. From these seven sisters have sprung a numerous progeny and among them were several men of influence and eminent ability. Among them may be noted Hon. Joseph Farr, late of Norwalk, Ohio, James Farr, late of New York, Drs. James and John Gilmore of Nunda, N. Y. Mrs. Van Brocklin was a remarkable natural mathematician, being prompt and accurate in mental computation of all the business transactions of her husband, often correcting the errors of merchants who used pen and paper. Mr. Van Brocklin was a farmer but always evinced a lively interest in public affairs.

Their children in the order of ther ages were Gilbert, Jane, Ann, Eliza B., John S., James W., Margaret, Martha and William White. The first six were born in Johnstown, and the two youngest in Pompey. When they moved to Pompey in 1821, they first located on a farm near Elihu Barber, but soon disposed of this and purchased of Robert Campbell the farm next east of where Grace Greenwood wás born. Here they lived till the day of their death. Mrs. Van Brocklin died Aug. 29, 1855, at the age of sixty-eight. Nicholas Van Brocklin died March 1st, 1872, in the 86th year of his age, never having used eye glasses and having read the bible five times through the last five years of his life. His son John Shields, and two of his daughters Eliza B., and Martha still reside on the old homestead.

Gilbert engaged in agricultural pursuits at first, and subsequently became a successful occulist. He married Emma Withey, of Port Byron. While on a journey from Buffalo, where he resided, he died in Chicago in 1853. Jane Ann married John King, a farmer of Pompey, and they reside near what is known as the block school house. An only living daughter, Mary, lives with her parents. Their only son David owns and occupies the Asa H. Wells farm near Pompey Hill. Margaret Van Brocklin died at the age of three years, soon after her parents came to Pompey.

James W. is a carpenter and joiner, and has built many dwellings in Pompey. In 1844 he married Tirza Tiffany, by whom he has six children, Mary, Julia, Wm. H., James, Charles and Frank. The first three are married. He owns and occupies the Bennet farm near Pompey Hill.

Wm. W., the youngest, worked his way through college, graduating at Hamilton, in the class of 1850. He taught school several years, commencing at Port Byron, N. Y., at the age of sixteen. Subsequently he taught in Fabius, Pompey and Syracuse. Studied law in the office of Gardner and Burdick, and was admitted to practice in 1853. Since that time he has followed law and farming, and now is the only resident lawyer of Pompey, owning and occupying the

Daniel Gott residence at Pompey Hill, which he purchased of Robert Ellis in 1874. He married in 1850, Lucy Aylworth, a grand-daughter of Rev. Jas. P. Aylworth, and daughter of Hon. O. Aylworth, late of Fabius. They have no children living.

DAVID WILLIAMS.

The subject of this notice was born in Halifax, July 16th, 1782, and when nine years old came to Pompey. At the age of twenty-one, he married Mary Eastman, who was born July 4th, 1782. The day after their marriage Mr. Williams killed a bear. With the exception of five years they have ever since their marriage resided in Pompey, till last fall, (1875,) when Mr. Williams died at the advanced age of ninety-three. He was a farmer and lived about a mile and a half north of Watervale. Mrs. Williams' father, Timothy Eastman, served seven years in the war of the revolution. Mrs. Williams is still living with her son, Hiram D., on the old homestead. One other son Horace resides in Michigan, and these constitute all that remain of the family. Two brothers of David also early came to Pompey, and settled on and near the corners where Egbert Avery now resides. They too, were farmers and remained residents of Pompey, till their death. One of them was Nathan, the father-in-law of Hon. Wm. G. Fargo, and the other was Daniel. They all bore the reputation of honest, upright citizens.

ASA WELLS.

Asa Wells was born in Colchester, Conn., Aug. 6th, 1774. In the spring of 1803, he came to Pompey and built a log house at Pompey Hill, on the place occupied by the late Daniel March at the time of his death. In 1807, he located east of Pompey Hill on the farm east of and adjoining the Daniel Wood farm. Here also he erected a log house in a small clearing in the woods. So small was the clearing that it was necessary to remove his children and wife from the

Asa Wells

house in falling the large trees. Mr. Wells was an excellent mathematician and practical surveyor. He with a corps of assistants laid out the road running north from the Academy to Manlius, and being no house on the way they camped out at night. He assisted the Senior Geddes in surveying for the Oswego canal. His father being an officer in service during the whole period of the revolutionary war, he inherited a military ambition, and for many years was an officer in the militia. When Sacket's Harbor was threatened by the British, he being then a captain of militia, his whole company volunteered to go if he would lead them, which he did. Afterwards he held the office of colonel of the militia for several years. In the civil service he held various important trusts. Was for a long time a Justice of the Peace, represented his town in the Board of Supervisors, was member of the State Assembly, and Judge of the County Court. He died in February, 1859, at the age of 79 years.

Chlœ Hyde Wells, wife of Asa Wells, died in January, 1872, aged 92½ years, retaining her faculties to the last.

Their children now living are Mrs. J. B. Pitkin of Oswego, Mrs. J. F. Ostrander, now of Mantorville, Minnesota, who was for many years a teacher in the schools of Pompey, Mrs. Morris Beard of Pompey, Levi Wells of Pompey, who has been for 32 years a Justice of the Peace. He also represented the town of Pompey for eighteen years in the Board of Supervisors, and became a living encyclopedia of the records of the Board. He was an honest, faithful and efficient officer. Like his father he was a practical surveyor.

Dr. Lucien B. Wells, of Utica, N. Y., was an early convert to the principles and practice of Homœopathy. He has been an active pioneer in the advancement of that system of medicine and in 1870 was chosen President of the Homœopathic State Medical Society. Since writing the above sketch, Levi Wells has gone to join his aged parents across the river of death upon the land of Immortality. He died March 31st, 1872, in the triumph of the christian's faith. In his death the community lost a citizen of the highest type of integrity and virtue, and the loss was sincerely mourned by all.

HENRY SEYMOUR,

Was born at Litchfield, Connecticut, in 1781. He was a son of Major Moses Seymour of that place, who was an officer in the army of the revolution, and for many years a member of the Legislature of that State; and who died in 1827, at the age of 84.

Major Seymour had five children, namely, one daughter, Mrs. Marsh, of Litchfield, (who lived to be 94 years of age,) and four sons, Horatio Seymour, of Middlebury, Vermont, United States Senator, from 1821 to 1833, Ozias Seymour, of Litchfield, sheriff of Litchfield county, Moses Seymour a lawyer, who also resided at Litchfield, Epaphro Seymour, of Brattleboro, Vermont, President of the Brattleboro Bank, and Henry Seymour, the subject of this notice.

Henry Seymour moved to Pompey Hill at an early day and entered into business as a merchant. By his integrity, sound judgment, and executive ability, he soon became so well and favorably known that from 1816 to 1819, and again in 1822, he was elected State Senator from that part of the State, then called the Western District. In 1818, he was nominated and chosen by the Assembly a member of the "Council of Appointment," which council had the appointing of a great portion of the civil, military, and judicial officers of the State. On the 24th of March, 1819, while the Erie and Champlain Canals were being constructed, he was made by the Legislature one of the Commissioners in charge of those works, with DeWitt Clinton, Stephen Van-Renssalaer, William C. Bouck, Samuel Youngs, and Myron Holley. Mr. Seymour held this office and was actively engaged in the discharge of its duties until the year 1833, having in the meantime and about the fall of the year 1819, moved with his family from Pompey Hill to Utica. In 1833

Henry Seymour

he resigned the position of Canal Commissioner, and was chosen President of the Farmers' Loan and Trust Company of the city of New York, and continued its President until his death.

The change from an active life in the country to the sedentary life of an office in the city of New York, destroyed his health, and he died at Utica in 1837. His wife survived him, living at the family residence in Utica, until her death in 1859. She was born at Monmouth, New Jersey, Feb. 18, 1785, and was a daughter of Colonel Jonathan Forman of that place, who at the age of 19, left Princeton College to join the revolutionary army, which he entered as lieutenant, and in which he served throughout the war, rising to the rank of Lieutenant-Colonel.

The mother of Mrs Seymour, was a Ledyard, a niece of the Col. Ledyard who was in command at Fort Griswold, opposite New London, at the time of its capture and the massacre of its defenders by the British. About the year 1797, Col. Forman moved with his family to Cazenovia, then a frontier settlement in Madison county. At that time there was no wagon road west from Whitestown, and in many places they were obliged to cut open the way, and it is said that the carriage of this party was the first conveyance of the kind that passed beyond the site of Whitestown. Col. Forman drove to Chittenango, and from there the family proceeded to Cazenovia on horseback. Col. Forman was accompanied by his brother, Major Samuel Forman, who subsequently resided in Syracuse, living to the age of 96. Miss Forman was married to Henry Seymour at Cazenovia, in 1807, their children were six in number, all of whom are now living, namely, Mary the wife of Mr. Rutger B. Miller, of Utica, Horatio Seymour, of Utica, Sophia, widow of Mr. Edward F. Shonnard, of Yonkers, Westchester county, John F. Seymour, of Utica, Helen, widow of Mr. Ledyard Lincklaen, of Cazenovia, and Julia, wife Mr. Roscoe Conkling, of Utica.

HORATIO SEYMOUR.

Horatio Seymour, the eldest son of Henry Seymour, was born at Pompey Hill, in 1811. He studied law in the office of Judges Beardsley and Bronson, at Utica; was admitted to the bar and practiced a short time, but was soon diverted from this profession by the care of property left in his hands and by political studies and pursuits. As an advocate of the principles of the democratic party, he was elected a member of the assembly of this State in 1841; mayor of the city of Utica in 1842; chosen speaker of the assembly in 1845, and Governor of the State of New York in 1853-5.

In 1861, before the outbreak of the war, he endeavored to arrest it by counseling conciliatory measures towards the South. After the commencement of hostilities, he denounced the rebellion, and declared that his party meant with all their "powers of mind and person to support the Constitution and uphold the Union, to maintain the laws and to preserve the public faith."

In 1862 he was again elected Governor of the State. Early in 1863, when a portion of the republican press was threatening to supercede President Lincoln, the President was assured by a messenger from Governor Seymour, that the democratic party of the State of New York would sustain him in the exercise of his Constitutional powers as President of the United States, against all comers. When arbitrary and illegal arrests were agitating the people of the State and endangering the cause of the Union, the firmness of his opposition to these violations of personal liberty, and the measures taken by him to enlighten the public on the dangers which might ensue from a disregard of the rights of the humblest citizen, changed the current of opinion among republicans, and tended largely to put a stop to such unwise and unlawful measures.

In 1863, when the southern army entered Pennsylvania, he was called upon by President Lincoln for volunteers to protect that State and repel the invaders; in response he

Horatio Seymour

forwarded troops with such promptness and energy that Mr. Stanton, Secretary of War, twice telegraphed the thanks of President Lincoln. The State of New York during his administration, furnished her full share of troops in the United States army. His policy was to restore the Union and at the same time to maintain the constitution of the State of New York and the rights of its citizens. In July, 1863, when a conscription upon the cities of New York and Brooklyn (which subsequent investigation proved to be unjust) caused the assemblage of an angry and frantic mob at the City Hall, Governor Seymour appeared on the steps of the City Hall, unprotected by any military force, and by a few words of assurance that he would protect their rights, induced the people to disperse. He was much criticised for addressing the excited multitude as his friends, but his words separated the well meaning from those in the mob whose intentions were evil, and some of them became conservators of the city.

He was president of the National Democratic Convention at Chicago, in August, 1864. He was again nominated in 1864 as the candidate for Governor of the State, but was defeated by Reuben E. Fenton. He was again president of the National Democratic Convention at New York, July 4, 1868, and nominated as its candidate for President of the United States, but was defeated by General Grant. Since that time Governor Seymour has devoted his attention chiefly to agricultural pursuits, and to the advancement of the farming interests of the country.

HENRY WALTER DePUY,

son of Jacob Rutson DePuy and Polly Clement, was born in Pompey, Sept. 1820. His first rudiments of education were obtained at the common district school, which were perfected at the "Old Academy."

He learned the art of printing of the Rev. D. D. Rudd, of Auburn, and soon edited and published the Fayetteville

Times, 1836. He next read law with the late Hicks Worden, and was admitted to practice. The profession was distasteful and he resumed journalism, and edited for a time the Cortland Democrat, and while yet a minor. He removed to Albion, Orleans Co., and while here married Theodosia Thomas, of Lewiston. He next sought the "Great West," and edited papers in Indianapolis, LaFayette, Ind., and Rockford, Ills., all we believe in support of the Liberty party.

He was the author of several biographical and historical works, among them "KOSSUTH and His Generals, with a Brief History of Hungary," with an introduction by HENRY J. RAYMOND. This work was submitted to the great Hungarian agitator himself, and carefully examined by Mr. PULSKY, his private secretary, who pronounced it the most correct account of the subjects treated of then extant. He was also author of "Louis Napoleon and His Times, with a Memoir of the Bonaparte Family;" and "Ethan Allen and the Green Mountain Heroes of '76, with the Early History of Vermont." He was private secretary to Governor SEYMOUR during his term of 1853–4, and subsequently served as consul to Carlsruhe, and was appointed secretary of legation at Berlin, which place he resigned to take part in the political struggle of 1860. He was appointed Secretary of Nebraska by President LINCOLN, and organized that Territory. He served as the first speaker of the Nebraska Legislature, and was also Indian agent to the Pawnees under President LINCOLN, devoting much time to an effort to reform the Indian service of the Government. He was a constant contributor to the political press and the author of several popular poems. Died in New York Feb. 2d, 1876.

ORAN---HISTORICAL.

In the vicinity of Oran, in Pompey, an old man remarkably well preserved and having a clear memory of the early history of that portion of the town lives, Elias Barnes, upon the farm upon which he was born in 1796. From Stockbridge, Mass., his father Asa Barnes came to Pompey, and purchased this farm in 1793. Phineas Barnes and Roswell Barnes, brothers of Asa, also came at the same time. In the early part of 1794 they brought their families, arriving at their new home March 5th, of that year, coming by the way of Albany and Utica. The land upon which they settled is upon Lot No. 11 of the original survey of the town. Job Bartholimew settled in 1793, upon the west part of the same lot. Daniel Thomas and Capt. Peck settled about the same time, on Lot No. 22. Thomas Foster and James Scoville, the father of Joseph Scoville, also settled near the present village of Oran, on Lot No. 11. Joseph Scoville now (1875,) owns the original farm upon which his father settled but lives on Lot No. 10. James Midler who was a revolutionary soldier, and the grand-father of Columbus C. Midler, of Pompey, and of Philip P. Midler of DeWitt, came with his brothers Christopher and Philip, about the year 1800, and occupied his soldier claim. Two sisters also came and one married a Mr. Horton, and the other, Betsey, married Daniel Candee, who is dead, but she now resides in Manlius. Geo. Clark who was the first merchant in Oran, and the first teacher, and who was the father of Brunson Clark, of Pompey, settled shortly after on the farm where Morgan Lewis now lives. Charles Thomas settled where Sandford Lewis resides. Deacon Hart Capt.

Pundason Avery and Wm. Barnes settled in the vicinity where S. B. Safford now lives. Shubel Safford, the father Silas B. Safford, settled on Lot No. 10. Francis Hale in 1802, purchosed of Judge Butler, and settled on Lot No. 12, Noah Palmer add Mr. Tripp of whom David Scoville purchased, had settled in this locality. Selah Goodrich reclaimed and settled the land where Mr. Bowen now lives.

The first hotel put up at Oran, was built by Job Bartholimew, about 1796, and by him kept till 1808. In 1809, another hotel was erected on the site of the present hotel, and was kept by Wm. Scoville. The first school house was erected at Oran, about 1800, and Geo. Clark was the teacher. A church was erected in 1808, and called "The Pleasant Valley Congregational Church." The first physician was Dr. Daniel D. Denison, who came about the year 1810, and remained till his death, about 20 years ago. He was the father of Dr. H. D. Denison and William Denison, of Syracuse, and D. D. Denison, of Oran. In an early day, Oran was a more thriving business place than at present, as well as most of the other villages in Onondaga county. About 1810, there were at Oran, two stores, two hotels, two blacksmith shops, a wagon maker shop, two tanneries, a grist-mill, a distillery, an ashery and more inhabitants than now.

REMINISCENCES.

The following papers, furnished by James W. Gould, of Syracuse, from the original manuscript among the old relics of his father, who was a pioneer of the original town of Pompey, are deemed worthy of a place in this book:

A RESOLVE OF THE SUPERVISORS AT THEIR MEETING IN SCIPIO.

Resolved, That the following recommendations be transmitted to the different towns in this county by their respective Supervisors, viz:—

WHEREAS, The Supervisors of the County of Onondaga have found many inconveniences by the various modes taken in the different towns in assessing the ratable property in the county, have thought it a duty to recommend to the assessors of each respective town next to be chosen in said towns, a mode of taking the valuation of property which appears to us the most elligible in our local situation, desiring this to be publicly read at the next annual town meeting, which uniform mode will render the next Board of Supervisors, our successors in office, more capable of doing justice in levying taxes in our infant State, viz:—Estimate as follows:

Improved lands of a medium quality,----------20s per acre
Working Oxen of a medium quality,---------£16 per yoke
Cows of a medium quality,--------------------£5 per piece
Young Cattle of 3 years old and under,--------20s per year
Horses of a medium quality,------------------£10 per piece
Colts, 3 years and under,----------------------40s per year
Hogs that will weigh 100 weight, ------------20s per piece

Negro Men.................................£50 per head
Negro Wenches,.............................£30 per head
Grist Mills, ...£50 per piece
Saw Mills,...................................£30 per piece

And those articles of an inferior or superior quality in proportion, and other ratable property in like proportion.

The Board further recommends to the consideration of the different towns, the following mode in taking the assessment, viz:—That each person holding ratable property shall give in to the assessor a list of his or her ratable property or estate, in writing, agreeable to the request of the assessor, which will be an avoucher for the assessor, and prevent any aspertions of injustice of being taxed unequally by those having that part of duty to do in society.

The Board also recommends to assessors that they completely make out their list of assessment by the first of May, as the law directs, so that the Supervisors may be enabled to proceed on their business at their first meeting, and save the county costs.

And further, we also recommend to the towns to adopt a uniform mode of granting a bounty on wolves, and render the reward of each man in his exertions for the destruction of these animals. Therefore, with submission, we think a reward of forty shillings, in addition to the bounty allowed by the county, to be adequate for the bounty of each wolf.

The Board submits the above recommendations to the consideration of the several towns within this county of Onondaga.

By order of the Board.

COMFORT TYLER, CLERK.

A true copy for the town of Pompey.

SCIPIO, December 20th, 1795.

We, the subscribers, inhabitants of Bloomingvale, in the town of Mexico, county of Herkimer and State of New York, taking into consideration the importance of the education of youth, as well to prepare them for a discharge of those religious duties which we owe our God, our neighbors and ourselves, as to gain that knowledge of letters which they may need to carry them happily and usefully through life, which is, (to use the expression of the celebrated Dr. Watts,) one of the greatest blessings that ever God bestowed on the children of men, have associated, and by these presents do enter into a solemn compact for the laudable purposes aforesaid, hereby pledging our good faith each to the other to carry the following objects into execution under the following regulations:—

First, That we will build a school house at Bloomingvale aforesaid, at or near the fork of the Genesee road with the road leading to Mr. Gold's, adjacent to the stream of water leading by the house of Mr. Rust; the size and fashion of which said house, and the time in which the same shall be completed to be determined on by a meeting for that purpose at the place aforesaid, on Monday, the second day of September next.

Secondly, That we will on the day aforesaid, appoint a committee, or otherwise provide to carry the result of our then regulations into execution.

Thirdly, That we will contribute to and bear an equal proportion, according to our number, in erecting and completing the said house.

Fourthly, That the said building when so completed shall be held and considered as our private property, jointly and severally; and that each proprietor shall be at liberty at any and all times, to dispose of his share to any person or persons who support the character or characters of good, wholesome citizens, first, however, giving the refusal to the association.

Fifthly, That as soon as the said building is completed we shall, if possible, procure a teacher for the said school, for such salary or salaries and in such way as may appear the most eligible to insure the objects of this association, which shall be made up and paid by us in such proportion as may be judged equitable and right.

Sixthly, That all future regulations and arrangements necessary to answer the above objects, shall be legal and binding on the whole, provided two-thirds of the association assent and agree thereto.

In testimony whereof we have hereunto set our hands, this twenty-second day of July, one thousand, seven hundred and ninety-three, (1793.)

MOSES DEWITT,
BENJAMIN MOREHOUSE,
ICHABOD LATHROP,
SAMUEL YOUNGLOVE,
DANIEL KEELER,
JEREMIAH GOULD,
THOMAS GASTON,
JOHN TILLOTSON,
THOMAS DIXON,
ELIJAH RUST,
COMFORT TYLER,
WM. HASKINS,
OLIVER OWEN,
JOSEPH WOODWORTH,
THOMAS WHITE.

Samuel Baker

Additional Biographies.

SAMUEL BAKER.

Samuel, eldest child of Nathaniel and Lydia (Tallmadge) Baker, was born at East Hampton, Suffolk County, L. I., October 2d, 1793. Died at Pompey, N.Y., Aug. 8, 1874.

The subject of this sketch, was the sixth in descent from Judge Thomas Baker, of East Hampton, L. I. It cannot be doubted that he received his training and character principally at the hands of his mother, Lydia Tallmadge. She was the daughter of one of the Deacons of Mr. Buel's church, of East Hampton, and was a woman of the greatest sweetness, simplicity, and yet strength of character. Deprived, as she was, for so many years of her life, of her hearing, and singularly retiring and modest in disposition, she was yet known throughout the town of Pompey, where so much of her life was spent, as ready for every good word and work.

In 1798, Mr. Nathaniel Baker and his family removed from East Hampton to Balston, Saratoga County. In 1806, they removed to Pompey. Deacon Baker used often to tell that as they drove into the village, coming from the Oriskaney reservation by the State road, leading from Cazenovia and Green's Corners, he saw the frame of the Academy standing gaunt and skeleton-like against the sky, as they drove past it. His father soon purchased the red building at the northwest corner of the green, which had been erected in part as a store house for grain purchased, and also the farm which has been ever since in the possession of the family.

As the Academy in Pompey was still unendowed and unfinished, young Baker was compelled to seek his education elsewhere. He pursued a full course of study at the Academy in Clinton, finishing his studies there with the last class which was sent forth before its charter as "Hamilton College" took effect. Returning to Pompey in about 1812, he proposed to devote himself to the profession of the law. He entered the office of S. S. Baldwin, Esq., where he pursued the study of the law for more than two years. Either the study or the surroundings, however, proved not to his taste. About that time, Mr. Morris desired his assistance for a time in his store; and he left the law office apparently for a few weeks only, but as it proved, for a permanent occupation. After a clerkship of considerable length in the store, he became interested in it, and subsequently, sole proprietor of it; though he called to his assistance at various times, Mr. N. Andrews, Mr. L. B. Pitcher, &c., finally retiring from the business in 1841; having then, as it was said, been employed as a merchant longer than any other person in the County. On the 21st of Sept., 1819, he was married to Philena Hascall, fifth daughter of Joseph Hascall, of Pawlet, Vt., for forty years Deacon of the Baptist church, there. She died August 17th, 1842. On the 3d Dec., 1826, Mr. Baker and his wife became members of the Congregational church in Pompey. On the 26th April, 1840, he was chosen one of the Deacons of the church, and officiated as such till the time of his death, having been absent, it is believed, but a single communion service, and that only a few weeks before his death.

At a very early period Mr. Baker was chosen one of the trustees of Pompey Academy, and served for many years in that capacity, being usually one of the Prudential Committee. Deacon Baker was a man of affable spirit, of sound judgment, a kind husband, and loving father; a citizen faithful in every relation of life. His life was, in fact, identified thoroughly with the church, of which he was for nearly 40 years one of the most laborious and useful members. He was, almost literally, never absent from his place in the prayer meeting and in the church. And no church could have a more thoroughly consistent or devoted member. He wore his religion as a daily garment. With him, christianity was not a theory, but a practical, heartfelt, daily experience. His whole nature was moulded by it, and his whole life was absorbed in it. It was at once his work, his life, and his joy. Most strictly conscientious, always pursuing the golden rule, it was not strange that no man should have aught to say against him. He who never spake ill of any one, might well enjoy the enviable distinction of having no one speak ill of him. The thoroughness of his conversion, reaching not only his moral nature, but extending to all his possessions, seemed to make it both easy and natural for him to live a truly christian life. This latter life was marked by no special exaltation or depression, but was calm, steadfast, consistent, faithful and always peaceful. His natural courtesy, his sterling good sense, and his equable temper, made him an admirable counsellor, a reliable friend, and a true peace maker. He married for his second wife Miss Eunice B. Birdseye, of Cornwall, Ct., who survives him. The children who survive him, (all of the first marriage,) are as follows:

1. Henry H. Baker, living in the homestead; 2. Catharine M., wife of Lucien Birdseye, of Brooklyn, N. Y.; 3. Tallmadge Baker, formerly a merchant in New York city, and now resident in South Norwalk, Ct.; 4. Mrs. Frances S., wife of Thomas Sherwood, Jr., of Kalamazoo, Mich.; 5. D. Kellogg Baker, merchant, of New York city; 6. James S. Baker, merchant, of New York city.

JESSE BUTLER.

Jesse Butler, son of Ebenezer Butler, Sen., was born in Bradford, Conn., Oct. 30, 1764.

He was married in 1786, to Miss Louisa Soper, by whom he had eight children—Riley, Merit, Lucinda, Orange, Gould, Louisa, Maria D., and Jesse S. The first three were born in Connecticut. Orange was the first white male child born within present limits of the town of Pompey.

Mr. B. came to Pompey in the Spring of 1792, and bought of his brother, Ebenezer Butler, Jr., one hundred acres of land. He remained through the summer, made a small clearing, and put up a small log house on the knoll near a spring of water, a little to the north of the house now, (1873) owned and occupied by Mr. Horatio S. Birdseye. He returned to Connecticut, in the fall of same year; and the next spring, March, 1793, returned in company with Geo. Catlin and their families, and made Pompey their home.

Their families and effects were brought hither on a sled drawn by oxen—of which each owned one. They wended their way from Whitestown, largely aided by marked trees. Each of the two women having young children to care for.

. During his life Mr. B. was a farmer—always in good health, rarely, if ever, gone from his home and family for 24 hours together. He and his wife kept house for 60 years.

In 1847 or 8, they sold the farm and moving to Fabius, spent the remainder of their lives with their daughter Louisa—Mrs. Ella W. Boss. Mr. B. died Nov. 30, 1856, aged 92 years. Mrs. Butler lived till the next April, 1857, when she died, aged 92 years and 9 months. She was one of the few original members of the Congregational church, in Pompey, and for more than 61 years and till her death, a communicant in that church.

Of their children, Riley Butler was born in Harwington, Conn. He was about five years of age when with his father, he came to Pompey. Was married in 1811, to Rachel Frisbee, of Harwington. He moved from Pompey to Albion, Orleans Co., N. Y., in 1824. His wife died at Albion, leaving six children. He afterwards moved to Mich., to a place about 18 miles from Detroit. He died about the year 1869. The children are now living in Chicago, and in the State of Mich.

Merit Butler was born in Harwington, Conn., April 10, 1790. He was three years of age when his father moved to Pompey. From that time till to-day, (March, 1876,) he has been a resident of Pompey. He lives to-day, being the last of the original settlers of this township, and perhaps, (it was so declared at last meeting of Pioneers,) the oldest resident of Onondaga Co. He still retains, at the age of 86 years, a strong physical constitution, and mental faculties unimpaired. His memory is very reliable. To him, more than to any other one individual, are we indebted for the facts and dates which make the Historical chapter of this book. He has an almost perfect recollection of the settlement and growth of Pompey village. At one time he knew every person residing within the town. He gives us names, dates, and circumstances; relating, as few can do, the history of Pompey, and of Onondaga Co.

He was married to Miss Sabina Bigelow, daughter of Josiah Bigelow, of Pompey, in 1813; by whom he had six children—Josiah B., who died in Syracuse, in 1855; Sarah L., wife of Rev. Geo. M. Peck, of Wyoming Conference, now living in Honesdale, Pa.; Ellen, wife of Carnie Heydon, living at Pompey; Amelia S., wife of U. H. Patterson, who died at Homer, in 1856; Ebenezer, for many years Principal of Seymour School, Syracuse, now Supt. Schools, Whitehall, N. Y.; and Wells M., still residing in Pompey.

Mr. Butler spent his youth on a farm; at age of 20, went to learn Blacksmithing, at which trade he worked for 40 years.

His wife died June 24, 1875, at the ripe age of 82 years and 8 mo. She will be remembered by the many who have been inmates of her household in their younger days, as the kind-hearted, benevolent, sympathizing friend; ever ready, with willing feet and hands to minister to the happiness of others.

Lucinda Butler married Dea. J. Curtis, of Elbridge. She lived in Elbridge many years. Afterwards with her husband moved to Malone, Ill., where she resided till her death. She left two children, Louisa and Maria. The first named is a prominent teacher in Chicago Public Schools—being Principal of a Ward school of that city.

Orange Butler was born at Pompey, March 5, 1794, graduated at Union College, and soon after entered the office of Hon. Victory Birdseye, with whom he pursued his legal studies till admitted to the bar—removing to Vienna, Ontario Co. He commenced the practice of law, but remained only a short time, when he settled in Gaines, Orleans Co. He was District Attorney of Orleans County for several years, and had a very extensve practice, being prominent in the famous Morgan trials during the anti-Masonic excitement.

Full of enterprise, he removed to Adrian, Mich. Soon becoming popular by his ability and affable manners, he was sent to the Legislature during the administration of Stephen T. Mason. Declining political preferment, he addressed himself studiously to his profession, establishing an enviable reputation as a sound lawyer and brilliant advocate. In 1849 he removed to Lansing, where he resided till time of his death in 1870. Abandoning his profession, for a number of years before his death he lived in agreeable retirement. He was an accomplished classical scholar and fine linguist; clear in judgment, cheerful, upright in all his intercourse with his fellow men. He lived to fill up the measure cf a long and useful life, being seventy-six years of age when called away.

He married Miss Wealthy Handy, of Pompey. They had five children—John, Chas. W., still residing at Lansing, Augustus S., deceased, Helen, wife of O. A. Jenison, and Augusta, wife of C. M. Beebe of Lansing.

Mrs. B. lived till within the present year, 1876, and during fall of 1875 paid a visit to Pompey, enjoying for the last time the scenes of her childhood's home.

Gould Butler was born in Pompey, lived many years in Onondaga Co., as an active business man—married Bathia Dodge. They had three children, Charles D., Caroline and Charlotte. He removed to Springfield, Ill., where he resided till May, 1849, when, in company with 20 others, he started "Over Land" for California. While crossing the Plains was taken ill of cholera, and died, May 16, 1849.

His wife survived him a number of years, and till about the year 1854.

Louisa Butler was born in Pompey. In 1825 was married to Ella W. Boss. About the year 1837 they moved to Fabius, where they have since resided. They have six children now living. The oldest, Henry W., is an artist, whose work is second to few in the profession. He, with four brothers and one sister, resides in Binghamton. Helen M., wife of J. Halloday, resides in Pompey.

Maria D. Butler was born in Pompey, Oct. 29, 1826, was married to Chas. E. Webb, who worked at wagon making in Pompey village, for over 40 years. They now reside in Syracuse; they have had six children, four now living; two lie buried at Pompey. Franklin H. has been since 1847 a resident of Hudson, N. Y., is now, and has been for many years editor and publisher of a weekly paper. Chas. E. married Miss Julia A. Bishop, of Pompey, is a carpenter, residing in Syracuse. Fannie married Mr. John Cadwell, of Fabius, and now resides in Western part of this State. James H. till recently lived in Syracuse.

Jesse S. Butler was born in Pompey. He was engaged as a merchant in Syracuse for many years. As a stirring business man he has few equals. He married Miss Amanda Bottom, of Syracuse, in which city he now lives. His children are William, Sarah, wife of Mr. Alfred Luther, and George W. The first two named residing in Syracuse. The last named died in the year 1870.

JOSIAH BIGELOW.

The subject of this notice was a native of the town of Holden, Mass., and when quite young emigrated to the town of Guilford, Vt. He was born in 1755, and married Sarah Culver, of Guilford, by whom he had six sons and three daughters. They came to Pompey in 1800, arriving on the 10th day of March. Mr. Bigelow had purchased of Samuel Beebe, of New York, five hundred and ninety acres of land opposite the Richard Hiscock place, which was the birth place and early home of L. Harris Hiscock and Frank Hiscock, who became distinguished lawyers in Syracuse, and of their brothers, Horace and Charles Hiscock. Mr. Bigelow, with his older boys, immediately commenced to fall the stately forest, and in three years they cleared one hundred acres of heavy timbered land. Up to 1803 all was prosperous, but that year was noted for the prevalence of the long fever. Most of Mr. B.'s family had it, and he died with it, Dec. 17, 1803. Mrs. Bigelow survived her husband only three years. Then comes a period of sad memories to the surviving members of the family. The time had come when brothers and sisters must separate—leave the paternal home and go among strangers. Soon they were where broad rivers and lakes rolled between them. Jacob Bigelow went to Concord, Mich., and Josiah to Massachusetts, and other members of the family were equally separated. Dr. Bigelow of Syracuse, who married a daughter of William Williams, formerly of Pompey, near Oran, is a descendant of this family.

DANIEL GOTT.

Although his name is incidentally mentioned in this volume in several places, this book would fail to meet the expectations of the public, without a biographical sketch of Daniel Gott. For so many years of his brilliant life was he identified with the history, growth and prosperity of Pompey, that he and his family occupy a large place in the memory and affections of the people. He was born July 10th, 1794, at Hebron, Ct., and died July 6th, 1864, at Syracuse. Within the measure of those years he acquired wealth, distinction and fame, and his memory will grow brighter as the

D Colt

years roll round and the asperities of life's conflicts are forgotten. His early education was limited only to enjoying the advantages which the common schools of his native town afforded. At the age of sixteen he commenced teaching, which he continued up to and including the first years of his residence in Pompey, having taught in the West room of the old Pompey Academy. At the age of nineteen he thought to learn the Clothiers trade, and for that purpose entered the service of his uncle, Ebenezer Snow. This not being congenial to his taste, he soon entered the office of Lawyer Gilbert of Hebron, Ct., and commenced the study ot the law. About the year 1812 he visted his uncle, Elihu Barber, in Pompey. It was probably then that he resolved to make Pompey his future home, and in 1817 he located permanently on the Hill and continued his studies with Daniel Wood, and after his admission to practice became the law partner of Samuel Baldwin, who afterwards located at Pompey West Hill, now LaFayette. On the 12th day of Sept., 1819, he was united in marriage to the widow of Stephen Sedgwick, of Pompey, a brilliant genius and eminent lawyer. Her maiden name was Ann Baldwin, a sister of Samuel and Charles Baldwin, a lady of large scholastic attainments and fine literary taste. By this union Mr. Gott also became the foster father of Henry J., John and Clarles B. Sedgwick, the second of whom died when a youth. Charles B. Sedgwick and Henry J. Sedgwick both lived to become eminent lawyers, and they have both held high and responsible positions in the State and Nation. Henry J. was a State Senator from 1844 to 1848, and Post Master at Syracuse under Buchanan's administration. Charles B. was member of Congress for two terms, from 1859 to 1863, and has acquired a brilliant record as a lawyer. Charles B. is the only survivor of three brothers, and his residence is in Syracuse.

Thus we find Mr. Gott at the age of twenty-five, with the care and responsibilities of a family devolved upon him and he assiduously applied his energies to the practice of his profession. Being both physically and mentally a man of remarkable power, he soon developed those qualities of indomitable energy, untiring industry and persuasive eloquence that won for him wealth and fame, and made him the peer of Noxon, Forbes, Jewett, Spencer, Sibley and extended his practice through the central Counties of New York. In 1828 he became afflicted with sore eyes, which seriously impaired his usefulness for about twelve years. At times so severe was this affliction, that he was obliged to confine himself to a dark room. It was during this time that his powerful and retentive memory came to his rescue, and enabled him at times to continue in business that otherwise he must have abandoned. In 1840 he became permanently cured, and his practice continued to increase till 1846, when he was elected a member of Congress, which office he held two consecutive terms. When in Congress he was the author of the famous "Gott Resolution" for the abolition of the slave trade in the District of Columbia. In 1851 he was nominated by the Whigs for Justice of the Supreme Court, and was defeated by Hon. Daniel Pratt, by a largely reduced majority. In 1844 he was on the Electoral ticket for Henry Clay. In 1853 he moved to Syracuse, where he resided till his death, continuing the practice of the law in company with his son Daniel F. Gott. His office was the law school of Pompey, and with the solicitude of a father he watched the progress of the numerous students who sought his instruction, and prompted by his genial and kind nature, and remembering the obstacles that he had encountered and overcome, he was ever ready to counsel, advise and encourage. Among the large number of gifted and eminent men who entered the legal profession from his office were Seabred Dodge, Charles Mason, John U. Pettit, Harvey Sheldon, Charles B. Sedgwick, Henry J. Sedgwick, Geo. H. Williams, LeRoy Morgan, L. H. Hiscock, Charles Foster, and these and all others who were students in his office bear concurrent testimony to his kindness and anxious solicitude for their honor and welfare. During his residence in Pompey, he was trustee of the Academy for many years, always laboring for its prosperity. He was a constant attendant of the Presbyterian church.

His children in the order of their ages, were Sackett, Ann, Amelia and Daniel F. The two eldest are dead. Sacket was never married, Ann married Hon. Geo. H. Woodruff, a graduate of Hamilton College, and a lawyer and writer of distinction of Joliet, Ills. He and one child survive. Daniel F. graduated from Hamilton College in the class of 1849, became the law partner of his father in Syracuse, married Sarah Clary, a daughter of the late Dr. Lyman Clary, of Syracuse, is Register in Bankruptcy, to which he was appointed in 1867. Amelia married Frank H. Hastings, a nurseryman of Rochester, N. Y. They have three children.

MORGAN.

LeRoy Morgan was the eldest son of Lyman Morgan, a farmer and one of the pioneers in the early settlement of Pompey, where he died February 24, 1864, universally respected for his consistent and upright life. Living about two and a half miles from the Academy, to the endowment of which he was an early contributor, his son LeRoy took every available occasion to attend this celebrated pioneer institution, and from it he graduated in 1830, at the age of twenty, having been born in Pompey, March 27th, 1810. At the age of eighteen he taught school in Volney, Oswego Co., at a compensation of $13 per month. The next year he taught in Delphi, in Pompey, where he became acquainted with Miss Elizabeth C. Slocum, a daughter of Mathew B. Slocum, and sister of Gen. Henry W. Slocum, whom he married in 1832. He also taught school in the Wells District and the Murray District in Pompey, in the years 1830 and 1831. Thus by his own labor he educated himself, teaching winters and attending the Academy summers. In 1830 he commenced the study of the law in the celebrated Law office of the late Hon. Daniel Gott, and Hon. Amasa Jerome, afterwards Judge of the Common Pleas and Surrogate of Onondaga County, also a native of Pompey, was his fellow student. There were also three other students in the same office, E. A. Baldwin, Q. O. Andrus, and the late Hon. H. J. Sedgwick. Remaining with Mr. Gott till 1831, he entered the office of Hon. S. L. Edwards, in Manlius, and there continued his studies till he was admitted to practice in the "Old Common Pleas" in 1832. The next year he was admitted to practice in the Supreme Court. In 1839 he located in Baldwinsville, where he continued in the practice of his profession till 1851. In 1843 he received the appointment of District Attorney of Onondaga County, which office he held with the exception of a few weeks, till the new constitution came into operation in 1848.

In 1851 he came to Syracuse to reside, and formed a Law partnership with the late Hon. D. D. Hillis, and this continued until the death of Mr. Hillis, which occurred in 1859. In the fall of the latter year Mr. Morgan was elected a Justice of the Supreme Court for the term of eight years, and at the expiration of his term was re-elected without opposition. He still resides in Syracuse.

DR. JEHIAL STEARNS.

Jehial Stearns was born in Rockingham, Vt., February 6th, 1790. His father was William Stearns, a respectable farmer, and a soldier of the revolution. From pecuniary considerations his early education was limited. At the age of sixteen he commenced his academic studies in Charlestown, N. H., and subsequently acquired the Latin language under various competent teachers. In 1809 he commenced the study of medicine under the direction of Dr. Oliver Hastings, a celebrated physician of Charleston, N. H. In 1811 was his first attendance of lectures at Dartmouth College, under Dr. Nathan Smith. Having graduated with honor, he located as a physician and surgeon in the town of Essex, Essex Co., N. Y., where he enjoyed a good degree of public patronage. In January, 1815, he came to Pompey, Onondaga Co., N. Y., where he was kindly and cordially received, and the growing town being in need of a physician, he was invited to remain, and he concluded to make Pompey his future home. Dr. Stearns ardently loved the practice as well as the science ot his profession, and by his assiduous devotion to its duties, his courteous manners and more than all his kind and ready sympathy for his suffering patients, he soon won reputation and success. He was never ambitious to be called a money making doctor, but considered his profession rather a charitable calling. His circle of practice if not so large as some of his compeers, was elligible and remunerative. Among the cotemporaries of Dr. S. in the profession, and who were likewise his friends, were Drs. Granger, Wm. Taylor, D. Denison, Upson H. B. Moore and others, whose professional standing was of a high order, and it is not too much to say that he was the equal of any of them.

Dr. Stearns had some experience in the war of 1812, and acquired skill and a taste for the practice of surgery, and this branch of his profession he made rather a specialty in his practice with a high degree of success, not only as an operator, but in exhibiting singular judgment in knowing where to operate. In 1822 he received the appointment of Surgeon of the 98th regiment of Infantry, under De Witt Clinton, Governor of New York, which he resigned Oct. 9th, 1830, united with the Onondaga Medical Society in 1817, of which he is a still a member, having served one term as its President, and one term of four years as delegate to the State Society. In 1826 he was elected Vice-President of the Onondaga Co. Medical Society. In 1839, January 21st, he was constituted Honorary member of the Medical Society of Geneva College, and by that College the Degree of M. D. was conferred upon him the same year. In 1840 the Cortland County Medical Society elected him an Honorary member, and in 1868 he became a member of the Onondaga County Historical Association. For many years he was an efficient and useful trustee of Pompey Academy, and is a member of the Presbyterian church at Pompey, with which he became connected soon after he came to Pompey, and in the prosperity of which he has always evinced a lively interest. On the 22d day of January, 1816, he was married to Nancy Hascall, a sister of Hon. Ralph Hascall, M. C., and of Rev. Daniel Hascall, who was a Baptist clergyman, and founder of the Madison University. She died July 11, 1856, and for a second wife, Dr. S. married May 9th, 1860, Serepta S. Shattuck, a daughter of Chester Shattuck, a pioneer of Pompey, and brother of Joseph Shattuck, whose biography is herein recorded. By his first wife he had two children, J. Hascall Stearns and Cornelia B. Stearns. The former was a pioneer Californian, and is a resident of San Francisco, but he has never forgotten his early home to which he pays his annual visits during the delightful summers of the old Hills, as regular as the seasons roll round. He is a bachelor, and not communicative as to his wealth, but their is little doubt that fortune has favored him to that extent that he might well afford to support a larger family.

Cornelia B. Stearns married Hon. John W. Dwinelle, of San Francisco, California. She died Oct. 25th, 1873, leaving her husband surviving her, and five children. In the order of their ages the children are, Ella C., the wife of Chas. Pond, of Providence, R. I. Anna Louisa, of San Francisco, Charles H., a graduate of Harvard College, largely engaged in agricultural pursuits. Herman, now a student in California College, and Florence, with her father in San Francisco. Mr. Dwinelle has been mayor of San Francisco, a member of the California Legislature, a lawyer of distinction and eminent ability, and a gentleman and author of high literary taste.

Dr. Stearns at the age of eighty-six still survives—a resident of Pompey Hill, and to a remarkable degree in the enjoyment of both his physical and mental faculties. Although nominally he has abandoned the practice of his pro-

Charles W. Stevens M.D. Richard F. Stevens M.D.

William H. Stevens

fession, he is often called to administer to the necessities of the afflicted.

HEZEKIAH W. STEVENS.

Hezekiah W. Stevens was born at Killingworth, Connecticut, in 1793. He came to Pompey in 1810, looking for a place to locate in the cabinet and chair business. He was a first-class mechanic, and was induced by Henry Seymour, Moses S. Marsh and others, to establish himself there. His first shop was located nearly opposite the Dr. Tibbals house. He was married by Rev. Jabez Chadwick, at the house of Henry Seymour, to Lois Field, who came to Pompey from Jericho, Vermont, and boarded several years in the families of Henry Seymour and Nathaniel Baker. They lived three years in the small house still standing opposite the Dr. Tibbals house, and afterwards built and occupied the house and shop between the Presbyterian church and Col. Hezekiah Hopkins' tavern. He was a man of excellent taste, successful in business, and many of the young married people received their "setting out" at his ware-rooms. Many pieces of furniture of his make are still to be seen in the old residences of the town. He was injured at the burning of Merit Butler's blacksmith shop, and died the following year, in January, 1828, at the age of 37. When Merit Butler had constructed the vane for the Presbyterian church steeple, Mr. Stevens covered it with gold leaf so thoroughly, that for sixty years it has glistened in the sunbeams, and it has been said their work stands *higher* than that of any of their successors. Henry Stevens, brother of Hezekiah, was at one time in the partnership with him. He married Phena Jerome, sister of Ira and John C. Jerome, and subsequently removed to Fabius, where he died, leaving several children, the only survivor being Mrs. Ann Wheaton, now residing there.

Hezekiah's widow with her second husband, Wm. C. Hendricks, and three sons, William H., Charles W. and Richard F., continued to occupy the family residence north of the church for many years. The house was sold to Geo. Merrell, and Mr. Hendricks and wife removed to the west. She died in 1853, at Elkhart, Indiana, and was buried in the family lot at Pompey. Mr. Hendricks subsequently married Emily Gould, of Jamesville, and now resides at Elkhart.

Wm. H. Stevens married Ann R. Bishop, who died at Buffalo, in 1852, and was buried in the family lot of her father near Oswego. He has resided sixteen years in the city of New York, engaged in the manufacture of parlor organs. One of his three children survives—Richard H. Stevens, residing in New York, engaged in the stationery trade.

Charles W. Stevens married Susan Dillon, at St. Louis, Missouri. He has resided in that city since 1840, engaged in the practice of medicine, and filled the Professorship of Anatomy twenty-four years in the Medical College. He was several years Superintendent of the St. Louis Insane Asylum. They have two sons, Frank H. and Charles D. Stevens.

Richard F. Stevens married Esther Prentiss in 1844, at St. Louis, where he resided several years engaged in the practice of medicine. He subsequently resided in Syracuse, N. Y., where his wife died in 1872, since which he has resided in the city of New York, and holds the office of Collector of City Revenue.

Of four children one survives, Jennie P. Stevens, now engaged in the study of medicine in the Woman's Medical College of New York city.

Of Incidents the Outgrowth of the Re-Union.

The influence of the re-union has been seen and felt in various ways since it occurred. It has given the town a notoriety and popularity not hitherto enjoyed. Every year since 1871, during the oppressively hot summer days, Pompey Hill has become the resort of those seeking pleasure and repose from the dust, heat and inconveniences of city life. Every year the number who seek its healthful heights increases.

The benefits of the Academy to the past generations of Pompey so plainly exemplified on that occasion, have created a sympathy in behalf of the venerable institution, and more closely endeared it to the citizens of Pompey, so that efforts are continually being made for its prosperity. Festivals and other means have been resorted to for the purpose of raising money to make needful repairs. Upon one occasion when an "Old Folk's Concert" was being held, August 21st, 1874, for the benefit of the Academy, William H. Stevens, Esq., of New York, unexpectedly came to town bearing a present to the Academy trustees of a miniature fac simile of the "Old Academy building." Taking advantage of the occasion the presentation was made at the concert, the following notice of which appeared in the Syracuse daily papers.

"On Friday evening, Aug. 21st, 1874, was a concert for the benefit of Pompey Academy. The entertainment was largely attended by the citizens of Pompey, and very many strangers who are here enjoying the rural pleasures of the country at this delightful season of the year. Among the distinguished visitors from abroad were Dr. Charles W. Stevens, of St. Louis, Mo., Charles Hayden, Esq., of Rochester, N. Y., Wm. H. Stevens, Esq., of New York, and Mrs. Charlotte Beardslee, of Syracuse, one of the pioneer teachers in the early days of Pompey. An interesting episode occurred at the conclusion of the first part. Wm. H. Stevens, Esq., of New York, was present at the Re-union in Pompey, June 29th, 1871, and upon that occasion hearing much said in reference to the old academy building which was torn down in 1834, to give place to the present structure, he conceived the idea of constructing a miniature fac-simile of the old building from memory. He was among the number who had been educated within its sacred walls. And drawing upon the recollections of his school boy days, he had finished his model and happened to return to his early home the very day the concert was to take place, bringing with him the miniature building as a gift to the present board of trustees. At the conclusion of the first part of the concert the trustees of the Academy were invited to take their place upon the stage, the audience and some of them not knowing for what purpose. They stood in the form of a semi-circle, in the center of which upon a stand, Mr. E. Butler, of Whitehall, N. Y., a native of Pompey, soon placed the gift. Mr. Stevens also stood upon the stage. Around and behind them stood the singers in the costume of one hundred years ago. Mr. Butler then in behalf of Mr. Stevens, made the following presentation speech :—

GENTLEMEN : I appear before you to-night, honored with a pleasing part of this evening's entertainment. I have before me a model of the "Old Pompey Academy" building, which was erected in 1801; within whose walls during more than a third of a century, were educated, perhaps, more men who have lived and become famous as governors, legislators, judges, lawyers, physicians, generals of the army, ministers of the gospel, missionaries to foreign climes, poets, orators and eminent civilians, than any other similar institution in this or any other State. Three years ago when was held on yonder "green" the grand re-union of the sons and daughters of Pompey, when they came from far and near to meet again at the old home hearth-stone as they grasped the hand of cherished friends, you remember how the old academy was the central theme of every conversation. Around it clustered the pleasant memories and reminiscences of the past; to it they turned with the fond eye of memory, and beheld anew the classic walls, paying to it a deference akin to adoration. Among the number who that day met with us and enjoyed the festive occasion was one who on his return to his home in New York, resolved from memory to reproduce in miniature, the old structure entire. He has during his leisure moments labored upon it, and to-day as he returns again to visit the home of his boyhood, does he bring with him this memento, and as others have in words so feelingly dedicated their affection to this institution, so he now dedicates this the offspring of his handiwork. In the name of our former townsman, Mr. Wm. H. Stevens, of New York, the architect and builder of this fac-simile of the old Academy building, I do now present this gift, asking that it remain in the archives of your institution so long as Pompey Academy shall exist, and it in the future it shall happen, as happen it may, that the organization as now existing shall cease, it is his wish that you or your successors shall present it to the Onondaga County Historical Association. Please accept as the offering of the devoted love of a noble heart to its cherished Alma Mater.

Mr. Stevens then explained the construction of the model, after which Wm. W. Van Brocklin, Esq., responded as follows:

Mr. Stevens:—In behalf of the trustees of Pompey Academy and in behalf of this entire community, whose interests in this institution it is their duty to cherish and protect, I return you most sincere and heartfelt thanks for this beautiful gift so suggestive of the thousand golden memories of the "olden time." And to you Mr. Butler, I return thanks for the appropriate and feeling language you have been enabled to use in the presentation of this perfect model of the old Academy building, and for the stirring memories you have awakened of the transcendent blessings and benefits which have resulted from the establishment of this institution to the early settlers of Pompey and their descendants.

But above all, we give thanks to our God, the great preserver and benefactor of humanity, whose Providence has so unexpectedly dropped down among us our former townsman on this interesting occasion, bringing this priceless gift appearing at this opportune time, when an old folks concert is in progress for the benefit of that institution, whose first edifice is here reproduced in miniature from memory; and our thanks are further due to the great architect of the universe, for the gift of memory, that has enabled you my brother so faithfully and vividly to call up from the storehouse of your memory all the details and minute peculiarities that characterized those classic halls whose walls echoed to the tread of a Dodge, a Mason, a Marsh and a Seymour, enabling you to construct it with that artistic skill that challenges the admiration and gratitude of all acquainted with the old building, who have had the good fortune to examine this. So perfect is it, that I understand the Hon. Luther R. Marsh said when admiring its just proportions and elaborate finish, that the only thing lacking, was the birchen rod of the venerable Joshua Leonard. I confess that language is too poor to express the thoughts and emotions that crowd upon my mind in viewing this memento of the past. The emotional sentiments which the occasions calls up are of kin to those inspired by the beautiful lines of the enraptured poet.

"How dear to my heart are the scenes of my childhood,
When fond recollection presents them to view
The orchard, the meadow, the deep-tangled wild wood,
And every loved spot which my infancy knew."

And those other immortal lines around which cluster a thousand fonder and dearer memories.

"I love it, I love it, and who shall dare
To chide me for loving that old arm chair,
Have you learned the spell a mother sat there,
And a sacred thing was that old arm chair."

The lessons too, which this event teaches, are of the most important character, and among them I may name the lasting impressions and unfading memories ot our early life. If our brother can in this matchless little building, so vividly portray all the lineaments of the school-room where forty years ago he spent the happy hours of life's bright morning, how important that in the youthful mind be instilled those principles of righteousness, truth, temperance, virtue and integrity that shall make the child through all the future years of life feel strong to resist the temptations that are scattered all along the pathway of life. For, rest assured, temptation will assail us through all the coming years, until the dawn of eternity shall appear.

Thanking you again for this priceless treasure, which we will ever cherish in our inmost heart, with the kindest feeling of respect for the donor, we wish you prosperity and joy through all the coming years of life, and unalloyed happiness through all the boundless cycles ot eternity.

Since the re-union, frequent notices of the healthful clime and beautiful scenery of Pompey have appeared in the newspapers. From among the number we clip the following beautiful poem, which some time after the re-union, appeared in one of the Syracuse papers.

TO POMPEY.

All day in fancy I have seen
Thy green clad hills, vast and eternal,
O'er looking all the vale between,
And rising toward the skies supernal.

All day I've roamed thy woodlands o'er,
And seen with fancy's glowing vision
Thy quiet streets, and fields so fair,
Fairer to me than fields Elysian.

Below thee in the distance seen,
The city's spires are brightly gleaming,
The whirr and clang of busy life
Within its crowded streets are teeming;
But tho' old hills upreared so high,
Escape the city's din and clashing,
The few within thy cool retreats
Enjoy the long, bright days now passing.

A happy home is mine beside
Oswego's brightly flowing river,
Yet, will my heart e'er yearn for thee,
My childhood's home, for aye and ever,
I tire of all this flat lowland,
I long for thy dear lights and shadows,
I want to climb thy rugged hills
And wander in thy quiet meadows.

I want to gaze upon thy scenes,
In Autumn's light serene, and mellow,
And watch thy graceful waving trees,
All beautiful, though sere and yellow,
But ah, for me, it may not be,
What need is there to murmur longer,
My feet must wander far away,
E'en while my love for thee grows stronger.

And I may roam in other lands,
May cross the deep and boundless ocean,
My heart shall ne'er forget that love,
While life its pulses keep in motion.
And oh, when all life's cares are o'er,
And swift from me is memory flying,
Old Pompey may thy hills arise,
To greet my eyes when I am dying.

SICILY SPRAGUE.

Of the Organization of the Re-Union.

In addition to the officers and committees whose names appears in the foregoing pages, mention should have been made of the marshal of the day and his assistants, whose duties were very laborious, and discharged with a skill and promptness which commanded the approbation of all.

The marshal was M. R. Dyer, and his assistants Samuel W. Jerome, Moses T. Robinson, Dwight Kershaw, Wm. J. Mason and Fred. A. M. Ball. The following additional names appear upon the programme published at the time, who were on the Committee of Arrangements: Chas. W. H. Wood, S. S. Walley, Geo. Hopkins, Geo. R. Vail, Rodney Hill and D. G. Southard, and the following on the Committee of Reception: J. R. Fenner, Wilfred M. Scoville, Bronson Clarke and John P. Robinson.

The following named ladies and gentlemen were omitted, who deserve to be remembered for untiring efforts in the preparations for the day. Wakeman G. Sprague, who was charged with making all necessary purchases in Syracuse, E. S. Dawson who was treasurer of the Re-Union fund, Mrs. Henry S. Doolett, Mrs. Jane E. O'Donaghey and Mrs. Wm. W. Van Brocklin, who were on committee to prepare refreshments, to make decorations and to arrange the tables.

CONCLUSION.

Having finally had charge of the publication of this volume, I esteem it a privilege and feel it a duty that I owe to the publication committee, to write a few explanatory words in conclusion. It will be observed that many biographical sketches are wanting to make the volume complete. Among the number omitted may be mentioned the Jeromes, Judds, Murrays, Marshes, Newmans, Northrups, Duguids, Candees, Woods, Woodfords, Hiscocks, Blowers, Loseys and many others, from whom have arisen distinguished and eminent citizens, mention of whom would be fully sufficient to fill another volume of the size of this. For this the committee are not at fault, as over four years ago, public notice was repeatedly given through "The Press," of the work in contemplation, and asking for contributions of sketches; moreover I have personally sought and importuned many to furnish sketches or at least the data, to enable me to write them up. It will not be overlooked, I trust, that the labor of the committee has been arduous and unremunerative. At one time it was a question whether the work would ever be accomplished, and it doubtless would have been given up had not Gov. Seymour and Hon. Wm. G. Fargo generously come to our assistance with material aid. It will be noticed also that the directory promised has been omitted. This is an intentional omission to avoid too large a volume for our resources. The embelishments are furnished by those whose lithographs adorn the work or by their friends. The old Academy, together with the inside view are from the fac simile made by Wm. H. Stevens, of New York, and but for his conception, would have been lost to history. It is to be hoped that the disadvantages under which we have labored, will avoid many criticisms which under other circumstances might be justly indulged.

WM. W. VAN BROCKLIN.

Pompey, June 17, 1876.

CONTENTS.

BIOGRAPHICAL SKETCHES.

ADDITIONAL BIOGRAPHICAL SKETCHES.

ERRATA.

At page 18, line 11 for transcendant, read transcendent.
At page 19, line 12 for salutory read salutary.
At page 22, line 8 for censtantly read constantly.
At page 25, line 25 for Mrs. P. P. Miller read Mrs. P. P. Midler.
At page 29, line 29 for grap read grasp.
At page 34, line 10 and 11 for Hepey Beeber read Hepsey Beebe.
At page 37, line 7 for snow read sorrow.
At page 67, line 13 for county read country.
At page 95, line 19 for descendents read descendants.
At page 96, line 23 for prepair read prepare.
At page 121, line 7 and 19 for Barrow read Barrows.
At page 125, line 33 for nostalgic read nosologic.
At page 130, line 35 for my house read my home.
At page 172, line 5 for Jabesh read Jabez.
At page 183, line 27 and 28 for Berry & Almer read Perry & Abner.
At page 185, line 32 for was read were.
At page 187, line 15 for graineries read granaries.
At page 187, line 22 for no read so.
At page 192, line 16 for Jehial Stears read Jehial Stearns.
At page 192, line 22 for Dr. Stevens read Dr. Stearns.
At page 201, line 29 for southwest read southeast.
At page 203, line 4 for Dr. L. W. Park read S. W. Park.
At page 209, line 24 for Henry B. Slocum read Henry W. Slocum.
At page 213, line 17 for second Wm. C. read Wm. G.
At page 261, line 8 for 1705 read 1795.
At page 297, line 2 for Schroppel read Scrœppel.
At page 302, line 6 for Doxanna read Roxanna.
At page 307, line 5 for Joseph read Josephine.
At page 86, line 31 for the glory read thy glory.
At page 86, line 32 for half forgotten read hast forgotten.
At page 87, line 2, for shaft read shafts.
At page 87, line 27 for plentitude read plenitude.
At page 176, line 29 for sholes read shales.
At page 254, line 17 for Berment read Bement.
At page 257, line 35 for Grandentia read Gaudentio.

www.ingramcontent.com/pod-product-compliance
Lightning Source LLC
LaVergne TN
LVHW020927110826
845150LV00004B/788

* 9 7 8 1 4 2 5 5 5 3 5 4 8 *